HIDDEN
IN THE
MIX

HIDDEN IN THE MIX

The
African American
Presence in
Country Music

DIANE PECKNOLD, EDITOR

Duke University Press   Durham and London   2013

© 2013 Duke University Press. All rights reserved. Printed in the United States of America on acid-free paper ♾. Designed by Courtney Leigh Baker and typeset in Arno Pro, Veneer, and Trade Gothic by Tseng Information Systems, Inc.

Library of Congress Cataloging-in-Publication Data
Hidden in the mix : the African American presence in country music /
Diane Pecknold, ed.
pages cm
Includes bibliographical references and index.
ISBN 978-0-8223-5149-8 (cloth : alk. paper)
ISBN 978-0-8223-5163-4 (pbk. : alk. paper)
1. African Americans — Music — History and criticism.   2. Country music —
History and criticism.   3. African American country musicians.
I. Pecknold, Diane.
ML3479.H53 2013
781.642089'96073 — dc23   2013005284

"Playing Chicken with the Train: Cowboy Troy's Hick-Hop and the Transracial Country West" was previously published in *Southern Cultures* 16, no. 4 (Winter 2010). Reprinted with permission. www.southerncultures.org.

Contents

Introduction

COUNTRY MUSIC AND

RACIAL FORMATION

Diane Pecknold

Country music's debt to African American influences and musicians has long been recognized. In his canonical history of country music, first published in 1968, Bill Malone opened with the frank acknowledgment that country was distinguished from its European ballad roots by "influences from other musical sources, particularly from the culture of Afro-Americans," and emphasized the fact that "country music — seemingly the most 'pure white' of all American musical forms — has borrowed heavily" from African Americans.[1] Other historians have been equally quick to point out the role relatively unknown African American musicians have played in shaping the styles and repertoires of the most important performers in the country canon: the partnership between Lesley Riddle and A. P. Carter that produced much of the Carter Family's repertoire; the influence of African American blues musicians and railroad hands on Jimmie Rodgers; Hank Williams's tutelage as a young man with the street musician Tee Tot Payne; the expansive influence of Arnold Shultz on the guitar playing of western Kentuckians such as Bill Monroe and Ike Everly.[2] However, such acknowledgments, as Pamela Foster has pointed out, tend most often to imagine the role of African Americans chiefly as influences on their white peers, and thereby obscure from view the African American performers and audience members who not only lent their blues sensibilities and chord progressions to white country musicians but played country and old-time themselves.[3]

Over the past several decades, scholars have begun to redress this emphasis on "influence" by recovering the presence of a series of rich, varied, and geographically diffuse black country traditions, not only in the precommercial era but in the twentieth century as well. Foster's groundbreaking books on African American involvement in country music, *My Country: The African Diaspora's Country Music Heritage* and *My Country, Too*, persuasively argued that African American participation in the playing and production of country music has been more a rule than an exception. Work by Cecelia Conway, Karen Linn, Kip Lornell, Paul Oliver, and others, has demonstrated that the African American banjo tradition profoundly influenced nearly all American popular music, including country, and that it survived well into the mid-twentieth century in places like Virginia, North Carolina, and Mississippi, as did a robust string-band tradition.[4] Recent revivals of black banjo and string-band music by ensembles like the Carolina Chocolate Drops and the Ebony Hillbillies and on CDs such as Otis Taylor's *Recapturing the Banjo* attest to the continuation of those traditions into the twenty-first century. The harmonica player DeFord Bailey, the first instrumentalist to achieve individual star status at the Grand Ole Opry, was belatedly elected to the Country Music Hall of Fame in 2006, based in part on the work David Morton and Charles Wolfe had done in recalling the magnitude of Bailey's popularity.[5] The tradition of African American singing cowboys in the 1930s and 1940s, including Herb Jeffries and Louis Jordan in one of his many incarnations, is similarly finally receiving its due.[6]

While the burgeoning literature to which this collection contributes has very usefully helped to restore the history of black participation in country music, little of it offers us substantial help in unraveling what becomes, as a result, an obvious paradox: that country music includes a long-standing tradition of black participation and contribution but remains nonetheless "white" music. Standard encyclopedic treatments of the genre still yield opening statements defining it in explicitly racial terms, as "a type of music derived primarily from the traditional folk idioms of the white rural southeastern United States" or "a style of 20th-century American popular music that originated among whites in rural areas of the South and West."[7] So why does this mythology persist in spite of ample evidence to the contrary? What ideological work does the erasure of country music's multiracial origins and history accomplish?

As Aaron Fox points out, it is too simplistic to argue either that "country's whiteness simply speaks for itself as evidence of a foundational racism" or that "its whiteness is a historical accident."[8] One aim of this volume is thus to examine how the genre's whiteness was produced and is maintained, to imagine country music not merely as a cultural reflection of a preexisting racial identity but as one of the processes by which race is constituted. The social history of working-class white southerners told through the standard mythology of country music omits not only African American engagements with the genre but also the role of race and racism in southern white working-class experience. Too often the country imaginary presents the poor white southerner simply as the downtrodden working man, without reference to the way class and regional identity intersected with hierarchies of race and gender; without reference, for example, to the way Jimmie Rodgers or Elvis Presley answered the challenges southern industrialization and urbanization posed to white working-class masculinity through their appropriation of tropes of musical blackness.[9] We need not indulge in "an unquestioning fondness for pre–Civil War Dixie," as one reporter suggested contemporary country music often does, to construct an imagined South that "represents a view of history that erases both America's black population and the suffering on which the South was built."[10] As Geoff Mann argues, country remains white in large part because its nostalgia proposes "a cultural politics of time" that suppresses specific histories of racism and domination to produce a pose of "dehistoricized innocence" and "naïve victimhood" that allows whites to lament their own loss of privilege without acknowledging ever having held it.[11]

Recent scholarship calls attention to country's role in constructing white identity and to the ongoing ideological work required to maintain the fiction of the genre's "natural" whiteness.[12] Karl Hagstrom Miller has convincingly shown that, as it emerged out of a variety of commercial and vernacular practices into a cohesive genre, country music *became* white, and did so in relation to a shifting landscape of social and symbolic practices that supported white hegemony. The fiction that divergent musical practices reflected racial difference offered cultural legitimacy to the increasingly strict imposition of Jim Crow segregation. In turn, the social boundaries policed by segregation ensured that black and white musical practice in the South would, in fact, diverge more sharply in both commercial and vernacular arenas.

In his examination in this volume of early black artists whose work was released in hillbilly record series, Patrick Huber explains how the recording and marketing practices of the phonograph men maintained the fiction that the generic separation of hillbilly and race reflected racial difference. But he also reveals how much uncertainty attended this process, suggesting that, while they almost certainly sought to conceal the racial identity of the black artists they released in hillbilly catalogues, a label's A&R (artists and repertoire) men did not necessarily make racial difference the dominant factor in assessing genre difference. Huber thus demonstrates that, even as record companies' advertising strategies capitalized on the romantic mythology that hillbilly music reflected an authentic and distinct white southern culture, their own production practices gave the lie to such beliefs.

That the work of naturalizing racial difference through genre distinctions remained incomplete even through the zenith of the Jim Crow social order is evidenced by the confusion surrounding the success of Ray Charles's 1962 album, *Modern Sounds in Country and Western Music*. As my own essay suggests, the music industry's search for a generic framework in which to understand the album pointed to the instability of racialized genre conventions but also showed how class and regional associations contributed to the maintenance of racial difference. Ultimately observers elided the racial dynamics of *Modern Sounds* and emphasized instead its importance in recasting the class identity of white, working-class southerners, an interpretation that drew in part on Charles's own musical conflation of race and class.

Erika Brady's examination of the contested legacy of Arnold Shultz similarly illuminates the ways that class and race intersect in the construction of country's whiteness. Though Shultz is widely revered among the pickers of the region, local resistance to crediting him with the "invention" of Kentucky's Travis-style thumbpicking simultaneously expresses both hostility to largely middle-class white outsiders who seek to impose their own historical narratives on the community and fear of being cast as racist appropriators. Brady's analysis suggests the ways music's racial discourses can also operate to elaborate class identity, not necessarily by asserting whiteness as a form of cultural capital but by declaring the value of subaltern, insider class knowledge and cultural ownership against the knowledge produced by authoritative outsiders. The ways class status and conflict have shaped different audience communities' divergent interpretations of Charles and Shultz thus recall Stuart Hall's famous contention that, whatever its autonomous power as an ordering ideology or individual or group identity, race can also be "the modality through which class is . . . lived."[13]

One consequence of country's laboriously enforced whiteness has been the particularly acute difficulty African American country musicians have faced in negotiating racism and notions of racial difference in their artistic and personal lives. Jeffrey A. Keith's account of the life and career of the Kentucky fiddler Bill Livers demonstrates how the visible presence of African American country artists nonetheless frequently serves to reaffirm the genre's whiteness. Livers's fiddling talent afforded him avenues of social mobility that were off-limits to his peers because of racism, but white musicians often viewed him as the embodiment of their own conceptions of race and black identity. Early in his career they regarded him as a comedic mascot whose presence served to confirm white supremacy by counterexample; later he served as a symbol of simplicity and naturalism that bolstered white musicians' own claims to rural authenticity. And although Livers was widely admired for his fiddling talent, he was never free from the requirements of social deference that racism demanded in his own Kentucky community.

Such constraints are echoed by Charles Hughes's account of the career of Arthur Alexander, whose 1962 hit "You Better Move On" figured as a charter moment in the development of southern soul but whose involvement in and contributions to the country canon have been less widely acknowledged. While Alexander joined the Dot roster and participated in the Combine songwriting collective with Dolly Parton, Kris Kristofferson, and Ray Stevens, Music Row executives felt they could not market his blend of country and soul because it sounded "too black," while R&B stations shied away from his country connections.

Clearly, like much of American culture, country music has been a form of "playing in the dark," of using notions of blackness to elaborate and provide affective depth to white identity. To stop at this observation, however, threatens to recapitulate the very racial hegemony it seeks to expose, obscuring the subjectivity of the black artists and fans who fashion their own identities partly through their practice of country music. Indeed popular and critical representations of country have focused so intently on its whiteness that it has become difficult to imagine a form of black engagement that does not call racial identification into question. (This inability to imagine blackness and country as coming together in any sensible way is, appropriately enough, reflected by the fact that Microsoft Word flags the combination of *black* and *country* in a single adjectival phrase as a grammatical error.) In movies like *Nashville, Boogie Nights*, and *Borat*, black country artists and fans are played for laughs at the expense of supposedly racist white country devotees or of African American buffoons whose unease with their own racial identity is figured through their love of country. The idea of a meaningful African American connection to country is so synonymous with the humorously bizarre that when the director David LaChappelle sought to expeditiously embody surrealism in his "Fantasy Ranch" commercial for Burger King, he offered the image of Darius Rucker playing a jingle-ized version of "Big Rock Candy Mountain" in a sequined cowboy outfit (a maneuver that ultimately demonstrated the unpredictability of the mutual circulations of race and music when Rucker actually became a country star).[14]

The tropes of both racial identity dysphoria and surrealism prevalent in popular culture representations also persist in critical discourse on black engagements with country. One online review of the rapper Snoop Dogg's album *Ego Trippin'* (2008), which included a duet with Willie Nelson dedicated to Johnny Cash, demonstrated the ease with which pop culture stereotypes are woven into critical dismissal. "At age 36, is Snoop Dogg going through a mid-life crisis?" the review's subtitle asked before its author remarked, "Somewhere in the making of . . . *Ego Trippin'*, Snoop appears to have lost his way. . . . [His] evolution—admitted MTV star . . . gangsta rapper . . . Cher imitator . . . Morris Day singer . . . set reppin' Crip . . . Hollywood scenester . . . back to gangsta rapper . . . loving and faithful husband (er, sortve) . . . gangsta again—wouldn't be complete without one last confusing musical costume change: Country singer."[15] As is often the case, Snoop Dogg's interest in country becomes, in this assessment, not just another symbol of his confusion about who he "really" is but the quintessential marker of alienation from a genuine black self.

Even positive scholarly, critical, and journalistic explorations of African American engagements with country have perpetuated distinctions that problematize the black country tradition even as they seek to restore it. Dozens of popular press articles over the past decade have repeated the litany of African American engagements with country and precountry styles, a line that runs from black string bands and DeFord Bailey through Chuck Berry, Ray Charles, and the Stax sound, to Charley Pride and Stoney Edwards, to Cowboy Troy, Rissi Palmer, and Darius Rucker. But even after rehearsing this trajectory, they invariably frame their inquiries in terms of the genre's enduring whiteness. "Country music may be the largest segregated corner of American music today," noted Bruce Feiler in one of the earliest of such articles, before puzzling with forthright dismay over Nashville's continued exclusion of African American artists, the industry's slighting of black listeners, and the popular failure to acknowledge African American contributions to country.[16] "Country is often seen as the whitest, most segregated of all styles: the redneck soundtrack of the racist South," reported another, before offering profiles of several African American country hopefuls.[17] Thus even as they work to reveal black engagements with country, such treatments simultaneously reinforce the whiteness the genre has come to symbolize. Among both sympathetic and cynical critics, black country artists and fans are imagined, as Adam Gussow suggests in his contribution to this collection, as always already exceptional, racially scandalous, and transgressive.

One goal of this volume is to question the related notions of racial and musical authenticity implied by such assessments. In this regard it joins an ongoing debate about the category of "black music." Guthrie Ramsey describes this debate as centering on the degree to which musical "retentions" representing the persistence of "African sensibilities . . . in the Americas and the Caribbean" continue to "exist and unite the African diaspora culturally and spiritually."[18] Scholars such as Samuel Floyd, Amiri Baraka, and Portia Maultsby have argued for the persistence of specifically African styles, techniques, and musical tropes across diasporic cultures, but also more globally for a set of "musical tendencies," "mythological beliefs," and "interpretive strategies" that form an identifiable "African cultural memory."[19] As Ronald Radano and Paul Gilroy have pointed out, however, such arguments frequently result in a conception of "black music" that posits it as being "expressive of the absolute essence of the group that produced it" and correlates "an enduring black musical presence with the myth of a consistent and stable socio-racial position of 'blackness.'"[20]

But the essentialism sometimes proposed by the concept of black music cuts both ways. Rejecting the very idea of black culture, Gilroy suggests, is "tantamount to ignoring the undiminished power of racism itself and forsaking the mass of black people who continue to comprehend their lived particularity through what it does to them."[21] Whether or not its claims to representationality or Africanness are fabricated, music has served as a foundational material in constructing the bulwark of shared cultural identity from which various groups within the African diaspora, in radically divergent historical, economic, and social circumstances, have staged their struggles against the brutalities of structural racism. Thus the stakes of analyzing the relationship between music and racial identity are at least as much about our own investments and the dynamics of contemporary racial hegemony as they are about originary musical traditions or the degree to which such traditions reflect a consistent cultural essence or sensibility.

This collection should not be read as seeking to undermine the notion of black culture or black music, either by asserting that country really is "black" music or by merely exploiting the counterintuitive juxtaposition of the genre's white racialization with the social identities of its black artists, entrepreneurs, and fans. Instead these essays attempt to address the shifting and multifaceted ways in which resilient black identities are fashioned through musical production, whether that music is construed as "black" or not. Seen from this position, the production of black music, both materially and as a concept, is offset from potentially essentialist understandings of race. The specific instances and changing forms of black participation in country music over the twentieth century suggest that there is ample middle ground between a conception of black music that assumes the expression of a fixed socioracial position and one that obscures how the consistent imposition of racism, in its many and flexible forms, has shaped the lived experience of blackness throughout the African diaspora of the West, and thus the needs, desires, and commitments expressed through its musical practices.

The telling re-racialization of one African retention central to the sound of country music illustrates the need to remember that music helps to constitute race rather than expressing an essence that precedes it. Examining the decline of the banjo in black dance music between 1900 and 1930, and its concomitant transformation into an aural signifier of whiteness in old-time country, Tony Thomas urges us to consider the lived experiences of changing social and material conditions as being at the center of the "blackness" of any musical culture. Thomas rejects persistent assertions that African Americans abandoned the banjo in reaction to its associations with racist blackface minstrelsy, arguing instead that the five-string banjo most commonly played in old-time string bands became obsolete when the guitar proved better suited to newer blues singing and dancing. That the banjo became irrelevant to black popular music in the United States while it persisted in white-dominated old-time and then country music, he argues, reflects the cultural effects of the new spatial and social relationships of Jim Crow segregation and the growth of a particularly white agrarian nostalgia during industrialization and urbanization.

Even within a system of apartheid as ubiquitous and powerful as Jim Crow, however, local social dynamics created different trajectories of cultural transmission and different identities produced through music. Kip Lornell recounts his own journey in uncovering the rich tradition of community-based "old-time country music" played by African Americans in the Piedmont of North Carolina and Virginia, documenting the "easy mix" of blues, old-time, and gospel that persisted into the mid-twentieth century in the region and showing how that mix was part of the fabric of African American social experience in church, end-of-school celebrations, square dances, and fiddle contests. "Old-time country" remained popular because it was a functional, integral part of the fabric of everyday life for Lornell's informants and one process through which their subjectivity as black people was produced, in spite of the increasingly white racialization of its commercial variants.

By the end of the civil rights era, country was, in the words of Aaron Fox, "widely understood to signify an explicit claim to whiteness . . . as a marked, foregrounded claim of cultural identity," thanks in large part to politicians like George Wallace and Richard Nixon, who mobilized the music as part of an effort to "use the emotional issues of culture and race to achieve . . . a 'positive polarization' of American politics" without resorting to overt racism.[22] Yet it continued to serve as a tactical cultural resource that could also signify very differently. Extending the analysis of Al Green's country repertoire begun in his monograph *Soul Covers*, Michael Awkward argues here that Green's invocations of "country" on *The Belle Album* allowed him to synthesize "his mannish brashness and his 'feminine' vulnerability, as well as seemingly incommensurable elements of the national cultural landscape."[23] The result was a post–civil rights version of black masculinity rooted in the specific history of the exodus from the rural South to the urban North, and an expression, in the intensely personal vocabulary of faith, temptation, longing, and self-possession, of how the effects of structural racism might be lived as individual feeling. For Green, " 'country' and its cultural specificities," as he understood them, signified an artistic identity more authentic and more connected to a shared historical experience of race than the smooth Philadelphia soul style with which he had become an established star.

Together Thomas, Lornell, and Awkward demonstrate that the relationship between country music and black identity has frequently been shaped not by abstract confrontations with racism as an ideology but by the locally specific lived social worlds that evolved within and against racism's institutional manifestations. For all of its local particularities, however, the American system of racial hegemony also circulates globally as a powerful symbolic resource, sometimes in unexpected ways. Jerry Wever's investigation of the thorny identity politics of U.S. country music in St. Lucia emphasizes the historically contingent relationship between music, race, and nation in the United States by reframing it in a global context. Though the popularity of the music prompts concern among intellectuals who see it as both racist and colonialist, Wever shows that St. Lucian fans have selectively pulled on country's repertoire for those songs and styles that accord with their own Afro-Creole dance and musical traditions. Dancing the habanera beat to country music, he argues, demonstrates the instability of the genre's whiteness in the U.S. context by preserving and celebrating its Creole origins and gestures to the unpredictable ways in which the sounds of the Black Atlantic continue to resonate in a global postcolonial culture.

Wever's reframing, with its emphasis on the tension between the elite and the popular, also serves as a reminder that postcolonial and, in the United States, post–civil rights social orders have reconfigured what Paul Gilroy identifies as the antiphony of black culture, creating a world in which "calls and responses no longer converge in the tidy patterns of secret, ethnically encoded dialogue," in part because the intersections of race, class, and power also converge in less and less tidy patterns.[24] As Adam Gussow suggests, efforts to defend and disrupt racialized music categories may both rely on "a residual nostalgia for the certainties, and scandals, of the color line." Yet both the Afro-Creole curations of the St. Lucian dance floor and the spectacular transracialism staged by the U.S. hick-hopper Cowboy Troy (Coleman) redraw that line, not in the service of denying its continuing potency but as a way of locating its function as a contact border rather than a separating boundary. Placing Cowboy Troy in the long literary and cultural genealogy of the transracial West and the shorter genealogy of rap-country hybrids, Gussow argues that Coleman's deliberately menacing, racialized self-presentation and his direct confrontation of Nashville's cryptoracism is nonetheless delivered through a lens of spectacular transracialism, creating "a space in which 'blackness,' even while summoned up, is playfully amalgamated with its imagined Other."

In her examination of the songs and fiction of Alice Randall, Barbara Ching suggests that Randall's lyrics, frequently rendered by white artists, force the listener to imagine multiple and ambiguous racial identities and to hear the unanticipated ways those identities intersect with historical racism. In her novel *Pushkin and the Queen of Spades*, Randall similarly juxtaposes violence and commonality, love and theft, in part through the black female protagonist's love of country music and her use of it to "translate" her life for her son. Such work, Ching and Gussow argue, directly addresses the history of American racism while using the terrain of country music as a staging ground for denaturalizing racial difference.

If racial discourse has served as a proxy for class distinction in contexts as diverse as civil rights–era Nashville and the thumbpicking community of western Kentucky, Randall's interventions, as Ching points out, target not only racial dichotomies but also class-cultural hierarchies. Her ambiguous invocations rely in part on a reconfiguration of the relationship between race and class, both in country music and in American society, at the turn of the twenty-first century. The growth of the suburban black middle class (at least prior to the recession of 2008) and country radio's shift to middle-of-the-road, adult-oriented pop have converged to create a space in which black participation in country music requires no "dramatic provocation."

The most optimistic contemporary observers suggest that perhaps the trends of the past decade, including rap-country collaborations such as the duets of Snoop Dogg and Willie Nelson and Nelly and Tim McGraw, the Muzik Mafia's "music without borders" stance, and a handful of persistent African American country aspirants like Rissi Palmer and Darius Rucker will add "diversity to this lily-white genre."[25] But even when critics hail the mixture of racially marked musical styles and bodies, few have the temerity to suggest, even playfully, as the *New York Times* critic Kelefa Sanneh did, that perhaps "in an age of rapping cowboys and hip-hop-loving country crooners," "twangy" dirty south hip hop collaborators Paul Wall and Killa Kyleon should "get a chance to flash their platinum teeth on CMT" with their song "Country Boy."[26]

Such a suggestion will undoubtedly raise hackles, even among those who wish to break down the racialization of genres by exploring music that circulates across boundaries of racial and musical difference; the twanging guitar accents, title, and southern regionalism of "Country Boy" come nowhere near making it a "country" song in stylistic or marketing terms. This reticence points to the fact that the connections between race and genre rely on a host of critical and scholarly discourses about purity, authenticity, and commercialism that are not explicitly about race. As Christopher Waterman has pointed out, "Performers, genres, texts, and practices not consonant with dominant conceptions of racial difference have . . . often been elided from academic, journalistic, and popular representations of the history of American music," and one of our aims here is to undermine the critical distinctions that have supported racialized genre boundaries and cast black engagements with country as both historically marginal and aesthetically suspect.[27]

The general hostility to crossover as inherently inauthentic is perhaps the most notable of these distinctions. One telling example of the implicit racialization of this discourse appears on a countdown of "the oddest — and most successful" pop-country crossovers offered on the AOL country website "The Boot." By opening its discussion with a reference to the "Vegas showgirl eying Nashville's greener pastures" in Alan Jackson's 1994 song "Gone Country," the editors frame their discussion in terms of the calculated, inauthentic commercialism Jackson was protesting. And while the site asserts that the tradition of pop crossovers into country "goes back to Tony Bennett's cover of Hank Williams' 'Cold, Cold Heart,'" and that some country crossovers may be born "of genuine affection for the genre," it also reminds readers that crossovers are frequently produced by artists seeking "to jump-start a flagging career." As is often the case, the rhetorical categories of the bizarre, the inauthentic, the commercially suspect, and the racially transgressive become conflated: African American artists constitute a full 25 percent of the list, a proportion well out of keeping with their representation in the ranks of pop-country crossovers.[28]

Several of the essays in this collection thus unapologetically expand on and contest the musical and social practices that define the boundaries of "country" and suggest that one reason race has remained so central to genre definitions is that racial crossover destabilizes the very concept of genre, reliant as it often is on homological conceptions of audience cultures. Charles Hughes traces the multiple connections between Nashville, Muscle Shoals, and Memphis—what he calls the country-soul triangle—emphasizing the institutional affinities and circulation of artists across generic boundaries. While he forcefully argues that the southern soul sound was at least as important to country music's development as country influences were to southern soul, he also demonstrates that the African American participants who profoundly shaped the triangle's musical exchange were relegated to roles that kept them out of view and on the margins of the country industry.

David Sanjek more explicitly engages with the notion of racial crossover in his discussion of Henry Glover's legendary production work. Glover, he argues, helped the country artists he produced avoid the racial masquerade that typified many white versions of R&B hits, instead encouraging artists like Moon Mullican and the Delmore Brothers to create what he sometimes called "advanced" or "new" country, a style that leavened traditional country arrangements with the emerging sounds of R&B. The music he and his artists produced within a strictly country marketing scheme presaged the destabilization of racially bounded genre categories occasioned by the arrival of rockabilly. Like Hughes, Sanjek reveals both the permeability and the tenacity of racialized genre boundaries by interrogating the relationship between notions of musical and racial authenticity.

IN 2008 BARACK OBAMA closed the Democratic National Convention, and his speech accepting the party's nomination for president of the United States, with Brooks and Dunn's "Only in America." At least as represented in *Rolling Stone*, Obama was no fan of country music; the eclectic iPod playlist the magazine described included exemplars of nearly every genre of American popular music except country and Broadway musicals. Yet his use of country music at this pivotal point in his campaign indicated a good deal about the racialized meanings of country music and both the persistence and the instability of its whiteness. During the primary contest, Obama's ability to reach white, working-class voters—the demographic most often associated with country music—was vigorously questioned; indeed the presumed racism of those voters was frequently cited as a reason he might be a weaker potential nominee than his opponents. In this light, the party's use of the song can be read simultaneously as a (perhaps premature) declaration of victory in reconstituting the New Deal coalition across racial lines and as a concession that race continues to constitute that coalition's most significant point of political fracture, making it desperately necessary to de-race Obama by associating him with the whitest of white American culture in order to allay racist fears about angry black men.

But such explanations seem necessary, and make sense, only if we accept country's whiteness and Obama's blackness as fixed and natural. Otherwise the song was a nearly perfect reflection of the candidate's biography and aspirations. Its title directly recalled his observation at the 2004 Democratic National Convention that "in no other country on earth is [his] story even possible." Its assertion that in America "we all get a chance" and its suggestion that any child on a city school bus "just might be president" perfectly mirrored the biographical narrative Obama outlined for himself throughout his campaign. Even the original video for the song echoed Obama's desire to stake out a racial middle ground: as the faces of the children on the bus come into focus, their black-and-white images switch from positive to negative, so that every child appears momentarily as both black and white. It would be as naïve to see black performances of country as a musical panacea for bigotry as to suggest that the election of a black president marks the end of American racism. But perhaps we would read country's racial (and class) politics, and this particular moment in its history, most accurately as a palimpsest in which the surface script of binary races and cultures can only partially obscure the contested and complex nature of racial formation.

Notes

1. Malone, *Country Music USA*, 5.

2. Zwonitzer and Hirshberg, *Will You Miss Me When I'm Gone?*; Porterfield, *Jimmie Rodgers*; Escott, Merritt, and MacEwen, *Hank Williams*; Smith, *Can't You Hear Me Callin'*.

3. Foster, *My Country*, vi.

4. Conway, *African Banjo Echoes in Appalachia*; Linn, *That Half-Barbaric Twang*; Lornell, "Pre-Blues Black Music in Piedmont North Carolina"; Lornell, "Non-Blues Secular Black Music in Virginia"; Oliver, *Songsters and Saints*; Wells, "Fiddling as

an Avenue of Black-White Musical Interchange"; Wolfe, "Rural Black Stringband Music," 32–35; Waterman, "Race Music"; Carlin, *String Bands in the North Carolina Piedmont*; Rosenberg, "Ethnicity and Class."

5. Morton and Wolfe, *DeFord Bailey*.

6. Allmendinger, *Imagining the African American West*, 66–83; Leyda, "Black-Audience Westerns and the Politics of Cultural Identification in the 1930s"; and Adam Gussow in this collection. For a good narrative overview of black country traditions and their influence on soul music particularly, see Hoskyns, *Say It One Time for the Broken Hearted*.

7. "Country Music," *Encyclopedia Americana*, Grolier Online, http://ea.grolier.com.echo.louisville.edu/article?id=0110880-00; "Country Music," *Encyclopedia Britannica Online*, http://www.britannica.com/EBchecked/topic/140388/country-music.

8. Fox, "White Trash Alchemies of the Abject Sublime," 50.

9. Bertrand, "I Don't Think Hank Done It That Way"; Feder, "'Song of the South,'" 110–43.

10. Martin Hodgson, "The Hidden Faces of Country," *Observer* (London), July 16, 2006.

11. Mann, "Why Does Country Music Sound White?," 89.

12. Mann, "Why Does Country Music Sound White?"; Miller, *Segregating Sound*; Feder, "'Song of the South'"; La Chapelle, *Proud to Be an Okie*; Thomas, "There's a Whole Lot o' Color in the 'White Man's' Blues"; Thomas, "The Color of Music"; Ching, "The Possum, the Hag, and the Rhinestone Cowboy"; Ching, *Wrong's What I Do Best*; Campbell, *Music and the Making of a New South*.

13. Hall, "Race, Articulation, and Societies Structured in Dominance," 55.

14. "Cowboy Hootie Sings for Burger King BK," Adland: The Commercial Archive, http://commercial-archive.com/node/118841. The commercial's original irony was compounded when, in the fall of 2008, Rucker released *Learn to Live*, a full-length country album for Capitol Nashville. The album and its first single, "Don't Think I Don't Think about It," both hit number 1 on the country charts.

15. "Album Review: *Ego Trippin'*," idk, http://idknada.wordpress.com/2008/04/06/album-review-snoop-doggs-ego-trippin.

16. Bruce Feiler, "Has Country Music Become a Soundtrack for White Flight?," *New York Times*, Oct. 20, 1996.

17. Hodgson, "Hidden Faces of Country."

18. Ramsey, "Editor's Introduction," vi.

19. Maultsby, "West African Influences and Retentions in U.S. Black Music," 25–26; Floyd, *The Power of Black Music*; Baraka, *Blues People*.

20. Gilroy, "Sounds Authentic," 114; Radano, *Lying Up a Nation*, 3.

21. Gilroy, "Sounds Authentic," 126.

22. Fox, "White Trash Alchemies of the Abject Sublime," 44; Carter, *The Politics of Rage*, 379–81.

23. Awkward, *Soul Covers*.

24. Gilroy, "Sounds Authentic," 134.

25. Bobby Reed, "Examining the Color of Country Music," *Chicago Sun-Times*, July 2, 2006.

26. Kelefa Sanneh, "Ebony and Ivory Learn to Share Country Home," *New York Times*, May 5, 2005.

27. Waterman, "Race Music," 167.

28. Brian Manfield, "Gone Country: Crossover Crooners," The Boot, http://www.theboot.com/2008/06/05/gone-country-snoop-dogg.

PART ONE

PLAYING IN THE DARK

Black Hillbillies

AFRICAN AMERICAN MUSICIANS

ON OLD-TIME RECORDS, 1924–1932

Patrick Huber

In the summer of 1930 Ralph S. Peer, RCA-Victor's A&R (artists and repertoire) man, arranged a working holiday in Hollywood for Jimmie Rodgers,
the nation's leading hillbilly recording star. There, working at a relaxed pace
during the three weeks between June 30 and July 17, Rodgers recorded fifteen selections at the newly completed Victor Hollywood Studios on Santa
Monica Boulevard. Several of these sides would become among his most
famous recordings, including "Blue Yodel No. 8 (Mule Skinner Blues)," "Pistol Packin' Papa," and "My Blue-Eyed Jane." But the most celebrated recording Rodgers made in Hollywood, what his biographer Nolan Porterfield
calls the "pièce de résistance" of these sessions, turned out to be "Blue Yodel
No. 9," recorded on July 16 and composed by Rodgers himself. Originally
titled "Standin' on the Corner," "Blue Yodel No. 9" was a standard twelve-bar
blues featuring Rodgers's signature yodeling refrains and comprising verses
in which Rodgers, adopting the persona of a Beale Street hustler, boasts of his
sexual prowess, his expensive clothes, and his handiness with a .44 Special.[1]

On September 11, 1931, fifteen months after its recording, "Blue Yodel
No. 9" was released on Victor 23580, coupled with "Looking for a New
Mama," in the label's "Old Familiar Tunes and Novelties" series, among
other records intended for sale chiefly to southern white record buyers.[2]
Considering Rodgers's primary audience, RCA-Victor's release of the record
in its flagship label's hillbilly series made commercial sense. At the same
time, however, this decision effectively obscured the extraordinary inter-

racial collaboration that produced this now-classic recording, for accompanying Rodgers on "Blue Yodel No. 9," as is now commonly known, were the brilliant young trumpeter Louis Armstrong (1901–71) and his estranged second wife, the pianist Lillian Hardin Armstrong (1898–1971). The exact details of how this remarkable session came together are now unfortunately lost to history.[3] But regardless of its origins, it ranks as one of the most famous recording sessions in the history of American popular music, touted by country music and jazz scholars alike as a seminal event that brought together two of the twentieth century's greatest musical entertainers at the peak of their artistic abilities. And the recording itself, one of thirteen blue yodels that Rodgers recorded between 1927 and his death in 1933, represents an amalgamation of musical styles: a standard twelve-bar African American blues composed of floating verses, sung in a nasally white Mississippi drawl, that featured both vaudeville-inspired yodeling and New Orleans–style jazz accompaniment. Indeed the inclusion of "Blue Yodel No. 9" in the most recent editions of both Brian Rust's *Jazz Records, 1897–1931* (1982) and Robert M. W. Dixon, John Godrich, and Howard Rye's *Blues and Gospel Records, 1890–1943* (1997) indicates, as Porterfield has observed, that this particular Rodgers recording transcends the genre of what we today call country music. Although "Blue Yodel No. 9" may stand out as one of the truly great American recordings, Rodgers's collaboration with the Armstrongs was only one of at least twenty-two racially integrated hillbilly recording sessions that occurred before 1933. And Louis and Lillian Armstrong were only two of the nearly fifty African American singers and musicians who appeared on commercial hillbilly records between 1924 and 1932.[4]

Country music scholars have long acknowledged the significant African American influence on country music prior to World War II, in the form of ragtime and blues, vocal and instrumental styles, musical mentors, and even the West African–derived banjo itself. But they have far less often recognized the actual participation of African Americans in the recording of this music, then called "hillbilly music" or, alternately, "old-time music."[5] Since at least the mid-1950s, scholars and discographers have been aware of a handful of prewar hillbilly recordings featuring racially integrated bands or African American artists, but these records have received surprisingly little scholarly attention, and have generally been treated either as historical anomalies or as interesting but otherwise unimportant curiosities.[6] And much misinformation continues to circulate, even within country music books and liner notes to CD anthologies published within the past decade. For example, in the booklet accompanying Yazoo's seven-CD boxed set, *Kentucky Mountain*

Music: Classic Recordings of the 1920s and 1930s (2003), the chief annotator makes the bogus claim that Taylor's Kentucky Boys, an otherwise all-white string band featuring a black fiddler, represents "the only group to record in the 1920's and 30's with an interracial construct." Elsewhere another eminent music scholar declares that this band's April 1927 sessions rank as "the first integrated recording sessions in American music history; jazz could not claim an integrated session until 1931"; both halves of this statement are patently false.[7]

The chief reason for these historical inaccuracies, as well as the primary obstacle impeding research in this subject, has been the lack of a comprehensive discography of prewar hillbilly records. But now, thanks chiefly to the publication of Tony Russell's monumental *Country Music Records: A Discography, 1921–1942* (2004), which was more than twenty years in the making, the fuller history of African Americans' participation on early country music recordings can begin to be told. Russell's reference work and its race records counterpart, Dixon, Godrich, and Rye's *Blues and Gospel Records, 1890–1943*, allow scholars to compile an accurate and fairly complete discography of all of the known commercial hillbilly records on which African Americans performed before World War II.[8] And what this newly emerging discography reveals is that African Americans actively participated in the hillbilly recording industry almost from its very beginning.[9] To be sure, records featuring African American artists were far from common, constituting only about 1 percent of the approximately eleven thousand hillbilly records released in the United States before 1933, but their numbers are far greater than most country music scholars and fans have generally appreciated. Between 1924 and 1932 black and white artists collaborated at twenty-two racially integrated sessions that produced sixty-nine recorded masters (see appendix A).[10] Additionally fourteen different African American artists or acts recorded forty-three known selections that appeared on hillbilly records during this same period (see appendix B). Altogether forty-nine African American musicians participated in the recording of at least 112 masters for the hillbilly recording industry before 1933. These recordings were released, in various series, on a total of 204 domestically issued sides, and of these sides, no fewer than 178 of them appeared on hillbilly records or on records otherwise intended for sale in the hillbilly market.[11]

Examining these prewar records on which African Americans performed can tell us much about the commercial hillbilly music of the 1920s and 1930s. Far from being merely historical anomalies, these records not only document the remarkable, though too-often-unacknowledged participation of

African Americans in this genre of American music, but they also reflect the significant amount of interracial musical cooperation and exchange that produced these recordings. Far more than being merely interesting and important examples of interracial musical collaborations, these prewar records also expand and deepen our understanding of the hillbilly recording industry during its formative period. They indicate that the commercial hillbilly music recorded before 1933 was far more complex and diverse than the narrow marketing categories created by talking-machine firms suggest. Finally they offer important and tantalizing glimpses into the unspoken perceptions and production decisions that guided the recording and marketing of such records, areas of inquiry for which much, if not most, of the industry-generated documents have been lost, discarded, or destroyed.[12]

These African American records raise a number of intriguing and important questions about the prewar hillbilly recording industry that produced them. For example, how, in an age of pervasive racism and Jim Crow segregation, did so many racially integrated sessions occur? Whose idea was it to record white and black musicians together, and why? How was it that a commercial music genre, which from its earliest advertisements was so deliberately and overtly linked to whiteness, came to include more than 175 records featuring African American artists? In promoting these records, did companies attempt to conceal the racial identity of these African American artists from the southern white consumers who supposedly constituted the chief market for hillbilly records? While it remains difficult, if not impossible to formulate definitive answers to such questions, studying these records suggests new ways of thinking about and understanding commercially recorded hillbilly music prior to 1933.[13]

WHEN U.S. TALKING-MACHINE companies began to record and market blues and old-time music during the early to mid-1920s, they effectively began the process of transforming southern vernacular music, heard for decades at fiddle contests, dances, house parties, tent shows, and other social gatherings, into immensely popular commercial products. This music, the product of more than three centuries of vibrant cross-racial exchange and adaptation, was profoundly and inextricably multiracial, but talking-machine companies, in an effort to streamline their marketing efforts, separated the music of black and white southerners into special categories of "race" and "hillbilly" records. First commercially recorded in 1920, race records encompassed blues, jazz, gospel numbers, and sermons marketed to African American consumers across the nation. Hillbilly records, first recorded in 1922 and so named in order to capture the music's supposedly white rural southern origins, consisted chiefly of southern fiddle tunes, string-band numbers, old parlor ballads, and religious songs, and were marketed primarily to rural and small-town white consumers, particularly in the South. But contrary to the claims of Donald Clarke and other music historians, this industrywide practice of separating the music into two racially encoded categories had little to do with the existence of de jure racial segregation in the American South. Rather this decision was motivated primarily by practical and commercial considerations. Dividing race and hillbilly records into special series allowed talking-machine companies to target specialized markets of consumers more effectively with their advertising and marketing campaigns. Moreover such series also made it easier for the firms' jobbers (local or regional distributors) and retailers to select from an entire catalogue of several thousand records those releases that would most appeal to their customers. This division was, however, premised on the racialist beliefs of northern white middle-class executives who assumed, as the folklorist Bill Ivey has written, that "consumers select music based upon race" and that "musical style and race are inextricably linked." What began as merely marketing categories soon evolved, for all intents and purposes, into musical genres, as the sociologist William G. Roy has noted, and the generic labels of *race* (first applied in 1921) and *hillbilly* (first used in 1925) would remain the sound-recording industry's dominant terms to describe black and white southern vernacular music until *rhythm and blues* and *country and western* replaced them shortly after the end of World War II.[14]

In developing these two musical genres, talking-machine companies applied many of the same methods and policies that they had been successfully using since at least 1904 to market foreign-language records to various immigrant communities in the United States. Chief among these was the practice of dividing catalogues into separate series of discrete, numerical blocks of records designed to target particular groups of consumers. Originally, most companies had released records of blues and old-time music in their standard domestic popular series, usually "without racial designation," as Roy notes. In 1921, however, OKeh inaugurated the first race series, its 8000 series, and within two years Paramount and Columbia, eventually followed by Vocalion, Brunswick, and Victor, established similar series for their African American records. This marketing practice was soon applied to hillbilly records. Around January 1925, the Columbia Phonograph Company became the first to establish a special series for what it defined as "old-time music" when it created its famous 15000-D "Familiar Tunes — Old and New" series (originally "Old Familiar Tunes"), the counterpart to its 14000-D race series. Prior to the mid-1930s, all of the major record labels involved in the hillbilly music field except for Gennett released such records in specially designated numerical series that paralleled their special numerical blocks of race records (see table 1.1).[15]

To obtain new material for their expanding race and hillbilly record catalogues, talking-machine companies either invited southern artists to record in their northern studios or, increasingly after the adoption of the electrical recording process in 1925, sent mobile crews to record these artists on portable equipment at southern field sessions, particularly in Atlanta, Dallas, Memphis, and New Orleans. Although talking-machine firms usually marketed the recordings of black and white southern artists in separate record series, their crews typically recorded the selections for their race and hillbilly catalogues on the same "recording expeditions," as they were called at the time, using the same temporary studios for both groups but often scheduling sessions for black and white musicians on different days or sometimes different weeks.[16]

In hindsight, the artificial categories of "race" and "hillbilly" records did far more than help talking-machine firms organize their inventories and rationalize their marketing and distribution efforts. These classifications also contributed to what Christopher A. Waterman, in his provocative essay in *Music and the Racial Imagination* (2000), has called "the naturalization of racial categories" within American popular music. Through their advertisements, record catalogues, and monthly supplements, record companies imbued both race and hillbilly records with certain social and cultural meanings that were intimately connected to race and racial difference.[17] For example, the literature developed to promote hillbilly records emphasized the supposedly white, Anglo-Celtic origins of the music heard on these discs by portraying it as the authentic folk expression of southern mountaineers. As the 1928 *Brunswick Record Edition of American Folk Songs* explained, "The only True American Folk Songs . . . are the songs of the Southern Mountaineers. Like the minstrels of old, the modern Bards of our southern mountains go about singing the simple songs of the people's own making, relating the gruesome details of a local murder, the latest scandal of the community, the horror of a train wreck, the sorrow of unrequited love, etc." The associated marketing labels for hillbilly series, such as OKeh's "Old Time Tunes," Brunswick's "Songs from Dixie," and Vocalion's "Old Southern Tunes," as well as the quaint pastoral images of the barn dances, log cabins,

TABLE 1.1. Race and Hillbilly Series of the Major U.S. Record Labels, 1924–1935

Label	Series numericals	Series title	Years of activity	Approx. no. of releases
BRUNSWICK				
Race	7000 series	NA	1927–32	234
Hillbilly	100 series	"Songs from Dixie"	1927–33	497
COLUMBIA				
Race	14000-D series	NA	1923–33	681
Hillbilly	15000-D series	"Familiar Tunes— Old and New"*	1924–32	783
OKEH				
Race	8000 series	NA	1921–35	967
Hillbilly	45000 series	"Old Time Tunes"	1925–34	580
PARAMOUNT				
Race	12000 series	NA	1922–32	1,157
Hillbilly	3000 series	"Olde Time Tunes—Southern Series"**	1927–32	324
VICTOR				
Race	V-38500 series	NA	1929–30	132
Hillbilly	V-40000 series	"Native American Melodies"†	1929–31	336
Race	23250 series	NA	1931–33	183
Hillbilly	23500 series	"Old Familiar Tunes & Novelties"	1931–34	359
VOCALION				
Race	1000 series	NA	1926–33	746
Hillbilly	5000 series	"Old Southern Tunes"‡	1927–33	497

Sources: Robert M. W. Dixon, John Godrich, and Howard Rye, comps., *Blues and Gospel Records, 1890–1943*, 4th ed. (Oxford: Clarendon Press, 1997 [1964]), xxiii–xl; Tony Russell, *Country Music Records: A Discography, 1921–1942*, with editorial research by Bob Pinson, assisted by the staff of the Country Music Hall of Fame and Museum (Oxford: Oxford University Press, 2004), 9–26; Charles K. Wolfe, "The Bristol Syndrome: Field Recordings of Early Country Music," in *Country Music Annual 2002*, ed. Charles K. Wolfe and James E. Akenson (Lexington: University Press of Kentucky, 2002), 207.

* Columbia's 15000-D series was originally called "Old Familiar Tunes."

** Paramount later called its 3000 series "Old Time Songs" and, alternatively, "Old Time Numbers."

† Beginning in May 1930 until the series termination in January 1931, Victor referred to its V-40000 series as "Old Familiar Tunes & Novelties," and the firm later used this title for its subsequent 23500 series.

‡ In its catalogues and promotional literature, Vocalion also variously described its 5000 series as "Special Southern Records," "Old Time Tunes," "Old Southern Melodies," and "Old Time 'Fiddlin' Tunes' and Southern Melodies."

FIGURE 1.1.
Front cover of *Old Time Edison Disc Records* brochure, ca. 1928. Author's collection.

and stands of mountain pines that often graced the covers of hillbilly record catalogues and promotional brochures, all hearkened back to a preindustrial rural South, particularly a Mountain South, that was deeply embedded in the American popular imagination. But within this sentimentalized advertising landscape, African Americans were almost nowhere to be found, except for an occasional image, such as the plantation scene of "happy darkies" featured on the cover of a ca. 1928 *Old Time Edison Disc Records* brochure (fig. 1.1). In fact promotional literature sometimes explicitly defined hillbilly music in direct opposition to the African American–inflected jazz and popular offerings that composed the bulk of record sales during the 1920s. A 1927 newspaper advertisement for Columbia's "Familiar Tunes — Old and New" series, for example, promised to satisfy the musical tastes of those record buyers who "get tired of modern dance music—fox-trots, jazz, Charleston—and long for the good old barn dances and the 'Saturday night' music of the South in plantation days." Amid the widespread concerns that Henry Ford and other cultural conservatives harbored about the morally corrupting influences of jazz music and modern dances, copywriters and illustrators tried to present hillbilly music as a wholesome, white Anglo-Saxon alternative to the growing sensuality and crudeness that seemed to define the nation's mass culture. And it was as a result of being defined in opposition to these other genres of popular music that hillbilly music gained much of its social significance and meaning in Jazz Age America.[18]

The truth, of course, is that much of the music found on the hillbilly records of the 1920s and early 1930s was the product of decades or even centuries of dynamic cultural interplay between white and black musicians, and many of the songs and tunes issued on these records were of black origin or borrowed from black tradition. Occasionally record catalogues and monthly supplements even mentioned these cross-racial borrowings. Victor's 1924 *Olde Time Fiddlin' Tunes* brochure, for example, remarked that on its record of two "wonderful old Negro Spirituals," former governor Alf Taylor and His Old Limber Quartet rendered the selections "exactly as they took [them] from the lips of the old Negro master of the hounds." But the accompanying photograph of the string band made clear that these records were decidedly white interpretations of traditional black songs. Although talking-machine companies occasionally issued African American artists' recordings in hillbilly series, no photographs of these recording artists, to my knowledge, ever appeared in the promotional literature for these records. With few exceptions, old-time record catalogues and advertisements disseminated images of an idyllic white rural Mountain South that existed outside of modern urban America, a closely knit, socially homogeneous and harmonious world free from flappers, foreigners, and African Americans. Talking-machine companies' use of these "whitewashed" textual messages and pictorial images effectively concealed the interracial character of much of the music heard on prewar hillbilly records and thereby rendered practically invisible African Americans' involvement in early commercial country music.[19]

DESPITE THE SEPARATE racially based record series and marketing strategies that talking-machine companies established, a close investigation of the discography of prewar hillbilly records reveals a surprising amount of inter-

llaboration at recording sessions. Although the pervasive racism
gation of the Jim Crow South discouraged such interactions, black
southerners occasionally played music together in a variety of
private settings, including at one another's homes, at neighbor-
es and house parties, on theater stages, and even in studio waiting
rooms at recording sessions.[20] Inside recording studios, however, such interracial collaborations proved to be relatively rare, even within the thoroughly
multicultural field of jazz, before the mid-1930s. But within hillbilly music—
a musical genre that has often been perceived as unsophisticated, culturally backward, and even politically reactionary—racially integrated sessions,
while by no means common, occurred with greater frequency than in any
other genre of American popular music except for vaudeville blues (the first
integrated session for which dates at least to May 1921).[21]

Between 1927 and 1932 white and black musicians participated in at least
twenty-two racially integrated recording sessions that produced hillbilly
records. Some of these sessions seem to have been spontaneous events resulting from the coincidental presence of white and black artists at a particular field session. Others appear to have been carefully planned collaborations,
such as the April 1927 Gennett sessions involving Taylor's Kentucky Boys,
a studio string band from Garrard and Jessamine counties, in south-central
Kentucky. Named for its manager, Dennis W. Taylor, the band featured an
African American fiddler, Jim Booker (1872–1940), from Camp Nelson, in
Jessamine County, who was the son of a former slave, himself a fiddler. On
April 26, 1927, in what was the first known racially integrated recording session in country music history, Booker and two white members of the band,
banjoist Marion Underwood and guitarist Willie Young, recorded a pair of
traditional southern fiddle breakdowns, "Gray Eagle" and "Forked Deer," at
the Starr Piano Company's studios in Richmond, Indiana. At a second session later that same day, Booker collaborated with Underwood and a white
singer, Aulton Ray, to produce two additional sides, "Soldier Joy" (sic) and
"Maxwell Girl" (a variant of the well-known "Buffalo Gals"). The Starr Piano
Company released all four of these recordings on its flagship label, Gennett, and advertised them in its 1928 Gennett Records of Old Time Tunes catalogue, where copywriters described these selections variously as "Old Time
Playin'" and "Old Time Singin' and Playin'."[22]

In August 1927, four months after his debut sessions, Booker returned to
the Starr studios, along with his younger brothers, guitarists Joe (1890–1966)
and John (1892–1986), to record again with Taylor's Kentucky Boys. Also accompanying them was a mandolin-playing neighbor, Robert Steele (1882–

1962), who was also African American. On August 26 and 27, the Booker brothers and Steele, either individually or in various combinations, waxed fourteen sides as members of this otherwise all-white string band. Six of these interracial recordings featured the fiddle duets of Jim Booker and Fiddlin' Doc Roberts, as he was billed on records, the most famous and extensively recorded Kentucky fiddler of the prewar era.[23] Besides recording as a member of Taylor's Kentucky Boys, Jim Booker also recorded two numbers at the August 27 session with his brothers and Steele in an all-black string band called the Booker Orchestra. Although Gennett did not follow the industry practice of issuing old-time records in a special dedicated series, company files indicate that these two recordings, "Salty Dog" and "Camp Nelson Blues," were "made for Hillbilly" and thus intended to be marketed to southern white consumers. Collectively the twenty Gennett sides on which Jim Booker or one of his brothers performed chronicle a portion of the rich African American fiddling and string-band traditions that existed in south-central Kentucky in the first decades of the twentieth century. Significantly these recordings also reveal that white and black old-time musicians in the region shared a common repertoire and similar performance style, and music historians have particularly noted the tightly knit interplay between Booker's fiddling and Underwood's banjo playing on "Gray Eagle" and "Forked Deer."[24]

Three months after these sessions with Taylor's Kentucky Boys and the Booker Orchestra, the Starr Piano Company studios hosted another racially integrated session involving two more Kentucky recording artists promoted by the talent scout Dennis W. Taylor. In November 1927 Taylor took Welby Toomey, a white Garrard County singer, and Sammy Brown (dates unknown), an African American multi-instrumentalist from Lexington, to the Starr studios in his Model T Ford. A barber by trade and the son of an English immigrant father, Toomey had first heard Brown playing as a one-man band on the streets of nearby Versailles, Kentucky, and, in a 1969 interview, recalled that Brown had six fingers on each hand. On November 22, in Richmond, Brown recorded three blues songs, including "The Jockey Blues," on which Toomey recalled performing. According to Godrich, Dixon, and Rye's *Blues and Gospel Records, 1890–1943*, an unidentified second voice does appear on this recording, based on surviving Gennett session sheets, but it is practically inaudible on the recording, except for one point when it seems to mimic a neighing horse. If Toomey's recollections are accurate, this may indeed have been his sole contribution on this recording. In any case, immediately following this session, Brown backed Toomey on four sides of religious and parlor songs, playing the guitar and occasionally the harmonica and an instrument identified in the Gennett files as a "jazzbo" (presumably the makeshift instrument, common in early jazz and jugs bands, that consisted of a kazoo attached to the body of some brass instrument such as a saxophone or a trombone). None of Toomey's four collaborations with Brown was ever released, however, although two of Brown's selections, including his purported side with Toomey, were issued on Gennett and two subsidiary labels for the race records market.[25]

Although the integrated lineups of Taylor's Kentucky Boys and Toomey-Brown appear to have been studio bands that existed only to make records, other interracial recording sessions grew out of long-standing musical partnerships. One such series of sessions involved the legendary Louisiana duo of the white Cajun fiddler Dennis McGee and the French-speaking black Creole accordionist and singer Amédé Ardoin (1898–prob. 1942), who performed together at dance halls and private house dances in southwestern Louisiana for more than two decades. The two men met in 1921 while sharecropping for the same landlord near Chataignier, in Evangeline Parish, and they soon struck up a musical partnership out of which, considering the racial climate of the era, evolved a rather intimate friendship. Encouraged by their landlord, McGee and Ardoin began playing together for white *fais do-dos* in the neighborhood. Ardoin, who was greatly admired for his expressive singing and syncopated, blues-inflected accordion playing, was much sought after for local dances and other social gatherings in both white Cajun and black Creole communities. But his musical partnership with McGee challenged the racial customs of Jim Crow Louisiana, and playing for white audiences often posed serious, even dangerous problems for the diminutive Ardoin. Another Cajun fiddler, Wade Frugé, recalled that he had to obtain the host's permission to bring Ardoin to certain house parties, and that sometimes at these parties "a lot of them old Frenchmen would start drinking homebrew and they'd try to cause trouble for Amédée [sic]." Indeed, one popular local account attributes Ardoin's psychological breakdown and eventual death in a Pineville, Louisiana, mental asylum to a severe beating he received from two white thugs for reportedly breeching conventional racial etiquette at a house dance he was playing for near Eunice around 1940. What had so outraged his two assailants, according to the story, was that Ardoin had accepted a handkerchief to wipe the sweat from his brow that had been offered to him by the daughter of the white homeowner.[26]

Together Ardoin and McGee teamed up to make twenty-two recordings for the Columbia, OKeh, Brunswick, and Bluebird labels between 1929 and

1934. The duo cut their first recordings together on December 9, 1929, at a joint Columbia-OKeh field session in New Orleans under the direction of the OKeh A&R man and talent scout Polk C. Brockman. At this historic session, Ardoin and McGee waxed six Cajun waltzes and two-steps, with the accordion and fiddle sharing the lead, including the now-classic "Two Step de La Prairie Soileau (Prairie Soileau Two Step)" and "Two Step de Eunice." All of these sides, credited on the record labels only to Ardoin, were released in both Columbia's and OKeh's small special series of Acadian French, or Cajun, records. Less than a year later, the duo returned to New Orleans, where they recorded ten sides for the Brunswick label at the Roosevelt Hotel on November 20 and 21, 1930. Unlike Columbia and OKeh, Brunswick did not employ a special numerical series for its Cajun records. Instead the firm released all of these titles, which consisted of waltzes, one-steps, two-steps, and blues, under the billing of McGee and Ardoin in its "Songs from Dixie" series. Two of them, "Amadie Two Step" and "La Valse a Austin Ardoin," were also issued on the Canadian Melotone label, presumably for the French Canadian market. The duo's final session together occurred on August 8, 1934, in San Antonio, Texas, and produced six sides for RCA-Victor's budget-priced Bluebird label. Today music scholars consider McGee and Ardoin's classic recordings to be among the most influential in the history of Cajun music, and nearly all of the songs found on them have become standards within the Cajun repertoire. And, reflecting the multiethnic nature of his dance music, Ardoin is widely acknowledged as one of the principal architects of both modern-day Cajun and zydeco music.[27]

Another racially integrated recording session that emerged out of a long-standing musical relationship occurred at a 1927 Charlotte, North Carolina, recording session, under the direction of Victor's A&R man Ralph S. Peer. There, on August 9 and 10, Victor's mobile unit recorded eight numbers by the Georgia Yellow Hammers, a white Gordon County, Georgia, string band that had made its recording debut earlier that February. Accompanying the band on the trip to Charlotte, but apparently in a separate automobile, was a Gordon County duo called the Baxters, composed of fiddler Andrew Baxter (ca. 1872–1955), an African American farmer who was reportedly half Cherokee, and his son, Jim (1898–1950), a singer and guitarist. "They could play breakdowns; they could play blues; they could play church music; they could play *anything*," recalled Gus Chitwood, whose father, the fiddler William "Bill" Chitwood of the Georgia Yellow Hammers, sometimes performed at local dances and picnics with the Baxters. In Charlotte the Georgia Yellow Hammers and the Baxters recorded separately. But on "G Rag," the Georgia

Yellow Hammers' final recording of its August 9 session, Andrew Baxter replaced the band's regular fiddler, George "Bud" Landress, who instead provided a humorous spoken introduction to the instrumental. Although Baxter sometimes performed with members of the Georgia Yellow Hammers back home at social gatherings in Gordon County, their collaboration on "G Rag" appears to have been a spontaneous event that originated in the recording studio that day.[28]

Although most of the racially integrated recording sessions before 1933 that produced hillbilly records appear to have involved musicians who played together at least on occasion, others seem to have been collaborations between white and black musicians who may have known one another but who never performed together outside of the recording studio. In the summer of 1927, a few weeks before the Atlanta session at which the Georgia Yellow Hammers recorded with Andrew Baxter, Ralph S. Peer and two recording engineers visited Bristol, Tennessee, the first stop on a three-city southern recording expedition. Between July 25 and August 5, during the now-legendary 1927 Bristol Sessions, Peer and his crew recorded seventy-six selections, including the debut recordings of Jimmie Rodgers and of the Carter Family, who would become the two most popular hillbilly recording acts of the pre–World War II era. Among the seventeen other acts that participated in these sessions was the Johnson Brothers, two white vaudeville musicians probably from nearby Johnson City, Tennessee. The duo, guitarist Charles Johnson and his brother Paul Johnson, a singer, steel guitarist, and banjo player, had recorded for Peer at Victor's main studios in Camden, New Jersey, less than three months earlier, and, impressed by the musicianship of the brothers, Peer appears to have personally invited them to record again, at the Bristol sessions. On July 28, 1927, in a vacant warehouse on State Street in Bristol, the Johnson Brothers waxed a half-dozen selections, four of which featured instrumental accompaniment by an obscure musician named El Watson (dates unknown), who was probably also from Johnson City. Watson, the lone African American artist to record at the 1927 Bristol sessions, played the harmonica on the Johnson Brothers' recording of "The Soldier's Poor Little Boy." On the three other selections, "Two Brothers Are We," "A Passing Policeman," and "I Want to See My Mother (Ten Thousand Miles Away)," Watson backed the duo on the bones, a percussion instrument popular among minstrel and medicine show performers. Although the Johnsons may have known Watson in Johnson City, his accompaniment of this white brother duo at this session appears to have been an improvised collaboration that occurred only at Peer's suggestion. At the session immediately following this one, Charles Johnson returned the favor, sitting in as the guitarist for Watson's recording of the harmonica blues instrumentals "Pot Licker Blues" and "Narrow Gauge Blues." Since the firm had not yet established dedicated series for either its race or its hillbilly records, Victor released both of Watson's sides, as well as three of those of the Johnson Brothers, in its 20000 domestic popular series.[29]

Like the Johnson Brothers' 1927 recording session with El Watson, most of Jimmie Rodgers's collaborations with African American sidemen appear to have been impromptu events, arranged on the spur of the moment either by Ralph S. Peer or perhaps even, as his biographer Nolan Porterfield suggests, by Rodgers himself. Besides his historic 1930 recording of "Blue Yodel No. 9" with Louis and Lillian Armstrong, Rodgers participated in at least three other racially integrated recording sessions, two of which occurred during a June 1931 RCA-Victor field session in Louisville, Kentucky. On June 11, at the first of these interracial sessions, Rodgers recorded the bawdy "Let Me Be Your Side Track" with the St. Louis blues guitarist Clifford Gibson (1901–63). For unknown reasons, however, Peer decided to release another version of the song, recorded immediately following this one, on which Rodgers supplied his own guitar accompaniment. Discovered in RCA's vaults in 1990, the unissued take featuring Gibson's guitar accompaniment—a recording that Porterfield has hailed as "like no other performance of this era"—was finally released more than sixty years later on Bear Family's six-CD boxed set *Jimmie Rodgers: The Singing Brakeman* (1992). On June 16, 1931, five days after his session with Gibson, Rodgers cut "My Good Gal's Gone Blues," accompanied by the all-black Dixieland Jug Blowers (credited on the Bluebird record as the Louisville Jug Band), a five-man Victor studio group that included vocalist and jug blower Earl McDonald (1885–1949) and fiddler Clifford Hayes (1893–1941), both of whom were veterans of Louisville's flourishing jug band scene and often played for white patrons at high-society parties and hotel dances during Derby Week.[30]

Far less is known about Rodgers's fourth, and earliest known, interracial session, but according to Porterfield, it resulted from an incident that took place during RCA-Victor's August 1929 field session in Dallas. On Saturday night while in town for the five-day session, Rodgers went out carousing to "a dancehall in the black section of east Dallas," where he heard an African American jazz band that he enjoyed, and he promptly recruited the musicians to accompany him on a recording at his Monday session. On August 12, at the temporary studio set up in the Jefferson Hotel's banquet hall, Rodgers recorded one side, a vaudeville stage version of the well-known ballad

"Frankie and Johnny," accompanied by this unknown, five-man band, which consisted of cornet, saxophone, piano, banjo, and string bass. Although one of Rodgers's regular session guitarists, Billy Burkes, recalled that "the band sounded real good with Jimmie," Peer decided to shelve this recording. He opted instead to release Rodgers's solo version of this song, made two days earlier, which featured Rodgers's own simple guitar accompaniment. Unfortunately, the wax master of Rodgers's take with the jazz band has long since been lost or destroyed.[31]

Columbia's response to Jimmie Rodgers, the yodeler Roy Evans, also recorded multiple sessions with African American accompanists, including a session that yielded two hillbilly selections. A once relatively famous but now almost forgotten vaudeville and radio singer whom Columbia billed as "the Eccentric Voice" and "the Yodelin' Man," Evans recorded, as best as can be determined, more than two dozen sides under his own name between 1928 and 1931 and even starred in an eponymous MGM movie short in 1929. Evans made his recording debut at an Atlanta field session on April 11, 1928, waxing at least three sides, including a two-part yodeling number, "Weary Yodelin' Blues," for which he claimed composer credits and which, the researcher Chris Ellis speculates, was "probably intended as Columbia's answer to Victor's hit," Rodgers's "Blue Yodel," released some two months earlier. Columbia released this doubled-sided blues disc in both its hillbilly series (on 15252-D) and its domestic popular series (on 1380-D). On June 18 Evans recorded again, this time in New York City, cutting two sides featuring his yodeling skills, "Dusky Stevedore" and "I Ain't Got Nobody (and Nobody Cares for Me)." He was accompanied by Jay Cee "J. C." Johnson (1896–1981), an African American session pianist who also recorded with Ethel Waters, Mamie Smith, and Lonnie Johnson, among others. A native of Chicago, Johnson composed nearly a hundred songs, including "Empty Bed Blues" (1928), which Bessie Smith popularized, and, teaming up with lyricist Andy Razaf and composer Thomas "Fats" Waller, his most famous composition, "This Joint Is Jumpin'" (1938), which was featured in the 1978 Broadway musical *Ain't Misbehavin'*. Johnson himself had cowritten the standout song of Evans's session, "Dusky Stevedore," in collaboration with Razaf. As it had with its two-part "Weary Yodelin' Blues," Columbia released these two Evans sides as a coupling for the hillbilly records market, in its "Familiar Tunes Old and New" series (on 15272-D); "Dusky Stevedore," tapped for special promotion, was also issued in the label's domestic popular series (on 1449-D). But Evans never achieved the stardom that Columbia had hoped for him, and his foray into yodeling was short-lived, at least on commercial recordings. On most of the remainder of his sides, Evans was relegated to singing uncredited vocal choruses on jazz records by white bands such as the Charleston Chasers, Rube Bloom and His Bayou Boys, and the Mississippi Maulers. After his recording contract ended around 1931, he fell into obscurity, seemingly without a trace.[32]

Little more is known about the enigmatic Evans; interestingly, even his racial identity remains uncertain, a puzzle that is made all the more complicated—and fascinating—as a result of his genre-defying recordings. On July 26, 1928, a little more than a month after he recorded his two sides with J. C. Johnson, Evans waxed two sides with the great black stride pianist James P. Johnson providing the accompaniment, "Syncopated Yodelin' Man" and "Jazbo [sic] Dan and His Yodelin' Band." These two numbers were released as a coupling not in Columbia's hillbilly series, as Evans's previous four sides had been, but in the label's race records series (on 14359-D), as well as on 1559-D, in the label's domestic popular series. According to Nick Tosches, the famed jazz sideman Garvin Bushell, who played clarinet on a couple of Evans's 1928 sides, remembered Evans as a black man and, in an interview done decades later, described him as a "tall brownskin fellow." But the evidence concerning Evans's racial identity is conflicting. On the one hand, Columbia took out a full-page advertisement for Evans's "Dusky Stevedore," complete with a photograph of Evans himself, dressed in a black tie and tuxedo, on the front cover of the *Phonograph and Talking Machine Weekly* for August 8, 1928. For the label to feature Evans and his latest record so prominently on the front cover of this important trade journal would have been out of the ordinary if the yodeler had been African American, and the photograph itself reveals Evans as having a fair complexion and Caucasian features.[33]

On the other hand, Columbia also promoted Evans's recording of "Dusky Stevedore," as well as his "Weary Yodelin' Blues," in elaborate, illustrated advertisements in the nation's leading African American newspaper, the *Chicago Defender*, on August 11 and June 16, 1928, respectively. (It also advertised his race record, "Syncopated Yodelin' Man," in the newspaper on October 27, 1928.) Record companies occasionally advertised the discs of white popular singers and band leaders in large, splashy ads in the *Defender*, but such publicity for a hillbilly disc by a presumably white artist was almost unprecedented. This unusually aggressive ad campaign in the black press, combined with Bushell's recollection and Evans's early known piano accompanists, all seem to suggest that he may have been African American. But regardless of his actual racial identity, Evans merits inclusion in this essay, either as a

e yodeler who recorded a disc with a black accompanist for Columbia's
ᴴiliar Tunes Old and New" series or as an African American singer who
ᴴwo of his records issued in this series.³⁴

ᴴt no hillbilly singer crossed the color line to record with African American musicians more often than Jimmie Davis, best known as the popularizer
of the classic song "You Are My Sunshine" and as the two-term Democratic
governor of Louisiana (1944–48, 1960–64). Between 1929 and 1933 Davis,
then working as the clerk of the Shreveport Criminal Court, recorded sixty-
eight sides for RCA-Victor, many of which featured double-entendre blues
that differed markedly from the sentimental and gospel numbers that he
would later, beginning in 1934, record for Decca. Davis launched his recording career as a Jimmie Rodgers imitator; he was well-schooled in the African American blues of northwestern Louisiana, and two of his semiregular
accompanists during his tenure with RCA-Victor were the black Shreveport blues guitarists Ed "Dizzy Head" Schaffer (dates unknown) and Oscar
"Buddy" Woods (ca. 1900–1956). Both Schaffer and Woods played the standard guitar as well as the steel guitar, which they laid across their lap horizon-
tally, producing a rich sound of whining, sustained notes by sliding a bottle
neck across the guitar's strings in a melding of Mississippi Delta and Hawaiian guitar styles. In fact Schaffer's and Woods's guitar playing so closely resembled each other's that they were practically indistinguishable, and as a
result, as Tony Russell has observed in his booklet notes to Bear Family's
five-CD boxed set *Governor Jimmie Davis: Nobody's Darling but Mine*, "the
identity of the guitarists [at certain sessions] is a matter for speculation."
On May 20, 1930 at a Memphis field session, in what was probably their first
recording venture together, Davis waxed "She's a Hum Dum Dinger from
Dingersville" accompanied by Schaffer on steel guitar and Woods on guitar
for RCA-Victor's "Native American Melodies" series. The following day, the
two African Americans collaborated on a pair of blues guitar duets, "Fence
Breakin' Blues" and "Home Wreckin' Blues," under the name the Shreveport
Home Wreckers, for the firm's 23250 race series.³⁵

Over the next two years, Schaffer and Woods, either individually or in
tandem, accompanied Davis on seventeen additional recordings at field sessions in such far-flung southern cities as Memphis, Charlotte, and Dallas.
Among the most famous of the resulting sides were the inventively raunchy
"Sewing Machine Blues," "Red Nightgown Blues," and "Davis' Salty Dog,"
all of which were recorded at the Jefferson Hotel in Dallas on February 8,
1932, with Schaffer on steel guitar and Woods on guitar. The most unusual
product of Davis's interracial collaborations, however, was "Saturday Night

Stroll," recorded at this same Dallas session, on which Davis and Woods actually sang a duet, "a circumstance," Tony Russell remarks, "without parallel, I think, in country music discography."[36] Davis's 1932 Dallas session with Schaffer and Woods marked the end of pre-1933 racially integrated hillbilly recording sessions and, along with McGee and Ardoin's 1934 RCA-Victor session in Dallas, was one of the last in the field of hillbilly recording before World War II.

It might surprise some readers to learn that so many racially integrated sessions occurred within the hillbilly recording industry prior to 1933. After all, most hillbilly recording artists, like other rural and working-class white southerners of their generation, tended to strongly support racial segregation and white supremacy. In fact several hillbilly musicians, including Fiddlin' John Carson and Blind Alfred Reed, are known to have been members of the revived Ku Klux Klan and to have performed at Klan-sponsored functions. And despite his early multiple recording sessions with black guitarists, Jimmie Davis ran for a successful second term as Louisiana governor in 1960 on a segregation platform, albeit perhaps chiefly for calculated political reasons, in which he vowed to defend the state's public schools from federally mandated desegregation. Interestingly, the Starr Piano Company, the firm responsible for recording the first racially integrated sessions in both jazz and country music history, also pressed dozens of custom recordings with titles such as "Why I Am a Klansman" and "The Fiery Cross" for Indiana klaverns of the Ku Klux Klan—a revealing commentary on both the business practices of 1920s record companies and the schizophrenic nature of Jazz Age race relations.[37]

Yet, despite the influence of racism and segregation, many southern white artists exhibited a deep fascination with African American music, and, moreover, much of their musical style and repertoire reflects a considerable African American influence. Jimmie Rodgers, the Carter Family, Jimmie Tarlton, Frank Hutchison, Dock Boggs, and Austin and Lee Allen, to name only a handful, all borrowed heavily from African American musical traditions, and in a few cases these borrowings resulted from long-standing relationships and even friendships with African American musicians. Occasionally, as previously noted, white and black southerners played music together informally, and that they might also make commercial recordings together is understandable. Upon closer examination, then, the release of African American records in hillbilly catalogues is not so surprising after all.[38]

But several other factors also help account for the appearance of African American musicians on hillbilly records during the 1920s and early 1930s.

For one, before the arrival of mass-marketed, factory-made guitars in rural southern culture around the turn of the twentieth century, the fiddle was, as the music scholar Marshall Wyatt has noted, the "dominant folk instrument of both races." This influential instrument, which was introduced into the seventeenth-century southern colonies primarily from the British Isles, played in combination with the banjo, which was imported with West African slaves, formed the basic instrumental arrangement for both white and black string bands in the American South throughout the nineteenth century and into the first decades of the twentieth.[39] Moreover, before the blues craze of the 1910s and 1920s, both black and white string bands tended to perform the same or similar "common stock" repertoires that included both traditional numbers and more recent Tin Pan Alley selections, as Tony Russell has demonstrated. Among these were instrumentals such as "Sourwood Mountain," "Bile Dem Cabbages Down," "Turkey in the Straw," "Buffalo Gals," and "Arkansas Traveler"; ballads such as "Casey Jones" and "John Henry"; blues ballads such as "Don't Let Your Deal Go Down," "Salty Dog," and "Lonesome Road Blues"; and popular songs of more recent vintage such as "Bully of the Town" and "At the Darktown Strutters' Ball." Even after the blues eclipsed them in popularity, though, these common stock songs and tunes remained central to the repertoires of African American musicians and bands in some pockets of the South well into the 1950s.[40] However, talking-machine company executives likely assumed that string-band recordings of such common stock songs and tunes, even if performed by African American artists, would appeal more to southern white consumers than to African American consumers. Firms therefore often classified these nonblues, old-time black recordings for distribution and sale in hillbilly series because such recordings seemed to conform to record company executives' perceptions of the musical tastes of rural and working-class white southerners.

In a decision that seems to run counter to their marketing efforts to promote hillbilly music as a distinctly white musical expression, talking-machine companies occasionally released African American records in their hillbilly series. Prior to 1933, in addition to the selections produced at racially integrated sessions, at least forty-three recordings featuring African American artists appeared in these hillbilly series that were usually reserved for white artists (see appendix B). The first such artist to have his recordings so issued was Sam Jones (prob. ca. 1881–?), a Cincinnati street singer and one-man band whom Columbia billed as Stove Pipe No. 1, a nickname apparently derived from the length of stovepipe through which he blew, as if it were a jug, to provide rhythmic accompaniment to his guitar playing. On

August 20, 1924, Jones recorded six common stock tunes at the firm's New York City studios, accompanying his vocals with guitar and, with the aid of a neck rack, both harmonica and stovepipe: "John Henry," "Lonesome John," "Cripple Creek and Sourwood Mountain," "Turkey in the Straw," "Arkansas Traveler," and "Fisher's Hornpipe." Around March 1925, Columbia released two of these selections, the coupling of "Lonesome John" and "Fisher's Hornpipe," in its 15000-D "Old Familiar Tunes" series—only the twelfth record released in the label's fledgling hillbilly series.[41] Another African American act whose records appeared in this same series was the Wheat Street Female Quartet, an a cappella quartet from Atlanta who waxed four spirituals in their home city on January 29, 1925. Two of its selections, "When the Saints Go Marching In" / "Go Down Moses," were issued in Columbia's 14000-D race catalogue, while the other two, "Wheel in a Wheel" / "Oh! Yes!," appeared in the label's 15000-D hillbilly catalogue. Two days after this quartet recorded, another local African American artist, the Reverend C. D. Montgomery (dates unknown), took his turn before Columbia's recording horn in the makeshift Atlanta studio. There he waxed a two-part sermon, interspersed with his own solo singing, titled "Who Was Job?" These two sides, the sum total of Montgomery's recorded output, likewise appeared in Columbia's "Old Familiar Tunes" series. Collectively, these three discs, all recorded for Columbia by relatively obscure recording artists, represent the earliest examples of African American records being deliberately classified for the hillbilly market.[42]

One of the most famous African American artists to have some of his recordings released in hillbilly series was the harmonica virtuoso DeFord Bailey (1899–1982), the first African American star of WSM-Nashville's celebrated radio barn dance, the Grand Ole Opry. Born in Smith County, Tennessee, some forty miles east of Nashville, Bailey grew up in a large farming family hearing and performing what, in interviews late in his life, he called "black hillbilly music." In mid-1926, while working as an elevator operator in Nashville, Bailey landed a regular spot on WSM's newly established radio program, then called the WSM Barn Dance. Billed as "the Harmonica Wizard," he specialized in startlingly realistic impressionistic pieces such as "Pan American Blues," on which he simulated the chuffing and whistles of that famous Louisville and Nashville steam locomotive, and "Fox Chase," on which he imitated a pack of yelping hounds running a fox. On the strength of such numbers, Bailey became one of the program's most popular entertainers, and in 1928, according to Charles K. Wolfe, "he made twice as many appearances (forty-nine in fifty-two weeks) as any other Opry regular." Since photographs of him rarely appeared in WSM publicity materials, most Opry listeners probably never realized that he was African American. Bailey performed on the show for fifteen years until WSM management summarily fired him in 1941. Not until Charley Pride joined the show in 1993 would the Grand Ole Opry have another regular African American cast member.[43]

Bailey made his first recordings some nine months after joining the Grand Ole Opry. George D. Hay, WSM's radio director and the Opry's founder, arranged for him to record at a Columbia field session in Atlanta on April 1, 1927, but neither of the two sides from his debut session was ever released. Less than two weeks later, Bailey recorded again, this time for Brunswick. On April 18 and 19 he waxed eight harmonica solos, including his signature pieces, "Pan American Blues" and "Fox Chase," at the firm's New York City studios. All of these sides were issued in either Brunswick's hillbilly series or that of its subsidiary Vocalion label. Half of them appeared simultaneously in both. A year and a half later, Bailey also participated in the historic 1928 Victor field session in his adopted hometown of Nashville, the first commercial recording session in the city that less than three decades later would emerge as the undisputed capital of the country music recording industry. Of the eight sides he recorded there on October 2, however, only three were ever issued. Victor issued two of these, "Ice Water Blues" / "Davidson County Blues," in its newly inaugurated race series. The third track, "John Henry," not issued until the spring of 1932, was simultaneously released in Victor's race and hillbilly series, coupled with a harmonica solo by an African American, Noah Lewis (of the Memphis Jug Band), on the race record (Victor 23336), and with a harmonica solo by the white D. H. "Bert" Bilbro on the hillbilly record (Victor 23831). Victor officials' decision to market Bailey's harmonica blues instrumental to both black and white consumers was unusual, although not unprecedented, especially during a period when the financial straits of the Great Depression had greatly curtailed the firm's field-recording excursions to the South and thus the acquisition of new material for their race and hillbilly catalogues. But in releasing Bailey's "John Henry," which the firm's executives must have believed had racial crossover appeal, Victor benefited economically by reaching two markets while incurring the production costs of recording only one selection.[44]

Another superb African American harmonica player who had recordings issued in his label's hillbilly catalogue was the obscure William McCoy (dates unknown). McCoy was probably from Dallas, and the title of one of his recorded sides, "Central Tracks Blues," is actually derived from a local reference to Deep Ellum, the African American district in Dallas whose proximity to the Houston and Texas Central Railroad earned it the nickname "Central Track." Little else is known about him, however, other than the details of his recording sessions. Between 1927 and 1928 McCoy recorded a total of six sides at three Columbia field sessions, all of them in Dallas. His first two harmonica solos, recorded on December 6, 1927, were "Mama Blues" and "Train Imitations and the Fox Chase." On the former, McCoy uncannily mimics a baby's voice on the harmonica; on the latter, combining two popular themes of mouth-harp players, he imitates the sounds of both a railroad locomotive and a fox hunt. Talking-machine company executives must have assumed that such novelty harmonica pieces, devoid, as they were, of any racial connotations, would appeal to both white and black record buyers, because, as with DeFord Bailey's "John Henry" on the Victor label, McCoy's two numbers simultaneously appeared in both Columbia's 14000-D race series (14302-D) and its 15000-D hillbilly series (15269-D). On May 12, 1928, Columbia advertised McCoy's race record in the *Chicago Defender*, where the caption beneath a cartoon of a dancing harmonica asserted, "Mama Blues—A snappy little, happy little, jazzy tune on the mouth harp. Mama won't be blue when she hears this number. On the other side, William McCoy toots out a set of 'Train Imitations' that rival a Dixie Flyer. Whistle, siren, choo-choo—they're all there! Hear 'Train Imitations' and see if you recognize them!" Based on the examples of Bailey and McCoy, it appears that, unlike commercial recordings of the banjo (an instrument that, after the turn of the twentieth century, African Americans increasingly abandoned in favor of the guitar), those of the harmonica (an instrument that retained a high level of popularity among both black and white southerners during the 1920s), offered far greater possibilities for racial cross-listing in record catalogues—or at least the labels' A&R men presumed they did.[45]

Perhaps the most unusual racially cross-listed recording issued in a hillbilly series prior to 1933 was Brunswick 487 in the label's "Songs from Dixie" series: "Lucky Strike" / "Wrigley's en Batterie," recorded at a November 17, 1930, session in New York City. Both of these sides, described on the record label as "chansonnette Créole avec piano" and "monologue Créole," respectively, were recorded in Haitian Creole, the island's indigenous language based chiefly on French. The artist who produced these sides, the singer Théophile Salnave (1890–ca. 1969), was a Haitian immigrant from Port au Prince who arrived in the United States in late September 1930, only about six weeks before he recorded this pair of selections; he later returned to his native island country and became a popular radio singer known by the nicknames "Zo" and "Zo bouke chen" on Haiti's Radio Caraïbes.[46] It is difficult to account for Brunswick's decision to release Salnave's record in its "Songs from Dixie" series, but since the label had no dedicated Cajun series and instead integrated such records into its hillbilly series, perhaps company executives mistakenly assumed that Salnave's recordings were Acadian French performances. Then again, releasing Salnave's record in the label's hillbilly series may have been a deliberate decision by Brunswick executives who believed it might appeal to Acadian French-speaking record buyers.

Although several African American solo artists and vocal ensembles made records that appeared in hillbilly catalogues, nearly two-thirds of racially cross-listed artists were black string bands, most of whose repertoires featured at least some pre-blues common stock songs and tunes. Among these string bands was the previously mentioned Booker Orchestra, whose sole Gennett record, "Salty Dog" / "Camp Nelson Blues," though not technically released in a hillbilly series (since the label had none), was promoted in the hillbilly market. Another African American string band, the James Cole String Band, had two of its traditional fiddle breakdowns, "I Got a Gal" and "Bill Cheatem," recorded on June 25, 1928, at an Indianapolis field session, released in Vocalion's hillbilly series. Virtually nothing is known about this band, which appears to have been based in Indianapolis, and until only recently even the race of these musicians remained in question. In his 1993 liner notes to Document's *The Tommie Bradley–James Cole Groups, 1928–1932: Complete Recorded Works in Chronological Order*, Dick Spottswood admits that James Cole, the fiddler and leader of this string band, might not be the same James Cole, an African American, who recorded more than a dozen sides for Gennett between 1930 and 1932 as a member of an all-black string band sometimes billed as James Cole's Washboard Four. Convincing evidence recently uncovered by Tony Russell, however, suggests that these were one and the same artist.[47]

Only slightly less obscure is the African American guitar-and-mandolin duo of Joe Evans (dates unknown) and Arthur McClain (dates unknown), sometimes billed on their race selections as "the Two Poor Boys," who had two of their sides issued for the hillbilly market. The geographical origins of these two artists is not known for certain, but Evans, a guitarist who worked as a shoeshine man and street singer on Vine Street in Knoxville, may have been a native of that city. McClain, who appears to have played both the mandolin and the fiddle, may originally have been from Alabama. Between 1927 and 1931 Evans and McClain recorded nearly thirty sides, chiefly for the American Record Corporation (ARC), including versions of the Mississippi Sheiks' 1930 best-selling race record, "Sitting on Top of the World," and Tom Darby and Jimmie Tarlton's enormously popular hillbilly hit of three years earlier, "Birmingham Jail." ARC usually released Evans and McClain's recordings under the designation of race records on its complex of Banner, Oriole, Perfect, and Romeo dime-store labels. But one of the duo's numbers, "Old Hen Cackle," recorded in New York City on May 20, 1931, was coupled with "Sourwood Mountain," recorded the following day, for release under the billing of Colman (*sic*) and Harper on both the Oriole and Perfect labels in the "Old Time Tunes" category.[48]

Another African American string band from Knoxville also recorded two instrumentals that were classified for the hillbilly market. The band, composed of fiddler and mandolin player Howard "Louie Bluie" Armstrong (1909–2003), blind guitarist Roland Martin (prob. ca. 1875–?), and Martin's younger stepbrother, string bass player Carl Martin (1906–79), entertained at dances, political rallies, weddings, and even funerals for both white and black audiences. Discovered by a local talent scout, the band made its recording debut on April 3, 1930, at a joint Brunswick-Vocalion field session held in WNOX's radio studios, located in Knoxville's St. James Hotel. This session produced two instrumentals with localized titles, "Vine Street Drag" (a misspelling of the actual title, which, according to Armstrong, was "Vine Street Rag") — which was loosely based on the 1896 Tin Pan Alley "coon song" known as "The Bully of the Town" — and "Knox County Stomp," which features passages of Armstrong's trademark pizzicato, a technique borrowed from classical violinists in which he plucked the fiddle strings. Vocalion issued the coupling simultaneously in both its race and hillbilly series but under different artist credits. On Vocalion race records, "Knox County Stomp" / "Vine Street Drag" were credited to the Tennessee Chocolate Drops, while on the firm's hillbilly records, the same two sides were listed as being by the Tennessee Trio — an example of how record companies deliberately disguised the identity of African American artists on old-time records behind racially neutral pseudonyms.[49]

The African American mandolin-and-guitar duo of Nap Hayes (prob. 1903–93) and Matthew Prater (dates unknown), who were possibly from around Vicksburg, Mississippi, also made recordings that were marketed in hillbilly series. On February 15, 1928, this virtually unknown pair recorded four duets at an OKeh field session in Memphis. Two of these recordings, "Nothin' Doin'" and "Prater Blues," consisted of standard twelve-bar blues, but the other two, "Somethin' Doin'" and "Easy Winner," were loosely based on Scott Joplin rags, rare instances of any of the so-called King of Ragtime's compositions being recorded for either race or hillbilly discs. "Somethin' Doin'" contained strains of Joplin's 1903 cakewalk march titled "Something Doing," while "Easy Winner," despite sharing its name with the composer's 1901 rag "The Easy Winners," was actually based on another Joplin composition, "The Entertainer," a two-step rag published in 1902.[50]

On four additional selections at this session, the famous St. Louis–based African American blues singer and guitarist Alonzo "Lonnie" Johnson (prob. 1894–1970) joined Hayes and Prater to form a trio. Between 1925 and 1932, in addition to his extensive solo recording career, Johnson also worked as a talent scout and studio guitarist for OKeh, accompanying blues singers such as Alger "Texas" Alexander, Victoria Spivey, and Clara Smith, as well as jazz bands such as Louis Armstrong's Hot Five and Duke Ellington and His Orchestra.[51] Although best known for his superb guitar work, much of which laid the foundation for the emergence of urban blues, the New Orleans–born Johnson was also a highly skilled fiddler who had begun playing the instrument in his family's string band around the age of fourteen. On the four sides he made with Hayes and Prater, including "Memphis Stomp" and "Violin Blues," Johnson demonstrates his smooth, sophisticated fiddling. The two other sides featuring his violin work, renditions of the Tin Pan Alley hits "Let Me Call You Sweetheart" and "I'm Drifting Back to Dreamland," went unissued. Of the six issued sides from Hayes and Prater's 1928 Memphis session, only two of them, "Violin Blues" and "Prater Blues," appeared in OKeh's race series, where they were credited to the Johnson Boys. The other four sides, including "Memphis Stomp" with Johnson on violin, were released in OKeh's "Old Time Tunes" hillbilly series: "Somethin' Doin'" / "Nothin' Doin'" appeared under the billing Nap Hayes and Matthew Prater, while "Easy Winner" / "Memphis Stomp" was credited to the Blue Boys. Apparently these six sides represent Hayes and Prater's entire commercially released body of work.[52]

The African American group whose records most frequently appeared in hillbilly series was the Mississippi Sheiks, the most successful black string band of the Great Depression. Between 1930 and 1935 the band recorded nearly one hundred sides for a series of record labels, including OKeh, Paramount, Columbia, and Bluebird (fig. 1.2). Based in Jackson, Mississippi, then an important regional blues center, the group evolved out of the family band of the large Chatman (sometimes Chatmon) clan, who hailed from the hill country around Bolton, twenty miles west of Jackson. The core members of

Race » OKeh » Records
ELECTRIC

Song

Sensations

by

◆ ## The Mississippi Sheiks ◆

8885   ⎰SHE AIN'T NO GOOD—Vocal; Violin and Guitar Acc.
10 in. 75¢⎱HONEY BABE LET THE DEAL GO DOWN—
      Vocal; Violin and Guitar Acc.

Lonnie Johnson *sings and plays* « « «

8886   ⎰ANOTHER WOMAN BOOKED OUT AND BOUND TO GO—
10 in. 75¢   Vocal with Guitar
     ⎱I JUST CAN'T STAND THESE BLUES—Vocal with Guitar

Bo   Carter

8887   ⎰PIN IN YOUR CUSHION—Vocal with Guitar
10 in. 75¢⎱I LOVE THAT THING—Vocal with Guitar

FIGURE 1.2. OKeh race records advertisement featuring the Mississippi Sheiks and Bo Carter, ca. July 1931. Courtesy of Old Hat Records.

heiks were fiddler Lonnie Chatman (ca. 1890–1943) and
, lead singer and guitarist Walter Vinson (1901–75; also
Vincson, Vincent, and Jacobs). Occasionally Chatman's
Armenter "Bo" Chatman (1893–1964) — better known on
— and Vivian "Sam" Chatman (1897–1983), joined them
. Formed around 1921, the band took its name report-
the 1921 Tin Pan Alley hit "The Sheik of Araby" (which
inspired by Rudolph Valentino's box-office smash of that
same year, *The Sheik*). The Mississippi Sheiks often entertained at dances and
parties for both white and black crowds throughout central Mississippi, and,
as a result, their repertoire featured a wide assortment of American music,
including blues, old-time breakdowns, waltzes, fox-trots, Tin Pan Alley
songs, and jazz tunes, all of which reflected the band's versatility as superb
all-around entertainers. On February 17, 1930, Vinson and Chatman, accompanied by Bo Chatman, made their first recordings together as the Mississippi Sheiks at an OKeh field session in Shreveport, Louisiana. This session
produced the band's biggest-selling hit, "Sitting on Top of the World," composed by Vinson, which was released in OKeh's race series and soon became
a Mississippi Delta and, later, a Chicago blues classic. During the mid- to late
1930s, several western swing bands, including Bob Wills and His Texas Playboys and the Light Crust Doughboys, also covered the song.[53]

Over the next five years, the Mississippi Sheiks recorded more than eighty
additional sides for OKeh and various other labels, most of which were marketed in these labels' race series to African American record buyers. But at
least a dozen of the band's sides were listed, always under racially ambiguous
pseudonyms, in OKeh's "Old Time Tunes" series. Two of the band's eight
selections from its February 1930 debut session, "The Sheik Waltz" / "The
Jazz Fiddler," were released as a coupling for the hillbilly market under the
billing Walter Jacobs and Lonnie Carter. Four other titles, recorded that June
in San Antonio, Texas, likewise appeared in OKeh's hillbilly series, this time
credited to Walter Jacobs and the Carter Brothers. Members of the Mississippi Sheiks also recorded in various other combinations under different
names, and one of these spin-off bands, the Mississippi Mud Steppers, made
recordings at a December 1930 OKeh field session held at the King Edward
Hotel in Jackson, Mississippi. There the mandolin player Charlie McCoy
(1911–50), a former neighbor and longtime colleague, teamed with Vinson and Chatman to record a half dozen instrumentals, including "Jackson
Stomp" and "Alma Waltz." All six of these sides appeared in OKeh's hillbilly

catalogue, but none of the accompanying promotional literature alluded to the race of the band members who had recorded them.[54]

ALTHOUGH IN RETROSPECT it may seem surprising that nearly 180 recordings featuring African American artists appeared in hillbilly series or on records intended for sale in the hillbilly market, one factor that helps to account for these marketing decisions is that hillbilly catalogues before 1933 were themselves remarkably diverse. For example, Brunswick's "Songs from Dixie" series, which ran from 1927 to 1933, included selections by African American string bands, Cajun duos, French Canadian harmonica soloists, Creole Haitian singers, and Minnesota polka bands. Other labels' hillbilly series contained recordings of New England old-time fiddlers, hotel dance orchestras, Hawaiian guitarists, popular vaudeville singers, Irish melodeon players, singing cowboys, western swing bands, Mexican groups, and even a Russian balalaika troupe. To be sure, country music scholars generally acknowledge such diversity but usually only in passing, with little substantive discussion of it. Within the field of country music studies, the dominant focus on more "traditional" (and therefore "authentic") recordings and on the precommercial Anglo-Celtic roots of this music has tended to elide this racial and ethnic diversity, particularly African Americans' involvement in the commercial recording of hillbilly music.[55]

African American participation in the commercial hillbilly recording industry encourages us to conceptualize early country music not as an organic folk tradition but rather as a culturally constructed commercial music, an "invented tradition."[56] As Richard A. Peterson points out, the commercialization of southern white vernacular music was not simply a matter of recording and then offering for sale records of a coherent, preexisting musical genre. Instead, like all commercial musical genres, it had to be invented—through a negotiated process that involved a multitude of production and marketing decisions. And the categories of "old-time music" and "hillbilly music" that talking-machine companies settled on to sell this music were as much marketing labels as anything else.[57] Moreover it appears that the racial division separating race and hillbilly records was far more elastic and permeable than most music scholars have generally appreciated. Contrary to what some have written, the classification of African American records for the hillbilly market indicates that when A&R men assigned new releases to a particular catalogue, the criteria of repertoire and performance style figured in their decisions as much as, or perhaps even more than, the race of the recording artist. And it is worth emphasizing that in releasing such records in their hillbilly catalogues, talking-machine companies were not so much reflecting a pre-existing musical genre as they were constructing a new one.

In accounting for the release of African American records in hillbilly series, it is also important to bear in mind that African Americans were not the only racial group to cross the musical color line institutionalized by the nation's talking-machine industry. Although it remains beyond the scope of this essay, it is worth noting that occasionally white old-time musicians, including Riley Puckett, Clayton McMichen, Frank Luther, Carson Robison, and Hoke Rice, either had their recordings issued in race series or accompanied black singers and musicians at integrated sessions that produced race records.[58] Perhaps the most famous example of a hillbilly record being racially cross-listed for the race market involves the Allen Brothers, a white Chattanooga guitar-and-tenor-banjo duo who specialized in bawdy blues songs. In December 1927 Columbia released the brothers' second record, "Chattanooga Blues" / "Laughin' and Cryin' Blues," in its 14000-D race series instead of its 15000-D hillbilly series, in which their first record had appeared. Whether by accident or design, this decision reportedly so incensed the Allen Brothers that they retained an attorney to bring a lawsuit against Columbia for $250,000 for "damaging their reputations." "We were trying to get into vaudeville back then," Lee Allen explained decades later. "It would have hurt us in getting dates if people who didn't know us thought we were black." The Allen Brothers recorded at only one more session for Columbia, in April 1928 in Atlanta. A few weeks later the duo dropped their suit and terminated their recording contact with the company, and then signed on as exclusive artists with Victor, for whom they went on to record fifty-seven sides over the next four years. The Allen Brothers' threatened lawsuit not only underscores the significance of racial categories in the 1920s Jim Crow South; it also illuminates the powerful role that the recording industry's marketing labels of race and hillbilly records played in shaping both recording artists' and consumers' perceptions of these commercial genres.[59]

Precisely because record retailers and buyers used the industry's marketing labels of *race* and *hillbilly* largely as racial markers, talking-machine companies at times resorted to a kind of commercial subterfuge when releasing records by black artists in hillbilly series and, conversely, by white artists in race series. This stratagem primarily took the form of pseudonyms crafted, seemingly deliberately, to disguise the racial identity of racially cross-listed artists. To be sure, the use of artist credit pseudonyms was a common industry practice, and during the 1920s record companies often issued the same master recording on several different labels, even within the genre of popular music. When companies did so, they usually employed pseudonyms for the artist credits on their cheaper, budget-priced labels in order to protect their higher-priced premium labels. For example, the Starr Piano Company released Ernest V. Stoneman's 1927 recording of "The Poor Tramp Has to Live" under his own name on its flagship Gennett label, which sold for seventy-five cents, but when it issued the same recording, pressed from the very same master, on its cheaper Champion label, which sold for about half that price, it was credited to Uncle Jim Seaney. On the firm's "stencil" labels of Silvertone, Supertone, and Challenge, which were manufactured for Sears, Roebuck and Company, the selection was listed as by Uncle Ben Hawkins.[60] The firm's marketing decision here was purely economic and had nothing to do with race. But for racially cross-listed records in hillbilly and race catalogues, such a decision seems to have been about nothing but race. On these records, such fictitious artist credits assumed special importance, because companies were attempting to conceal not only the actual name of a recording artist but also, and more important, the artist's racial identity. Within the field of hillbilly records, scattered evidence indicates that talking-machine firms often disguised the identity of the African American artists who appeared in these series, particularly if they were relatively well known as race recording artists, just as those same firms concealed the identity of white hillbilly artists whose selections appeared on race records. In fact companies regularly assigned pseudonyms to racially cross-listed artists even on their premium flagship labels, when such pseudonyms would otherwise have been unnecessary. Firms also substituted pseudonyms for the actual names of racially cross-listed artists even when a recording was issued on only a single label and there was no economic imperative to shield their higher-priced labels from the competition of their cheaper subsidiary labels. Considering the lack of documentary evidence, accounting for motivations behind these commercial decisions is difficult and therefore only speculative, but perhaps talking-machine company executives believed that if the racial identities of these artists were publicly known, given prevailing racial attitudes, white consumers might decline to purchase hillbilly records featuring black artists, and that black consumers might likewise reject race records featuring white artists. But anecdotal evidence does not bear out these commercial concerns. In terms of their actual consumption patterns, southern record buyers of the 1920s were far more omnivorous than record company executives generally seemed to comprehend, and interviews with elderly black and white musicians reveal that many of them purchased records intended specifically for sale to other racial and even foreign-language ethnic groups. Still, much of this appears to have been lost on talking-machine firms, which focused their promotional efforts on marketing race records to African Americans and hillbilly records to rural and working-class white southerners.[61]

Also intriguing in regard to this issue of racial masquerade is a studio portrait of Taylor's Kentucky Boys circa 1927 that Gennett used in its promotional literature. As a recording unit, this otherwise all-white string band of revolving members, as previously noted, featured the African American fiddler Jim Booker, who performed on "Gray Eagle" and "Forked Deer" at the band's April 1927 debut sessions. But in the publicity photograph of the band that appeared in the 1928 *Gennett Records of Old Time Tunes* catalogue above the listing for these two selections, the man shown holding the fiddle is not Jim Booker but rather the band's white manager, Dennis W. Taylor (fig. 1.3). Booker's absence from the studio portrait raises the question of whether Gennett executives consciously sought to conceal his membership in the band from their white customers. Without attributing a source, Charles K. Wolfe claims that "when it came time to make a band photo for the Gennett catalogue, Jim Booker was not invited and in his place Dennis Taylor posed, holding a fiddle he didn't know how to play; the image the catalogue presented was that of an all-white stringband." But Richard Nevins posits another, perhaps more plausible explanation for Booker's absence. In the liner notes to the *Kentucky Mountain Music* boxed set, Nevins suggests that the portrait may not have been taken at the time of the band's recording sessions and that when it was actually taken Booker was unavailable to sit for the photograph with his two band mates. Without knowing the source of Wolfe's claim, we cannot entirely discount it, but neither can we dismiss Nevin's reasonable speculation. Bolstering Nevin's theory is the fact that, although the photograph includes banjoist Marion Underwood, the guitarist is not Willie Young but apparently Aulton Ray, who, although he recorded at the band's April 1927 sessions, did not perform on either "Gray Eagle" or "Forked Deer."[62] Ultimately we cannot conclusively explain Booker's absence from this studio portrait. But this line of inquiry raises interesting, though perhaps ultimately unanswerable questions about both the extent and motivations of companies' efforts to conceal the identities of African American artists on hillbilly records, and about whether or not white record buyers actually realized, or even cared, that African American artists occasionally performed on the hillbilly records they purchased and enjoyed.

Taylor's Kentucky Boys

TAYLOR'S KENTUCKY BOYS

FORKED DEER—*Old Time Playin'* } 6130
GRAY EAGLE—*Old Time Playin'* } .75

JOHN STROM AND HOW

SKANSEN WALTZ—*International—Fiddle & Accordion* } 6231
WALTZ BY THE RIVER—*International—Fiddle &*
Accordion } .75

GRANDPA'S COURTSHIP—*Waltz—International—*
Accordion, Concertina, Tuba, Acc.
Joseph Soukup & Joseph Peroutka } 6207
GRASSHOPPER POLKA—*International—Fiddle, Accordion* } .75
John Strom and How }

FIGURE 1.3. Listing of Taylor's Kentucky Boys' "Gray Eagle" and "Forked Deer," along with a studio photograph of the band, from the *Gennett Records of Old Time Tunes* catalog, 1928. Author's collection.

Beyond the use of racially ambiguous pseudonyms and misleading advertising materials, prewar African American hillbilly records also provide insights into the commercial perceptions and production decisions of the talking-machine companies' almost exclusively white executives. While a rich literature on post–World War II country music's business history has emerged in the past two decades, the relative dearth of extant corporate documents has prevented scholars from generating comparable studies about the prewar hillbilly music industry.[63] But the industry's creation and development of separate racialized record series are essential to understanding hillbilly music as a commercial genre. While prewar hillbilly, race, popular, and classical record series appear to modern-day scholars and fans to be discrete, organic genres that sprang naturally from the musics themselves, the truth is that these genres, like all commercial musical genres, were culturally constructed categories that were continuously being redefined during the 1920s and 1930s by record label executives charged with creating and sustaining a profitable market for their companies' discs. In hindsight, it seems obvious that Jimmie Rodgers's "Blue Yodel No. 9," despite its "hot" jazz accompaniment, would have been classified as a hillbilly record. But the recordings of African Americans and other racial and ethnic minority artists that were classified for the hillbilly market helps us to understand that these record series do not reflect preexisting natural genres but rather constitute constantly evolving musical categories that emerged from a negotiated historical process.

An excellent example of the cultural construction of hillbilly music as a commercial genre can be found in Columbia's "Old Familiar Tunes" series, which assembled a broad spectrum of seemingly unrelated artists and selections in the 783 discs issued in this series between 1925 and 1932. Although this series overwhelmingly featured recordings by white southern musicians, it also contained records by an African American songster (Stove Pipe No. 1), an African American women's gospel quartet (Wheat Street Female Quartet), and an African American minister (Rev. C. D. Montgomery). All three of these records appeared within the first twenty-five releases in Columbia's "Old Familiar Tunes" series, and, in issuing them in this series, company executives must have believed that these selections represented a legitimate part of the emerging genre of hillbilly music. At the very least, they assumed that these records would appeal to this series' presumed audience of southern white record buyers. But these African American records also remind us that Columbia executives, groping to define the boundaries of this fledgling series and understand the market for these records, were constructing their hillbilly catalogue release by release, without the benefit of being able to hear or envision a fully developed musical genre. The creation of hillbilly music therefore was always an ongoing and incomplete process, and the genre should be understood and studied as such, as a historical process and not as a finished product, the complete discography, that today's scholars and fans have the advantage of seeing in its entirety.[64]

Of course, this process of developing a hillbilly series and assigning particular records to it began long before a phonograph record was ever commercially released, with A&R men's decisions of where and when to hold field recording sessions, whom to recruit to audition and then to select to make recordings, and which of their musical numbers to record.[65] But important decisions also occurred at company headquarters after these performances had been captured on wax masters. After returning from a one- or two-month, multiple-city recording expedition, A&R men faced the time-consuming, laborious task of evaluating the test pressings (produced from the original wax masters) of perhaps three hundred to four hundred different titles, for each of which two or perhaps even three different masters, or "takes," might have been recorded. This screening process involved listening to all of these pressings, evaluating them, choosing which musical selections to release, and then determining which of the two or three takes of that particular selection contained the most appealing performances or the fewest imperfections. Only after making these production decisions did executives begin to consider how best to market their chosen selections. Here A&R weighed a number of important considerations, including the type of song or tune it was and the performance style in which it was rendered, the perceived appropriate consumer audience for a particular record, and the imperatives of expanding a particular catalogue or of meeting consumer demand for a particular title or kind of selection (vocal duets, fiddle tunes, comical songs, etc.). For companies that had such active series, most of the selections of vernacular music made on these southern recording trips were destined for either the race or the hillbilly series, depending largely but by no means solely on the race of the recording artists. As we have seen, A&R men occasionally cross-listed white artists in race series and black artists in hillbilly series, or even simultaneously released records in both series. And it bears emphasizing that, in making these relatively subjective production and marketing decisions, talking-machine company executives played an enormously influential role in shaping and defining hillbilly music as well as race music, not only for contemporary consumers but also, decades later, for scholars and collectors.[66]

With limited evidence to drawn upon, we cannot reconstruct the precise aesthetic and commercial considerations that informed record company executives' myriad production and marketing decisions. But surviving company ledgers and files offer fascinating glimpses of this process and particularly the subjectivity and sometimes even the uncertainty involved in the assignment of new releases to particular record series. To assist them in their record-keeping tasks throughout the various phases of the production process, talking-machine company officials used in-house forms, called "label copy notices," which contained basic information about a phonograph record's production and marketing, including the date for its scheduled release, the monthly catalogue supplement in which it would be announced, and the catalogue series in which it would be issued. It is not uncommon to find studio ledger sheets and label copy notices on which an official has switched the assigned record series for a forthcoming release. One example of this involves the eight selections recorded by the black blues singer and guitarist Mississippi John Hurt at his debut February 14, 1928, session for OKeh in Memphis. In his native Carroll County, Mississippi, Hurt often performed with a white neighbor, fiddler Willie Narmour, at dances when Narmour's regular accompanist, guitarist Shell Smith, was unavailable; indeed it was Narmour who had recommended Hurt to an OKeh A&R man scouting for local talent, which led to Hurt's recording session. Company file cards indicate that Hurt's selections were originally intended for release in the label's "Old Time Tunes" series. But the cards were altered to change the series designation to "race." Only two of Hurt's initial eight sides were eventually issued: "Frankie," backed with "Nobody's Dirty Business," appeared in OKeh's 8000 race series. Likewise "World in a Jug" and "Sunny Southern Blues" — credited to the white singer and guitarist "Big Road" Webster Taylor (the Mississippi Mule Skinner), who recorded them in Chicago in April 1929 — were originally scheduled for release in Vocalion's 5000 hillbilly series but ultimately appeared in the label's 1000 race series. On a few occasions, as already noted, talking-machine companies even released records deemed to have cross-racial appeal, such as those by DeFord Bailey, William McCoy, and the Tennessee Chocolate Drops, simultaneously in both their hillbilly and races series. In 1931, to cite a final example, RCA-Victor not only released a record by Jack Cawley's Oklahoma Ridge Runners, a white string band, simultaneously in both the firm's race and hillbilly catalogues, but the firm also retitled the selections. On Victor 23540, intended for the hillbilly market, the titles appeared as "Guitar Duet Blues" / "Slow Guitar Blues," but on the race record (Victor 23257), aimed at African American consumers, the same sides were credited to Buster and Jack and retitled, for unknown reasons, "Cross Tie Blues" / "Pouring Down Blues."[67]

We cannot entirely discount the possibility that at least some African Americans' records found their way into hillbilly catalogues in error, the result of shoddy record keeping, unfamiliarity with southern vernacular music, poor understanding of southern dialects, or some mistaken assumption on the part of a record company executive. But the release of most such African American hillbilly records appears to have been based on deliberate and carefully considered decisions. Some rather strong evidence, albeit concerning the marketing of white hillbilly artists in race series, exists to support this claim. In Gennett ledgers, for example, a company official has crossed out the description "Old Time Playin'" for the banjoist G. C. Osborne's "Token [sic] In Blues" (probably a misspelling of "Taken In Blues"), recorded in Richmond, Indiana, in April 1928, and appended a note: "Use as race inst[ead]." Gennett files contain a similar note for "Separation Blues," which the West Virginia guitarist Jess Johnston recorded in November 1931: "Can Use Race Another Name." That is, one of the label's executives was recommending that the recording either be issued for the race records market using a pseudonym for Johnston, or issued simultaneously for both the hillbilly and race market using a pseudonym for Johnston on the latter release. Ultimately Gennett decided not to issue Johnston's recording at all, but both of these notes indicate that officials were clearly aware that they were breaching the industry's own established racial categories in considering the release of white artists' records for a race market aimed at African American consumers.[68]

Collectively the 178 known hillbilly recordings on which African Americans appeared between 1924 and 1932 add considerably to our understanding of the formative decade of commercially recorded hillbilly music. These sides, particularly those that resulted from integrated recording sessions, document a significant amount of interracial musical exchange and cooperation between white and black southern musicians at the height of Jim Crow segregation. Moreover these recordings chronicle the participation of nearly fifty African American artists in the nation's fledgling hillbilly recording industry, and thus provide a better historical context for understanding Charley Pride and the handful of other African American singers who have emerged in the Nashville country music industry within the past four decades. Although records by black artists represent only a tiny fraction of the total number of hillbilly records released before 1933, they nonetheless challenge our standard narrative of early commercial country music and encourage us to consider more closely the racial as well as ethnic diversity of the artists who performed on these recordings, the role of talking-machine companies in shaping and defining this musical genre, and the industry's perceptions of both this music and its presumed audience. In particular these records reveal that firms' efforts to advertise and market hillbilly music as a distinctly white southern musical expression were frequently at odds with their actual production decisions regarding the release of these records and the content of their record series. Country music scholars have overwhelmingly favored the former, nostalgia-tinged, publicity-based interpretation of hillbilly music, stressing the traditionalism, authenticity, and southern white rural origins of this music, but the latter conception, based on the actual production of these records and not on advertising images, represents a far more historically accurate reflection of hillbilly music as a commercially recorded musical genre prior to 1933.

Notes

For critical reading, encouragement, and suggestions, I thank Kathleen Drowne, Lance Ledbetter, Kevin S. Fontenot, Steve Goodson, David M. Anderson, Michael T. Bertrand, Tony Russell, Luke Horton, Jack Norton, Chris O'Neill, Pen Bogert, Jack Bond, James Akenson, Diane Pecknold, Paul A. Huber Jr., and the late Archie Green. I also acknowledge the librarians at Wilson Library on the campus of Missouri University of Science and Technology for their indispensable assistance in securing interlibrary loan materials.

1. Porterfield, liner notes, *Jimmie Rodgers*, 29; Porterfield, *Jimmie Rodgers*, 250–61. "Blue Yodel No. 9" can be heard on the *Jimmie Rodgers* boxed set.

2. Porterfield, *Jimmie Rodgers*, 409; Russell et al., *Country Music Records*, 804. According to RCA-Victor files, Rodgers's Victor recording of "Blue Yodel No. 9" sold slightly more than 25,000 copies, comparatively high sales figures given its release during the depths of the Great Depression. During the 1930s this title was reissued twice on Montgomery Ward's mail-order label and, as was typical of much of the popular Rodgers's catalogue, also appeared on an assortment of international labels marketed chiefly in the British Isles, Australia, and India.

3. Nolan Porterfield has speculated that this studio collaboration was arranged by Rodgers's producer and manager, Ralph S. Peer, who became acquainted with Armstrong in the mid-1920s when the jazz trumpeter recorded for Peer's then employer, OKeh Records. The jazz historian Dan Morgenstern, in contrast, has claimed that Armstrong and his wife recorded at Rodgers's personal invitation. In the end, however, the origin of this unique session remains, in the words of Armstrong's biogra-

phers Max Jones and John Chilton, "one of jazz's unsolvable riddles." In fact despite the distinctive "hot" trumpet solo on the record and the effortlessness with which the trumpeter follows what Morgenstern calls "Rodgers's somewhat unpredictable bar lines," jazz scholars and record collectors had long disputed Armstrong's presence on "Blue Yodel No. 9" until the trumpeter himself confirmed it in 1949. The identity of the pianist on the recording remained in question even longer, with some discographers assuming that it was Armstrong's close friend and frequent sideman Earl "Fatha" Hines, but Porterfield found conclusive proof when he discovered a typewritten lyric sheet for the song containing a scribbled note at the bottom of the page, apparently in Rodgers's own hand, that read, "Recorded in Hollywood 7-16-30 / Louis Armstrong Trumpet, Lillian on Piano."

At the time of the session, Louis Armstrong had only recently arrived in California, where he was headlining shows as the featured soloist in the orchestra at Frank Sebastian's New Cotton Club, a swanky nightclub located across from the MGM Studios, in the Los Angeles suburb of Culver City. Armstrong's estranged wife Lillian, who had played piano at several of his now-classic Hot Five and Hot Seven sessions for OKeh, had come to Hollywood for one final attempt to salvage their stormy six-year marriage. Her efforts proved futile, however, and "Blue Yodel No. 9" marked their last recording collaboration, as well as Louis Armstrong's last side as a blues accompanist. See Porterfield, *Jimmie Rodgers*, 258–60; Morgenstern, liner notes, *Louis Armstrong*, 23, 50; Jones and Chilton, *Louis*, 235–36; Meckna, *Satchmo*, 12, 40, 257.

4. Waterman, "Race Music," 171; Rust, *Jazz Records*, 2:1328; Dixon, Godrich, and Rye, *Blues and Gospel Records*, 767; Porterfield, *Jimmie Rodgers*, 72. Also worth noting is that the Rock and Roll Hall of Fame and Museum has selected "Blue Yodel No. 9" as one of the "500 Songs That Shaped Rock and Roll." See the Rock and Roll Hall of Fame and Museum website, http://rockhall.com/exhibits/one-hit-wonders-songs -that-shaped-rock-and-roll/.

5. As late as 1968, for example, the historian Bill C. Malone could write in his landmark study *Country Music U.S.A.*, "Although Negro songs and styles have moved freely into country music, Negroes have not. One of the striking characteristics of country music has been the almost total absence of Negro performers" (27).

6. The scholarly literature on these prewar African American hillbilly records consists almost entirely of scattered passages in books, articles, and CD liner notes. But for some of the most important studies, see Russell, *Blacks, Whites, and Blues* (pages cited here refer to the edition published as part of Oliver et al., *Yonder Comes the Blues*); Wolfe, "Rural Black String Band Music"; Wolfe, "Black String Bands"; Morton and Wolfe, *DeFord Bailey*; Ivey, "Border Crossing"; and Wald, *Escaping the Delta*, especially 48–53.

7. See, for example, Nevins, liner notes, *Kentucky Mountain Music*; Wolfe, *The Devil's Box*, 8; Rumble, "The Artists and the Songs," 29.

8. It is worth noting that, in his meticulously researched *Country Music Records*

aphy, Tony Russell mentions but does not provide the discographical de-
r most of the racially cross-listed African American recordings (i.e., those in
dix B) discussed in this essay, even though these records were issued in hill-
series. Instead he refers readers to Dixon, Godrich, and Rye's *Blues and Gospel*
rds, which does include the complete extant session information about these
records. Thus it is necessary to use this reference work in conjunction with Russell's
in order to compile a complete list of African American artists who appeared on prewar hillbilly records. See Russell et al., *Country Music Records*, 5.

9. Ivey, "Border Crossing," 8. Despite the existence of *Country Music Records* and
Blues and Gospel Records, however, research in this area remains particularly challenging, because most of the talking-machine companies that manufactured old-
time records before 1933 are now defunct, and their business records containing
so much of the information essential to prewar discographies are no longer extant.
Those studio ledgers, label copy notices, and other industry-generated documents
that have survived contain invaluable data for discographers, record collectors, and
scholars, but much of the personnel information, particularly for string bands and
vocal quartets, is often incomplete or entirely absent. Even when all the personnel
for a particular recording session are provided, it is often frustratingly difficult, if
not impossible, especially in cases of common surnames like "Smith," "Jones," and
"Johnson," to locate a particular artist in census records and other public documents
and to determine his or her race with any degree of certainty. As this essay makes
abundantly clear, the release of a particular record in a talking-machine company's
race or hillbilly series is by no means a reliable indicator of the race of the artist or
artists who made that recording.

For more than three decades now, for example, scholars and record collectors
have debated the racial identity of Bayless Rose, the superb guitarist who recorded
eight solo blues and rags under his own name for Gennett Records in 1930. Although
the compilers of *Blues and Gospel Records* have pointed out that Rose's participation
in other Gennett sessions with known African American musicians suggests that
he was almost certainly African American, the publication of Christopher C. King's
2004 article in *78 Quarterly* indicates that the debate about Rose's racial identity
remains unresolved. The racial identities of other, no less obscure recording artists, including Bud Alexander, Eugene Ballenger, Lysle Byrd, Gace Haynes, Wesley
Long, Palmer McAbee, Frank Roberts, and Fiddlin' Slim Sandford, also remain in
question. Even with scholars' access to an ever-expanding collection of digital census records and other public records, the racial identity of some prewar hillbilly
and blues recording artists may never be determined conclusively. King, "Bayless?
Bailey?," 59–68; Dixon, Godrich, and Rye, *Blues and Gospel Records*, 557, 771, 1072;
Russell, *Country Music Records*, 150, 414, 513, 526, 755, 813.

10. These figures exclude those racially integrated sessions involving white hillbilly
musicians that resulted in the release of race records, a subject related to, but beyond
the scope of, this essay. But for examples of these, see note 58 below.

11. Included in this total of 178 recordings are those issued on Gennett, which, although the label did not employ a discrete hillbilly series, did designate these records as "Old Time Playin'" and "Old Time Singin' and Playin'" for sale chiefly to white southern and Midwestern consumers. Excluded, however, are those recordings that appeared, either simultaneously or exclusively, in popular, race, or Cajun series. Additionally, not reflected in this total are fifteen sides that were issued on records sold in the foreign market, particularly in the English-speaking nations of Great Britain, Canada, Australia, and India. See appendixes A and B for complete discographical details.

The two appendixes are based primarily on Russell's *Country Music Records* and Dixon, Godrich, and Rye's *Blues and Gospel Records*, and although I believe I have identified all of the known prewar hillbilly records on which African Americans performed, further research may expand both of these lists. These pioneering artists rightfully deserve more scholarly attention, and one of my sincerest hopes for this essay is that it will stimulate additional research into this significant but heretofore largely ignored aspect of early country music history. To assist in this scholarly endeavor, I have listed in the notes here the titles of currently available CD anthologies and boxed sets on which many of the recordings discussed in this essay can be heard. Within the past decade, nearly 90 percent of these recordings have been reissued on CD, and the availability of these records will certainly facilitate future research and writing about African Americans' participation in the prewar hillbilly recording industry.

12. Much of Tony Russell's and Charles K. Wolfe's pioneering work on these prewar African American recordings, in contrast to my essay here, focuses on what these records reveal about the otherwise murky and sketchily documented history of southern vernacular music prior to the rise of the blues and hillbilly recording industries in the 1920s. Collectively these records provide important insights, Russell and Wolfe have argued, into the shared musical repertoire of white and black southerners in the late nineteenth century and early twentieth. Furthermore a significant percentage of these records feature pre-blues songs and tunes performed by African American string bands, and, as Wolfe has noted, offer rare glimpses into what he calls "the lost worlds" of African American fiddlers and string bands, so common throughout the rural South before World War II but seldom represented on the commercial recordings of the 1920s and 1930s. See Russell, *Blacks, Whites, and Blues*; Wolfe, "Rural Black String Band Music," 3–4; Wolfe, "Black String Bands," 15–18; Wolfe, *The Devil's Box*, 77.

13. A brief explanation of the historical periodization of this essay is in order. Coverage in this essay begins with 1924, the year of the first known hillbilly recording by an African American, and ends in 1932, the year of both a drastic decline in the national sales of phonograph records and the last southern field-recording sessions for two years. That year also serves as an appropriate cut-off date for this essay, because thereafter only one African American artist (Amédé Ardoin), to my knowl-

edge, participated in an integrated hillbilly recording session or otherwise made recordings that were issued in prewar hillbilly series. By 1935, in fact, all six of the major pre-Depression record labels had discontinued both their race and hillbilly series. Henceforth most of the surviving labels generally integrated blues, gospel, jazz, and hillbilly records into a single numerical series, which sometimes included popular vocal and dance selections as well. See Dixon, Godrich, and Rye, *Blues and Gospel Records*, xxiii–xxxix; Russell et al., *Country Music Records*, 9–26.

14. Ivey, "Border Crossing," 9–11; Malone, *Southern Music, American Music*, 4–10; Lipsitz, *Rainbow at Midnight*, 309–12, 316; Laird, *Louisiana Hayride*, 36–46, 50–54; Peterson, *Creating Country Music*, 195–96; Roy, "'Race Records' and 'Hillbilly Music,'" 271–75, 277–78; Clarke, *Rise and Fall of Popular Music*, 135. On the origins of these two series, see also Foreman, "Jazz and Race Records, 1920–1932"; Dixon and Godrich, *Recording the Blues*; Green, "Hillbilly Music"; Malone, *Country Music U.S.A.*, especially pp. 31–91; Miller, *Segregating Sound*, especially 187–214. Miller's superb book is indispensable in these matters.

The pioneer record producer and music publisher Ralph S. Peer later claimed credit for creating both of the marketing labels *race records* and *hillbilly records*. As an A&R man for OKeh between 1920 and 1926, Peer had supervised the experimental June 1923 Atlanta field session at which Fiddlin' John Carson had recorded "The Little Old Log Cabin in the Lane" and "The Old Hen Cackled and the Rooster's Going to Crow," the first commercially successful recordings of what, in 1925, came to be called "hillbilly music." Peer had also assisted OKeh's musical director Fred W. Hager at the August 1920 New York City recording session at which Mamie Smith had recorded "Crazy Blues," which marked the advent of commercial blues recordings by African Americans. As Peer put it bluntly in a 1959 interview, "I invented the hillbilly and the nigger stuff." See Green, "Hillbilly Music," 206–10, 213–14; Laird, *Louisiana Hayride*, 43, 48; Ralph S. Peer interview by Lillian Borgeson, Hollywood, California, ca. January–May 1958, tape recordings in the Southern Folklife Collection, Louis Round Wilson Library, University of North Carolina at Chapel Hill.

15. Spottswood, *Ethnic Music on Records*, 1:xxviii; Gronow, "Ethnic Recordings," especially 5, 7, 36; Miller, *Segregating Sound*, 180–84, 187–89; Roy, "'Race Records' and 'Hillbilly Music,'" 270–71, 274; Dixon, Godrich, and Rye, *Blues and Gospel Records*, xxiii–xxxix; Green, "Hillbilly Music," 215; Russell et al., *Country Music Records*, 3–4, 9–26; Cohen, *Long Steel Rail*, 37–38. Although U.S. talking-machine companies had been releasing foreign-language records on the domestic market since at least 1893, the first discrete numerical series for such records dates to 1904, when Columbia created a special series for its Spanish records. See Spottswood, *Ethnic Music on Records*, 1:xxviii.

16. The best overviews of talking-machine companies' practice of staging field-recording sessions in the South are Wolfe, "The Bristol Syndrome," and Russell, "Country Music on Location." But see also Wolfe, "Ralph Peer at Work"; Wolfe, "Early Country Music in Knoxville"; Wolfe and Russell, "The Asheville Session";

Lornell and Mealor, "A & R Men and the Geography of Piedmont Blues Recordings"; Lornell, "Spatial Perspectives on the Field Recording of Traditional American Music"; Wolfe, "The Legend That Peer Built"; Wolfe, "The Rest of the Story."

17. Waterman, "Race Music," 167; Ivey, "Border Crossing," 10–11; Laird, *Louisiana Hayride*, 41–42, 46–51; Miller, *Segregating Sound*, 187–214. Talking-machine company executives' decision to organize southern vernacular music along the color line profoundly shaped consumers' and, decades later, scholars' understanding of southern vernacular music. Within the historical literature on southern music, for example, this division led to the development of wholly separate fields of musical scholarship for blues studies and country music studies. Furthermore the industry's use of the categories race and hillbilly records led to the "naturalization," to borrow Waterman's term, of what were artificial but seemingly commonsense divisions within southern vernacular music, and obscured the complex interracial interplay that produced the musical antecedents of these two commercial genres. See Ivey, "Border Crossing," 10–11; Laird, *Louisiana Hayride*, 41, 50–51, 53; Waterman, "Race Music," 167.

18. *Brunswick Record Edition of American Folk Songs* 1 (October 23, 1928): 1 (reprinted in Archie Green, "Commercial Music Graphics #41," *John Edwards Memorial Foundation Quarterly* 13 [Summer 1977]: 75–78); Titon, *Early Downhome Blues*, 235–41; *Burlington* (N.C.) *Daily Times*, May 20, 1927; Patrick Huber, "Inventing Hillbilly Music: Record Catalog and Advertising Imagery, 1922–1929," paper presented at International Country Music Conference, Nashville, Tenn., May 27, 2005 (in author's possession). The hillbilly music historian Archie Green suggests two possible explanations for Edison's use of this plantation image to illustrate its recordings of white hillbilly fiddle and string-band records: "Possibly, Edison publicists had issued separate envelope stuffers for both categories of old time discs (hillbilly and race), and perhaps the cover drawing reproduced here simply was used at one time for both sets of brochures. Alternately, the actual person who collated record titles and art work might have noted that among the songs offered by Ernest Stoneman . . . were included 'Hand Me Down My Walkin' Cane,' 'Watermelon Hanging on the Vine,' 'Bully of the Town,' and 'Kitty Wells.' These numbers were representative of black-face stage material that had entered white folk tradition, and, hence, could be illustrated by a wide variety of drawings" ("Commercial Music Graphics," 25–26). Green's latter speculation seems to be closer to the truth, since in my research I have located a few additional examples of talking-machine companies employing similar images of African Americans to advertise hillbilly records. Victor Records' *Old Time Melodies of the Sunny South* brochure (Camden, N.J.: Victor Talking Machine Co., October 1926), for example, features a plantation scene designed apparently to conjure up associations between these "old-time" recordings and a mythical Old South, and thereby to underscore the quaint, old-fashioned, southern nature of the music found on these discs.

19. Victor *Olde Time Fiddlin' Tunes* catalogue (October 1924); Ivey, "Border Crossing," 10–11; Laird, *Louisiana Hayride*, 41, 50–51, 53.

20. Sudhalter, *Lost Chords*, 43–44. On white and black southerners performing music together at stage shows, dances, and other public gatherings before 1933, see, for example, Calt, liner notes, *Mississippi John Hurt*; Seroff, "Polk Miller and the Old South Quartette"; Wald, *Escaping the Delta*, 48; Barker and Taylor, *Faking It*, 30–31. In a 1969 interview, the white Kentucky fiddler Dock Roberts recalled that during a chance encounter at his first Paramount session in April 1927 he and the African American blues guitarist Blind Blake played a few impromptu numbers together in a Chicago recording studio waiting room. See Dock Roberts interview by Harlan Daniel and Archie Green, Richmond, Ky., September 8, 1969, tape recording in the Southern Folklife Collection; Green, "A Discography/Biography Journey," 199.

21. Sudhalter, *Lost Chords*, 43–44. During the early to mid-1920s, the recording of "vaudeville," or "classic," blues involved an extensive number of racially integrated sessions, and among the white popular and jazz musicians who accompanied African American female singers at these sessions were Eddie Lang, Roy Smeck, Ted Lewis, Benny Goodman, Jimmy Durante, and Jimmy and Tommy Dorsey, to name only a handful. In what appears to be the earliest such session, the white Original Dixieland Jazz Band accompanied blues singer Lavinia Turner on an unissued take of "Jazz Me Blues" for Victor on May 3, 1921. See Dixon, Godrich, and Rye, *Blues and Gospel Records*, 936, and the sessions listed in the discography's "Index to Accompanists" under these and other white musicians' names. An even earlier such session, the February 14, 1920, session at which Mamie Smith, accompanied by the all-white Rega Orchestra, recorded "That Thing Called Love" and "You Can't Keep a Good Man Down," at OKeh's studios in New York City, is listed in Dixon, Godrich, and Rye's *Blues and Gospel Records*. This session, however, preceded the one at which Smith waxed "Crazy Blues," which is generally considered the record that marked the advent of classic blues recording. See Dixon, Godrich, and Rye, *Blues and Gospel Records*, 828.

Several racially integrated recording sessions, including a series of 1909–10 sessions involving Carroll Clark, accompanied by banjoist Vess L. Ossman, and another, also from 1909, involving Polk Miller and His Old South Quartette, predate the classic blues sessions mentioned above. The historian Tim Brooks has identified an even earlier recording session, perhaps the first of its kind, featuring white and black artists: a series of six minstrel-skit cylinders recorded circa 1894 for the New Jersey Phonograph Company by the Spencer, Williams, and Quinn Minstrels. This four-man troupe, led by Len Spencer, was composed entirely of white members, except for George W. Johnson, a pioneering black recording artist best known for his popular cylinders, "The Whistling Coon" and "The Laughing Song." See Brooks, *Lost Sounds*, 37–38, 163–67, 215–33.

22. Bogert, "Ramblin' around Kentucky, Part 1," 1, and "Part 2," 1; Russell et al., *Country Music Records*, 894–95; Dixon, Godrich, and Rye, *Blues and Gospel Records*, 904; Wolfe, *Kentucky Country*, 27–28; Wolfe, *The Devil's Box*, 71; Nevins, liner notes, *Kentucky Mountain Music*; Rumble, "The Artists and the Songs," 29; Kennedy, *Jelly Roll, Bix, and Hoagy*, 150–51, 159–61; *Gennett Records of Old Time Tunes* (Richmond,

Ind.: Gennett Records, 1928), 6, 11 (reprinted in *Gennett Records of Old Time Tunes: A Catalog Reprint,* JEMF Special Series, No. 6 [Los Angeles: John Edwards Memorial Foundation, n.d.]). All four of these sides can be heard on both *Kentucky Mountain Music* and *String Bands, 1926–1929: Complete Recorded Works in Chronological Order* (Document DOCD-5167). Jim Booker's fiddling closely resembled that of white fiddlers from the area, and the recordings he made as a member of Taylor's Kentucky Boys reveal the intertwined white and black musical traditions of south-central Kentucky. Today Booker is still renowned in that region of the state, and many of his signature tunes, some of them learned directly from him, continue to circulate there among white old-time fiddlers. See Titon, *Old-Time Kentucky Fiddle Tunes,* 126, 128, 133–36, 149, 174–77, 207, 210, 220.

23. Russell et al., *Country Music Records,* 752–53, 895; Dixon, Godrich, and Rye, *Blues and Gospel Records,* 904. Dock Philip Roberts, his actual name, was a tobacco farmer and champion fiddler from near Richmond, Kentucky, and between 1925 and 1934 he performed on more than two hundred hillbilly recordings. His music was deeply influenced by several local African American fiddlers, particularly a Richmond fiddler and bandleader named Owen Walker (1857–1933) who entertained at local dances and social gatherings around the time of World War I. Walker played blues, waltzes, and old-time pieces, and was, in the words of his admiring disciple Roberts, "the fiddlingest colored man that ever was around in Kentucky. He played like a white man, only he could beat a white man." Scholars have estimated that Roberts learned perhaps as much as almost three-quarters of his repertoire from Walker, including "Old Buzzard" and "Waynesburgh," which Roberts recorded at these August 1927 sessions. See Cohen, "Tapescript: An Interview with Doc Roberts"; Wolfe, *Kentucky Country,* 29; Wolfe, *The Devil's Box,* 67–69, 72; Russell, liner notes, *Fiddlin' Doc Roberts,* on which eight of Roberts's August 1927 recordings with the Bookers can be heard.

24. Bogert, "Ramblin' around Kentucky, Part 1," 1, and "Part 2," 1; Dixon, Godrich, and Rye, *Blues and Gospel Records,* 93; Wolfe, *The Devil's Box,* 72; Wyatt, liner notes, *Violin, Sing the Blues for Me*; Nevins, liner notes, *Kentucky Mountain Music. String Bands, 1926–1929* and *Violin, Sing the Blues for Me* each contains one of the Booker Orchestra's recordings. The Kentucky blues scholar Pen Bogert, as well as the discographical data included on *String Bands, 1926–1929,* claims that fiddler Jim Booker does not perform on the two Booker Orchestra sides. In the absence of more conclusive proof, however, both this paragraph and the entry for the band in appendix B reflect the conclusions found in Dixon, Godrich, and Rye, *Blues and Gospel Records,* the standard discography in the field.

25. Russell et al., *Country Music Records,* 912; Dixon, Godrich, and Rye, *Blues and Gospel Records,* 116; Cohen, "Tapescript: Interview with Welby Toomey," 63–65; Russell, *Blacks, Whites, and Blues,* 180–81. Sammy Brown's two issued sides from his session, the coupling of "Barrel House Blues" and "The Jockey Blues," can be heard on *Country Blues Collector's Items, 1924–1928* (Document DOCD-5169).

26. Savoy, "Dennis McGee," 11–12; Doucet, "Amédé Ardoin's Blues," 2–4; Tisserand, *Kingdom of Zydeco*, 51–65; Savoy, *Cajun Music*, 46; Mattern, "Let the Good Times Unroll," 99; Brasseaux, *Cajun Breakdown*, 82–84.

27. Russell et al., *Country Music Records*, 61–62; Snyder, "Amédé's Recordings," 10–13. All twenty-two of the McGee-Ardoin recordings can be found on *Mama, I'll Be Long Gone: The Complete Recordings of Amede Ardoin, 1929–1934*, two-CD set (Tompkins Square TSQ 2554), while all ten of the duo's 1930 recordings have been reissued on both *"I'm Never Comin' Back"* and *Cajun Country, Vol. 2: More Hits from the Swamp*, four-CD boxed set (JSP JSP7749). Despite claims to the contrary, though, Ardoin was not the first black Creole from southwestern Louisiana to make commercial recordings. That historic honor belongs rather to the fiddle-and-accordion duo of Douglas Bellard and Kirby Riley, who made four recordings at an October 2, 1929, recording session in New Orleans, for the Vocalion label, nearly ten weeks before Ardoin made his debut recordings there, for Columbia. But since Vocalion did not issue Bellard and Riley's discs in its 5000 hillbilly series, as might seem appropriate, but rather assigned them to its 15000 popular series, the duo's recordings are neither considered here nor listed in appendix B. See Russell, "The First Recording of Black French Music?," 20; Russell et al., *Country Music Records*, 99.

28. Russell et al., *Country Music Records*, 367; Dixon, Godrich, and Rye, *Blues and Gospel Records*, 44; Wiggins with Russell, "Hell Broke Loose in Gordon County, Georgia," especially 13; Russell, liner notes, *Black Fiddlers*; Bastin, *Red River Blues*, 38–40; Rumble, "The Artists and the Songs," 29–30; Wyatt, liner notes, *Violin, Sing the Blues for Me*; Wyatt, liner notes, *"Folks, He Sure Do Pull Some Bow!,"* 23. "G Rag" can be heard on *From Where I Stand* and *"Folks, He Sure Do Pull Some Bow!"* The historian John Rumble, writing in the liner notes to the landmark boxed set *From Where I Stand: The Black Experience in Country Music* (1998), claims that Bill Chitwood was responsible for bringing the Baxters along on the 1927 Charlotte recording trip. It appears more likely, however, that Phil Reeve, the Georgia Yellow Hammers' steel guitarist and business manager, arranged for the Baxters to audition for Victor, since the father-and-son duo were currently under his management as well. See Rumble, "The Artists and the Songs," 30; Bastin, *Red River Blues*, 39.

29. Russell et al., *Country Music Records*, 463; Dixon, Godrich, and Rye, *Blues and Gospel Records*, 998; Wolfe, "The Bristol Sessions," 45–47, 52–53; Wolfe, liner notes, *The Bristol Sessions*. This collection contains the Johnson Brothers' previously unissued "A Passing Policeman," on which El Watson plays the bones. All four of the duo's sides with Watson, plus his two sides with Charles Johnson, can be heard on *The Bristol Sessions: The Big Bang of Country Music*, five-CD boxed set (Bear Family BCD 16094 EK).

30. Russell et al., *Country Music Records*, 805–6; Dixon, Godrich, and Rye, *Blues and Gospel Records*, 767; Russell, *Blacks, Whites, and Blues*, 208; Mazor, *Meeting Jimmie Rodgers*, 56–57; Porterfield, *Jimmie Rodgers*, 292–93, 297–99; Porterfield, liner notes, *Jimmie Rodgers*, 30. Both of Rodgers's interracial collaborations from this 1931

Louisville field session can be heard on this collection. Rodgers, a Meridian, Mississippi, native and former brakeman for the Mobile and Ohio Railroad, grew up hearing the work songs and blues of black railroad section gangs while employed as a water boy, and was deeply influenced by the African American musicians, particularly bluesmen, of his native state. For the best biographical account of Rodgers, see Porterfield, *Jimmie Rodgers*.

31. Porterfield, *Jimmie Rodgers*, 211, 400; Russell et al., *Country Music Records*, 801.

32. Mazor, *Meeting Jimmie Rodgers*, 68–69; Ellis, liner notes, *Blue Yodelers, 1928–1936*; Tosches, *Where Dead Voices Gather*, 164–67; Rust, *Jazz Records,1897–1942*, 1:513. Nine of Evans's performances, including two from the soundtrack of his 1929 MGM film, can be heard on *Blue Yodelers, 1928–1936*, released in 2005, but neither "Dusky Stevedore" nor "I Ain't Got Nobody (and Nobody Cares for Me)" is among them, and, to my knowledge, neither of these two recordings has been reissued, either on LP or CD. Incidentally the following year J. C. Johnson participated in a far more famous integrated recording session. On April 30, 1929, Johnson played piano on two sides for OKeh, "Jet Black Blues" and "Blue Blood Blues," as part of a band billed as Blind Willie Dunn's Gin Bottle Four, led by guitarist Eddie Lang. The other members of this pseudonymous mixed-race studio band were guitarist Lonnie Johnson, cornetist Joe "King" Oliver, and vocalist and percussionist Hoagy Carmichael. See Tosches, *Where Dead Voices Gather*, 150; Visser, liner notes, *Lonnie Johnson*.

33. Rust, *Jazz Records*, 1:513; Tosches, *Where Dead Voices Gather*, 165–67. Tosches appears to be confused about Evans's session with James P. Johnson, which he claims occurred on June 15, 1928. According to the discographer Brian Rust, this session actually occurred on July 26, 1928; the front cover of the August 1928 issue of *Phonograph and Talking Machine Weekly* bearing the photograph of Evans is reproduced in Bastin, *Never Sell a Copyright*, 310.

34. Columbia advertisements, *Chicago Defender*, June 16, August 11, October 27, 1928, in "Blues Ads from the *Chicago Defender*: An Index Compiled by Elijah Wald," http://www.elijahwald.com/chidef.html; Tosches, *Where Dead Voices Gather*, 166–67. To my knowledge, the only other hillbilly record to receive such a prominent advertising treatment in the *Chicago Defender* was one of the blind duo Lester McFarland and Robert A. Gardner's Vocalion discs. See Vocalion advertisement, *Chicago Defender*, April 9, 1927. For the purpose of categorizing Evans's hillbilly record in my discography, I have assumed that he was Caucasian and have therefore listed his recordings of "Dusky Stevedore" and "I Ain't Got Nobody (and Nobody Cares for Me)," which feature J. C. Johnson's piano accompaniment, in appendix A as the products of a racially integrated recording session.

35. Russell et al., *Country Music Records*, 299; Dixon, Godrich, and Rye, *Blues and Gospel Records*, 200, 794; Wolfe and Lornell, *The Life and Legend of Leadbelly*, 91; Laird, *Louisiana Hayride*, 36, 38, 71–73; Oliver, "Jerry's Saloon," 89–94; Russell, *Blacks, Whites, and Blues*, 206–9; Russell, liner notes, *Governor Jimmie Davis*, on which "She's a Hum Dum Dinger from Dingersville" can be heard.

36. Russell et al., *Country Music Records*, 299–300; Dixon, Godrich, and Rye, *Blues and Gospel Records*, 200–201; Russell, *Blacks, Whites, and Blues*, 208; Russell, liner notes, *Governor Jimmie Davis*, which contains all fourteen of Davis's other issued sides with Schaffer or Woods or both of them. *Jimmie Davis: Midnight Blues, 1929–1933* (Acrobat ACOA 4220) reissues eleven of Davis's blues numbers with these two Shreveport guitarists. At two Charlotte sessions, on May 27 and 28, 1931, another of Davis's regular sidemen, the white guitarist Ed "Snoozer" Quinn, joined Schaffer to provide the accompaniment on six Davis sides. Quinn, an early jazz guitarist who grew up in Bogalusa, Louisiana, was a former member of the Paul Whiteman Orchestra. See Russell et al., *Country Music Records*, 299–300; "Snoozer Quinn: A Pioneering Jazz Guitarist from Bogalusa, Louisiana," http://snoozerquinn.com/?page_id=389.

37. Wiggins, *Fiddlin' Georgia Crazy*, 114; Rounder Collective, "Life of Blind Alfred Reed," 114; Russell, liner notes, *Governor Jimmie Davis*; Russell, *Blacks, Whites, and Blues*, 158; Kennedy, *Jelly Roll, Bix, and Hoagy*, 36–38, 75–76, 159. The first racially integrated recording session in jazz history occurred on July 17, 1923, when the celebrated black Creole composer and pianist Ferdinand "Jelly Roll" Morton accompanied the all-white New Orleans Rhythm Kings at Starr's studios in Richmond, Indiana. This integrated studio band recorded again the next day, and, although discographers continue to dispute the exact number of sides on which Morton actually played, these sessions produced at least four and possibly as many as six recordings, including "Milenberg Joys" and "London Blues." See Sudhalter, *Lost Chords*, 43–45; Kennedy, *Jelly Roll, Bix, and Hoagy*, 73–76, 159.

38. On the extensive black-white musical exchange that shaped hillbilly music and its vernacular antecedents, see, for example, Russell, *Blacks, Whites, and Blues*; Cohen, "Folk Music Interchange"; Otto and Burns, "Black and White Cultural Interaction in the Early Twentieth Century South"; Wolfe, "A Lighter Shade of Blue"; Lipsitz, *Rainbow at Midnight*, 312–13; Wells, "Fiddling as an Avenue of Black-White Musical Interchange."

39. Wyatt, liner notes, *"Folks, He Sure Do Pull Some Bow!,"* 10; Wolfe, "Rural Black String Band Music," 3–4; Wolfe, "Black String Bands," 15–18; Lornell, "North Carolina Pre-Blues Banjo and Fiddle"; Zwigoff, "Black Country String Bands"; Conway, *African Banjo Echoes in Appalachia*, especially 111, 155; Carlin, *String Bands in the North Carolina Piedmont*, especially 14–17, 20–23, 31–42; Durman, "African American Old-Time String Band Music," 797–98, 801–2. Dena J. Epstein has traced the instrumental pairing of the fiddle and banjo within African American tradition back as far as 1774. See Epstein, *Sinful Tunes and Spirituals*, 115.

40. Russell, *Blacks, Whites, and Blues*, 163–65; Wolfe, "Black String Bands," 16; Lornell, "North Carolina Pre-Blues Banjo and Fiddle," 25–26.

41. Russell et al., *Country Music Records*, 879; Dixon, Godrich, and Rye, *Blues and Gospel Records*, 495; Russell, *Blacks, Whites, and Blues*, 168–69; Tracy, *Going to Cincinnati*, 8–33. "Lonesome John" and "Fisher's Hornpipe" can be heard on both *Stovepipe No. 1 and David Crockett / Tub Jug Washboard Band: Complete Recorded Works in*

Chronological Order, 1924–1930 (Document DOCD-5269) and *Cincinnati Blues* (Catfish KATCD 186).

42. Russell et al., *Country Music Records*, 637, 948; Dixon, Godrich, and Rye, *Blues and Gospel Records*, 651, 1007. The Wheat Street Female Quartet's "Wheel in a Wheel" and "Oh! Yes!" can be heard on *Vocal Quartets: Complete Recorded Works and Supplements, Vol. 7: S/T/V/W, 1925–1944* (Document DOCD-5543), while both parts of the Reverend C. D. Montgomery's "Who Is Job?" have been reissued on *Atlanta, Ga., Gospel, 1923–1931: Complete Recorded Works in Chronological Order* (Document DOCD-5485).

43. Rumble, "The Artists and the Songs," 27–28; Morton and Wolfe, *DeFord Bailey*, especially 17, 47–49, 121–30; Wolfe, *A Good-Natured Riot*, 119–29.

44. Russell et al., *Country Music Records*, 87–88; Dixon, Godrich, and Rye, *Blues and Gospel Records*, 31; Rumble, "The Artists and the Songs," 27–28; Wolfe, *A Good-Natured Riot*, 122–24; Morton and Wolfe, *DeFord Bailey*, 50–59. All nine of Bailey's sides issued in hillbilly series can be found on *Harp Blowers: Complete Recorded Works of John Henry Howard, DeFord Bailey, D. H. "Bert" Bilbro, George Clarke, 1925–1936* (Document DOCD-5164).

45. Russell et al., *Country Music Records*, 531; Dixon, Godrich, and Rye, *Blues and Gospel Records*, 570; Oliver, *Story of the Blues*, 54; "*Chicago Defender* Blues Advertisements: William McCoy," Big Road Blues: Vintage Radio Blues and Writing, http://sundayblues.org/archives/185; Licht, "Harmonica Magic," 214–15. McCoy's "Mama Blues" and "Train Imitations and the Fox Chase" can both be heard on *Texas Black Country Dance Music, 1927–1935: Complete Recordings* (Document DOCD-5162).

46. Russell et al., *Country Music Records*, 818; Laird, *Brunswick Records*, 2:807; Nzengou-Tayo, "Haitian Callaloo," 175. Unfortunately, to my knowledge, neither of these two Salnave recordings have been commercially reissued.

47. Russell et al., *Country Music Records*, 217; Dixon, Godrich, and Rye, *Blues and Gospel Records*, 166; Wyatt, liner notes, *Violin, Sing the Blues for Me*; Wyatt, liner notes, "*Folks, He Sure Do Pull Some Bow!,*" 23–24; Rumble, "The Artists and the Songs," 30–31; Tony Russell, email messages to the author, December 9 and 10, 2007; Spottswood, liner notes, *The Tommie Bradley–James Cole Groups, 1928–1932*, on which both "I Got a Gal" and "Bill Cheatem" can be heard. The former title also appears on both "*Folks, He Sure Do Pull Some Bow!*" and *Richer Tradition: Country Blues and String Band Music, 1923–1942*, four-CD boxed set (JSP 7798), while the latter can be found on *The Cornshucker's Frolic: Downhome Music and Entertainment from the American Countryside, Vol. 1* (Yazoo 2045).

48. Dixon, Godrich, and Rye, *Blues and Gospel Records*, 250; Russell, *Blacks, Whites, and Blues*, 166–67; Zwigoff, liner notes, *Early Mandolin Classics*; Cherry, liner notes, *Vintage Mandolin Music, 1927–1946*, on which "Old Hen Cackle" appears. Both "Old Hen Cackle" and "Sourwood Mountain" have been reissued on *The Two Poor Boys: Joe Evans and Arthur McClain, 1927–1931, Complete Recorded Works in Chronological Order* (Document DOCD-5044).

49. Russell et al., *Country Music Records*, 898; Dixon, Godrich, and Rye, *Blues and Gospel Records*, 908; Wolfe, "Early Country Music in Knoxville," 31; Wyatt, liner notes, *"Folks, He Sure Do Pull Some Bow!,"* 24; Wyatt, liner notes, *Violin, Sing the Blues for Me.* "Knox County Stomp" can be heard on *"Folks, He Sure Do Pull Some Bow!"* and on *Richer Tradition*, while "Vine Street Drag" appears on *Violin, Sing the Blues for Me.* Both titles have also been reissued on *Carl Martin, 1930–1936 / Willie "61" Blackwell, 1941: Complete Recordings in Chronological Order* (Document DOCD-5229). Several scholars have argued, probably correctly, that the guitarist on these two sides is not Roland Martin but rather Armstrong's younger brother Roland Armstrong (ca. 1913–?). But in the absence of definitive proof, both this discussion and the entry for the band in appendix B reflect the personnel details found in Dixon, Godrich, and Rye, *Blues and Gospel Records.*

50. Russell et al., *Country Music Records*, 414; Dixon, Godrich, and Rye, *Blues and Gospel Records*, 368; Russell, *Blacks, Whites, and Blues*, 167–68; Cherry, liner notes, *Vintage Mandolin Music, 1927–1946*; Wyatt, liner notes, *Violin, Sing the Blues for Me*; Wyatt, liner notes, *"Folks, He Sure Do Pull Some Bow!,"* 9; Zwigoff, liner notes, *String Bands, 1926–1929*, on which all four of Hayes and Prater's issued mandolin-and-guitar duets discussed above can be heard. "Easy Winner" also appears on *Richer Tradition* and on *Vintage Mandolin Music, 1927–1946.*

51. Dixon, Godrich, and Rye, *Blues and Gospel Records*, 458–64. Johnson went on to record a series of now-classic guitar duets, released in OKeh's race catalogue under the billing Lonnie Johnson and Blind Willie Dunn, with the famed white jazz guitarist Eddie Lang between November 1928 and October 1929. See Dixon, Godrich, and Rye, *Blues and Gospel Records*, 461–62.

52. Russell et al., *Country Music Records*, 109; Dixon, Godrich, and Rye, *Blues and Gospel Records*, 368; Russell, "Keys to the Bushes," 19; Russell, *Blacks, Whites, and Blues*, 168; Wyatt, liner notes, *Violin, Sing the Blues for Me*; Wyatt, liner notes, *"Folks, He Sure Do Pull Some Bow!,"* 9–10, on which "Memphis Stomp," featuring Lonnie Johnson's fiddling, can be heard. It can also be found on *Lonnie Johnson: Complete Recorded Works 1925–1932 in Chronological Order, Vol. 3* (Document DOCD-5065).

53. Calt, Kent, and Stewart, liner notes, *Mississippi Sheiks*; Cohn, liner notes, *Honey Babe Let the Deal Go Down*; Smith, liner notes, *Mississippi Sheiks*; Wyatt, liner notes, *"Folks, He Sure Do Pull Some Bow!,"* 13–15; Dixon, Godrich, and Rye, *Blues and Gospel Records*, 642.

54. Russell et al., *Country Music Records*, 453, 629; Dixon, Godrich, and Rye, *Blues and Gospel Records*, 642–45, 973; Rumble, "The Artists and the Songs," 31–32; Cherry, liner notes, *Vintage Mandolin Music, 1927–1946*; Wyatt, liner notes, *Violin, Sing the Blues for Me*; Wyatt, liner notes, *"Folks, He Sure Do Pull Some Bow!,"* 13–15. "The Sheik Waltz" and "The Jazz Fiddler," recorded at the Mississippi Sheiks' February 1930 debut session, can both be heard on *Mississippi Sheiks: The Complete Recorded Works in Chronological Order, Vol. 1* (Document DOCD-5083 — DOCD-5086) and on *The Mississippi Sheiks: Sitting on Top of the World* (Snapper SNAP 61). The four "Old Time

Tunes" titles from the band's June 1930 recording session in San Antonio appear on *Walter Vinson, 1928–1941: Complete Recordings in Chronological Order* (Document BDCD 6017). Four of the Mississippi Mud Steppers' six recordings discussed above have been reissued on *Mississippi String Bands and Associates, 1928–1931* (Document BDCD 6013); the remaining two sides appear on *Charlie McCoy: Complete 1928–1932 Recordings in Chronological Order* (Document BDCD 6018).

55. Russell et al., *Country Music Records*, 5; Ivey, "Border Crossing," 10–11.

56. For a discussion of this concept, see Hobsbawm, "Introduction: Inventing Tradition," 1–14.

57. Peterson, *Creating Country Music*, especially 4; Mark Humphrey, "What Is Old-Time Music?," in booklet accompanying the 2002 video *Legends of Old Time Music* (Vestapol 13026).

58. For examples of white hillbilly artists' records being classified for the race market, see Russell et al., *Country Music Records*, 55, 199, 208, 773, 893, 976; Dixon, Godrich, and Rye, *Blues and Gospel Records*, 12, 94, 127, 156, 905. For examples of blues records produced at integrated recording sessions involving white hillbilly artists, see Russell et al., *Country Music Records*, 196, 745; Dixon, Godrich, and Rye, *Blues and Gospel Records*, 43, 303, 492, 735, 1018.

59. Russell et al., *Country Music Records*, 55–57; Dixon, Godrich, and Rye, *Blues and Gospel Records*, 12; Wolfe, "A Lighter Shade of Blue," 233–37; Laird, *Louisiana Hayride*, 50; Miller, *Segregating Sound*, 220.

60. Cohen, "Computerized Hillbilly Discography," 188–89; Russell et al., *Country Music Records*, 17, 874.

61. For accounts of African Americans purchasing, or at least listening to, prewar hillbilly records, see, for example, Pollak, "John Jackson's Good-Time Blues," 26; Evans, "Black Musicians Remember Jimmie Rodgers," 12–14; Brauner and Pearson, "John Jackson's East Virginia Blues," 10–13; Pearson, "Archie Edwards," 22–26.

62. *Gennett Records of Old Time Tunes*, 11; Wolfe, *The Devil's Box*, 71; Nevins, liner notes, *Kentucky Mountain Music*.

63. Here, though, the studies of Archie Green, Charles K. Wolfe, and Richard A. Peterson provide important exceptions. See, for example, Archie Green's pioneering articles in his "Commercial Music Graphics" series that appeared in the *John Edwards Memorial Foundation Newsletter* (later the *John Edwards Memorial Foundation Quarterly*) between 1968 and 1985; Charles K. Wolfe's articles and essays cited in note 16; and Peterson, *Creating Country Music*. For studies that focus on the business and production practices of the postwar country music recording industry, see, for example, "The Unseen Hand," 2–3; Ivey, "The Bottom Line"; Jensen, *The Nashville Sound*; Pecknold, *The Selling Sound*.

64. Russell et al., *Country Music Records*, 14. On Columbia's "Familiar Tunes — Old and New" series, see Wolfe, "Columbia Records and Old-Time Music."

65. The commercial recording of race and hillbilly records during the 1920s certainly opened doors for a diverse range of talented musicians of both races, but

talking-machine companies' decision to create separate race and hillbilly catalogues closed doors for an inestimable number of musicians whose music did not seem to fit A&R men's perceptions of either of these two musical genres. From this historical distance and without much evidence to go on, we cannot know, for example, how many African American string bands, after auditioning to make recordings, were rejected by these A&R men. Nor can we know to what extent A&R men, ever mindful of record sales, encouraged African American artists to replicate successful formulas or to record selections that neatly conformed to their own perceptions of race records and the market for these records.

String bands represented one of the oldest African American pre-blues musical traditions, but record companies — operating under the assumption that blues and gospel records sold better to African American audiences, or that this older string-band music had little commercial appeal for them, or that both of these premises were true — recorded relatively few black string bands for either race or hillbilly series before World War II. One of the leading historians of African American string bands, Charles K. Wolfe, has estimated that talking-machine companies released perhaps only fifty records of prewar black string-band music between 1920 and 1942, compared to some twenty thousand records of blues and gospel music for that same period. Wolfe does not define what he means by a string band, but surely his figure represents a serious undercount; the Mississippi Sheiks alone produced almost that many issued records between 1930 and 1935. The number of prewar commercial recordings of black string-band music is admittedly small, but if we count all fiddle-based bands, including duos, trios, and jug bands, it surely exceeds five hundred records, and the actual number may be closer to one thousand. Wolfe's point, however, is an important one: as a result of A&R men's aesthetic and commercial considerations, African American string bands were greatly underrepresented on prewar commercial phonograph recordings, which makes the handful of surviving performances of these neglected bands on hillbilly records all the more valuable for understanding this once flourishing but now nearly lost African American musical tradition. See Laird, *Louisiana Hayride*, 36–37; Wolfe, "Black String Bands," 15, 17; Dixon, Godrich, and Rye, *Blues and Gospel Records*, 642–45.

66. "Commercial Music Documents: Number Five"; Cohen, "'I'm a Record Man,'" 49; Wolfe, "Columbia Records and Old-Time Music," 118–25, 144.

67. Wolfe, "Columbia Records and Old-Time Music," 119; Calt, liner notes, *Mississippi John Hurt*; Barker and Taylor, *Faking It*, 30–31, 35–36; Russell et al., *Country Music Records*, 199, 893; Dixon, Godrich, and Rye, *Blues and Gospel Records*, 127, 418, 905.

68. Russell et al., *Country Music Records*, 464, 670.

Appendix A

Racially Integrated Hillbilly Recording Sessions, 1927–1932
(in Chronological Order)

RECORD LABELS

BB	Bluebird
Bell	Bell
Br	Brunswick
Ch	Champion
Chg	Challenge
Co	Columbia
CoSs	Columbia (Switzerland)
Eld	Electradisk
Ge	Gennett
Her	Herwin
HMVIn	His Master's Voice (India)
HMVPg	His Master's Voice (Portugal)
Me	Melotone
MW	Montgomery Ward
OK	OKeh
RZ	Regal-Zonophone (Britain and Ireland)
RZAu	Regal-Zonophone (Australia)
Sil	Silvertone
Spr	Superior
Spt	Supertone
Sr	Sunrise
Twin	Twin (India)
Vi	Victor
ZoAu	Zonophone (Australia)

The names of African American singers and musicians appear in italics.

TAYLOR'S KENTUCKY BOYS

Jim Booker, fiddle; Marion Underwood, banjo; Willie Young, guitar.

RICHMOND, INDIANA, APRIL 26, 1927

12741-A	Gray Eagle	Ge 6130, Ch 15315, Sil 5082, Sil 8183, Spt 9170
12742	Forked Deer	Ge 6130, Ch 15300, Sil 5082, Sil 8183, Spt 9170, Chg 302

MARION UNDERWOOD AND AULTON RAY

Jim Booker, fiddle; Marion Underwood, banjo; Aulton Ray, vocal.

RICHMOND, INDIANA, APRIL 26, 1927

12747	Soldier Joy	Ge 6205
12748-A	Maxwell Girl	Ge 6205, Ch 15332, Sil 5084, Sil 8150, Spt 9250, Chg 335, Her 75550

JOHNSON BROTHERS

Paul Johnson, vocal; accompanied by *El Watson*, harmonica-1/bones-2; own steel guitar-3/banjo-4; Charles Johnson, guitar.

BRISTOL, TENNESSEE, JULY 28, 1927

39722-3	Two Brothers Are We — 2, 3	Vi 21243
39724-2	A Passing Policeman — 2, 3	Vi unissued
39729-3	The Soldier's Poor Little Boy — 1, 4	Vi 20891
39731-2	I Want to See My Mother (Ten Thousand Miles Away) — 2, 3	Vi 20940

Victor 20891 and 21243 released under the billing of Johnson Brothers with Tennessee Wildcats.

GEORGIA YELLOW HAMMERS

Andrew Baxter, fiddle; Ernest Moody, banjo-ukulele; Phil Reeve, guitar; Clyde Evans, guitar; Bud Landress, speech.

CHARLOTTE, NORTH CAROLINA, AUGUST 9, 1927

39783-2	G Rag	Vi 21195

FIDDLIN' DOC ROBERTS

Dock Roberts, fiddle; accompanied by *John Booker*, guitar.

RICHMOND, INDIANA, AUGUST 26, 1927

13038	Arkansas Traveler	Sil 5079, Sil 8185, Spt 9172
13039	Buck Creek Gal	Chg 15500, Sil 5077, Sil 8180, Spt 9164, Chg 307
13040	Black Eyed Susie	Ge 6257, Ch 15396, Sil 5077, Sil 8180, Spt 9164, Spr 386
13041	Old Buzzard	Ge 6336, Ch 15449, Sil 5079, Sil 8185, Spt 9172, Chg 303
13042	Waynesburgh	Ge 6257, Ch 15449, Sil 5078, Sil 8182, Spt 9168

13043	Cripple Creek	Ge 6336, Ch 15396, Sil 5078, Sil 8182, Spt 9168, Chg 303, Spr 348, Bell 1171

TAYLOR'S KENTUCKY BOYS

Jim Booker, fiddle; Dock Roberts, fiddle; *John Booker*, guitar.

RICHMOND, INDIANA, AUGUST 27, 1927

13044, -A	Turkey in the Straw	Ge rejected
13045, -A	Old Hen Cackled and the Rooster Crowed	Ge rejected
13046-A	Sourwood Mountain	Sil 8179, Spt 9165

MARION UNDERWOOD

Marion Underwood, vocal; accompanied by *Jim Booker*, fiddle; Dock Roberts, fiddle; *Robert Steele*, mandolin; own banjo-1; *John* or *Joe Booker*, guitar.

RICHMOND, INDIANA, AUGUST 27, 1927

13051	Down in the Valley	Ge rejected
13052	Little Old Log Cabin in the Lane	Chg 331
13053	That's What the Old Bachelor's Made Of—1	Chg 331

FIDDLIN' DOC ROBERTS

Dock Roberts, fiddle; accompanied by *Joe Booker*, guitar.

RICHMOND, INDIANA, AUGUST 27, 1927

13054	Billy in the Low Ground	Ge 6390, Ch 15500, Sil 8178, Spt 9176, Spr 386, Bell 1188
13055	And the Cat Came Back	Ge 6390, Sil 8179, Spt 9165, Chg 307, Spr 348, Bell 1171

WELBY TOOMEY

Welby Toomey, vocal; accompanied probably by *Sammy Brown*, guitar, harmonica-1, "jazzbo"-2.

RICHMOND, INDIANA, NOVEMBER 22, 1927

GEX-971, -A	You Must Unload—1	Ge rejected
GEX-972, -A	The Faded Coat of Blue	Ge rejected
GEX-973, -A	Sadie Ray—1	Ge rejected
GEX-974, -A	A Lone Summer Day—2	Ge rejected

ROY EVANS (THE YODELIN' MAN)

Roy Evans, vocal; accompanied by *J. C. Johnson*, piano.

NEW YORK, NEW YORK, JUNE 18, 1928

146553-1	I Ain't Got Nobody	Co 15272-D
	(and Nobody Cares for Me)	
146554-3	Dusky Stevedore	Co 15272-D, Co 1449-D

JIMMIE RODGERS

Jimmie Rodgers, vocal; accompanied by *unknown*, cornet; *unknown*, saxophone; *unknown*, piano; *unknown*, banjo; *unknown*, string bass.

DALLAS, TEXAS, AUGUST 12, 1929

| 55344-3 | Frankie and Johnny | Vi unissued |

AMÉDÉ ARDOIN

Amédé Ardoin, vocal; accompanied by Dennis McGee, fiddle; own accordion.

NEW ORLEANS, LOUISIANA, DECEMBER 9, 1929

111384-2	Taunt Aline (Aunt Aline)	Co 40514-F, OK 90014
111385-2	Two Step de Mama	Co 40514-F, OK 90014
	(My Mother's Two Step)	
111386-2	Madam Atchen (Mrs. Atchen)	Co 40515-F, OK 90015
111387-1	Two Step de la Prairie Soileau	Co 40515-F, OK 90015
	(Prairie Soileau Two Step)	
111388-2	La Valse ah Abe (Abe's Waltz)	Co 40511-F, OK 90011
111389-2	Two Step de Eunice	Co 40511-F, OK 90011

JIMMIE DAVIS

Jimmie Davis, vocal; accompanied probably by *Ed Schaffer*, steel guitar; *Oscar Woods*, guitar.

MEMPHIS, TENNESSEE, MAY 20, 1930

59952-1	She's a Hum Dum Dinger	Vi unissued
	(from Dingersville)	
59952-2	She's a Hum Dum Dinger	Vi V-40286, BB 1835, BB B-5005,
	from Dingersville	Eld 1963, Sr S-3128, MW M-4283

JIMMIE ROGERS

Jimmie Rodgers, vocal/yodeling; accompanied by *Louis Armstrong*, trumpet;
Lillian Hardin Armstrong, piano.

HOLLYWOOD, CALIFORNIA, JULY 16, 1930

54867-2	Blue Yodel No. 9	Vi 23580, MW M-4209, MW M-4724, RZ MR3208, ZoAu EE300, RZAu EE300, Twin FT8832, HMVPg MH194, CoSs MZ315

MCGEE AND ARDOIN

Dennis McGee, fiddle; *Amédé Ardoin*, accordion/vocal.

NEW ORLEANS, LOUISIANA, NOVEMBER 20, 1930

NO-6717-	Amadie Two Step	Br 576, Me M18050
NO-6718-	La Valse a Austin Ardoin	Br 576, Me M18050
NO-6719-	Blues de Basille	Br 531
NO-6720-	La Valse a Thomas Ardoin	Br 531
NO-6721-	Two Step d'Elton	Br 513
NO-6722-	La Valse de Gueydan	Br 513
NO-6737-	Valse des Opelousas	Br 559, Br 80083
NO-6738-	One Step des Chameaux	Br 559, Br 80083

MCGEE AND ARDOIN

Dennis McGee, fiddle; *Amédé Ardoin*, accordion/vocal.

NEW ORLEANS, LOUISIANA, NOVEMBER 21, 1930

NO-6735-	Valse a Alcee Poulard	Br 495
NO-6736-	One Step d'Oberlin	Br 495

JIMMIE DAVIS

Jimmie Davis, vocal; accompanied probably by *Ed Schaffer*, steel guitar-1;
Oscar Woods, guitar-3.

MEMPHIS, TENNESSEE, NOVEMBER 29, 1930

64754-2	Penitentiary Blues—1, 3	Vi 23544
64775-2	Arabella Blues—1, 3	Vi 23517, BB B-5496
64759-1	A Woman's Blues—1	Vi 23544
64759-2	A Woman's Blues—1	Vi unissued
64760-2	Bear Cat Mama from Horner's Corners—1, 3	Vi 23517, BB 1835, BB B-5005, Eld 1963, Sr S-3128, MW M-4283

JIMMIE DAVIS

Jimmie Davis, vocal/speech-1; accompanied by *"Dizzy Head"* (*Ed Schaffer*), steel guitar/vocal-2; Snoozer Quinn, guitar-3.

CHARLOTTE, NORTH CAROLINA, MAY 27, 1931

69358-1	Down at the Old Country Church—1, 2	Vi unissued
69358-2	Down at the Old Country Church—1, 2	Vi 23628, MW M-7361, ZoAu EE331
69359-1	She's a Hum-Dum Dinger— Part 2 (From Dingersville)—3	Vi 23587, BB B-5751
69359-2	She's a Hum-Dum Dinger— Part 2 (From Dingersville)—3	Vi unissued
69360-1	Market House Blues—3	Vi 23620
69361-1	Get on Board, Aunt Susan—3	Vi 23620, BB B-5319, Sr S-3400
69362-1	Midnight Blues—3	Vi 23601, BB B-6249, HMVIn N4399

JIMMIE DAVIS

Jimmie Davis, vocal; accompanied by *"Dizzy Head"* (*Ed Schaffer*), steel guitar-1; Snoozer Quinn, guitar.

CHARLOTTE, NORTH CAROLINA, MAY 28, 1931

| 69367-1 | There's Evil in Ye Children, Gather 'Round—1 | Vi 23573, BB B-5319, Sr S-3400 |

JIMMIE RODGERS

Jimmie Rodgers, vocal/yodeling; accompanied by *Clifford Gibson*, guitar.

LOUISVILLE, KENTUCKY, JUNE 11, 1931

| 69424-2 | Let Me Be Your Side Track | Vi unissued |

JIMMIE RODGERS

Jimmie Rodgers, vocal/yodeling; accompanied by the Louisville Jug Band (Dixieland Jug Blowers): *Clifford Hayes*, fiddle; *George Allen*, clarinet; *Cal Smith*, guitar; *Freddie Smith*, guitar; *Earl McDonald*, jug.

LOUISVILLE, KENTUCKY, JUNE 16, 1931

| 69449-1 | My Good Gal's Gone Blues | Vi unissued |
| 69449-3 | My Good Gal's Gone—Blues | BB B-5942, MW M-5014, Twin FT1925 |

JIMMIE DAVIS

Jimmie Davis, vocal; accompanied by *Ed Schaffer*, steel guitar; *Oscar Woods*, guitar-1/vocal-2/speech-3.

DALLAS, TEXAS, FEBRUARY 8, 1932

70656-1	Saturday Night Stroll—2	Vi 23688, MW M-7363
70657-1	Sewing Machine Blues—1	Vi 23703, BB B-5751
70658-1	Red Nightgown Blues—1	Vi 23659, BB B-5699
70659-1	Davis' Salty Dog—1, 2, 3	Vi 23674

Source: Compiled and adapted from Tony Russell, *Country Music Records: A Discography, 1921–1942*, with editorial research by Bob Pinson, assisted by the staff of the Country Music Hall of Fame and Museum (New York: Oxford University Press, 2004); Robert M. W. Dixon, John Godrich, and Howard Rye, compilers, *Blues and Gospel Records, 1890–1943*, 4th ed. (1964; Oxford: Clarendon Press, 1997); and Brian A. L. Rust, compiler, *Jazz Records, 1897–1942*, 5th revised and enlarged ed., 2 vols. (1961; Chigwell, Essex, England: Storyville Publications, 1982).

Appendix B
Recordings by African Americans Issued in Hillbilly Record Series, 1924–1931 (in Alphabetical Order)

RECORD LABELS

Ba	Banner
Br	Brunswick
BrC	Brunswick (Canada)
Co	Columbia
Ge	Gennett
Ha	Harmony
OK	OKeh
Or	Oriole
Pe	Perfect
Ro	Romeo
Vi	Victor
Vo	Vocalion

DEFORD BAILEY
DeFord Bailey, harmonica solo.

NEW YORK, NEW YORK, APRIL 18, 1927

E-22475*/76	Pan American Blues	Br 146, Vo 5180

NEW YORK, NEW YORK, APRIL 19, 1927

E-22501*/02	Dixie Flyer Blues	Br 146, Vo 5180
E-22503/04*	Up Country Blues	Br 147, BrC 434
E-22505/06*	Evening Prayer Blues	Br 148, BrC 435, Vo 5147
E-22507/08*	Muscle Shoals Blues	Br 147, BrC 434
E-22509/10*	Old Hen Cackle	Vo 5190
E-22511	Alcoholic Blues	Br 148, BrC 435, Vo 5147
E-22512	Fox Chase	Vo 5190

NASHVILLE, TENNESSEE, OCTOBER 2, 1928

47111-2	John Henry	Vi 23336, Vi 23831

BOOKER ORCHESTRA
Jim Booker, fiddle; John or Joe Booker, fiddle; John or Joe Booker, guitar; Robert Steele, kazoo.

RICHMOND, INDIANA, AUGUST 27, 1927

13047-	Salty Dog	Ge 6375
13048-	Camp Nelson Blues	Ge 6375

JAMES COLE STRING BAND

James Cole, fiddle; probably Tommie Bradley, guitar; probably Eddie Dimmitt, mandolin; unknown, string bass; unknown, vocal.

INDIANAPOLIS, INDIANA, JUNE 25, 1928

IND-650-;	I Got a Gal	Vo 5226
E-7480-		
IND-651-;	Bill Cheatem	Vo 5226
E-7481-		

JOE EVANS AND ARTHUR MCCLAIN

Joe Evans, probably guitar; Arthur McClain, probably mandolin.

NEW YORK, NEW YORK, MAY 20, 1931

| 10658-2 | Old Hen Cackle | Ba 32264, Or 8095, Pe 12751, Ro 5095 |

NEW YORK, NEW YORK, MAY 21, 1931

| 10663-2 | Sourwood Mountain | Ba 32264, Or 8095, Pe 12751, Ro 5095 |

Oriole and Perfect discs released under the billing of Colman (*sic*) and Harper.

HAYES AND PRATER

Nap Hayes, guitar; Matthew Prater, mandolin; Lonnie Johnson, fiddle-1.

MEMPHIS, TENNESSEE, FEBRUARY 15, 1928

400238-A	Memphis Stomp — 1	OK 45314
400241-B	Somethin' Doin'	OK 45231
400242-B	Easy Winner	OK 45314
400243-B	Nothin' Doin'	OK 45231

OKeh 45314 released under the billing of the Blue Boys.

SAM JONES (STOVE PIPE NO. 1)

Samuel Jones, vocal-1/guitar/harmonica/stovepipe.

NEW YORK, NEW YORK, AUGUST 20, 1924

| 81937-3 | Lonesome John — 1 | Co 15011-D, Ha 5137-H |
| 81941-2 | Fisher's Hornpipe | Co 15011-D, Ha 5137-H |

Columbia sides released as by Stove Pipe No. 1 (Sam Jones).

WILLIAM MCCOY

William McCoy, harmonica solo/speech

DALLAS, TEXAS, DECEMBER 6, 1927

145334-2	Mama Blues	Co 14302-D
		Co 15269-D
145335-1	Train Imitations and the Fox Chase	Co 14302-D
		Co 15269-D

MISSISSIPPI SHEIKS

Walter Vinson (Jacobs), guitar/vocal-1, Lonnie Chatman, fiddle.

SHREVEPORT, LOUISIANA, FEBRUARY 17, 1930

| 403803-A, -B | The Sheik Waltz | OK 45436 |
| 403804-A, -B | The Jazz Fiddler—1 | OK 45436 |

OKeh 45436 released under the billing of Walter Jacobs and Lonnie Carter.

Walter Vinson (Jacobs), guitar; Lonnie Chatman, fiddle; Bo Chatman, guitar.

SAN ANTONIO, TEXAS, JUNE 10, 1930

404133-B	Sheiks Special	OK 45468
404134-B	Dear Little Girl	OK 45468
404135-B	Mississippi Low Down	OK 45482
404136-B	That's It	OK 45482

Both OKeh 45468 and 45482 released under the billing of Walter Jacobs and the Carter Brothers.

Probably Walter Vinson (Jacobs), guitar-1/probably guitar-2; probably Charlie McCoy, probably banjo-mandolin; possibly Lonnie Chatman, fiddle-3, unknown, speech-4.

JACKSON, MISSISSIPPI, DECEMBER 15, 1930

404714-B	Jackson Stomp—1, 4	OK 45504
404715-B	Farewell Waltz—1	OK 45532
404716-B	Vicksburg Stomp—2	OK 45519
404717-B	Morning Glory Waltz—1	OK 45532
404718-A	Sunset Waltz—4	OK 45519
404719-B	Alma Waltz (Ruby Waltz)—1, 3	OK 45504

All sides released under the billing of Mississippi Mud Steppers.

REV. C. D. MONTGOMERY

Rev. C. D. Montgomery, speech with singing (no congregation)

ATLANTA, GEORGIA, JANUARY 31, 1925

140317-1, -2	Who Was Job? Part 1	Co 15023-D, Ha 5153-H
140318-1, -2	Who Was Job? Part 2	Co 15023-D, Ha 5153-H

THÉOPHILE SALNAVE

Théophile Salnave, vocal-1/piano-1, speech-2.

NEW YORK, NEW YORK, NOVEMBER 17, 1930

E35406-A, -B	Lucky Strike — 1	Br 487
E35407-A, -B	Wrigley's en Batterie — 2	Br 487

TENNESSEE CHOCOLATE DROPS

Howard Armstrong, fiddle; Roland Martin, guitar; Carl Martin, string bass.

KNOXVILLE, TENNESSEE, APRIL 3, 1930

K-8066-	Knox County Stomp	Vo 1517, Vo 5472
K-8067-	Vine Street Drag	Vo 1517, Vo 5472

Vocalion 5472 released under the billing of the Tennessee Trio.

WHEAT STREET FEMALE QUARTET

Female vocal quartet, unaccompanied.

ATLANTA, GEORGIA, JANUARY 29, 1925

140300-1	Wheel in a Wheel	Co 15021-D, Ha 5151-H
140301-1	Oh! Yes!	Co 15021-D, Ha 5151-H

Source: Compiled and adapted from Tony Russell, *Country Music Records: A Discography, 1921–1942*, with editorial research by Bob Pinson, assisted by the staff of the Country Music Hall of Fame and Museum (New York: Oxford University Press, 2004); and Robert M. W. Dixon, John Godrich, and Howard Rye, compilers, *Blues and Gospel Records, 1890–1943*, 4th ed. (1964; Oxford: Clarendon Press, 1997).

Making Country Modern

THE LEGACY OF *MODERN SOUNDS IN
COUNTRY AND WESTERN MUSIC*
Diane Pecknold

Ray Charles's *Modern Sounds in Country and Western Music* (1962) is the soul of paradox. First, there's the apparently obvious, though actually somewhat misleading, incongruity of a black man recording an album in the musical style most closely associated with the aggressive performance of whiteness and even with overt racism at one of the most racially charged moments of the twentieth century. Then there's the genre confusion arising from the fact that the Genius of Soul recorded the first million-selling album of country songs, and the record-keeping conundrum that, in spite of its platinum status, the album is not generally designated as the first million-selling country record. (That honor is reserved for Waylon and Willie's compilation album *Wanted: The Outlaws.*) Nor is it inconsequential for the cultural logic of country's image that the two central events that contributed to what Bill Malone calls "the national 'discovery' of country music in the sixties" were segregationist George Wallace's deployment of it in his gubernatorial and presidential campaigns and Ray Charles's astonishing commercial success in incorporating it into a decidedly integrationist musical statement.[1] As Charles once said of his stint as a hillbilly piano player in Florida at the height of Jim Crow, "Can you feature that?"[2]

A less immediately apparent paradox, though, lies in the way the country music industry both embraced and excluded the album, and in the way this worked a special kind of alchemy that transformed a record most obviously about the porousness of racially marked musical boundaries into a record that commented primarily on class and region. Although it did not imagine the album as a country record or Charles as a country singer, the industry enthusiastically promoted *Modern Sounds* to broadcasters and broadcast advertisers as proof that country and its audience were, like Charles, thoroughly modern. No longer backward hillbillies or ignorant hayseeds, the industry argued, country's core audience of white southern rural-to-urban migrants had become the industrial blue-collar middle class, and they were a lucrative broadcasting demographic that could not be ignored.[3]

However opportunistic this transformation might have been, it was consistent both with Charles's performances on *Modern Sounds* and with his own conflation of race and class in discussing his reasons for doing the project. By the time he made the album, Charles had been consciously playing around the edges of racialized genre boundaries since the late 1950s. Even in his earliest days as a musician in Florida, he recalled, he learned the differences in the kinds of material white and black audiences requested and the different ways in which music targeted to white and black audiences was treated. "During my day," he recounted in his autobiography, "there were two types of sounds. Least that's how we country folk viewed it. You had race records . . . colored artists only. . . . On the other hand, there was music from the radio." In opposing *race* to *radio*, Charles made the first term a descriptor of both race and class. He similarly emphasized the relative class positions of black and white repertoires when he pointed out that musicians who wanted to earn tips in white clubs learned the songs most often requested there, particularly swing standards and jazz adaptations of Tin Pan Alley and Broadway tunes such as Cole Porter's "Ace in the Hole" and Woody Herman's version of the movie theme song "Laura." Charles viewed such standards as a necessary component of his repertoire if he hoped to eke out a living as a musician, and besides, he recalled, "it was easy for [him]" because it fit with his own eclecticism and wide range of influences.[4]

By the mid-1950s Charles had established himself as a successful rhythm and blues performer, but he still struggled financially and professionally. His dissatisfaction with the working conditions of a club performer became more acute, and he began to think about shifting his position in the dichotomy between race and radio music. "It'd be nice to play Carnegie Hall," he recalled thinking, "to record a country song . . . to sing with violins and cellos." For Charles, this terrain was marked by both race and class. Black singers such as Nat Cole and Dinah Washington had moved from jazz to pop vocal status, in Washington's case also partially with the use of country repertoire, but "us rhythm-and-blues musicians," Charles said, were viewed as less sophisticated and polished. "[We] had had a label slapped on us—strings were out."[5] And, like most R&B artists, Charles was well aware that white artists were regularly finding commercial success by appropriating musical styles and repertoire from which their black innovators could not fully profit because of segregation and discrimination. While he "gave those ofay boys some credit for having good ears," he also regarded the inclusion of songs like "Cow Cow Boogie" and "Pistol Packin' Mama" in his own repertoire as a reappropriation of popular white interpretations of black styles.[6]

Given his experience with the differences between white and black audience tastes, his practical analysis of the racial dynamics of the music industry, and the ease with which he could navigate the material that sat at the intersection of jazz, rhythm and blues, and pop, Charles began to experiment with other combinations of styles that were popularly coded as "black" and "white." Though a far less impressive success than his pop breakthrough hit, "What'd I Say," the first song he placed on the pop charts was actually "Swanee River Rock," an adaptation of the Stephen Foster minstrel tune "Old Folks at Home."

There are a number of ways to imagine the meaning of such forays first into minstrel material and then into country: as an implicit acknowledgment of the role of racial and racist performance in American popular music; as a conscious incursion into "white musical space"; or as a sincere, if somewhat jarring gesture to some of the common roots of white and black popular music.[7] Charles combined all three as he fashioned his pop crossover identity. "Swanee River Rock," for instance, inescapably drew attention to the complicated tensions between interracial appropriation and homage inherent in American music. The song opened with the echoing resound of a sharp conga beat, sonically recalling the talking drums that so fascinated and terrified white slave owners. When he began to sing, Charles's call received immediate response from the hand claps and voices of his backup singers, and the whole song, in spite of its lugubrious lyrics, was set to a lively syncopated beat that mocked the singing persona's longing for the old plantation, now only implied, as Charles dropped the plantation lyrics. Charles thus turned Foster's nostalgic lament into a rollicking, hand-clapping gospel stomp that reappropriated the racist stereotypes of the blackface stage in a sly nod both to the historical roles race and racism played in shaping American popular music and to the tenacity and creativity of African Americans who made popular music an important cultural defense against racism.

Charles allowed that minstrelsy was a "strange" point of departure for a single, particularly from an artist who, in Peter Guralnick's formulation, had come to symbolize "the unabashed celebration of negritude without the covering mask of religion."[8] But, as he would frequently remark later with regard to country music, the song formed part of a set of "melodies [he]'d been hearing [his] whole life," and he saw no reason why he could not turn them to his own uses. He would return to minstrel songs on his 1960 *Genius Hits the Road* LP for his new label, ABC.[9]

In his autobiography, Charles depicted this work as mere experimentation, "little jive ideas [he] wanted to try out."[10] His willingness to take on such material reflected his belief in his ability to transcend genre, but he frequently placed his individual eclecticism in a framework that also called attention to the shared roots and continuous exchange between musics that were racially coded as "black" and "white." Minstrelsy was one such shared root, but Charles understood popular music as a process of natural cross-racial exchange, however unfairly the economic fruits of that exchange were divided. In spite of a frequently expressed sense of racially specific black and white musicality, he also regularly told interviewers in the most direct terms that the racialization of music was social rather than stylistic. "I'm not sure I made all those black and white distinctions you're always hearing about," he later said of his early club career. When one interviewer asked him to define the distinction between "a black band like Chick Webb's and a white one like Tommy Dorsey's, [he] said, 'Oh, about a hundred dollars a week.'"[11] His comment to Peter Gurlanick, "You take country music, you take black music, you got the same goddam thing exactly," was probably reductive even of his own opinion. However, like his forays into minstrel repertoire, it indicated that he saw himself as being able to transcend racialized genre boundaries not only because of his talent and varied influences but because the boundaries themselves were vast borderlands of shared traditions rather than clearly demarcated lines.

Whether Charles viewed his early recordings of country songs as a transgression of white musical space, as an acknowledgment of the instability of racialized musical genres, or as a means of musical class mobility, the style of *Modern Sounds* and his use of country repertoire were also consistent with emerging soul trends that would ultimately produce the southern soul of Stax and Muscle Shoals. Ivory Joe Hunter had scored a moderate pop crossover with his cover of Ray Price's "City Lights," one of several country songs he recorded in R&B versions in the 1950s. Otis Williams and the Charms had done an R&B cover of the Delmore Brothers' "Blues Stay Away From Me" for King Records as one of the series of R&B-country cross-pollinations produced by the label under the direction of Henry Glover. The most successful precursor to *Modern Sounds*, though, came from Charles's old label, Atlantic. Shortly after Charles left, *Billboard*'s editor Paul Ackerman had persuaded Jerry Wexler to sign the relatively unknown Solomon Burke and to have him record in his first session a country ballad called "Just Out of Reach," which had been cut by Faron Young, Patsy Cline, and T. Texas Tyler with little success. Wexler originally declined to release the single and harbored doubts as to whether "there would be much of a market for a straightforward country song by an r&b singer," but the single soared to the top ten on the R&B charts and hit number 24 on the pop charts, maintaining a chart presence for seven weeks at the end of 1961, just as Charles was preparing to go into the studio for *Modern Sounds*.[12] Of the many R&B covers of country material in the latter half of the 1950s, Burke's smooth baritone and teardrop breaks, as well as the choral backing vocals that accompanied him, most closely approximated Charles's approach by situating the rendition as much in the new countrypolitan style of the day as in the R&B and gospel backgrounds of the performers.

What distinguished *Modern Sounds in Country and Western Music* from earlier blends of R&B or jazz and country, by Charles and by other black artists, was his insistence on the genre label. Because the album was conceived as a concept statement originally intended to be marketed without singles, its title meant that the genre-crossing of *Modern Sounds* could not be misinterpreted simply as pop or "good music." Though Charles later wrote that he decided to record *Modern Sounds* "not for show, not for shock, but for [his] own pleasure," and that he wasn't aware of "any bold act on [his] part or any big breakthrough," he clearly intended the album as a significant crossing of genre boundaries, in social as well as musical terms. As Daniel Cooper has pointed out, Charles "impelled listeners to deal with the implications of *his* having made [a collection of country songs]. Other blacks had played country music, but none in recent times had so openly claimed it by name."[13] It was perhaps for this very reason that ABC-Paramount initially tried to discourage Charles from recording country, expressing fear that it might alienate his black fans. The success of "Just Out of Reach" must have allayed their doubts about the commercial potential of the sound, but the direct confrontation of racially coded genre boundaries contained in the album title was far more likely to offend those black fans who might perceive it as a bizarre embrace of white racism and those white fans who might view it as trespassing on segregated ground.

Though it ultimately supported Charles's decision to do the album, the label did not initially intend to release any singles from it. But when the white pop singer and teen movie idol Tab Hunter released a single of "I Can't Stop Loving You" backed with "Born to Lose" that duplicated the Charles versions, ABC rushed "I Can't Stop Loving You" into production as a single. Within a month, both the album and the single reigned at number 1 on the *Billboard* charts. One Atlanta distributor reported of the single, "People who don't even own record players are buying it," and regional distributors in some parts of the South were selling fifty thousand and sixty thousand of the singles each week.[14] In the end, "I Can't Stop Loving You" spent eighteen weeks on *Billboard*'s Hot 100 chart, five of them at number 1. The album held the top spot for fourteen weeks and remained on the album chart for *two years*. Charles and ABC-Paramount quickly released a follow-up album called *Modern Sounds in Country and Western, Vol. 2*, and it too climbed the charts, topping out at number 2.[15]

For many years, however, this immense commercial success was largely forgotten, as was the critical role *Modern Sounds* played in the development of the country industry. When the Country Music Foundation released a three-CD set of country music by twentieth-century African American artists, *Modern Sounds* was not only absent from the track list — an exclusion that could be attributed to licensing problems — but received only a single passing mention in the extensive liner notes, an oversight that more directly reveals the obscurity into which the album had fallen in the popular narrative of the genre's history.[16] But the album was released at a particularly pivotal moment in the industry's evolution. By 1962 the trade had weathered the worst of the lean years during which rock and roll dominated the radio and commercial charts. The first hits of the Nashville Sound era had been released, and the number of hours devoted to country radio programming was already increasing, but the industry was still on fragile footing. The attention the album brought to country music radically altered the genre's fortunes. In the early 1950s pop covers of Hank Williams songs by Tony Bennett, Dinah Washington, and others had helped to establish Nashville as a music publishing center. A few years later, the success of Elvis Presley's early RCA recordings under Chet Atkins had given Steve Sholes the prestige to turn Nashville into a major recording center. In just the same way, the enormous success of Ray Charles's country covers allowed Nashville to advance its vision of country-format radio as a thoroughly modern, respectable, and profitable enterprise, and that image decisively moved the genre from margin to mainstream, from a denigrated niche market to the most programmed format in the country.

Modern Sounds transformed the cultural value of country music and the image of Music Row, both in the popular imagination and in the conventional wisdom of the music industry. When the trade publication *Broadcasting* magazine ran one of its first major features on country music, "A Big New Sound Blows out of Nashville," the article appeared under a half-page picture, not of Hank Williams or even countrypolitan avatar Jim Reeves, but of Ray Charles, accompanied by the caption, "The Nashville Sound is sweeping the charts in national music popularity—propelled by best-selling records cut by performers like Ray Charles."[17] In a piece that similarly touted the country boom and contended that Charles "almost single-handedly put the craze in high gear," *Variety* quoted producer Owen Bradley's opinion that the genre's best sales in more than a decade were due to "barriers . . . broken by individuals like Ray Charles . . . by such people passing on their acknowledgement of the music to the public."[18]

Such observations were not limited to the trades. In an article on Ferlin Husky's three-day engagement at Tokyo's Copacabana, *Pacific Stars and Stripes* neatly summarized the modern patina Charles bestowed on country. Reproducing Husky's claim that patrons at similar "society spots" in the United States "pretend they don't know what [he's] doing because they're not supposed to like country and western music," the magazine suggested, with more than a little bit of ambivalence, that country's lowbrow reputation was being rehabilitated: "Like it or not, there's no getting around the fact that country and western music is in the middle of a big boom in the U.S. Such top acts as Nat Cole, Ray Charles, and Connie Francis have recorded C&W LPs that are selling like the proverbial stack of hotcakes."[19] Even a "good music" paragon like Andy Williams staked his future on the enduring popularity of pop-country hybrids he thought Charles's album presaged. Explaining how he would make his new television variety show even better than the summer replacement series he had hosted two years earlier, Williams told a reporter, "I feel the next basic trend in pop music is country music that verges on pop music—things like Ray Charles' big album, 'Modern Sounds in Country Music' [*sic*]. So I want to do some things in that vein."[20]

Although the newsletter of the Country Music Association noted in May 1962 that Ray Charles had "reached a new pinnacle in a new realm . . . the Americana land of Country Music," in general the album's success was greeted as evidence of country's influence on pop rather than as a landmark in the development of country music as a genre.[21] This position, however, suppressed a widespread uncertainty over what the album might suggest about the country audience's willingness to embrace a soul-country hybrid. Early trade press write-ups on the record's first hit single, "I Can't Stop Loving You," contended that "according to deejays it was selling in all markets, pop, r&b, and country," and noted that both the album and the single were selling particularly well in traditional country markets such as Atlanta.[22] "ABC-Paramount readily admitted that when the album and single began selling they were amazed at the quantity of disks being sold in country music strongholds," *Billboard* reported. "No one could possibly have forecast the huge quantities of records that were sold throughout the South and Southwest. These had to be bought not only by the usual Charles devotee and teen-age pop fan," the paper speculated, "but by whole hosts of consumers who had never bought a Charles record before," by which the magazine apparently meant country fans, at least in part.[23] Apparently the Texas-based country and gospel distribution company Starday was also convinced that country fans were excited not only about the album but about Charles as an artist. In the spring of 1962 Starday ran a feature ad in the Nashville trade paper *Music Reporter* announcing that its Third Annual Country Music Spectacular Sale would include bargain prices on albums by Cowboy Copas and Leon McCauliff, a compilation called *Banjo in the Hills*, and *The Original Ray Charles*, a collection of his Swingtime singles of the late 1940s through the early 1950s released in the aftermath of *Modern Sounds*.[24]

The confusion about just which market Charles was reaching was also evident on the popularity charts of the *Music Reporter*. Throughout the spring and summer of 1962, the paper listed "I Can't Stop Loving You" only on the R&B airplay charts, correctly reflecting country radio's disinterest in the single. But on the facing page, the editors consistently listed the album at the top of their "big C&W albums" chart, a discrepancy that pointed to a possible disjuncture between the tastes of deejays and those their audience expressed through their record buying.[25] In fact although it eventually won him a Grammy for Best R&B Male Vocal Performance, the song climbed the R&B radio charts relatively slowly and, according to Charles, met with resistance from black deejays which was overcome only when the single became too popular to ignore, a perception that again calls into question the initial source of the single's popularity.[26]

In their search for a genre framework that would allow them to assess the commercial potential of *Modern Sounds*, the trades quickly turned to another prominent instance in which the race of the performer, the racialized genre codes of the performance, and the apparent social identity of the audience did not seem to match: the rise of Elvis Presley. *Billboard*'s speculation about the success of *Modern Sounds* in country strongholds was reminiscent of

RCA's early assessment of Presley's "That's All Right" single on Sun. RCA originally took note of Presley in part because the single sold to country fans, not on the basis of the B-side cover of Bill Monroe's "Blue Moon of Kentucky," but on the R&B-influenced sound of the A side.[27] This parallel was explicitly expressed in *Billboard*'s early observation of sales trends on "I Can't Stop Loving You": "Feeling among dealers was that Charles' current single was one of the hottest records released in almost a year, and was equal in sales action to some of the early Presley disks."[28] The *Music Reporter* echoed the sentiment in announcing the Charles single's meteoric one-week ascent from number 41 to number 1 on that magazine's Big 50 chart: "Only one other artist has ever had a disk to jump so fast and he was Elvis Presley."[29]

In the wake of the album's success, a number of black artists recorded country material or came to Nashville to record pop. Solomon Burke regularly returned to the country material that had made him a star and, according to Jerry Wexler, "practically kept Atlantic alive between 1961 and 1964," in part with versions of the folk standard "Down in the Valley," the Eddy Arnold hit "I Really Don't Want to Know," and "He'll Have to Go," first made famous by countrypolitan Jim Reeves.[30] Burke's label mate Esther Phillips also scored pop crossover successes with "Release Me" and "I Really Don't Want to Know." On Stax, Carla Thomas recorded "I Fall to Pieces" and "I'm So Lonesome I Could Cry." Sam Cooke reached the pop, adult contemporary, and R&B charts with his version of "Frankie and Johnnie." Even the Supremes recorded an album of country and pop standards in 1963, though it did not see release until 1965. Some of this material struck critics and listeners as mere gimmickry, but the effects of Charles's success went beyond the suddenly fashionable trend of having black artists from other genres record established country hits. The country-soul fusions produced at FAME, Stax, American, and other studios in Memphis and Muscle Shoals proved to be the dominant sound in R&B for the remainder of the decade.

Ultimately, however, neither the music industry at large nor the country industry in particular understood the success of *Modern Sounds* as pointing to the formation of a new listening audience with an appreciation for a particular blend of "black" and "white" styles, as had Presley's rise a decade earlier. In spite of their staying power on the R&B and easy listening charts, the record's hit singles never received regular country radio airplay. Country deejays ignored the album and its singles in the annual "best of" polls published in the Nashville trade and fan press, though one *Billboard* poll of country jocks showed the album in their top-ten list of Favorite Country Music LPs.[31] The *Music Reporter*, which earlier had touted the record as reinvigorating not just country music but the profits of the entire music industry, did not even refer to *Modern Sounds* in its August retrospective look at 1962. A month later *Cash Box* magazine reported that *Modern Sounds* was the most programmed album in the nation, and grouped "I Can't Stop Loving You" together with Jimmy Dean's "Big Bad John" when it noted that two of the three most programmed singles were "of C&W origin." But it also entirely omitted both the single and the album from its list of "the Country Set's most programmed."[32]

The fledgling Country Music Association, however, embraced the album enthusiastically as a marketing stance that allowed the country field to claim mainstream respectability and a progressive, modern position on race. In the civil rights era, the notional framing of southern backwardness shifted from economic shortcomings to virulent racism. To the country industry and its fans, the image of the racist hick simply extended and updated long-standing images of southern cultural and economic backwardness, embodied most obviously in the figure of the hillbilly. Such imagery had been used to stigmatize country music for decades, minimizing both its cultural worth and its marketing potential. Many of the CMA's efforts during its early years were aimed at combating these stereotypes of southern backwardness, and *Modern Sounds* offered the association an opportunity to construct a different social narrative, one that situated disparaged southern white migrants within a national, middle-class, integrationist consensus.

When *Modern Sounds* was released, the CMA, still in its formative stages, had only recently undertaken its first major project: a radio marketing campaign that by 1970 would help to make country the most programmed genre in America. The CMA sought to counter the prevailing stereotype that country listeners were ignorant, barefoot hillbillies whether they still lived in rural areas or had migrated to the city. They hoped to cast their traditional audience in a new light: as country folk who made good in the big city, moved to the suburbs, and ascended into the burgeoning ranks of the blue-collar aristocracy that symbolized the democratizing (and nominally race-neutral) effects of universal consumerism in postwar America. To further this goal, the CMA initiated a series of lunchtime sales presentations to broadcasters and sponsors designed to reeducate them about the economic and cultural profile of the country audience. The presentations cited median household incomes for country listeners, dwelt on the results sponsors had achieved by advertising on country radio, and directly confronted stereotypes of country listeners as lowbrow and low class.[33]

In presenting its case for the modernization of the country industry and its audience, the CMA's sales presentations invariably cited *Modern Sounds* as the foundational moment of the "new" country music trend of the early 1960s. In the first presentation of the show, the narrator told his audience, "Country music is quote discovered unquote by the so-called pop music field every few years but the lid really blew off in mid-1962, when Ray Charles' 'Modern Sounds in Country Music' [*sic*] album hit the million sales mark in a hurry. . . . Following this, the entire world of show business seemed to go Nashville crazy."[34] A second version interpreted the album as more than just an economic charter; rather it was a metaphor for the nation's (and the country audience's) move toward a more enlightened view of race. In this show, after a brief demographic sketch of the audience as mainstream middle-class consumers, a discussion of the music opened with the assertion, "In one aspect of America's cultural life, integration has already taken place." With the specter of the southern rejection of racial justice just below the surface, the narration continued.

> As we check off the best selling and most programmed tunes today, we are impressed by a fact of both sociological and musical import. The songs we hear are patently the creative products of many different social and racial groups. The song, "I Can't Stop Loving You," written and performed by a country artist, Don Gibson, was performed last year by a blind Negro artist, Mr. Ray Charles, and walked off with some of 1962's top selling honours in both single and LP record products.[35]

The class connotations of this social narrative helped to establish both the respectability and the broadcasting marketability of the country audience and provided the foundation for country's transition to mainstream status within the popular music industry. Charles's sophisticated treatment of country, with its big band and swing arrangements, seemed less important to the industry as a statement of racial integration than of class status. In the CMA's conception, racial tolerance, figured through the embrace of *Modern Sounds*, became a particularly important sign of another kind of integration that was more central to its own concerns: the class and regional integration of its audience. The CMA's public relations campaign hoped to communicate that the modern sounds of country and western music Charles played would reach a fully modernized audience whose social progress was symbolized in part through participation in a theoretically racially neutral ethos of industrial consumer democracy.

However, this substitution of class for race was made available by Charles's own philosophy about his work and by the recordings themselves.

The album featured twelve country standards, including Ted Daffan's "Born to Lose," Don Gibson's "I Can't Stop Loving You," and Hank Williams's "Hey Good Lookin'," each performed in one of two main idioms. The first, arranged by Marty Paich, consisted of simple small-band string and vocal arrangements, as in the hit song "I Can't Stop Loving You." The other, arranged by Gerald Wilson, was characterized by fuller, syncopated swing arrangements including horns, as in the cover of "Hey Good Lookin'."

The first idiom combined pop arrangements with rhythm and blues vocal lines. The instrumentation of Charles's rendition of "I Can't Stop Loving You," for instance, is not dramatically different from the original version recorded by Don Gibson. Both rely on guitar, strings, and backing vocals to create a lush country pop sound. Musically Charles's version differs from Gibson's primarily in extending and emphasizing the pop elements: the guitar is less prominent, the string and vocal parts more so. But this arrangement would have been understood by many listeners, particularly those in the country music audience, as firmly situated within the countrypolitan style that had been pioneered by artists like Eddy Arnold, Ferlin Husky, Jim Reeves, and Gibson himself. By incorporating rich backing vocals and sweet strings, Charles did not introduce a radically new approach to country material. Instead he exaggerated the elements of the original country rendition that were widely perceived as being class-based and, through exaggeration, drew attention to the contest over class and cultural hierarchy embodied in the original version.

Although his arrangement was not a radical departure from the original, Charles was also interested in moving the arrangement and delivery of the songs beyond standard country conventions. As he later explained, "[I] wanted to take the country songs and sing them my way, not the country way."[36] Through his bluesy vocal timbre, syncopated phrasing, and aching melismas, Charles situated his own vocal identity firmly within the stylistic conventions of rhythm and blues. He *played* one potential version of straight country, but he made no effort to *sing* straight country. Instead he vocally emphasized his presence as a black R&B singer situated seamlessly, but very prominently, into a purely countrypolitan musical context. This performance combined the middle-class trappings of the Nashville Sound with the conspicuous persona of the urbane, sophisticated soul crooner, and thereby connected class mobility and racial pluralism as the central elements of the "modern" in *Modern Sounds*.

Charles's cover of Hank Williams's "Hey Good Lookin'" typified the second style of arrangement on *Modern Sounds*: a big band sound that emphasizes connections to swing and jazz. But here again Charles combined musical codes for class and race in such a way that musical integration virtually symbolized middle-class respectability. In one sense, Charles's version of "Hey Good Lookin'" simply repeated Williams's original mixing of "black" and "white" vernacular styles. Williams was so successful in the early 1950s in part because he reconnected with the blues elements that characterized the "authentic" core country tradition beginning with Jimmie Rodgers.[37] Williams made "Hey Good Lookin'" and other songs in his repertoire "swing" through syncopation and blue note effects taken from jazz and urban blues.

By performing the song with a heavily syncopated big band swing arrangement, Charles gestured to Williams's original incorporation of "black" musical elements, acknowledging the fundamental interconnections between rhythm and blues and country and grounding his own rendition in the core of the country repertoire in musical as well as lyrical terms. Yet by the late 1940s big band swing, in spite of its roots in black idioms, was primarily a middle-class white genre that symbolized the melding of black and white cultures within the emerging liberal consensus. By incorporating "whitened," middle-class swing rather than repeating Williams's original borrowing of lowbrow urban blues and jazz, Charles produced a rendition that subordinated racial difference to a narrative about class and appropriate versions of whiteness. In doing so, he prefigured the very same rhetorical strategies of racial pluralism and class respectability that animated the CMA's broadcast marketing campaign in the 1960s.

Ironically, though, as Charles's posthumous reputation has developed in the twenty-first century, that dynamic has been reversed, and the import of *Modern Sounds* in its original context has been revised to focus on race. This revision may be due to the long discography of country material that Charles continued to produce after *Modern Sounds*, including the single "Busted" and songs on the album *Country and Western Meets Rhythm and Blues* in the 1960s, as well as his albums in the 1980s for CBS's country division, which produced enough hits in a single decade to place him alongside artists such as Spade Cooley, June Carter, and Kris Kristofferson in terms of chart success, despite the fact that none of his work from the 1960s made the country charts.[38] These releases—particularly those on *Friendship* that featured Charles singing duets with country legends such as Willie Nelson and George Jones—allowed him to reposition himself; no longer an outside interpreter of country standards, he could now claim to be a mainstream country artist, both stylistically and institutionally (fig. 2.1). But if Charles had felt compelled to defend himself in his autobiography against charges of

FIGURE 2.1. Ray Charles appearing on a Willie Nelson television special in 1984. Though *Modern Sounds* never reached the country charts, Charles enjoyed mainstream country success in the 1980s thanks in part to duets with Nelson, George Jones, and other country stars. Image courtesy of Photofest.

privileging commercial over artistic aims when he recorded *Modern Sounds*, his country output in the 1980s was even more likely to be viewed as a sell-out. He had not placed a song in the top ten since the late 1960s, and his new direction was easily interpreted, even by sympathetic observers such as his biographer, as a "cold-blooded" calculation that country fans' storied loyalty to older artists could provide him with "a possible pasture for his old age."[39]

Thus in spite of his later work for the country market, it was because of the impact of *Modern Sounds*, an album that never made the country charts, that Charles found a new position in the country canon after his death. When the Grand Ole Opry presented a tribute to Brother Ray in 2006, the artists who reprised his work invariably referred not to his 1980s country hits but to *Modern Sounds*. Vince Gill opined, "Ray Charles single-handedly took some of the greatest country songs ever written, did them his way with his arrangements, and showed the world how soulful country music could be." When Martina McBride described Charles as "a vocalist who inspired so many artists including [her]self," she enlarged on the homage by reminding the interviewer that she had "recorded his version of 'I Can't Stop Loving You.'"[40]

While this belated acknowledgment of the album's importance was frequently framed in terms of the shift in the class status of country that it occasioned, the utility of positioning a black artist at the center of country music's history also clearly advanced contemporaneous efforts to de-whiten the genre. When Charles appeared with Travis Tritt on *Crossroads*, a CMT show dedicated to showing "the far-reaching roots of country music by pairing country artists with musicians from other genres," the official announcement of the episode suggested that, if Tritt was right that Charles should be in the Country Music Hall of Fame, it was because he had recorded an album of country songs "at a time when racial tensions hovered over the South," thereby "bringing in new fans to country music."[41]

Tritt's declaration clearly showed that many in the industry remembered the album as a landmark, but the redress of the collective amnesia surrounding *Modern Sounds* was made possible largely by an exhibit on Charles mounted by the Country Music Hall of Fame and Museum in 2006. Press reviews of the exhibit emphasized the fact that Charles had taken country uptown in class terms, but also consistently addressed the racial implications of a black man recording country music during the death throes of Jim Crow not as a symbol of the country audience's respectability but as a form of racial reconciliation: "The move seemed to validate the music of the Southern white working class during the heat of the civil rights era."[42]

Latter-day assessments of *Modern Sounds*, both as historical narratives and as contemporary interventions in the racial politics of country, have thus minimized the way the album's dynamics of racial crossover were subordinated to the class ambitions of the country industry, an elision that emerges when the revival of the album is placed in historiographical context. Titled "I Can't Stop Loving You: Ray Charles and Country Music," the Charles exhibit at the Country Music Hall of Fame and Museum followed on the heels of an acclaimed exhibit and accompanying Grammy-winning CD box sets that explored Nashville's rhythm and blues scene and the country musicians, studios, and songwriters who participated in it. It thus formed part of a larger effort—begun in the 1990s with the CD box set *From Where I Stand* and a special issue of the *Journal of Country Music* dedicated to African American artists and entrepreneurs—to reclaim the history of black engagements with country music. Yet negotiating the cultural politics of that reclamation project remains hazardous. The title of the exhibit gestured to the biggest hit from *Modern Sounds*, but it also focused attention mainly on the heroism of a black R&B artist tenaciously embracing a music he ought not to have loved because of its racist reputation. Moreover, by associating the wistfulness of the song with the subterranean black country tradition the museum has tried to reveal, it depicted that tradition as a lost but enduring romance that cannot and should not be relinquished. To the extent that *Modern Sounds* has become a musical representation of racial reconciliation, these associations subtly, and undoubtedly inadvertently, perpetuate the notion that such reconciliation is primarily a matter of black forgiveness rather than white atonement.

In 2007 Jamie Foxx appeared with Rascal Flatts on the CMA Awards to sing "She Goes All the Way," a song they had recorded together several months earlier. In sharp contrast to the popular understanding of Charles's persona in the 1960s, Foxx, who won an Academy Award for his portrayal of Charles in the biopic *Ray*, could now be introduced as the man who played "one of the greatest country singers of all time, Ray Charles." But if Foxx's presence as a symbol of Charles was cause for celebration, his presence as a contemporary black star on a country stage was clearly still subject to the same set of suspicions Charles had faced in the 1960s and required special legitimization. The CMA lauded the appearance as "the sort of one-of-a-kind performance the CMA Awards are known for," but it was also anxious to authenticate the performance as more than mere posturing, emphasizing that such a collaboration could create "magical moments that resonate with [their] audience and expand awareness of the format" only if "there is a meaningful and tangible connection between artists from seemingly diverse musical styles," a connection provided in this case by the fact that Foxx and the Rascal Flatts front man Gary LeVox had been roommates in the late 1990s.[43]

So maybe this is the ultimate paradox about *Modern Sounds in Country and Western Music*: that it changed everything about the class politics of country and virtually nothing about its racial politics. If the album's early success pointed to the prospect that country fans really were ready to relinquish the genre's insistent performance of whiteness, that possibility was quickly foreclosed. Instead it became a way for the country industry to symbolize the social mobility, economic clout, and cultural sophistication of its core audience of southern white migrants. And while the posthumous recuperation of Charles as a country artist evidences the industry's desire to reconfigure country's racial politics, it also attests to the continuing elisions of inequality that lay at the root of the album's original reception.

Notes

1. Malone, *Don't Get above Your Raisin'*, 237–38.
2. Charles and Ritz, *Brother Ray*, 87.

3. Pecknold, *The Selling Sound.*

4. Charles and Ritz, *Brother Ray*, 78, 85–86.

5. Charles and Ritz, *Brother Ray*, 152.

6. Charles and Ritz, *Brother Ray*, 72.

7. For an interpretation of what he calls Charles's calculated "trespassing" on white musical space, see Feder, "Song of the South," 175–90.

8. Charles and Ritz, *Brother Ray*, 195; Guralnick, *Sweet Soul Music*, 63.

9. Charles and Ritz, *Brother Ray*, 195.

10. Charles and Ritz, *Brother Ray*, 221.

11. Charles and Ritz, *Brother Ray*, 86.

12. Guralnick, *Sweet Soul Music*, 72.

13. Cooper, "Take Me Down to That Southern Land," 16.

14. "Atlanta Goes Ray All the Way," *Billboard*, May 19, 1962, 1; "Charles Continuing Disk Sales Climb," *Billboard*, May 26, 1962, 1.

15. Lydon, *Ray Charles*, 219–22.

16. Wynn, "This Is My Country," 21; Rumble, "The Artists and the Songs," 39.

17. "A Big New Sound Blows out of Nashville," *Broadcasting*, Jan. 28, 1963, 67.

18. "Tin Pan Valley's Peak Year," *Variety*, July 25, 1962, 89.

19. Al Ricketts, "On the Town," *Pacific Stars and Stripes*, April 19, 1963, 11.

20. Dick Kleiner, "Andy Williams Problem: 'Too Good in the Past,'" *Long Beach* (Calif.) *Independent Press-Telegram*, Sept. 23, 1962, 3.

21. "Ray Charles Records C&W All Time Greats," CMA *Close-Up*, May 1962, 4.

22. "New Charles Single Leads Sales Climb," *Billboard*, May 19, 1962, 1; "Atlanta Goes Ray All the Way," 1.

23. Jack Maher, "Ray Charles Carried the Ball — Then Everyone Else Began Scoring Big," *Billboard*, Nov. 10, 1962, 34.

24. *Music Reporter*, June 23, 1962, n.p.

25. *Music Reporter*, May 5, 1962, 26–27.

26. Charles and Ritz, *Brother Ray*, 223.

27. Guralnick, *Last Train to Memphis*, 123.

28. "New Charles Disk Leads Sales Climb," 1.

29. *Music Reporter*, May 26, 1962, 1.

30. Guralnick, *Last Train to Memphis*, 84.

31. Cooper, "Take Me Down to That Southern Land," 30.

32. "Country Tunes Crowd *Cash Box* Box-Score," CMA *Close-Up*, Sept. 1962, 1.

33. Pecknold, *The Selling Sound*, 153–57.

34. Joe Allison, "Presentation to the Sales Executives Club of New York," Country Music Association Sales and Marketing Programs, microfiche: fiche 1, Country Music Association Papers, Frist Library and Archive, Country Music Hall of Fame and Museum, Nashville; Joe Allison, "Presentation to the Nashville Chamber of Commerce," Country Music Association Sales and Marketing Programs, microfiche: fiche 2.

35. CMA sales presentation to Canadian Radio and Television Executives Club, Aug. 1963, quoted in CMA *Close-Up*, Sept. 1963, n.p.

36. Charles and Ritz, *Brother Ray*, 223.

37. Brackett, *Interpreting Popular Music*, 98.

38. Whitburn, *Top Country Singles*, 502.

39. Lydon, *Ray Charles*, 344.

40. Business Wire, "GAC's Grand Ole Opry Live Pays Tribute to Ray Charles," http://www.businesswire.com/portal/site/google/index.jsp?ndmViewId=news _view&newsId=20060601005794&newsLang=en.

41. "Crossroads: Ray Charles and Travis Tritt: About the Episode," CMT, http:// www.cmt.com/shows/dyn/cmt_crossroads/63660/episode_about.jhtml.

42. "Exhibit Explores Ray Charles' Country Side: R&B Genius' 1962 Album 'Modern Sounds' Cornerstone of Nashville Display," MSNBC.com, http://www.msnbc .msn.com/id/11657782.

43. "Jamie Foxx to Perform," *The 41st Annual CMA Awards*, ABC.com, http://abc .go.com/primetime/cmawards/index?pn=jamiefoxx.

Contested Origins
ARNOLD SHULTZ AND THE
MUSIC OF WESTERN KENTUCKY
Erika Brady

There's a favorite story about Arnold Shultz (1886–1931), the African American instrumentalist whose distinctive style impressed a generation of musicians white and black, in an area where virtuoso playing was already commonplace. As John Hartford tells it:

> In the fall of the year [Arnold] would take his guitar one morning, and simply walk out of the house and into the woods and sit down on a stump and play. After a little spell of that he would pick up and move on out into the forest where he would find a stump or somewhere else to sit and repeat the performance. Thus, if you were his family on the porch of the house you could hear him disappearing out through the woods with his music. And when he figured he was out of earshot he'd keep going and catch the local gas packet or some form of water transportation down Green River and up to Evansville where he could get deck passage on one of the Ohio boats. . . .
>
> He would winter in New Orleans and I'm sure he played music on the street, and of course this was the days of Jelly Roll Morton and his tremendous influence on all who heard him, and I'm sure Arnold spent not a small amount of time listening to music through a whorehouse window. Jelly Roll pioneered passing chords in ragtime, and you know Arnold could hear this and worked out the chords and their voicings

on the guitar to expand the harmonies of what he was playing on the street.

Then come spring he would find a northbound boat, connect up the river to Evansville and thence up Green River and come home through the woods stopping every once in a while to play some tunes (with passing chords) in to the breeze. Some fine morning the ladies on the porch look up and listen and one will say "I think I hear Arnold, away far away and faint but I believe that's him and he'll be home soon." And Arnold would play his way back to the house and home for the summer.[1]

Apparently unrecorded and unknown outside western Kentucky in his day, in recent years Shultz has commanded considerable attention from scholars and fans of bluegrass and Travis-style thumbpicking, two styles of music with deep roots in the area that have influenced popular music worldwide. Some treatments of Shultz virtually anoint him as the originator of these styles: "It All Goes Back to Arnold Shultz" is the title of a piece in the *Merle Travis Newsletter* in 1988, and a 1989 article in *Bluegrass Unlimited* asks, "Arnold Shultz: Godfather of Bluegrass?"[2] In light of this attention, the vignette of Shultz recounted by Hartford represents an origin myth *within* an origin myth: how a black performer came by the skills that would shape two important strands of white country music by undertaking a journey to yet another source of musical style: New Orleans, and the self-styled Father of Jazz himself, Jelly Roll Morton.[3]

Hartford's story represents a western Kentucky version of the iconic legend of Robert Johnson at the crossroads. The scenario embodies elements of mysterious absence, then reappearance, of a hero magically transformed; an epic quest to capture a rare gift, and a triumphant return to share it with those who stayed at home. If it lacks the dark occult edge of Johnson's supposed diabolical deal-making, it offers the possibility of the mildly transgressive (Shultz leaning in the whorehouse window, neither musical participant nor client) and the charm of a trip by water, so appealing to the river pilot Hartford that he practically charts out the itinerary. It is perhaps the nicest song Hartford never wrote. The story is well known enough to aficionados of western Kentucky roots music to have inspired an instrumental tune by the nationally known fingerstyle guitarist Pat Kirtley called "Arnold's Coming Home."[4]

The bare bones of the story seem to have originated with Shultz's own family, reaching wider recognition through a print account by the folklorist William E. Lightfoot from the musician's nephew, Malcolm Walker. In this interview, Walker recalls his uncle's habit of abrupt appearance and disappearance: "He traveled a whole lot. He would leave and we wouldn't know where he was. He didn't write or anything. But, somehow or another, we'd all be around the house there and the first thing you knew, you'd hear that guitar. And you *knew* it the minute you heard it." Shultz would remain for a time, then take off again.

> "He'd play as he walked away?" [Lightfoot] asked.
> "That's right; that's the way he was."
> "And wander off?"
> "He'd just kind of ease on away."

Shultz's demise also offers an enigma: though the death certificate cites the cause of death as a mitral lesion, relatives as well as some white musicians in the area attribute his passing at the age of forty-five to poisoning by jealous members of his band.[5] This unsubstantiated story further reinforces the parallel with Robert Johnson, who also may or may not have been poisoned.[6]

The leave-taking scenario retold by Hartford, and indeed the whole of Shultz's story, seems to invite vivid embroidery; even Lightfoot, not generally given to scholarly hyperbole, compares the performer to a medieval minstrel, "spread[ing] his music wherever he went."[7] And Hartford follows his own flight of fancy with the rueful admission, "This is all pure speculation and dream on my part—except that he did play passing chords."[8] It is notable that the elaborated romantic variants of the story are most popular among musicians and scholars from outside the region. Indeed while Shultz's skill as a performer is widely acknowledged by musicians of western Kentucky, there is a quiet resistance to the preeminence given him in the more extravagant accounts of the origins of bluegrass and thumbstyle picking.

Arnold Shultz's name began to surface in print in the 1960s as educated young scholar-fans of bluegrass music initiated investigations into its sources, with bossman Bill Monroe as their point of departure. It was at this time that Monroe's loyal advocate and manager Ralph Rinzler tagged him with the enduring title "Father of Bluegrass."[9] In conversations and interviews with Rinzler from 1963 to 1965, as well as Alice Gerrard and Hazel Dickens from 1968 to 1971, Shultz emerges as a respected musician in the vicinity of Monroe's home in Rosine, who gave the teenager occasional work playing backup guitar at local dances. Rinzler quotes Monroe:

The first time I think I ever seen Arnold Shultz, this square dance was at Rosine, and Arnold and two more colored fellows come up there and played for the dance. . . . People loved Arnold so well all through Kentucky there. If he was playing guitar they'd go gang up around him till he would get tired. . . . There's things in my music that comes from Arnold Shultz, runs that I use a lot of in my music. . . . I tried to keep in my mind a little of it, what I could salvage to use in my music. Then he could play blues, and I wanted some blues in my music, you see.[10]

Noteworthy in this account is Monroe's recollection that Shultz was routinely hired to play the breakdowns and other tunes suitable for square dances, and that he was by no means the only black musician who did so. Monroe's comments on the blues indicate that, certainly in his own mind, Shultz's blues represented a stylistic expertise separate from the skill required for the square dances, one that Monroe admired and to a limited degree — "a little of it" — chose to incorporate in his own music. Finally, he cites Shultz's striking manner of linking core chords in a tune — "runs that I use a lot" — the linear equivalent of the passing chords cited by virtually every musician who had the opportunity to hear Shultz.

Monroe acknowledged a debt to Shultz, but a debt with boundaries: at no point did he attribute the paternity of bluegrass to his former associate — that was his *own* role, jealously guarded. It should also be pointed out that Monroe's music shows evidence of judicious borrowings from other African American sources, from jazz and jug bands to rhythm and blues.[11] Not only did Monroe respect and admire many aspects of black music, but his biographer Richard D. Smith argues that Monroe's behavior to blacks was well in advance of his time.[12] As his legend grew, however, Monroe reacted with increasing hostility to any perceived slight to his position as the wellspring of bluegrass as a unique musical form. He was evidently also irritable concerning the paternal attribution of Kentucky thumbpicking guitar to Shultz: he was heard to remark almost pettishly, "I want to know where this Arnold Shultz stuff got involved in thumbpicking. . . . Arnold didn't play thumbstyle."[13]

Shultz's influence on bluegrass music through his relationship with the teenage Bill Monroe is a relatively simple matter to unravel in comparison to the question of Shultz's influence on western Kentucky thumbstyle guitar, and the importance of getting this part of the story straight is essential to understanding the origins of a style of immense significance, not only to musicians in the region where it developed but to the larger world of country music and beyond. As a country music superstar of the late 1940s and 1950s, Muhlenberg County's Merle Travis took his version of Kentucky thumb-picking to the world. The music historian Mark Humphrey observed, "Without Merle, there would have been no Chet, and without those two, it's hard to imagine Scotty Moore or Carl Perkins or at least two subsequent generations of country and rockabilly guitarists."[14] A partial list of those acknowledging Travis's influence includes such diverse talents as Scotty Moore, Jerry Reed, Doc Watson, Lenny Breau, Marcel Dadi, and Albert Lee, as well as scores of unsung session and side musicians who have left their stamp on country, rock, and pop music. Like Charlie Christian in jazz, early thumb-style musicians in these genres powered the emergence of the guitar as a lead instrument in commercial recording. Many western Kentucky musicians and fans are profoundly invested in their regional identification with this style of music; they sponsor a National Thumb Pickers Hall of Fame, regular contests, and an annual schedule of events celebrating this aspect of their musical heritage.

This sense of investment is accompanied by a deep sensitivity concerning the question of its origin. Musicians currently involved in the style have their own origin myth. As they tell it, around 1918 a young musician named Kennedy Jones had played his thumb raw, hitting the bass notes on his guitar for hours while playing a square dance. The next morning he went down to a Central City music store and found a box of thumbpicks, at that time used exclusively for Hawaiian music. As he later recounted to the musician and music historian Mike Seeger, he told the owner, "Hand me down a guitar. I'm not gonna run off with it."

> So he handed it down to me, and I started pickin' with it. . . . Just a thumb and finger, that's all I used. I couldn't do a good job with it to start with, but it gave me a good idea that I could. I bought the whole box, turned the box up, and filled my pockets full with them.
>
> I started pickin', and oh, in about a week or two, I was really rockin'. Oh, I could just do it, and it would talk to you.

Relating this story in print, the journalist and local music historian Bobby Anderson reinforces the local importance this story is given by remarking portentously, "Perhaps the unidentified store owner who sold Kennedy Jones his first picks never realized what consequences this one remote incident would have on the world of music in years to come."[15]

In addition to expressing a particular view of the lineage of thumbstyle guitar, the prevalence of this story in response to the query "Where did Travis-style guitar come from?" underlines a further subtle but important distinction recognized among thumbpickers. Lightfoot admirably summarizes the salient musical characteristics: the use of the pick to create pulsating alternating bass line; the light, steady afterbeat; the syncopated and playful melodic line; the artful use of damping or choking strings to vary the timbre; the repertoire of characteristic ornaments and "licks"; and the application of the techniques to tunes from a broad range of musical genres.[16] All these elements are readily recognized among local pickers, but one absolute criterion supersedes all others: the true thumbpicker invariably uses the D-shaped pick that wraps around the thumb, as opposed to use of fingers alone or the teardrop-shaped flatpick known locally (and somewhat dismissively) as a "straight pick." Chet Atkins's longtime accompanist Paul Yandell, the superb guitarist who lit a fire under a number of unforgettable Louvin Brothers hits, puts it firmly:

> If Merle and Chet and Jerry Reed had never lived, I'm telling you, guitar playing would be so boring, nobody could play three licks. Everybody would be playing with a straight pick up in Kentucky, because that's where it all came from. Kennedy Jones is the father of it all. Now I know they give Arnold Shultz credit and all that, and I don't know about that. . . . One time Chet and I were playing at a benefit down at the Station Inn about fifteen years ago [ca. 1985], and I asked Bill Monroe about Arnold Shultz. . . . I said, "Did he play with his fingers? Use a thumbpick or anything like that?" And he said, "No, he played with a straight pick, used a Barlow pocket knife [to slide]."
>
> Kennedy Jones, Junior, told me that his daddy told him he'd been playing about ten years before he even met Arnold Shultz, and Kennedy Jones learned his first guitar from his mother. And Kennedy Jones was the first guy that started playing with a thumbpick, which was a major, major advancement, because you take somebody that plays thumbstyle and take their thumbpick off, you sound *completely* different.[17]

Like Yandell, most thumbpickers are literalists in this regard: they are not so much thumb-pickers as thumbpick-ers. Musicians who deviate from this norm — and a handful of local musicians white and black do so — may be much admired, but they are not *thumbpickers* in the strict sense. T-shirts and

FIGURE 3.1.
Arnold Shultz's headstone in Morgantown, Kentucky. Its inscription, which dedicates the stone "to thumb picking and finger cording," describes Shultz merely as "famous for his guitar picking," delicately finessing local sensitivities about the origins of thumb-picking style. Photograph by Andrew Barron.

posters connected with local events underline this distinction, on which one can commonly see the silhouette of a flatpick represented inside the iconic circle and slash expressing prohibition.

By this standard, Arnold Shultz was *not* a thumbpicker (fig. 3.1). Most accounts indicate that he either played a straight thumb-and-finger style without thumbpick or made use of a flatpick, in all likelihood the latter for dances and the former for blues and performances in more intimate settings.[18] In fact the use of the thumbpick appears historically to have been especially prevalent within the white musical community; indeed, to this day, use of the thumbpick is rare among local black musicians, even the few who now occasionally play with white thumbpickers.[19]

How, then, *did* Arnold Shultz play? Thanks to the vigorous sleuthing of William E. Lightfoot, Keith Lawrence, Charles Wolfe, and Wendell Allen, we know quite a bit about his music as well as his life story. Summarizing their findings, it is evident that he was a multi-instrumentalist, proficient on banjo, piano, and mandolin as well as guitar. Bill Monroe's brother Birch recalls him primarily as a fiddler: "He played a good old-time fiddle, I can tell you that."[20] Shultz was in fact both a blues and an old-time string-band music stylist, depending on the context in which he was called upon to perform.

Born to a musical family in Cromwell (or, by some accounts, the settlement of Taylor Mines near Beaver Dam), Ohio County, by the age of fourteen he was working in the mines with his father. By 1911, at the age of twenty-five, he was well established locally as a guitarist in a family band, playing for square dances in and around Ohio County with his Shultz cousins Ella (later Griffin) on fiddle, Luther on bass, and Hardin on banjo. According to Ella Griffin, "It was hillbilly music then, and it *was* hillbilly, too. But it was all I knew, all I had ever heard."[21] By the early 1920s, he was a featured performer in Forrest "Boots" Faught's dance band, playing lead guitar. According to Faught, "Arnold was the *only* man I ever saw [play lead guitar] in them days [1918]. And people thought that was *something*, you know, it was something unusual. And he was *good*! He absolutely played the first lead guitar that I ever heard played."[22]

Faught and others were dazzled by Shultz's versatility as well as his virtuosity: he could play straight old-time music, fingerstyle blues, and jazzy dance-band numbers, as well as slide guitar, using a bottleneck or knife blade. Above all, musicians were enchanted with the broad palette of chords with which he could expand the bland harmonic structure of most music popular at the time—the "passing chords" referred to by Hartford. And Shultz was generous in sharing his knowledge. Faught recalled a night in the shadow of the coal tipple at Render with a grass sack full of home brew: "Back then, everybody just used three chords (G, C, and D). That's about all anyone knew how to play. That night we was playing 'See You in My Dreams.' Arnold showed us where to put that A chord in there. From then on we used the A chord in 'See You in My Dreams' and a lot of other pieces."[23] "I'll See You in My Dreams" remains a standard in the thumbpicking repertoire to this day, offering musicians ample scope for far more than a simple II chord to vary the harmony. Above all, thumbstyle musicians attribute the sophistication of their use of chords to Shultz, by way of his influence on Ike Everly and, above all, Kennedy Jones.[24] Through these two musicians and their brilliant buddy Mose Rager, the tradition was passed to Merle Travis, from Travis to Chet Atkins, and from Chet Atkins to the world.

For many western Kentucky thumbpickers, the first awareness that Arnold Shultz was being credited as the originator of the style came with the release of the 1974 album collaboration between Chet Atkins and Merle Travis, *The Atkins-Travis Traveling Show*, in which country music deejay Hugh Cherry's liner notes opined that "the shadow of Arnold Shultz was with Chet and Merle," and gave a brief account of Shultz's influence on Mose Rager and Ike Everly, two important progenitors of the Muhlenberg sound.[25] As it happens, Rager never encountered Shultz, and the connection with Everly, though more direct, is hazy. Shultz's influence on him is likely to have been as much through Kennedy Jones as by face-to-face encounter, although there is evidence that Everly learned some interesting chord use from him.[26] Tommy Flint, an exemplary western Kentucky thumbpicker and mainstay of Mel Bay's stable of instructional manuals, was struck by the mention of the unfamiliar name of Shultz in the liner notes and asked Travis about it. Travis did not recall ever hearing the name of Arnold Shultz.[27]

In this light, the resistance of musicians from the region to attributing thumbpicking's origin to Shultz may be seen less as a stubborn effort to retain white precedence in the history of their music than as an attempt to keep the record straight — at least in their own terms — and free of overinterpretation by zealous outsiders. In his published account, Bobby Anderson sounds almost apologetic in his attempt to concede Shultz his due while giving credit where most members of the thumbpicking community would place it:

> There is a legend which persists today, one that perhaps will never die, that Arnold Shultz was the originator of the sound known today as the "Merle Travis Guitar Style."
>
> But the man, Kennedy Jones, to whom all credit has been given by the guitar legends of our day, dispels this legend. His words are not a dispute or a contradiction; they simply state a fact as only Kennedy Jones would have known it. In brief, Kennedy Jones learned the thumb-and-finger roll type of picking from his mother. . . . He did not, he emphasized, learn his thumbpicking style from Arnold Shultz. Their styles — both exceptional — were quite different.
>
> Yet, Kennedy Jones was always the first to praise Arnold Shultz as a great guitar player.[28]

This resistance is rendered all the more awkward by the racial dynamics of the question in a part of Kentucky with a long and intricate history of relations between blacks and whites that is far too easily oversimplified by outsiders. A careful examination of the historical relationships between black and white musicians in western Kentucky can provide a much-needed perspective on the documented role of Arnold Shultz and the perception of that role by later musicians of the region. Such an examination sheds light on the history of a specific geographical source of significant vernacular music. It may also lead to a more nuanced understanding of the interrelationship between forms of musical expression such as blues and hillbilly that have been too readily categorized in polarized and unexamined racial terms.

Much, for example, has been made of Shultz's participation in white musical ensembles. Richard D. Smith observes that his playing with Birch, Charlie, and Bill Monroe for square dances in the early 1920s took place "in the South, and nearly a decade before the Benny Goodman Trio with black pianist Teddy Wilson was hailed as the first racially mixed jazz combo to perform in public."[29] True enough, but such groups were far less a novelty than Smith's comparison suggests. Throughout the mid-South, mixed-race old-time and hillbilly groups were commonplace, drawing on the rich tradition of black as well as white string-band music. Both Charles Wolfe and Richard Nevins argue persuasively for a period "before southern music was split up into white country music and black blues-and-spirituals music . . . when [black] bands played for white and black audiences."[30] Citing such examples as Howard Armstrong of the Tennessee Chocolate Drops and the black east-central Kentucky fiddler Jim Booker (who played regularly with white master musicians such as Marion Underwood and Doc Roberts, leading and recording with the exceptional group Taylor's Kentucky Boys), Nevins suggests that through most of the nineteenth century black and white string-band musicians shared both style and repertoire. He sees the traditions diverging after 1910 and reconverging only briefly in the 1950s with the synthesis of rock and roll from rhythm and blues and country music.[31] DeFord Bailey represents yet another example of a black performer raised in the Tennessee string-band tradition where performers and audiences were both black and white.[32]

Largely due to the presence of the mining industry in the coalfields of western Kentucky, distinctive and complex patterns of interconnection and separation developed among white and black musicians. The reasons for this complexity derive in part from the geography and social history of the region. Even within the region, there are demarcations and distinctions of locus. Unlike regions dominated by the plantation economy, the average slave owner in the pre-Emancipation era had, on average, five enslaved individuals, with whom he and his family often worked side by side. Following Emancipation, economic factors shaped the density of the black population in the area: counties bounded by the Ohio River tended to be more attractive because of opportunities for employment. Counties with ample opportunity for mining employment were also attractive.[33] Rosine is located in

Ohio County, on the far western edge of the Western Kentucky Coal Field. In this area, coal represented only one of several means of subsistence, which also included timber farming and river transport. Hence the African American population of the county was relatively small, 4.7 percent in 1900 and 3.3 percent in 1930, in comparison to the more coal-dependent area of Muhlenberg County, epicenter of the thumbpicking style, where the proportions were 10.2 and 7.8 percent, respectively.[34] The geographer Wilbur G. Burroughs noted that whites dominated in those regions of rough topography with little or no coal mining and poor transportation.[35]

This is borne out in interviews conducted by Sara J. McNulty in the Rosine area in the 1990s. Looking back on her early childhood in Rosine in the early 1930s, Holly McGuiness remarks that she would have remembered Arnold Shultz had she met him, if only for the novelty of his skin color: "Back in those days, we never saw any colored people. And I remember the first colored person that I saw, and I thought—Hildred was in Mama's arms—and I thought she was screaming her head off. And I followed the poor black man, you know, he was fascinating to me, because, you know, we weren't around them. And I figure if I had ever seen Arnold, then I wouldn't have been so fascinated by this black person."[36] Notwithstanding the two "colored fellows" Monroe recalls joining Shultz at the dance in Rosine, Shultz clearly stood out in central Ohio County for his race as well as his musicianship.

Farther west, in Muhlenberg County, the role of Shultz and other black musicians must be evaluated in the larger picture of a more substantial and established African American presence, with a more extensive and better documented musical tradition. To offer an emblematic example of the multiple layers of contradictory social meaning and practice regarding race, when Merle Travis's father gave up tobacco farming and moved from Rosewood to Browder in Muhlenberg County, the family lived on what was called "the ol' Littlepage Place." Though Travis was a toddler when they moved in, and only seven when they moved on, he vividly recalled the ritual of rent day. "Our landlord was an old negro we called Uncle Rufus. He came to the back door and removed his hat to politely ask for the rent."[37] The role of "Uncle Rufus" as property owner did not absolve him from the accepted conventions of black deference in the 1920s South.

Lightfoot offers an excellent overview of the unique patterns of racial interaction shaped by the social and economic dynamics of the early twentieth century in the area of western Kentucky dominated by mining.[38] Black miners were employed in most of the large mines in Muhlenberg County beginning in the late nineteenth century; the United Mine Workers of America was the first major labor union in the United States to accept black members. Many black activists joined the effort to organize the industry in western Kentucky.[39] The cycles of hiring and layoff in the mining communities created periods when white and black workers had time on their hands, during which music provided welcome relaxation and distraction from the dangers and uncertainties of work underground.[40] Music also provided a possible escape from the mines; LaVerda Rager recalled that, when a grade-school teacher objected to Merle Travis bringing his guitar to school in Drakesboro, he coolly informed her that one day it was going to be his living.[41] The navigable waterways by which the coal was exported provided both a path to other worlds and a means by which exciting news and entertainment could arrive, both informally through the experience of black and white roustabouts and by the more professional efforts of showboat performers.[42]

Though common, interaction between white and black musicians was not unconstrained. Racial stereotyping was a given. The same resident of Rosine who called Shultz "the best thing you ever seen" and observed that white audiences "worshipped that man," also remarked smugly concerning the tone of his voice when he made an insignificant request, "You *know* how they can whine."[43] The homes in mining settlements were grouped in seeming intimacy, each company house similar, regardless of the race of the inhabitants. The cultural geographer Claude Eugene Pickard describes "clusters of uniformly small houses attach[ed] to the railroad at irregular . . . intervals, giving an abnormally large number of villages, towns and cities in an essentially rural pattern."[44] But even within these small clusters, some degree of spatial separation was informally enforced. The memoirist Amy Longest described the Greenville Coal Company's arrangement for black workers in one Muhlenberg County mining community in the 1890s, while evoking the faintly sticky nostalgia of Stephen Foster's "Old Kentucky Home": "A row of ten 'box' houses . . . was built north of Powderly to accommodate the negroes, [and] there in summer evenings the soft, dreamy music of guitar or banjo could be heard while 'the curly headed pickaninnies played around the little cabin door' and the older children engaged in sports on the village green."[45]

White and black musicians might jam in one another's homes, but following a jam in a white man's parlor, a black musician would expect to eat alone in the kitchen.[46] Evening and weekend dances featuring black and white performers commonly took place in schoolhouses; during the day, of course, the education system itself was carefully segregated.[47] Dance halls and roadhouses might accept mixed-race performing ensembles, but even the rough ones such as Twin Hills in Rosine, Kincheloe's Bluff on the Green River, and Hollywood in Central City would have drawn the line at mixed-race couples. Nor were the interracial musical groups free from comment and occasional harassment. "Boots" Faught remembered:

> Back then [1920s] we would go to play for a dance and someone would say, "Hey, you've got a colored fiddler. We don't want that."
>
> I'd say, "the reason I've got the man is because he's a good musician. The color doesn't mean anything. You don't hear color. You hear music."[48]

Aside from the rough dance halls, perhaps the most contentious places for conflict involving black and white musicians were the occasional contests. Prizes for these events were generally not substantial: a sack of flour or a can of tobacco.[49] But Faught recalled one contest with the impressive incentive of fifty dollars and expenses paid to nearby Hopkinsville to be on the radio. "I'm pretty sure Shultz was there that night with an all-colored band. They was the best band there. If they had been white, they would have won that contest."[50] Then, as now, contests were an arena in which social issues other than musical excellence often played a part. Roni Stoneman still recalls with bitterness a contest in the late 1950s in which the judges frankly acknowledged her superiority but refused to give her the prize, a much coveted store-bought banjo, with the excuse "Because you're a girl."[51]

Perhaps because it placed performers within an unambiguous hierarchy of power, an undisputed area of black musicianship in the region was that of street performance, or "busking." Many residents of towns such as Greenville and Central City recall black street musicians, some anonymous and some as well known as Shultz.[52] Fiddler Christopher Columbus ("Uncle Lum") Martin, born a slave in 1847, was a fixture of the court square in Greenville for many years; he died in 1956 at the age of 109.[53]

Naturally the African American communities of Muhlenberg County and surrounding areas had their own musical activities, occasionally observed but largely unshared by their white neighbors. Churches were a fruitful source of organized effort in this regard, as were schools; according to the historian Leslie Shively Smith, all the black schools had choruses and glee clubs that performed throughout the county and for meetings of the Third District Teachers Association. Piano instruction was available to young black students from a number of teachers, including Annie Jenkins Stumm, who studied with W. C. Handy for two years at the turn of the century when she attended Oakwood Industrial School in Huntsville, Alabama.[54]

The Drakeboro Band was organized in 1924, trained by none other than DeFord Bailey.[55] Evidently unaware of Bailey's later fame as a founding member of the Grand Ole Opry and an isolated black presence in country music, Leslie Smith merely refers to him as "De Fort [sic] Bailey, a professional musician from Nashville." The band included two saxophones, a tuba, two clarinets, a trombone, and a drummer and performed for picnics and events throughout the county. Several members of this group went on to form H. O. Sutton and his Kentucky Foot-Warmers, a dance band featuring trumpet, banjo, trombone, saxophone, and drums. The Foot-Warmers played throughout western Kentucky and were frequent performers on WHOP in Hopkinsville.

It is in the context of this larger picture of the early twentieth-century music scene that Mose Rager's comment to Lightfoot concerning race relations in the region must be understood: "Man, we always got along this part of the country with Black people. There's some fine Black people, lives here in Drakesboro, and we've always got along, played music together, and, oh, have big gatherings. And we never did have any trouble."[56] Predictably tensions and boundaries were far more evident to the black musicians bound by them than to white musicians, however admiring and sympathetic.

That very admiration adds a further complexity to a measured evaluation of African American influence on thumbstyle guitarists of western Kentucky. Far from rejecting identification of black music as a threat to a purely white social construction of country music, many musicians embraced blues — or blues as they understood it — as a means of distancing themselves from what they perceived as the "three chords and a church lick" stylistic limitations of conventional country music. Many musicians from western Kentucky found permanent or temporary employment in country music an attractive alternative to working in the mines, including not only Travis but also Tommy Flint, Ike Everly, Odell Martin, Spider Rich, Charlie "Chicken Hawk" Murphy, Steve Rector, Royce Morgan, Paul Yandell (from far western Kentucky, but considered one of the thumbpicking "fold"), and others. The seemingly endless flow of musicians from the area sometimes prompted those hiring them to speculate whether something in the water of the region nurtured talent. A significant handful of these musicians participated in the rockabilly boom of the 1950s, when their pulsing rhythms and sophisticated playing underlined the relationship of the emerging music with jazz and rhythm and blues. But within this cadre, the availability of employment did not necessarily translate into full self-identification with country music and its offshoots.

No musician was more emphatic than Mose Rager in his espousal of blues as opposed to country as the idiom underlying his thumbpicking. Although he performed with Grandpa Jones (also from western Kentucky), as well as Curly Fox and Texas Ruby for a time, and played on the Opry from 1946 to 1947, his heart wasn't in the world of professional country music, and he returned to Drakesboro in the late 1940s to work for the Operating Engineers' local union and run several small businesses, including several grocery stores and a small barbershop. Despite abandoning a career in music, no single musician playing thumbstyle guitar has wielded more influence than Rager, both through the fame of his admiring younger friend Merle Travis and through innumerable lesser known but respected protégés since. When asked by Lightfoot, "Do you prefer blues to what's called 'hillbilly'?," Rager responded without hesitation, "Oh, yes, a *hundred* percent!"[57]

This attraction dated from his teens in the 1920s, hitchhiking around the country with his buddy Lester "Plucker" English. Rager recounted with delight Plucker's preference for jazzy pop tunes and stylings: "No country music man would have any use for him at all, if they knew how he was. Plucker said . . . rather than stay at a fine hotel and play hillbilly tunes all night long and do blue yodels and stuff, he said he'd rather sleep in a beer garden, sleep under a table. . . . These country pieces like Jimmie Rodgers' yodellin' and all that stuff. . . . We could *play* 'em all right, but I couldn't get him to."[58]

Although Rager never met Shultz, he readily listed a handful of other black guitarists of Muhlenberg County and surrounding areas who influenced him, including Mutt Smith, Jody Burton, and Jim Mason, whose duo with his brother on fiddle sounded to Rager like a swing orchestra.[59] When in the 1960s he discovered through Leon Moseley that Shultz's nephew Malcolm Walker was living in Owensboro, Kentucky, Rager accompanied Moseley and Moseley's talented young son Paul on a pilgrimage to the city and spent a happy afternoon trading stories and licks. Rager's wife, LaVerda, recalled that early on he picked up fancy runs and chords from Amos Johnson, whose "Amos Johnson Rag" would metamorphose into Travis's tribute to Rager, "Guitar Rag."[60] He admired the African American vocal stylings of singers such as Charles Brown and Ray Charles, and he himself performed in an interracial gospel quartet called the Gladiators in which Amos Johnson's son David ("Foots") sang bass. Rager's young followers picked up on his preference; Steve Rector remembers Rager listening with pleasure to the so-called dean of Muhlenberg County guitarists, Royce Morgan, jam with Tennessee jazz picker Doc Richardson. Rager exclaimed, "Man, man — that guy plays so black, makes the lightning bugs swarm in the daytime."[61]

Not all western Kentucky thumbstyle guitarists have been as vocal in their espousal of jazz and blues as Rager. Nevertheless, when asked about primary influences and inspiration, pickers first pay tribute to the locally canonical lineage of Mose Rager, Merle Travis, Chet Atkins, and Jerry Reed, then usually cite an eclectic range of musical influence and inspiration. Their responses are far more likely to include the likes of Django Reinhardt and Les Paul than country artists such as Maybelle Carter or Sam McGee or later luminaries such as Hank Garland and Doc Watson, though the work of these artists may be admired. At the many jams held in the area attended primarily by guitarists with roots in the region, the repertoire inevitably includes challenging Travis, Atkins, and Reed compositions that showcase the particular skills valued in the style, as well as a playlist of uptown jazz and swing standards from the 1920s and 1930s, such as "Sweet Lorraine" (Mitchell Parish and Cliff Burwell, 1928), "Sweet Georgia Brown" (Maceo Pinkard and Kenneth Casey, 1925), "I'll See You in My Dreams" (Gus Kahn and Isham Jones, 1924), "Up a Lazy River" (Hoagie Carmichael and Sidney Arondin, 1931), "Stomping at the Savoy" (Benny Goodman, A. Razaf, E. M. Sampson and Chick Webb, 1934), and "Honeysuckle Rose" (Fats Waller, 1934). Notably scarce are such commonplace country and bluegrass instrumentals as "Blackberry Blossom" or "Black Mountain Rag."

The ambiguity and ambivalence surrounding issues of origin in Travis-style thumbpicking or, for that matter, in bluegrass are by no means unique to western Kentucky. Real-life historical and social complexity ultimately undermines any causal "creationist" theory attributing the origin of a vernacular music style to one individual, or even one single clear and inviolate stream of cultural derivation. Regardless of their historical "truth," myths of origin offer only a reductionist illusion of certainty regarding the essential nature of traditional forms of expression, though these myths in themselves can provide important clues to meaning and identity within communities of musicians and listeners. There is no reason to set Arnold Shultz in opposition to either Bill Monroe or Kennedy Jones; the significance of each of these important musicians takes on different value, a different coloring, depending on the concerns and sympathies of the musical community.

As with all matters of race and culture in the United States, the interplay of black and white musical influence in the vernacular music of western

Kentucky is tantalizingly elusive. The root components are as difficult to isolate and identify as the harmony, melody, rhythm, and bass parts in a well-wrought thumbpicked tune or the parts in bluegrass gospel harmony. We can investigate, quote, and surmise, but in the end the precise character, like Arnold Shultz, "just eases away," leaving an unforgettable legacy of sound.

Notes

1. John Hartford, personal email communication, August 3, 2000. The influential singer-songwriter John Hartford ("Gentle on My Mind") had a strong attraction to the music of western Kentucky and spent much time tracing the origins of both bluegrass and Kentucky thumbstyle guitar.

2. Lightfoot, "It All Goes Back to Arnold Shultz"; Lawrence, "Arnold Shultz." It should be noted that these authors were far more cautious in their claims for Shultz than the titles suggest, and they were not necessarily responsible for the titles under which these articles were published. My debt to their efforts, along with those of Charles Wolfe, in amassing information concerning Shultz's life and legacy is immeasurable. See Wolfe, *Kentucky Country*. Lawrence's "Arnold Schultz" is a revised version of his 1980 article, "The Greatest (?) Guitar Picker's Life."

3. Few would cede to Jelly Roll Morton the role he ascribed to himself. In recent years, albeit not without controversy, jazz scholars have also begun to recognize the seminal role of many white musicians in the development of the music. See, for example, Sudhalter, *Lost Chords*.

4. Kirtley's instrumental cut can be heard on Pat Kirtley, *Rural Life* (Mainstring 9801).

5. Lawrence, "The Greatest (?) Guitar Picker's Life," 8; Paul Moseley interview by Erika Brady, Feb. 21, 2004, audiotape, in author's possession.

6. Pearson and McCulloh, *Robert Johnson*, 14–17. The authors capably deconstruct the highly romanticized stories that circulate concerning Johnson's life and death.

7. Lightfoot, "A Regional Musical Style," 132–33.

8. Hartford, personal email communication.

9. Smith, *Can't You Hear Me Callin'*, 171–72. Smith notes that Rinzler was not the first to dub Monroe "Father of Bluegrass." The phrase was current at least by the early 1960s, corresponding to the revival of Monroe's career through his exposure to campus and folk revival audiences. Nevertheless, as Smith points out, Rinzler exploited the title, and the monumental paternal image, to brilliant advantage.

10. Rinzler, "Bill Monroe," 208.

11. Smith, *Can't You Hear Me Callin'*, 31, 56, 299n23. Of course Monroe was by no means the only conduit by which African American influence entered bluegrass music, though musicians may have been more aware than audiences of elements of African American derivation. Neil Rosenberg suggests that part of the appeal of bluegrass in its early years was in white reaction against the influence of rock,

rockabilly, and rhythm and blues (*Bluegrass*, 16–125). He states bluntly, "The racist reaction to the new music . . . played a part in the growth of bluegrass music" (119).

12. Smith, *Can't You Hear Me Callin'*, 71–72.

13. Moseley interview by Erika Brady.

14. Humphrey, "Merle Travis," 208–9.

15. Anderson, *That Muhlenberg Sound*, 11–12.

16. Lightfoot, "A Regional Musical Style," 122.

17. Paul Yandell interview by Erika Brady, 2000, audiotape, in author's possession. Yandell's mention of Kennedy Jones's talented mother, Alice DeArmond Jones, raises an interesting secondary issue concerning the roots of thumbpicking: the role of turn-of-the-century women guitarists in the region who learned a thumb-and-finger "parlor" guitar style and provided the next generation of male pickers with their instrumental fundamentals. This element is summarized concisely in Wilson, liner notes, *Eddie Pennington Walks the Strings*, 5–10. Yandell himself was taught by a neighbor, Wanda Gunn, and still treasures the old guitar she gave him.

18. Lightfoot, "Mose Rager from Muhlenberg County," 18–19; Mose Rager interview by Larry Sykes, 1978, audiotape, Western Kentucky University Folklife Archive, Bowling Green.

19. Mose Rager interview by Joy Heingartner, 1976, audiotape, Western Kentucky University Folklife Archive, Bowling Green.

20. Lawrence, "The Greatest (?) Guitar Picker's Life," 6.

21. Lawrence, "Arnold Schultz," 40.

22. Lightfoot, "A Regional Musical Style," 132.

23. Lawrence, "The Greatest (?) Guitar Picker's Life," 5.

24. Lightfoot, "Mose Rager from Muhlenberg County," 18–19; Moseley interview by Brady.

25. Cherry, liner notes, *The Atkins-Travis Travelin' Show*.

26. Lightfoot, "A Regional Musical Style," 131.

27. Tommy Flint interview by Erika Brady, June 14, 2004, audiotape, in author's possession; Yandell interview by Brady; Moseley interview by Brady.

28. Anderson, *That Muhlenberg Sound*, 4–5.

29. Smith, *Can't You Hear Me Callin'*, 24.

30. Wolfe, liner notes, *Altamont, Black Stringband Music from the Library of Congress*.

31. Nevins, liner notes, *Before the Blues*, 2–7.

32. Morton and Wolfe, *DeFord Bailey*, 18.

33. Lucas, *A History of Blacks in Kentucky*, 2–4; Smith, *Around Muhlenberg County, Kentucky*, 181–82.

34. Pickard, "The Western Kentucky Coal Field," 28.

35. Burroughs, *The Geography of the Western Kentucky Coal Field*, 152.

36. Holly McGuinness and Flossie Hines interview by Sarah J. McNulty, March 9, 1992, audiotape, Kentucky Historical Society Archives, Frankfort.

37. Eatherly, *A Scrapbook of My Daddy*, 10, 8. Travis also recalled his father's discovery of a battered but once fine five-string banjo boarded up in a window casement of the old home.

38. Lightfoot, *A Regional Musical Style*, 125.

39. Smith, *Around Muhlenberg County, Kentucky*, 181.

40. Steve Rector interview by Erika Brady, Feb. 26, 2000, audiotape, in author's possession; Lawrence, "The Greatest (?) Guitar Picker's Life," 7.

41. La Verda Rager interview by Erika Brady, 2000, audiotape, in author's possession.

42. Lightfoot, "A Regional Musical Style, 133.

43. Flossie Hines interview by Sara J. McNulty, July 2, 1991, audiotape, Kentucky Historical Society Archives, Frankfort.

44. Pickard, "The Western Kentucky Coal Field," 106.

45. Amy Longest, "A Sketch of Powderly Past and Present, Pt. 3," *Record* (Greenville, Ky.), March 16, 1911.

46. McGuinness and Hines interview by McNulty.

47. Lawrence, "The Greatest (?) Guitar Picker's Life," 6–7.

48. Lawrence, "The Greatest (?) Guitar Picker's Life," 7.

49. M. Rager interview by Heingartner.

50. Lawrence, "The Greatest (?) Guitar Picker's Life," 7.

51. Stoneman, *Pressing On*, 42–43.

52. Lightfoot, "Mose Rager from Muhlenberg County," 19.

53. Anderson, *That Muhlenberg Sound*, 138; Smith, *Around Muhlenberg County, Kentucky*, 171.

54. Smith, *Around Muhlenberg County, Kentucky*, 174–75.

55. This episode is unreported in Morton and Wolfe, *DeFord Bailey*, which makes no mention of Bailey's activities as an itinerant music teacher during this period.

56. Lightfoot, "Mose Rager from Muhlenberg County," 23.

57. Lightfoot, "Mose Rager from Muhlenberg County," 26.

58. Lightfoot, "Mose Rager from Muhlenberg County," 15–16. Ironically Rodgers is generally recognized as having introduced significant African American stylistic elements to country music. On "Blue Yodel No. 9," he was accompanied by a fine jazz ensemble, including Louis Armstrong and Lillian Hardin Armstrong. Porterfield, *Jimmie Rodgers*, 123, 258–60.

59. Lightfoot, "Mose Rager from Muhlenberg County," 23–25.

60. L. Rager interview by Brady.

61. Rector interview by Brady.

Fiddling with Race Relations in Rural Kentucky

THE LIFE, TIMES, AND CONTESTED
IDENTITY OF FIDDLIN' BILL LIVERS

Jeffrey A. Keith

William "Bill" Livers (1911–88) was the last African American old-time fiddler from Kentucky. Throughout his life, Livers worked as a tenant farmer in rural Owen County, located in Kentucky's Outer Bluegrass region. His employment as a tenant on a white-owned farm was common for rural African Americans living in the Upper South during the early twentieth century, but his experiences as a renowned fiddler, storyteller, humorist, and showman made his life unique in many ways. These talents enabled Livers to transcend some of the social restrictions placed upon African Americans during the era of Jim Crow segregation. Moreover the social changes that occurred in the wake of the civil rights movement and the concurrent emergence of the counterculture movement allowed him to participate in some segments of white society with a surprising degree of intimacy. Yet Livers's identity was always contested. The residents of Owen County, both black and white, interpreted his role in the community differently from one another, while his own self-fashioned identity was contingent upon his social surroundings. An examination of his life allows for a glimpse into the complicated terrain of race relations and interracial cultural exchange in rural Kentucky. In fact Livers bridges these subjects, exemplifying both the possibilities and ultimately the limitations of African American participation in the rural societies that nurtured the vernacular music traditions of the Upper South.[1]

The life, times, and contested identity of Bill Livers speak to why country music "turned white" in rural America. Part of the reason, as Livers's biography illustrates, is that rural African Americans who performed as country musicians experienced confusing social pressures regarding the discomfiture of their publicly scorned status as black people and their publicly celebrated roles as artists who specialized in a musical style understood as regional or local in nature. In this sense, Livers's story is particularly significant because he lived through an era of pronounced social change that revealed these social tensions in his life and his community at large. The contest over his identity therefore became a topic of concern for those in his community who viewed both his musical contributions and his racial identity in competing ways.

This chapter weaves together a biography of Bill Livers and an exploration of his musical career as an old-time fiddler, highlighting three phases in the development of his entertainment persona and linking these to both the contest over his identity and the changes in rural Kentucky race relations over the course of the twentieth century. As a young adult, Livers played in an all-white group that featured him as a comic figure. Performing a role reflective of white supremacy's dominance in rural Kentucky during the mid-twentieth century, Livers seemingly conformed to the expectations of his white audiences when he fiddled in segregated venues, but his storytelling often provided him with a way of challenging racism through veiled critiques of the status quo. As an adult, he performed with a group of hippies who settled in Owen County during the late 1960s and the early 1970s. Serving as a social and cultural intermediary between these hippies and the community of Owen County, he played in a band that sought to fuse the counterculture movement with the rural culture of Kentucky. In the twilight of his life, Livers continued to perform music in venues catering to folk revivalists, and, most important, he formed a group that featured him as the bandleader. His individual celebrity earned him official recognition and public reverence as a repository of Kentucky's rural heritage.

Livers's talents as a fiddler and an entertainer allowed him to negotiate his position within the Owen County community, but his entertainment personae remained bound by the confines of white perceptions of African Americans in the Upper South. In this sense, both his early performances as a buffoonish mascot before all-white audiences and his subsequent performances as the embodiment of romantic primitivism before members of the counterculture movement stemmed from racial stereotypes held by the white residents of Owen County. On the other hand, these phases in his career made possible his eventual transformation into a revered icon of tradition and afforded him a level of personal dignity in social interactions that had been unimaginable for African Americans living in the Upper South at the time of his birth.

Bill Livers was born just outside of Owenton, the Owen County seat, on August 3, 1911. His parents, Lula Rose Thirsty and David "Dave" Livers, had a total of six children. Dave Livers worked as a sharecropper on various tobacco farms owned by local whites, and Bill remembered that his mother "used to go out and cook Sunday dinners for the big rich white folks all around Owenton."[2] Initially Livers was able to attend school, but the necessities of life required him to prematurely end his formal education. He stated, "I never got no further than the fourth grade.... [I] was doing pretty good, and then ... I had to help — come in and help make a living for the rest of them you know." He farmed tobacco alongside his father, and he modestly supplemented his family's income with possum hides, fish, and small game.[3]

In these ways, the Livers family wrestled with poverty long before the Great Depression wreaked havoc upon the economy. Livers recalled that his family often subsisted on cornbread and sorghum molasses. He recounted that "back there around 19 and 23 times was rough.... Back in them days meat was scarce."[4] In his later life, he offered humorous portrayals of these lean years. He joked about rats that picked locks with their tails to access the family's food supply.[5] He also remembered that while his mother prayed for sorely needed material goods, his father quipped, "While you got Him, hit Him up for a blackberry cobbler ... while you got the Old Boy going."[6] Characteristically Bill saw humor in tragedy, but life posed myriad challenges and difficulties for the family. They lived in a world dominated by white supremacy, and this was a fact he could not escape. His family's financial and material woes were rooted in the racial caste system of the South, and they faced difficulties similar to those experienced by African Americans throughout the region.

The tumultuous history of race relations in Owen County is strikingly similar to that of the Upper South at large. In 1860 Owen County was home to seventy free blacks, 1,660 slaves, and 10,989 whites.[7] The legacy of chattel slavery led to widespread violence during the Reconstruction Era. A *New York Times* headline on September 10, 1874, stated the situation in stark terms: "The Kentucky Kuklux: Official Report of the Owen County Outrages." The article reported that white mobs had killed over one hundred people and forced numerous others to flee; the rest of the county remained "under a reign of terror."[8]

By 1910, on the eve of Livers's birth, the African American population had dwindled to 943, while the white population had climbed to 13,305.[9] Many of the remaining African Americans resided either in tenant homes or in one of two predominantly black communities, New Liberty and Mountain Island. Interestingly, Mountain Island was left to freedmen by a former slave owner, and locals often referred to the land as "Nigger Island."[10] The popular use of this racist epithet illustrated the prevalence of racist thought in Owen County. Many white residents believed that blacks were inferior and actively sought to assert white supremacy.

Racial intimidation did not cease with the dawning of the twentieth century. During the 1930s a local black man was discovered to be having a consensual sexual relationship with a white woman. A mob of white men brutally castrated him and "left him for dead." The victim miraculously drove himself to an area doctor, and he survived his wounds. However, he lost his mind in the wake of the incident. He lived out his life in New Liberty as a visual reminder to local blacks about who possessed power in their community—and what could happen to those who challenged the status quo.[11]

Bill Livers was keenly aware of the limits that were placed upon him as an African American in rural Kentucky. Indeed he knew that the situation was dangerous. Once he remarked, "I been down to Long Ridge [a local community]. I used to go down there. I was about eleven years old, and they were always on me. . . . I was scared. . . . Boy, I was ready to move on out of there." As the story unfolds it becomes apparent why Livers was ready to flee the area, and who "they" were:

> Late one evening I was down there, and they caught me and tied me up for a long time. Finally they turned me loose . . . and then they put me in a wool sack and tied both ends. I couldn't get out and I couldn't kick out . . . and they put me in a dump truck and throwed a pile of dirt on top of me where I couldn't get out. And then, well, about three miles down the road . . . they dumped the truck right over the bank, you know. . . . I was down there half the night before they got me out of that sack. . . . I've had a lot of experiences in life like that.[12]

It was during this time that he discovered there were possibilities for interracial cultural exchange despite the clear limitations imposed by white racism.

Livers participated in a vernacular tradition of musical entertainment that transgressed racial boundaries in substantial yet limited ways. He delightedly remembered when, as a boy, he heard harmonica music on "one of those little old round records with the horn on it, you know, Edison put them out." He was especially moved by the music of the late 1920s and early 1930s; "Shakin' That Thing," "Casey Jones," and "St. Louis Blues" were among his favorite songs. He also commented on the experience of attending carnivals, fairs, and medicine shows that visited Owen County during their extensive tours throughout the South. These events exposed Livers to the exhilaration of live performances. Decades later he excitedly recalled the details of entertainers who made an impression on him:

> They called him Old Stovepipe. Always wore a great big stovepipe hat. Playing that French harp [harmonica] and I'll be doggone, pickin' that guitar all at the same time. And there was a guy come in here, he was about half Indian and a half colored fellow and he was a tap dancer. He was selling medicine. Big old Indian up there, had his feathers on and selling medicine. He was an Indian, you know. . . . Yeah, right up there in the courthouse yard in Owenton.

Clearly, "Old Stovepipe" and the "big old Indian" entertained Livers, but they also introduced him to the power of entertainment. These men were in command of their audiences, and they were "right up there in the courthouse yard" performing for all of the community. Similarly he commented that local black musicians, including the town shoeshine, played on the courthouse yard and "drawed the awfulest crowd."[13] This was empowerment. Music temporarily suspended social limitations, and the local African American shoeshine became the celebrated center of attention for the entire community, white and black.

By the mid-1930s Livers had moved away from his family and was working as a tenant farmer on Clarence Orr's tobacco farm. One day Orr gave him a left-handed fiddle, and he began to teach himself how to play music. He recalled, "Nobody taught me a thing. I just had a song in mind and I said I was either going to play or just keep sawing until I sawed the thing up or done something with it, and I just kept on until I learned 'Old Kentucky Home.'"[14] Livers later switched to a right-handed playing style, but this adjustment hardly tempered his passion for music and entertainment.

In many ways, Livers was continuing a family tradition. His paternal great-grandfather, Virgil "Virge" Livers, had been a multi-instrumentalist, capable of performing on the fiddle, guitar, and banjo. Albert and Claude Livers, Virge's sons, also played music; Albert was a banjoist and Claude could play both the mandolin and the fiddle. These three traveled Owen County by mule to perform at area dances and parties. Bill taught himself family melodies such as "Old Virge," "Up and Down Old Eagle Creek," and "Looking through the Knot Hole in Pa's Wooden Leg," and he learned new songs from the radio and traveling performers.[15] Perhaps this was also when he began to develop his arsenal of entertainment tricks. He learned to light a cigarette inside his mouth, kick the top of a door jamb without straining, and leap over a handkerchief as if it was a jump rope.[16] In short, it was during these Depression years that he harnessed the power to make his audiences smile.

Livers performed throughout Owen County for house parties, dances, and clubs. Rural Kentucky was rigidly segregated, yet he was able to operate on both sides of the color line. He remembered playing at the only African American venue in the area: "Miss Ella Morgan run that place down there . . . that great big old house down there. That's the only place colored folks had. They'd dance in there."[17] However, most frequently he entertained white audiences. At these events he likely had to conform to audience expectations about the behavior of African Americans, but the specifics of these performances are unclear. According to one secondhand report, he donned blackface while performing at a local dance.[18] It is also apparent that during the 1940s he fiddled at several integrated bootlegging taverns. His nephew, James "Jimmy" Ware, would occasionally accompany his uncle to these shows. Ware recalled, "I was just a kid, and . . . I would go in with Uncle Bill and this guy that ran the place. He'd come out from behind the bar and get me by the hand, lead me back [behind the bar and] . . . get me a coke. . . . I sat there on a nail keg . . . and Uncle Bill, he'd be back there playin' in that bootleg joint." Ware further remembered that at this time Livers was performing with an all-white band called the Owen County Idiots.[19] This band continued to play together for several years, and they eventually changed their name to Bill Livers and the Holbrook Idiots.[20] It is difficult to ascertain who might have attended their shows because Owen County was dry; bootlegging clubs were illegal operations and left no record of their clientele. We can assume, however, that the band dynamics at these shows reflected the social mores of the Upper South during the pre–civil rights era. Livers may have been an excellent entertainer, but he was still an impoverished, black tenant farmer living in a white-dominated world.

The tension between Livers's roles as a frequent entertainer for the white community and as a social "inferior" within society at large was visible in his experiences with the Holbrook Idiots. Their performances enabled him to enter otherwise inaccessible venues within the white community, and his

FIGURE 4.1. This promotional photograph of Bill Livers and the Holbrook Idiots conveys the comedic and playful style of the group. Courtesy of Owen County, Kentucky, Public Library.

fiddling talents were undoubtedly rewarded with applause. The band's stage name set up Livers as the leader of a white group of "idiots." Yet this belies the fact that he might have been the butt of the joke. In retrospect, many people, white and black, have wondered whether Livers was taken advantage of by his fellow musicians. One white friend even speculated that the Idiots' show was akin to "minstrelsy" and that Livers was "the comic."[21] The only extant promotional photograph of the band lends itself to this interpretation (fig. 4.1). Livers is prominently placed in the middle of the image, wearing a ragged hat and with an unkempt beard. He is flanked by two whites with deadpan expressions. Beside Livers stands a third white man who appears to be laughing and looking in Livers's direction. As a result, this picture conveys ambiguous meanings, inviting viewers to see Livers as either the band's frontman or its mascot.

Livers experienced similarly contradictory impulses when he interacted with members of the white community who presumably lauded his talents as an entertainer. He often accompanied the most prominent tobacco farmers in the county on trips to Lexington, Kentucky, where they sold their annual crops. He even shared a hotel bed with one of the farmers.[22] This level of intimacy implies equality, but it seems unlikely that he was genuinely regarded with a spirit of egalitarianism. Was he their court jester, or was this a unique, though not unprecedented, instance of interracial camaraderie in the Jim Crow South? Another vignette from Livers's life suggests that the former was more likely than the latter. Bettina and Kirk Somerville recalled that a group of local whites failed to treat Livers "like he was a hundred percent person" when they happened upon him after an evening of drinking alcohol. Livers had committed an offense against a member of the party, and they felt that he should be punished. They forced him into the trunk of their car and drove to Chicago.[23] The Somervilles' recollection of the event ends at this moment, but the incomplete story successfully illustrates a larger point: Livers was harassed even after he became a local celebrity.

Livers was victimized and exploited by some Owen County whites, but he should not be interpreted as a passive figure. In fact he was the opposite. His talents as an entertainer could not eclipse the racist ideology of the Upper South, yet they provided him with a venue to expose and challenge the racist perceptions of white society. He crossed the color line, and by doing so he challenged the validity of its existence. Moreover he often entertained white audiences with stories that attacked the foundation of their presumed superiority by mocking their power or escaping their punishment.[24]

Livers frequently told several stories that placed him in control of gullible white people or their property, and one tale is particularly rich with meaning. A wealthy white man called "old man Majors" hired Livers to drive him in his Model T into Owenton. This allowed Majors to relax and enjoy a cigar along the way. Livers had never driven a car before, but he took the driver's seat after Majors foolishly assumed he would be an appropriate chauffeur. The vehicle flew out of control, and they crashed at a high speed. Livers described how the impact "drove that cigar back in ol' man Majors, plumb to the fire. You oughta saw him tryin get that fire out. Course his head hit the windshield and drove that derby over his ears. You oughta saw him tryin to get it off."[25]

The story is hilarious in its entirety, but the humor works on several levels and often at cross-purposes. White listeners could laugh at Livers's buffoonery and his ineptitude as a driver. On another level, the tale could be heard as didactic, reaffirming white superiority and ridiculing the belief that a black man could successfully steer (control) a white man's vehicle (society). Yet the humor reaches its climax when Majors is unmasked as a fool and outwitted by the man he expects to control. In some tellings, the story subtly suggested both the ways white supremacy denied education and opportunity to African Americans and also the ways this victimization could become the basis for everyday resistance. Livers sometimes tacked a dialogue onto the story's ending that made this message more explicit: "[Majors] said, 'You going to have to pay for this.' I said, 'Mister, I ain't got a dime.'"[26] In this telling, Majors had caused his own troubles. His assumption that a black man is his natural servant places Majors on a collision course with disaster, and the power and deference guaranteed to him in a white-dominated society evaporate in part because of the very inequities that society imposed. He is choked, deafened, and crippled by three signs of his affluence: the cigar, the derby, and the Model T. When he demands that his money, and his dignity, be restored, he momentarily becomes the victim of the poverty systematically imposed on African Americans from rural Kentucky. In every version, Livers quickly escapes from the scene of the accident, unscathed and without loss. In fact he gains a story.

Livers rarely discussed his opinions about race in an open or unveiled fashion, yet elements of his racial self-identity can be deciphered from an intriguing episode that occurred during his midlife. In the 1960s he began working as a tenant on Miriam and C. W. Cobb's tobacco farm. His living quarters on the farm had served as a slave blockhouse during the antebellum era. Jimmy Ware recalled that the blockhouse possessed several horrific reminders of slavery. Iron chains appeared to be growing out of one nearby cedar tree where traders had chained up their slaves; over the subsequent century the tree had grown around and swallowed the majority of the chain's links, so that the remainder seemed to sprout like branches from the trunk. In the side yard there was a stump that was worn as smooth as a tabletop; this had been the auctioning block. Ware recalled that Livers found a way to laugh about his grim surroundings, and his humor took the form of a defiant gesture against Kentucky's legacy of chattel slavery.[27]

Ware and Livers were working together in the yard surrounding the blockhouse when Livers decided to expand the list of farm chores that had been handed down by Miriam Cobb. Ware recalled the scene:

We moved two or three stumps up there for Miss Miriam and we chewed them up, you know, with dynamite. . . . Uncle Bill said, "When we get through we gonna move up and down the house too." I said, "What do you mean?" He said, "You wait and see. . . . I'll fix that stump there." So he went down there and he got an auger. He drilled down in it, put a half-stick of dynamite in it, dug around there, and blowed that stump. He said, "Now they ain't sellin' no more!" I can see that stump now.[28]

As the dynamite exploded, Livers and Ware were aware of the connection between this stump and the racism that pervaded Owen County. They also knew that the enslaved matriarch of their family, "Ms. Thirsty," had been forced to walk from Virginia to Kentucky when her master migrated to the Bluegrass State.[29] Perhaps they were celebrating the destruction of a relic that represented her bondage. Regardless, Livers again used humor to exhibit his frustrations with the state of race relations.

Livers's decision to destroy the auction block was reflective of larger social changes that were taking place during the 1960s and 1970s. The civil rights movement made great strides over these years, but it barely registered in the insular community of Owen County. During the early 1970s, Kirk Somerville, a white man, asked Raymond Sims, a local African American, about the situation. "Have you seen any change . . . in your life because of Dr. King?" he asked. Sims responded, "No, I've lived here all my life."[30] For most residents of rural Kentucky, it seems, racist ideology remained an entrenched feature of an otherwise bucolic landscape.

This persistent racism did not make rural Kentucky wholly immune to changing times. During the late 1960s and early 1970s an influx of young hippies created a new social environment in the small community of Monterey, located at the southern tip of Owen County. "The Owen County hippies," a moniker still used in the region today, came to Monterey in search of a "back to the land" experience. The rural setting of central Kentucky suited them well. Homes and land were cheap, Frankfort and Owenton were conveniently nearby, and the thriving rural culture of the region provided an alternative to mainstream America and its modern values, while the peaceful area offered these hippies refuge from the social tumult that accompanied the Vietnam War. They came from various places: some were return migrants who were born in Kentucky, others were transplants, and many were transients who stayed briefly before moving on to other hippie communities. Most of the Owen County hippies were middle class and college-educated, many were artists, and all of them were white.[31]

Livers and these hippies developed a symbiotic relationship. He provided them with access to the region's vernacular music and local culture, and they provided him with a new environment of social liberalism and racial tolerance. Several of the hippies were strongly influenced by the folk revival of the 1960s. They were interested in learning songs and stories from Livers to attain a better understanding of the values and traditions of rural America. In turn, the Owen County hippies exposed Livers to the counterculture movement of the era. John Harrod, a hippie who moved to Owen County after returning from Oxford as a Rhodes scholar, stated the situation in clear terms. "It gave [Bill] a new lease on life.... He loved us and we loved him.... We were sort of seeing life through his eyes a little bit, and, you know, Bill became a hippie.... He fit right in."[32] Though all participated in the larger community of Owen County, during the 1970s a subculture developed around the town of Monterey, and Livers became a vital link between this hippie scene and the community at large.

By the early 1970s Livers was working and living on William L. Cammack's tobacco farm, and his tenant home was the site of many fish fries that exemplified the unique social milieu of Owen County during the late Vietnam War era. These fish fries served as carnivalesque play spaces where the societal norms of the past seemed suspended and integrated crowds participated in wild frolics that embodied the social possibilities of rural Kentucky. Andrew Cammack, son of the farm's owner, recalled the remarkable spirit of these events:

> It was just great — the variety of people that came. There were hippies and, you know, college kids, and then there were local "rednecks" and there were local older people . . . that Willie [Bill] entertained from years ago. And just a lot of music and never enough fish, never enough beer. . . . People would just get lit, just crazy. . . . That was sort of the [period of] free love, and people would be screwing out in the field. . . . It was just so much fun and just such a variety of people — black, white. It was a really good mix. . . . There may have been a few people in Owenton who would've said, "I'm not gonna go out there." . . . And would think, "I have a little more class than that." But what I liked about it so much was that it was classless — that everybody got out there and everybody just got down.[33]

Livers's fish fries are of monumental significance to his story. They reflected the changing social dynamic of the late twentieth century and provided a venue in which local community members could temporarily cast off social expectations and create a new, "classless" environment. These events represent the introduction of a liberal ideology to rural Kentucky, one that permitted an unprecedented degree of interracial interaction. Livers had long

FIGURE 4.2. This photo, taken in the era of the Progress Red Hot String Band, shows Bill Livers (center) with fellow musicians John Harrod (left) and Eric Larson (right). Courtesy of John Harrod Collection.

been a participant in white culture, but by the mid-1970s he was able to interact with whites on his own terms. This was reflected in the fish fries at his tenant house, and these novel opportunities produced friendships between Livers and members of the Owen County community that allowed him to forge a new entertainment persona.

During the late 1970s Livers joined John Harrod and several other hippies to form the aptly named Progress Red Hot String Band (fig. 4.2). This group performed for audiences in Owen County, and they played at Lexington venues frequented by University of Kentucky students. They developed a show that incorporated Livers and Lily May Ledford, a female banjo player from Powell County, in a celebratory showcase of old-time musicians from Kentucky. Harrod and his fellow hippies would perform the first set by themselves, a second set featured Livers, and a third set spotlighted Ledford.[34] Livers was a featured member of a band that sought to celebrate him rather than mock him. Yet his role in the band was still imbued with meaning. His participation allowed the Owen County hippies to broadcast their liberalism and rebel against the middle-class white society in which they were raised. Indeed this sense of mutual liberation was contagious, and the

Lexington crowds often raucously embraced the band's implicit message: a celebration of Kentucky's diverse cultural heritage.

The mood of the Progress Red Hot String Band's Lexington shows was reminiscent of Livers's fish fries, and they brought new people into the burgeoning hippie scene of central Kentucky. These events also strengthened the growing bond between Livers and the Owen County hippies. John Harrod recalled that Livers "just loved being part of this Monterey hippie scene and going in and being part of the hippie scene in Lexington. . . . It got him away from home." For the first time, Livers was able to publicly interact with white musicians and audiences without deferring to them. He had been accepted into the hippie subculture, and he began to participate in activities associated with the counterculture movement of the 1970s. Already known to be a heavy drinker, he started to occasionally smoke marijuana, and he began to embrace free love. Harrod leaped to the latter subject when he described the composition of the Lexington audiences: "There were a lot of girls, and you could go home with them too. . . . All those pretty . . . girls would flirt with [Bill], and, you know, he'd get a few kisses out of them. . . . It made him awful happy, though. He always hugged on people and told them how much he loved them. . . . Those were the hippie days. It was a big love fest [with] Bill in Lexington."[35] Remarkably these acts of interracial sexual experimentation took place without provoking racist responses, and Livers began to publicly advertise his sexual liberation.

Kirk Somerville made a common observation about Livers: "Bill was a kisser." After the arrival of the Owen County hippies this became a conspicuous aspect of his persona. He kissed everyone with his "open mouth"—man or woman, black or white.[36] This degree of sexual freedom was remarkable for a black man in rural Kentucky. Fifty years earlier, when Livers was an adolescent, an African American man had been castrated for having a private, consensual relationship with a white woman. By the time Livers was in his sixties, however, he was capable of freely expressing love for all of his newfound friends. This marked a sea change in the sexual mores of some Owen County residents, and it led to even greater levels of interracial intimacy between Livers and members of the white community.

In the mature years of his life, Livers became increasingly open about his vigorous sexuality. Bettina Somerville recalled that he frequently made advances toward local women. She specifically recalled the events surrounding a day when Livers and her husband passed time rendering lard and drinking whiskey. Both men ended up extremely inebriated. Bettina had to help her husband to bed, and then she and another woman drove Livers back to his tenant house. He sat between them and was "kissing and feeling all the way" home. At this point in time, interracial sex was not unheard of in Owen County. Livers and a white woman made love in a wheelbarrow during a midafternoon Fourth of July celebration. One witness of the event stated, "It wasn't that hard to see what was going on, but people were sort of looking the other way."[37] Put simply, Livers's adherence to the free love ethic of the 1970s vividly exposed the possibilities of interracial intimacy in the Upper South. As a local entertainer he gained access to an increasingly tolerant and liberal population of white people, and this subculture exposed him to sexual experiences that were taboo in earlier decades.

During the late 1970s and early 1980s, Livers's celebrity as an entertainer spread far beyond the borders of Owen County. The Progress Red Hot String Band changed its membership, switched their stage name to the Bill Livers String Ensemble, and developed a regional reputation. They performed at festivals throughout the Upper South and were increasingly incorporated into the national folk revival scene. They performed at the Folklore Society of Greater Washington, D.C., in January 1979, and Mike Seeger, a prominent revivalist, attended the concert.[38] In 1982 Livers performed at the World's Fair in Knoxville, Tennessee. The ensemble performed for the Indiana Folklore Society in Bloomington and at the John Henry Music Festival in Charleston, West Virginia.[39] Livers became a hero for revivalists throughout the region. He was viewed as an embodiment of the "folk," and this allowed him to fulfill his final entertainment persona.

The Bill Livers String Ensemble did not simply spotlight Livers—the band was his and he was the star. He was no longer in the company of "idiots," nor was he a member of a larger group seeking to celebrate an idealized conception of rural Kentucky's culture. Rather Livers was the band's sole focus, and he became increasingly popular throughout Kentucky as a result of his successes. In the late 1970s he performed a concert on the grounds of the Kentucky governor's estate, and afterward he and Governor Julian Carroll enjoyed a drink together inside the mansion.[40] In the 1980s Governor Martha Layne Collins commissioned Livers a "Kentucky Colonel," the highest honor awarded by the Commonwealth of Kentucky and a rare title for blacks during the early and mid-twentieth century.[41] Livers had gained respect from members of his community, the political leaders of his home state, and enthusiasts of vernacular music throughout the nation.

Although Livers received fame and accolades during the twilight of his life, he was never able to overcome the racial expectations that were ingrained in him during the era of Jim Crow segregation. In those years he was faced with the burden of crafting his image to suit his surroundings, and this tendency stayed with him until his death. It was even apparent in his fiddle playing. John Harrod recalled, "He played to an expectation . . . that he wasn't supposed to be a good fiddler. Over the years, the really amazing thing was the way Bill played ten times better when he was not in Owen County and when he was around other good fiddlers." In Owen County, Livers deferred to his fellow musicians on the grounds of their supposed racial superiority. On one occasion, Harrod accompanied Livers to Jarvie Hall's house for a fiddling session. Hall, a local white fiddler, began exchanging fiddle tunes with Livers. After one tune, Livers looked at Hall and lamented, "I wish my color would change then I could play like you." The statement shocked Harrod, but he recognized the comment as part of a "pattern" of behavior he had observed over "a long period of time."[42] Harrod believed Livers disingenuously downplayed his skills so that he would not threaten someone who historically stood in a higher station on account of his race.

This pattern of social deference provides insight into Livers's racial self-identity. His behavior was contingent upon his immediate surroundings, and he operated within a web of limitations despite the relatively liberating powers of his music. As a result, his social demeanor was as variable as his fiddle playing. For instance, none of his white friends remembered that he ever got angry, but Jimmy Ware recalled that his uncle possessed a quick and violent temper: "Everybody talk about how sweet a person Bill Livers was, [but] he had one of the viciousest tempers you've ever seen."[43] Livers was also known to put on a "Stepin Fetchit routine" around certain whites. Harrod remembered, "It was like he felt different about who he was."[44] In these ways, Livers would conform to the social expectations of his immediate surroundings as a defense mechanism against the pervasive ideology of white supremacy.

Livers moved between different social spheres within Owen County by continually crafting his identity to suit various situations, and occasionally these spheres collided. This placed him in awkward social predicaments. For example, in the late 1970s he was invited to play music for some of the prominent tobacco farmers whom he formerly had accompanied to Lexington. He decided to bring his band mates with him, and a bizarre scenario unfolded. John Harrod recalled the situation:

> We all went with Bill to play for this big party. . . . Obviously there were
> a lot of prostitutes there . . . it was pretty sleazy. It was just a weird

scene—there was something strange about it, and, finally, they asked us to leave. . . . They wanted to keep Bill there for themselves. They didn't want us, so Bill had this dilemma. He was really uncomfortable and apologetic and didn't know what to do. . . . We said, "Bill, you don't have to stay." But he decided that he would stay. Like he'd better stay or he owed it to them. . . . I sort of felt like Bill was really being exploited in a way—the fact that they didn't want us there—like we would get in the way of something.[45]

This statement is shrouded in mystery and speculation, but it illustrates a larger point about Livers's identity. He was aware of the complexities of his past, and he felt that he could not break free from the expectations of those around him. This also alludes to another crucial point: Livers's identity was contested between various segments of the Owen County community.

Many people described Livers in richly symbolic language, and these portrayals provide a glimpse at how various community members perceived his identity within different contexts. For instance, many members of Owen County's native white community saw him as an accommodating African American. One white resident recalled that Livers "could have been another Steppenfetchit . . . just by being himself."[46] The irony of this statement was unintentional. Livers was celebrated by much of the white community for his continually happy, jovial, and deferential demeanor. Another white native of Owen County wrote in his journal that Livers's "favorite expression . . . was 'yes, suh.'"[47] This use of dialect might reveal that Livers was appreciated not only for his perennial good humor but also for his supposedly authentic representation of "blackness." Indeed he fulfilled the expectations of the white community, and many whites lauded his adherence to the racial status quo of the Upper South.

The hippie community of Monterey viewed Livers in an entirely different way, but they described him with equally colorful language. He was both celebrated as the embodiment of a traditional way of life and idolized as a symbol of total liberation. Harrod compared the relationship between Livers and the hippies to the relationship between Mark Twain's "Huck and Jim," evoking images of adventure, friendship, and an escape from civilization.[48] In a similar vein, Kirk Somerville recalled, "If you were around [Bill], whoever you were, he would . . . grab you and he would give you that kiss . . . [and] you wanted that kiss. You wanted whatever it was that he had. You wanted that spark."[49] Somerville described Livers as "the freest man on earth," both "a sprite" and "the devil's assistant."[50] This characterization of

Livers as a romantic "Other" is ironic and powerful, for the hippies considered him both a member of their community and a person who was different from them, a view clearly informed by perceptions of racial difference that pervaded all segments of society in the Upper South. In fact Sommerville and his fellow hippies held up Livers as a symbol of freedom largely because of his ability to challenge the limitations placed upon him by a racist society. Livers seemed a living contradiction, and this only exaggerated his supposed mastery of freedom.

Many revivalists also celebrated Livers for his "folk" roots. The historian Benjamin Filene argues that revivalists "yearn[ed] to identify with folk figures, but that identification [was] premised on difference. Roots musicians [were] expected to be premodern, unrestrainedly emotive, and noncommercial."[51] This matches the sentiments voiced by some regional folk revivalists. For instance, an article in *Southern Exposure* titled "Child of the Lord" described Livers's use of language as "smooth as homemade sorghum, soft as country rain." The authors then added, "Nature is an integral part of Bill's world."[52] Indeed both revivalists and hippies presented Livers as an exotic "folk" hero, and his "premodern" ways were exalted as signs of his authenticity.

Owen County African Americans, on the other hand, were conflicted about Livers's identity as well as his role in their community. He had a strained relationship with much of his family, and some blacks considered him to be a scoundrel.[53] Yet others viewed him in a positive light. These conflicting perceptions are apparent in the reflections of black residents. Jimmy Ware fondly remembered that Livers played pranks on his black friends and often turned to the black community for emotional support.[54] In stark contrast, another African American remembered that some blacks felt Livers was "a bit of a 'Tom'" because he spent the majority of his time with or entertaining whites.[55] Many African Americans came to associate rural vernacular music with the twin legacies of slavery and Jim Crow segregation.[56] This placed Livers in the ironic position of being both celebrated and criticized by the black community for his abilities as a musician. Nonetheless he remained a prominent member of the black community throughout the twilight of his life.

Bill Livers passed away in his tenant home on February 2, 1988. Appropriately, he died with a grin on his face.[57] He had been suffering from an unknown ailment that was likely emphysema. A longtime cigarette smoker, he complained of "smothering" in his final days.[58] He died a poor black tenant farmer, but he had also become a local legend. In order to preserve his memory, the Monterey community organized a "Headstone Potluck" fundraiser to purchase a tombstone.[59] Their fundraising efforts proved so successful that they were able to afford Livers's headstone and make a memorial donation to the Owen County Children's Fund.[60]

The tombstone was placed on Livers's gravesite in Maple Grove Cemetery, an African American graveyard. The fact that he was buried in a segregated cemetery illustrates the constraints placed upon him by the social standards of rural Kentucky. He had challenged many racial boundaries, and his skills as an entertainer had enabled him to access much of Kentucky's white society. Still, the tumultuous history of race relations in the Upper South bound him within a web of limitations that he could not escape. Yet his memory lived on in Owen County, and his identity remained a contested topic between those who remembered him.

Perhaps the most intriguing contest over Livers's perceived identity took place years after his burial. In the early 1990s Robert Cull began selling commemorative blankets at the North Park Pharmacy, Owenton's town drugstore.[61] Fiddlin' Bill Livers was the only individual whose image was included in the blanket's design. The image portrayed Livers in a dignified fashion, as an older man dressed in fine clothing and playing the fiddle. Thus an image of his final performance persona was forever linked to a visual representation of Owen County's history.

The discrepancy between the commemorative representation of Fiddlin' Bill Livers and the location of his gravesite is important, for it signifies his role as a transitional figure in the history of rural Kentucky race relations. The people of Owen County embraced the memory of Livers as a prominent participant in a tolerant and integrated society, yet these same people entombed his black body in an eternally segregated environment. Livers's influence as an entertainer created the community's collective memory of him, while social tensions within the community dictated his burial site. The realm of commemoration was the only place where these contradictions could be reconciled, and the contest over the identity of Bill Livers remained a testament to the region's complicated relationship with its past.

Notes

1. The differences between the terms *vernacular* and *folk* are significant. In *Romancing the Folk*, Benjamin Filene writes, "Terms like 'folk' and 'pure' [serve as] ciphers waiting to be filled: people imbue them with meanings that have cultural relevance and power to them." In other words, *folk* has often been used to connote a sense

of "authenticity" or "purity" that is misleading and, sometimes, destructive. In this essay, the term *folk* is used in reference to a constructed sense of authenticity and traditionalism; it is used sparingly and should be understood as unique from *vernacular*, which is relatively free from the controversy conjured up by *folk*. In this sense, and again borrowing from Filene, *vernacular* is a way of referencing songs and tunes "employing a musical language that is current, familiar, and manipulable by ordinary people." Occasionally I mention the "folk revival" or "folklore." These are also distinct from the word *folk*, as they have independent meanings that should be self-evident. Filene, *Romancing the Folk*, 2–4. The problematic nature of *folk* as a descriptive term, particularly in its dialectical relationship with *modern*, is elaborated in Kelley, "Notes on Deconstructing 'The Folk,'" 1402–4.

2. Andrews and Larson, "Bill Livers Recalls," 47; Andrews and Larson, "Child of the Lord," 17.

3. Andrews and Larson, "Bill Livers Recalls," 47.

4. Andrews and Larson, "Bill Livers Recalls," 47.

5. James Ware interview by Jeffrey A. Keith, October 23, 2004, digital recording in author's possession.

6. Andrews and Larson, "Child of the Lord," 16.

7. Department of the Interior, *Population of the United States in 1860; Compiled from the Original Returns of the Eighth Census* (Washington, D.C., 1864), 181.

8. Willis Russell, "The Kentucky Kuklux: Official Report of the Owen County Outrages," *New York Times*, September 10, 1874.

9. Department of Commerce, Bureau of Census, *Thirteenth Census of the United States Taken in the Year 1910*, Vol. 2: *Population 1910: Reports by States, with Statistics for Counties, Cities, and Other Civil Divisions: Alabama-Montana* (Washington, D.C., 1913), 747.

10. Elizabeth Campbell, "Cultural Resources Survey: Owen County, Kentucky," photocopy, Kentucky Folklife Program, 1996, Owenton Public Library, 17, 47.

11. Burnham Ware interview by Jeffrey A. Keith, October 23, 2004, digital recording in author's possession.

12. Bill Livers interview by John Harrod, September 6, 1976, audiotape in John Harrod's possession. There are no sources that corroborate this event, and Livers was known for telling stories that mixed reality with fantasy. The event was recounted between two comedic tales, but this story had no punch line.

13. Ware, "Kentucky Blues," 31.

14. Ware, "Kentucky Blues," 32.

15. Andrews and Larson, "Child of the Lord," 17; John Harrod interview by Jeffrey A. Keith, September 15, 2004, digital recording in author's possession. There were also at least three other African American fiddlers that once performed and lived in Owen County. Ambrose Smith, Louis Jenkins, and Wesley "Wes" Stafford all performed "black string band music" before Livers began his fiddling career. B. Ware interview by Keith.

16. Bettina and Kirk Somerville interview by Jeffrey A. Keith, October 23, 2004, digital recording in author's possession.

17. Ware, "Kentucky Blues," 33.

18. B. Ware interview by Keith.

19. J. Ware interview by Keith.

20. Holbrook is a community in Owen County.

21. Bettina Somerville, phone interview by Jeffrey A. Keith, November 17, 2004, notes in author's possession.

22. K. and B. Somerville interview by Keith. Livers sometimes joked about this experience. He was tall and skinny, and he always shared a bed with the largest of the tobacco farmers. Livers said that the man's belly propped the sheets so high that the experience was reminiscent of sleeping in a tent, except he was always afraid that he might be crushed to death while sleeping.

23. K. and B. Somerville interview by Keith.

24. In understanding Livers's story as an act of subversion, I owe a great intellectual debt to Levine's magisterial book. Levine examines the "folk" culture of African Americans in order to establish a past for "people who, though quite articulate in their own lifetimes, have been *rendered* historically inarticulate." In his time, Livers was certainly articulate. I hope this essay provides him with a voice in contemporary historical discourse. Levine, *Black Culture and Black Consciousness*, ix.

25. Andrews and Larson, "Child of the Lord," 18.

26. Livers interview by Harrod.

27. J. Ware interview by Keith.

28. J. Ware interview by Keith.

29. B. Somerville phone interview by Keith.

30. K. and B. Somerville interview by Keith.

31. Campbell, "Cultural Resources Survey," 16; Kirk Somerville phone interview by Jeffrey A. Keith, November 20, 2004, notes in author's possession.

32. Harrod interview by Keith.

33. Andrew Cammack interview by Jeffrey A. Keith, October 25, 2004, digital recording in author's possession.

34. Harrod interview by Keith.

35. Harrod interview by Keith.

36. K. Somerville phone interview by Keith.

37. K. and B. Somerville interview by Keith.

38. Harrod interview by Keith.

39. Bill Livers's résumé, typewritten, Community Files, Owenton Public Library, Owenton, Ky.

40. K. and B. Somerville interview by Keith.

41. E. D. Scott, "Memorial to Colonel William 'Bill' Livers," clipping, Community Files, Owenton Public Library, Owenton, Ky.

42. Harrod interview by Keith.

43. J. Ware interview by Keith.

44. Harrod interview by Keith.

45. Harrod interview by Keith.

46. Scott, "Memorial to Colonel William 'Bill' Livers."

47. Lawrence Smith, journal excerpt, manuscript, Community Files, Owenton Public Library, Owenton, Ky., 97.

48. Harrod interview by Keith.

49. K. and B. Somerville interview by Keith.

50. K. Somerville phone interview by Keith.

51. Filene, *Romancing the Folk*, 63.

52. Andrews and Larson, "Child of the Lord," 15–17.

53. Burnham Ware phone interview by Jeffrey A. Keith, October 16, 2004, notes in author's possession.

54. J. Ware interview by Keith.

55. B. Ware interview by Keith.

56. Filene, *Romancing the Folk*, 112.

57. J. Ware interview by Keith.

58. K. Somerville phone interview by Keith.

59. "Benefit Sat. at Monterey," *Owen County News Herald*, November 23, 1988.

60. B. Somerville phone interview by Keith.

61. B. Somerville phone interview by Keith.

PART TWO
NEW ANTIPHONIES

Why African Americans Put the Banjo Down

Tony Thomas

Twenty-first-century African Americans are picking up the five-string banjo. The black banjo revival has been led by the blues artists Taj Mahal, Otis Taylor, Corey Harris, and Alvin Youngblood Hart; by the African musical percussionist Sule Greg Wilson; by black old-time string bands like the Ebony Hillbillies and the Carolina Chocolate Drops; by the soul, jazz, and rhythm and blues bassists and guitarists turned banjoists Al Caldwell and Don Vappie; and by scholar banjo players like Rex Ellis and myself. The 2005 Black Banjo Gathering at Appalachian State University in Boone, North Carolina, the 2005 release of *Recapturing the Banjo,* and the 2011 Grammy award for Best Traditional Folk Album for the Carolina Chocolate Drops CD *Genuine Negro Jig* highlight this reawakening.

Yet why did the five-string banjo, once played by African Americans urban and rural, North and South, nearly disappear among blacks? How did it become an instrument largely played by whites? Why did African Americans put the banjo down? Did black people stop playing the banjo because of an aversion to country music?

Some claim negative images of black banjo playing created by European American minstrelsy and racist propaganda led African Americans to abandon the banjo. However, no one can point to a single banjoist who gave up the banjo for this reason. On the contrary, African Americans deserted the banjo because they developed new music that required new instruments. In the hundred years after Emancipation new black musics swept across black

America, white America, and much of the rest of the world. First came ragtime, blues, and jazz, and in time, swing, gospel, and rhythm and blues followed. As these musics developed, they demanded different instruments from the older musics that the five-string banjo served. In both popular and folk music the banjo's foremost task was providing rhythm for dancers. As the dances changed with the changing music, they demanded rhythms that were not suited to the five-string banjo. For example, the blues led black folk to replace the banjo with the steel-stringed guitars. Even in the Appalachians, where five-string banjo playing held on the longest among black folk, Cecelia Conway explains, "Black banjo players became obscure as they had begun to put down their banjos by the 1920s and to set their songs to the then-inexpensive and readily available mail-order guitar, leaving the banjo to whites."[1]

Bluegrass and old-time revivalist music keep the five-string banjo alive among whites. Nostalgia for and celebration of a mystified view of the southern rural past are associated with these musics. However, African Americans reject any such nostalgia for the Jim Crow South and constantly seek newer, blacker musics. The banjo survived in bluegrass because European Americans in the South continued to dance to the rhythms created by the African and white fiddle and banjo music.

Black Banjo and Hillbilly and Country Music

African American music, including black banjo playing, developed in response to the specific needs and developments of black life. African American distance from country music reflects the fact that country music does not meet these needs, having been constructed and branded to meet the needs of a different demographic.

While slave masters forced blacks to play European American music, and freed and enslaved African Americans played both African and European music for white folks to gain tips and employment, black traditional and vernacular musicians continued to play for black dancers. While appropriating dances and musical forms from European Americans, African American dance nonetheless retained the traditions and functions of West African dance. As Samuel Floyd explains, the role of black music is

> as a facilitator and beneficiary of black dance. The shuffling, angular, off-beat, additive, repetitive, and intensive unflagging rhythms of shout and jubilee spirituals, ragtime, and rhythm and blues; the less

vigorous but equally insistent and characteristic rhythms of the slower "sorrow songs" and the blues; and the descendants and derivatives of all these genres have been shaped and defined by black dance, within and without the ring, throughout the history of the tradition. In the movements that took place in the ring and in dances such as the breakdown, buck dance, and buzzard lope of early slave culture, through those of the Virginia Essence and the slow drag of the late nineteenth century, on through those of the black bottom, Charleston, and lindy hop of the present century's early years, to the line dances of more recent days can be seen movements that mirror the rhythms of all of the black-music genres.[2]

Throughout the African American experience, such dancing has remained located in the most segregated sites in the New World. From the first arrival of Africans these dances were sometimes secret religious celebrations and cultural assertions of identity, which in themselves may have been crucial to the crystallization of black New World identities out of individual African ethnicities.[3] Later, as among whites, dances became sites where the sexes found partners, sought romances, and celebrated their physical affection and sensuality. Black dance evolved from group dancing to couple dancing and in the late nineteenth century and early twentieth into sensual dances like the slow drag and others seen as sexually scandalous by Victorian standards of propriety. Predominantly, dancing, partying, and "jooking" took place within black society. As Katrina Hazzard-Gordon explains:

Except for encounters in the workplace and marginal socialization among the middle class, blacks still maintain a high degree of autonomy, particularly in their social lives. Blacks still prefer their own forms of entertainment and leisure activity though they have struggled to strike down statutes and customs that have barred them from access to white-controlled public facilities. Both of these phenomena have been particularly true of dance arenas. In the century (117 years) since emancipation, Afro-Americans have established seven institutions for secular dancing and socializing. Four of these are exclusively Afro-American: the classical jook and its derivatives — the honky tonk, after hours joint, and rent party. . . . In addition, blacks in the urban environment have adopted three dance arenas that also appear in white communities, dance halls, membership clubs, and cabaret night clubs. These seven settings have provided the institutional context for the development of Afro-American social dance.[4]

Nurtured in these locations, black vernacular dance, while sometimes appropriating European and European American forms, retained West African approaches to dance and required music that retains significant West African components. Consequently, the African American musicologist and composer Olly Wilson contends, "the West African musical sphere should include Afro-American music as an important sub-group" because of the number of "common musical characteristics shared by West African and Afro-American musical cultures."[5] Black music thus developed separate laws of motion from white music. African American banjo players played different music from European American musicians, even if there was an interchange of tunes and playing styles. Social, economic, cultural, and sexual life changed over time as dances and music changed over time.

Yet European American music and black music were never completely separate from each other. Especially in the South, they always influenced each other in decisive ways. For example, many of the leading figures who defined early country music reflected the influence of new and old black musics. Jimmie Rodgers, who was strongly influenced by jazz, ragtime, blues, and popular music, recorded with black blues musicians such as the Memphis Jug Band and Louis and Lil' Hardin Armstrong. Moreover, despite its claims to tradition, country music has omnivorously devoured all sorts of musical influences from African American music and from popular music, which, over the time of country music's existence, has become increasingly influenced by black music. In the mid-1950s, this reached the point where musicians who began by defining themselves as country artists, such as Elvis Presley, Carl Perkins, and Jerry Lee Lewis, topped the rhythm and blues record charts before they were exiled to the category of rock and roll.

On the other hand, in the 1920s and 1930s black string-band musicians whose music had become outmoded among African Americans sometimes found that their old-time music found a reception among whites. They included a number of musicians who played the older string-band music for whites and the newer mixture of jazz, blues, ragtime, and popular music for blacks. For example, the Mississippi Sheiks, who were among the most famous black blues bands of the 1920s and 1930s, playing the best of the mixture of blues and popular ragtime with hints of jazz, performed old-time string-band music for white audiences.[6] While this reflects similarities between what had become outmoded music styles for many African Americans and music styles popular with some European Americans, it does not reflect identity between southern black and white music. Rather it reflects that by the 1920s, African American and European American vernacular music in the Southeast had developed at different paces and moved in different directions.

Some have suggested that DeFord Bailey's participation in the Grand Ole Opry demonstrated that during the hillbilly phase of country music's development, black music and white music in the South were not separate. While there was intense interaction between European American and African American music in the early twentieth-century South, Bailey's participation in the Opry merely continued the practice of having black people play black music for white people. Bailey, a black harmonica virtuoso, singer, and guitar and banjo player, performed on the Grand Ole Opry from the 1920s to 1941. Bailey asserted that he played black music. He told David C. Morton, "You can tell I'm a black man to hear me play. I got too many tangles in there. It's just natural."[7] Bailey's repertoire as recorded by Morton indicates this as well: along with a number of religious songs of black origin that are common to both African and European Americans, black blues tunes dominated his repertoire. Bailey probably learned many of these songs, such as "Gotta See Mama Every Night," "Kansas City Blues" ("I'm Going to Kansas City"), and "Sitting on Top of the World," from jazz and blues recordings.[8] Moreover a major reason Bailey and other artists appeared on the Opry was to attract black listeners, particularly potential black customers for National Life and Accident Insurance, the major sponsor for the Grand Ole Opry and owner of WSM, the station that broadcast the Opry. David C. Morton and Charles C. Wolf explain this: "A large portion of National Life's business consisted of small policies popular with both white and black low-income customers. Judge Hay [Opry emcee and director George D. Hay] told DeFord that 'half of National Life's money comes from colored people.' He said that DeFord had helped make those sales."[9]

From African Plucked Lutes to Jazz Banjos

Organic developments within the African American community drove the rise and decline of black banjo playing. Africans brought the banjo from the Caribbean and launched African American banjo playing. In *African Banjo Echoes in the Appalachians*, Cecelia Conway shows that both the minstrel and the traditional Appalachian frailing and clawhammer banjo styles, once widespread among white banjoists, derived from black banjo styles, themselves derived from African playing of African plucked lutes. Along with Kip

Lornell, Robert Winans, Rex Ellis, and other scholars, Conway has documented how black banjo playing persisted into the twentieth century in the Piedmont and Appalachian South.

In the nineteenth century and the early twentieth, urban and rural African Americans and European Americans played many types of popular and art music as well as folk music with the five-string banjo. Toward the close of the golden age of the five-string banjo at the turn of the century, the five-string banjo adorned Park Avenue mansions and Mississippi shotgun shacks.[10] Beginning in 1893 many banjo cylinder recordings were made of popular, minstrel, and ragtime music because the banjo's frequencies were well suited to the early Edison recording equipment.[11] In 1900 companies like Cole Brothers and Fairbanks crafted high-quality five-string banjos in Boston, while mass-market five-string banjos had long been cranked out of New York, Philadelphia, and Chicago.

Urban African Americans of the late nineteenth century embraced the five-string banjo. Writing on February 2, 1889, in *New York Age*, one of the city's black dailies, Florence Williams described hearing on an "uptown street" "the sweet strains of music set forth from a band of colored brethren consisting of a violin, banjo, guitar and clappers."[12] That September, the *Age* reported that on Emancipation Day in Jamaica, Queens, "a band of vocalists with guitars and banjos sang through the village in the afternoon, to the great delight of all who heard them."[13] On February 13, 1892, the *Age* reported on a Brooklyn gathering of black bicycle enthusiasts from Manhattan and Brooklyn, where "the music of a guitar, banjo and mandolin added pleasing harmony to the merry gathering, until the guests were moved to indulge in the Virginia reel."[14]

The banjo significantly influenced the development of ragtime. Abbott and Seroff suggest that the syncopated rhythms of black fiddle and banjo dance music inspired early ragtime in Kansas and Missouri.[15] Lowell Schreyer points to a genre of piano music imitative of the banjo that began after minstrelsy popularized the banjo as another root of ragtime.[16] Indeed Robert Cantwell suggests that one of the origins of ragtime itself was the adaptation of black syncopations to classic banjo by black banjoists. Cantwell writes, "It [ragtime] was simply the playing of the old plantation cakewalking song on the banjo in a three finger style."[17]

Banjoists were leading figures in ragtime. Formal ragtime pieces were composed for the banjo and transcribed for the banjo from piano compositions. While the spread of ragtime massively encouraged use of the piano, more ragtime banjo recordings were made than piano recordings, in part because the banjo was much more recordable than the piano on early record-ing equipment.[18] Schreyer points out that "the five stringed banjo's eclipse in public popularity coincided roughly with the end of the Ragtime Era. By the close of World War I, ragtime was out and jazz was in. The five stringed banjo was also out, while the tenor and plectrum banjos were in."[19]

With jazz came the popularity of banjos played with plectrums, including the six-string and tenor banjos. In the late 1920s and early 1930s most popu-lar music abandoned the tenor and the six-string banjos for the guitar. The development of four-beat swing, the production of larger guitars like the Gibson L-5, and improvements in amplification, first for theaters and dance halls and later for the guitars themselves, made guitars more attractive in jazz and other dance musics. In these years, among both European and Afri-can Americans, the guitar became a much more important instrument in the string bands that continued the old fiddle-banjo dance repertoire. The onset of the blues led to the replacement of the five-string banjo by the gui-tar, where the new music replaced black banjo-fiddle dance music. Among African Americans, the five-string banjo remained in small pockets in the Appalachian and Piedmont South, where black folk continued to dance the old dances. As Karen Linn explains, "The Southern Black banjo tradition was real, but it has nearly disappeared, due in large part to the loss of its perfor-mance context: black country dances in the rural South (for example square dancing and buck-and-wing)."[20]

By the late 1920s the black audience for old-time string-band music had declined, while the white audience remained. As mentioned earlier, some African musicians continued to perform old-time music for white audiences. Elijah Wald explains, "In the few cases where black fiddlers recorded old-time hoe-down numbers, these records tended to be issued in the hillbilly rather than the Race series."[21] However, string-band recordings marketed as "white" by black performers and recordings of "white" string bands that con-tained black musicians do not seem to have included any black five-string banjoists, only fiddlers, guitarists, and mandolin players. Among the more than twenty-five black musicians on white hillbilly recordings that Patrick Huber surveys in his contribution to this volume, the only banjoist is a man-dolin banjoist in the Memphis Jug Band who recorded with Jimmie Rodgers.

As Karl Hagstrom Miller has demonstrated, these recording companies had notions of genre and "ethnic" markets that often arbitrarily separated black music from southern white music.[22] Yet these notions did not prevent them from recording black blues, religious music, and preaching when they discovered a market for them. The recording companies did not record black old-time banjo players because they saw no market for that music among African Americans. Real changes in black musical taste supported this belief. Blacks did not buy white old-time banjo and string-band recordings because they could not buy black old-time recordings. Reports of black purchases of white hillbilly recordings chiefly refer to recordings by white artists like Jimmie Rodgers, whose music was highly flavored by ragtime, blues, jazz, and popular music, or artists like the Carter Family, who recorded a large repertoire of black-originated religious music.[23] This contrasts with the blues, a music black record buyers wanted. Before black blues recordings were widely available, black people had bought thousands of white blues recordings. Karl Hagstrom Miller explains, "Evidence suggests that African Americans purchased blues records by white artists when they were the only ones available. '[European American singer] Marion Harris has the manner so at her command that thousands of Negroes make a point of buying her records, under the impression that she is one of them," noted the author Abbe Niles in the introduction to W. C. Handy's *Blues: An Anthology*."[24]

The recording companies recorded black banjoists who played the musics African Americans sought, including scores of black string bands and the famous jug bands.[25] These bands featured few five-string banjos, but many tenor, six-string, ukulele, and mandolin banjos. Their music mixed country ragtime, blues, popular music, and jazz with traces of the older music.

Indeed the thirty-four recordings Gus Cannon made with three different recording companies between 1927 and 1930 constitute the only significant body of prewar commercial black five-string banjo recordings.[26] Even though Cannon would continue to play old-time banjo tunes like "Old Johnny Booker" and "Old Blue" until his death in the 1970s, the only old-time banjo song he recorded between 1927 and 1930 was his September 9, 1928, recording of "Feather Bed."[27] The banjo style that dominates his 1927–30 recordings is the three-finger guitar banjo style called classic banjo, not the down-picking style associated with old-time music. Twenty of Cannon's recordings were pure blues, while two other recordings had "blues" in their titles. Most of his other recordings were country ragtime, although he also recorded turn-of-the-century black show business songs.[28] From 1927 to 1930 three different record companies believed they could market this black banjo music to African Americans.

Across the first forty years of the twentieth century, most white musics followed the lead of the new black musics by abandoning the five-string banjo. In the Southeast, European American five-string banjo music declined in the first forty-five years of the twentieth century. Before the emergence of bluegrass, five-string banjoists in country music had largely been relegated to the role of the stereotypical rube comedian or old-time survivor typified by Uncle Dave Macon, Stringbean, and Grandpa Jones.[29]

White and Black Blackface Minstrels and Black Banjo Playing

It is often argued that an association between the banjo and white blackface minstrelsy's negative and degrading depiction of blacks caused African Americans to stop playing the five-string banjo. The music historian Bruce Bastin reflects this approach:

> The parody of the Negro in minstrelsy could be tolerated by blacks at a time of lesser social change. As social distance grew to physical and psychological distance, intensified beyond all earlier belief after 1896, this stereotyping, once tolerable as crude but harmless humor, became directly offensive. The banjo, ubiquitous instrument of the minstrel stage, embodied this stereotyping, just as later, the watermelon and headscarf would take similar roles. . . . By the turn of the twentieth century, blacks were reacting against the use of the banjo to parody aspects of their lives which were becoming increasingly less tolerable.[30]

Unlike Bastin, Linn does not tie the negative image of the banjo directly to minstrelsy. She understands that in the late nineteenth century European American minstrelsy was in its death agony. She writes, "Minstrelsy lost its dominance of the entertainment business in the 1890s, and by about 1920, professional minstrelsy was gone."[31] Yet elsewhere she writes, "The generally racist ideas that clung to the image of the black banjoist not only encouraged the abandonment of the instrument by blacks, in the end it discouraged the survival of the instrument, as a viable vehicle for music making in American culture."[32]

Linn supports this assertion with a quotation from Claude McKay's 1928 book *Banjo*. She quotes a character named Goosey, who says, "Banjo is bondage. It's the instrument of slavery. Banjo is Dixie."[33] Goosey's ideas did reflect one current of black opinion. Yet Linn fails to inform her reader that McKay's novel celebrates the banjo as a symbol of black assertion and pan-African solidarity. In fact McKay presents Goosey as a negative assimilationist foil to his protagonist, Banjo, who uses his banjo to struggle for pride and unity among black sailors from North America, the Caribbean, and Africa in Marseilles. Ramesh and Rani call Goosey "the Negro Elite spokesman" who at first "refuses to join the black orchestra because of the banjo."[34] Indeed Goosey ultimately joins the jazz orchestra. The most representative statement about the instrument in the book affirms:

> The Negros and Spanish Negroids of the evenly-warm, ever green and ever-flowering Antilles may love the rich chords of the guitar, but the banjo is preeminently the musical instrument of the American Negro. The sharp noisy notes of the banjo belong to the American Negro's loud music of life — an affirmation of his hard existence in the midst of the biggest, the most tumultuous civilization of modern life.
>
> Sing, Banjo! Play, Banjo![35]

In the first thirty years of the twentieth century, the most prominent images of black banjoists that African Americans were exposed to were not those of white blackface minstrelsy but those of the jazz and ragtime banjoists who propelled jazz bands and popular dance orchestras. Linn explains, "The banjo and banjo-like instruments, starting in the 1910s, became the dominant fretted string instrument of the professional dance orchestra."[36] Most chose the four-string tenor banjo, although many jazz banjoists like Johnny St. Cyr — who played with Fate Marable, King Oliver, Jelly Roll Morton, and Louis Armstrong — used six-string guitar banjos, while some, particularly in the last days of ragtime, used mandolin banjos.

As Linn points out, "Banjos played an important role in both the dance bands and the 'Negro Symphony Orchestra' of James Reese Europe," the leading black band leader in New York before World War I.[37] A photograph captioned "James Reese Europe with One of the Clef Club Bands, c. 1914–17" shows six banjos "from the cello to the piccolo" among only ten musicians.[38] A photograph of Europe's full-scale Clef Club Orchestra taken between 1910 and 1913 includes thirty-seven mandolins and *bandoris* (a banjo-mandolin combination also known as the banjoline) and nine tenor banjos.[39]

Black tenor and six-string banjoists of the 1920s and early 1930s included some of the most urban and urbane musicians of the time. Many went on to become major jazz guitarists, band leaders, and composers. They include Ellington's banjoist and later guitarist Fred Guy, Elmer Snowden, Zach White, Johnny St. Cyr, Noble Sissle, Ikey Robinson, Bud Scott, Lee Blair, and Freddie Green. Wald writes, "Numerous writers have stated that the banjo fell out of favor with black musicians because of its racist, minstrel associations, but this makes little sense when one considers that the most sophisticated black groups of the period, the orchestras of Louis Armstrong,

Duke Ellington, and Jelly Roll Morton, continued to use banjos until amplification made the guitar viable in a bigger band setting."[40]

Moreover claims that African Americans abandoned the banjo due to its association with minstrelsy ignore the fact that African American minstrelsy remained a vibrant part of black entertainment through these years. Abott and Seroff caution against confusing the African American minstrel companies of the late nineteenth century with their white predecessors. They explain, "Black minstrel companies stole the audience away from the pale imitators, thus opening a pathway of employment for hundreds of musicians, performers, and entrepreneurs." Further, "the parade bands with their 'street flash' and open-air concerts, and the canvas theaters, with their blues singers, jazz orchestras, vernacular dancers, and blackface comedians, brightened the lives of the entertainment-hungry southern masses."[41] Phil Pastras observes, "As onerous as the blackface stereotype seems by today's measure of political correctness, it actually involved a highly ironic interplay of racial identities." He writes that blackface "began among white minstrels as a racial caricature of blacks, but it was quickly picked up by black minstrels as a caricature of white people's stereotyped notions about blacks."[42]

Interviews of African American banjoists and blues musicians contain no discussion of minstrelsy as a reason for the abandonment of the banjo. Instead they often spoke of the shows as sources of the new musics. When the blues singer and guitarist Nat Reese from Mercer County, West Virginia, spoke with Barry Lee Pearson about *Silas Green from New Orleans*, a touring show that featured blackface comedy, he did not speak of abandoning the banjo due to minstrelsy. Instead Reese told Pearson, "They used to come to Mullens [West Virginia] all the time. They came down for ten years straight as I recall, because my dad used to take me to each one of them. They had blues musicians, guitar pickers."[43]

Black minstrelsy often offered the most up-to-date popular music, including jazz, ragtime, and blues. Many blues guitarists worked in black minstrelsy. For example, Blind Blake worked with George Williams's "Happy-Go Lucky Road Show in the winter of 1932–33," which William Barlow describes as "a traveling minstrel show."[44] Samuel Charters explains that in 1943 Muddy Waters joined the Silas Green Show, "playing harmonica to accompany blues singers," and he "occasionally sang a little himself."[45] Douglas Henry Daniels reports that one of the first public performances of the Oklahoma Blue Devils, a jazz band led by the great bassist Walter Page that came to include Eddie Durham, Count Basie, Lester Young, and Jimmy Rushing, was when they accompanied the "blackface comedian and vaudevillian Billy King in the road show 'Moonshine' . . . in the winter of 1923." Daniels writes, "The blackface figure in the Oklahoma City Black Dispatch advertisement reminded readers of the minstrel tradition that set the tone for the musicals, as it did for most Black entertainment during the jazz decade and for years prior to that."[46] The African American blues recording stars Gus Cannon and Jim Jackson appeared as blackface minstrels in medicine shows in the same years that their blues records were sold. Bengst Olsson's booklet accompanying the *Good for What Ails: Music for the Medicine Shows* compilation includes a picture of Jackson and Cannon in blackface in a 1920s medicine show.

The Silas Green show Nat Reese referred to was not a simple medicine show. As late as 1954 the Silas Green troupe traveled "in a convoy of six trucks, three house trailers, a bus, ten passenger cars and a station wagon."[47] Abott and Seroff quote a 1954 *Ebony Magazine* feature that reported that Silas Green, with "such diverse fare as a chorus line, table eaters, torch singers and lively situation comedy featuring blackface comedians," was "almost as much a part of Dixie as collard greens and barbecued ribs."[48]

Almost every one of the major singers of the 1920s "vaudeville" blues sang their blues in black minstrel companies. Writing of the Rabbit Foot Minstrels, one of the most popular troupes, Frederick Ramsey Jr. tells us, "The Rabbit Foot did well in the twenties and thirties because its star was the matriarch of all stage blues singers, Ma Rainey." The Rabbit Foots' "long summer itinerary brought the music of performers like Ma Rainey and, later, Bessie Smith to nearly every obscure corner of the South."[49] If the stigma of minstrelsy precluded black use of the banjo, why didn't it preclude the popularity of Bessie Smith, Ma Rainey, and Clara Smith, who began and sustained their careers in African American minstrelsy accompanied by jazz combos and pianists? Indeed, why didn't it prevent African Americans from playing the tenor banjo in jazz bands? Why didn't it stigmatize black minstrelsy itself?

This whole argument seems to presume that a major change in black music was caused by white racist attitudes generated by a waning medium aimed at whites, not blacks. If white minstrelsy and racist propaganda on banjos had this impact on black people, why didn't it produce similar negative feelings about the banjo among European Americans? No one has ever suggested that.

Yet by the middle of the twentieth century, some African Americans sought to distance themselves from the banjo. In part this reflected the cultural assimilationist strain of black opinion that seeks to distance African

Americans from African and black culture, particularly from those elements criticized by white racists. Langston Hughes captured this in his last work, "Black Misery," writing, "Misery is when your mother won't let you play your new banjo in front of the *other* race."[50] Hughes's poem suggests that the problem is not the banjo, but "the *other* race."

In part, black distance from the banjo reflected a rupture in the continuity of black banjo playing in the mid-twentieth century. The tuxedoed, urbane black jazz banjoists were the final images of black active banjoists widespread in African American life. With the death of jazz banjo in the 1930s, living images of black banjoists no longer refuted the racist images pouring out of dominant society. The real images of the remaining black five-string folk banjoists—Nathan Frazier as recorded by John Work III, Lucius Smith as recorded by Alan Lomax, or Murph Gribble as recorded by Stu Jamison—did not reach the black public. Instead popular culture widely circulated popular stereotypes of "darky" banjoists and minstrels, if it produced any images of African American banjoists at all. Indeed the waning of black banjo playing produced an even more dangerous misconception: that the banjo was a European American instrument and had never been African American.

The Blues, the Banjo, and the Guitar

Gus Cannon's 1927–30 recordings stand out. That no other black five-string banjoist had a comparable recording career suggests that by the 1920s, black blues and the five-string banjo had separated. Born in 1883, Cannon, who began playing at Mississippi Delta "balls" as a teenager in the mid-1890s, was a survivor from an earlier era in the blues business of the 1920s.[51]

In April 2005, at the Black Banjo Gathering in Boone, North Carolina, I interviewed Algae Mae Hinton, a black traditional blues singer, guitarist, dancer, and five-string banjoist from North Carolina, about the banjo and the blues. Here is that exchange:

> TONY THOMAS: Do you ever play the blues on the banjo or just on the guitar?
> ALGAE MAE HINTON: I play the blues on the guitar.
> TONY THOMAS: Never on the banjo?
> ALGAE MAE HINTON: I might could, but I'm a blues woman.[52]

Hinton spoke for the last generation of African American five-string banjoists and their contemporaries among blues players. They play the blues on the guitar and the piano and less often on the fiddle, the mandolin, and far less often on the tenor banjo, mandolin, plectrum, and ukulele banjos. The five-string banjo joins the guitar only in the musics of buck, flat foot, and square dancing. Traditional black five-string banjoists play few blues. When they do, the music usually combines blues harmony, verse structure, and words with rhythms that serve the old dances, not the new dances of the blues. As the blues, accompanied by new dances like the slow drag, replaced the older musics, the need for the five-string banjo disappeared.

Particularly in the cities, black guitar playing was widespread in the late nineteenth century.[53] However, the blues developed in the early twentieth century when inexpensive steel-string guitars became available in the rural South.[54] Steel strings had volume and sustain that gut strings did not have. They facilitated voice-like bending of notes and slide playing, both integral to blues guitar playing and difficult on steel-string banjos because of their lack of sustain. Gus Cannon did record a beautiful slide version of "Poor Boy, Long Ways from Home" in November 1928 for Paramount, but to play slide, he had to put dimes under the bridge of his banjo to create proper sustain.[55] To play a nonslide tune, Cannon had to remove the dimes, readjust the location of the banjo bridge, and totally retune the banjo, while a guitarist can play slide on a steel-string guitar without readjusting it.

In the first musical generation of blues players, African American banjo elders taught young guitarists the blues. For example, William Barlow explains that the blues singer, guitarist, and fiddler Big Bill Broonzy's uncle introduced Big Bill Broonzy to music when he was ten years old, around 1903.[56] Barlow writes, "Blecher played a five string banjo; his repertoire and the repertoires of his fellow musicians included many of the region's earliest folk Blues: 'Goin' Down the Road Feeling Bad,' 'Mindin My Own Business,' 'Crow Jane,' 'See See Rider,' and 'Joe Turner Blues.'"[57] The Virginia-born black blues guitarist Archie Edwards similarly reported that his father, who taught him to play, continued to play banjo songs on the guitar. Edwards told Barry Lee Pearson, "My dad used to play a lot of banjo songs on his guitar because he was a banjo picker. He would play 'Georgie Buck,' and 'Stack O'Lee,' and 'Cumberland Gap,' and an old song about the 'Preacher Got Drunk and Laid His Bible Down.' He used to play all those old things, you know. He used to play 'John Hardy'—he used to play that on his guitar."[58]

Yet the blues requires instruments that can engage in this dialogue with the singer's voice and, indeed, become an equal voice with that of the singer or other instruments. This is one reason the banjo disappeared from the blues while the fiddle and mandolin remained until the blues electrified in

David A. Jansen and Gene Jones point out that the guitar was superior to the banjo for the singer of blues, a chiefly vocal music:

> The hard sound of the banjo did not complement singing. The banjo was fine for clanging out a rhythm for dancing, but one had to sing over it rather than sing with it. The guitar's sound was softer and more flexible, and it allowed for subtlety and shading within a sung line. The guitar could practically sing back to the performer. And if the strings were fretted by a knife blade or the neck of a bottle, a guitar could bend a tone as a human voice could. The streetcorner bard had long ago found his voice in churches and cotton fields, and now, with the guitar, he found his sound. The "talking" guitar was the perfect accompaniment to his singing.[65]

The last generation of vernacular black five-string banjoists shared Hinton's approach to the blues, the guitar, and the banjo. The banjo rang for what remained of the flat foot, buck, and square dancing, while the guitar played the blues. In 1977 Bob Winans surveyed the repertoire of thirteen living Virginia and West Virginia banjoists. His sample included Bob Jones, "in his mid-forties" in 1979; John Jackson, born in 1924; Robert Stuart, born in 1916; Leonard Bowles (fig. 6.3), born in 1919; Irvin Cook (fig. 6.3), born in 1924; Lewis Hairston (fig. 6.2), born in 1929; John Lawson Tyree, born in 1914; Rufus Kasey (fig. 5.1), born in 1918; Homer Walker, born in 1904; Clarence Tross, born in 1884; James "Clinks" Fauntleroy, born in 1906; John Calloway, born in 1906; and Peter Bundy born in 1905.[66] All of these musicians, save Tross, were born after the blues and the guitar swept out of the Deep South. They were not strangers to the guitar. Jones's father played blues guitar; Hairston's uncle played guitar; Jackson was really a guitarist who sometimes played banjo, often in a style that reflected as much of his Piedmont guitar playing as any traditional style of banjo; Kasey's brother played guitar; Tyree's sister played guitar; Fauntleroy primarily played the guitar; and Uncle Homer Walker's brothers played guitar.[67] Some of these banjoists were blues guitarists, something they shared with black banjoists from North Carolina like Dink Roberts and Odell Thompson and the black banjoist Frank Covington from Delaware.

Yet they sang few blues on the banjo. Winans reported, "While most of the informants played a few Blues pieces on the banjo . . . such pieces are definitely a minor portion of any individual's repertoire."[68] The Digital Library of Appalachia provides recordings of seven of the black banjoists Winans surveyed: Bowles, Cook, Hairston, Tyree, Walker, Rufus Kasey, and Tross.

FIGURE 5.1. Traditional African American five-string banjoists like Rufus Kasey persisted in the Upper South into the late twentieth century. Here is Kasey on his front porch in Huddleston, Virginia, with his Kay banjo in 1997. His granddaughter Katina is on his left, and his granddaughter Reva is on his right. Photo by Jay Scott Odell.

Out of their seventy-eight five-string banjo tunes, only eight recordings are blues. All of the other recordings were traditional string-band tunes, religious songs, or, in the case of Hairston, songs from the bluegrass repertoire.

As I did when speaking with Algae Mae Hinton, the interviewers on the Digital Library were persistent in asking the black banjoists about the blues the black banjoists played. Winans also seemed to expect there to be more blues among these banjoists. He described the blues as "a genre of song that one might particularly look for from black musicians."[69] Yet, as Hinton said, the banjo was for old-time music; blues needed the guitar.

Moreover the blues songs played on the five-string banjo were rhythmically distinct from most guitar-based blues. The blues selections these banjoists play on the Digital Library may have the formal AAB structure of a twelve-bar blues, but none of them has the rhythm associated with black blues artists like Bessie Smith, Charlie Patton, Lonnie Johnson, or Muddy Waters. As if honed to fit the called dances of the banjo and the fiddle, they lack the harmonic and rhythmic variation and space for call and response dialog between singer and instrumentalist and dancer associated with other black blues. Although a trained student of blues and African American music might recognize much of the early African and African American prehistory of the blues in these performances, an untrained listener might associate these performances with bluegrass and the older banjo-fiddle string-band music.[70]

No one could dance to these tunes the slow drag that black urban and rural dancers identified with the blues. They danced the old-time flat-foot, buck, and square dances associated with fiddle-and-banjo-based string bands. They adapted the blues to old-time string band and square dancing. The end of the old dances and the old music came in part because the blues and other forms of black music and their associated dances conquered African American culture in the twentieth century, leaving the five-string banjo aside.

The European American Banjo Revival and Why Black Folk Have Not Revived the Banjo

The five-string banjo continued to play a role in white music of the American South because dance to rhythms like those of the old string bands did not disappear among southern white folk. The spread of bluegrass created a new living music that continued the five-string banjo playing among whites. Moreover the folk music revival and its old-time music spinoff generated new interest in banjo playing among European Americans, North and South.

Bluegrass crystallized in full form in 1945 in the recordings and Grand Ole Opry appearances of Bill Monroe's Bluegrass Band, with Earl Scruggs's five-string banjo at its center. Bluegrass consolidated changes in white southeastern string-band music that had been brewing since the southeastern country music industry began in the late 1920s. Along with its links to traditional white folk music, bluegrass incorporated innovations from jazz, western swing, blues, pop, and swing. Scruggs's banjo style fused contributions from jazz, classic, and vaudeville banjo with traditional banjo styles.[71] The flat-foot, square, and round dances of old-time music can be done to bluegrass reworkings of traditional banjo-fiddle band tunes like "Cripple Creek" and "Soldier's Joy," as well as to the many new "breakdowns" and "specials."

Starting in the 1950s urban European American interest in what came to be called "folk music" and old-time music revived five-string banjo play-ing and created interest in bluegrass among middle-class European Ameri-cans from the cities and the suburbs, North and South, and encouraged re-tention of traditional five-string banjo playing where it persisted. Once the folk crowd embraced it, bluegrass experienced an enormous boost in accept-ability and spread far beyond the Upper South. During the 1960s "folk" radio and television shows featured pop folk groups with the banjo like the Kings-ton Trio, old-time revivalists like the New Lost City Ramblers, and bluegrass bands like Monroe's Bluegrass Boys. The banjo rang in the sound tracks of movies like *Bonnie and Clyde,* on television shows like *The Beverly Hillbillies* and *Petticoat Junction,* on the long-lasting *Hee Haw* show that featured blue-grass banjoist Roy Clark, electric banjoist Buck Trent, and old-time claw-hammer player Grandpa Jones, and on syndicated bluegrass radio and tele-vision programs like the *Flatt and Scruggs Grand Ole Opry* show sponsored by Martha White Flour.

This resurgence reversed the decline of the five-string banjo. Yet bluegrass does not represent a return to the overall acceptance of the five-string banjo in almost every genre of music in all areas of the country among diverse so-cial strata that characterized the turn of the twentieth century. It is thus mis-leading to suggest that African Americans have abandoned the banjo while European Americans have continued to play it. Like blacks, most European Americans do not listen to or play musics that use the five-string banjo. The banjo has disappeared from most white musics and from black musics but has been retained by bluegrass and old-time revivalist music, two minority musics even among whites. This situation creates the misconception that the five-string banjo has always been a chiefly southern white instrument. The "hillbilly" stereotype identified with country music, especially bluegrass, nourished another misconception: that the five-string banjo had always been a primarily Appalachian instrument.

Old-time music and bluegrass reflect a feature of European American culture that African American musical culture does not share so strongly: nostalgia for past music in general and nostalgia for the rural southern past in particular. Elijah Wald explains that these cultural differences shaped the marketing of southeastern tradition-based music in the 1920s:

> There was a fundamental difference between the markets served by
> the early white country musicians and by the black street singers who
> followed. The white rural recordings were released in a series labeled
> "Old Time Tunes" or "Old Fashioned Tunes," reflecting the percep-

tion that their music was a treasured relic of past times. Many white Southerners had a fond attachment to the good old days "before the war," and the nostalgic advertising rubrics were designed to appeal to such feelings. This appeal would remain a commonplace of country-and-western music, and is still routinely invoked by Nashville stars in the twenty-first century.[72]

Many of these white record buyers no longer lived in the rural South but had moved to cities. Still others were not nostalgic for the rural South but for other pastoral settings real and imagined, in the United States and beyond.

Of course this does not mean that the actual musicians and musics marketed to whites as old-fashioned rural music were old-fashioned, southern, or rural. Vernon Dalhart, one of the best-selling singers in this market with his "Wreck of the 97," studied at the Dallas Conservatory of Music, moved to New York, where he "learned four Italian operas *in Italian* hanging on a strap on the subway," and landed his first role in "a production of Puccini's *Girl of the Golden West*" in 1911.[73] Jimmie Rodgers, often called the father of country music, played most of his recordings in the style of blues, ragtime, and jazz, using jazz horn players. The only banjo players on Rodgers's records played tenor and mandolin banjos; the only fiddlers played jazz and pop music violin, not traditional fiddling.[74]

Meanwhile bluegrass continues to incorporate its own innovations and influences from other musics, including singer-songwriter "folk" music, country, rhythm and blues, world music, and hip-hop, and is into its third or fourth generation of leading players, yet it still claims to reflect pre–World War II traditional roots. Many musicians that old-time music fans adore, like Dave Macon and Clarence Ashley, were veteran commercial performers who changed their style and image to suit the times. Yet many old-time music revivalists see old-time music as a pure folk alternative to commercial music, whether from Music Row or the Brill Building. Folk and old-time music enthusiasts are overwhelmingly white, middle class, college-educated (old-time fans often have advanced degrees), and of urban or suburban origin. Yet they often claim to represent the values of the rural, mountain, and small-town South of the first thirty years of the twentieth century. The segregation, terrorization, and degradation blacks faced are rarely part of old-time music and bluegrass enthusiasts' nostalgic notions of the rural South.[75]

Musical revivalism and nostalgia among whites have not been restricted to European American folk-based musics from the Southeast. Since several generations of recorded music have been available there has been a succes-sion of revivals: a "Dixieland" revival, two or three swing revivals, a ragtime revival (that curiously did not include the five-string banjo), a western swing revival, revivals of acoustic and electric blues, and revivals of rock and roll, as opposed to rock, along with revivals of doo-wop, acid rock, glam rock, soul, and disco. In country music, past generations of musicians successively try to remarket themselves as preservers of the "true" and "original" country music, while current musicians await their turn to raise the same banner for future audiences.

Even when these revivals have centered on African American musics, they have failed to attract many blacks. Unlike the popular nostalgia for the southern past that persists in European American culture, African American memory has not forgotten the nightmare of racist violence, exploitation, discrimination, and poverty of the Jim Crow South. Black culture celebrates escape from this oppression, not return to it. Much of black musical culture is propelled forward to new musics speaking for new times. Wald explains that in the 1920s, when the record industry began marketing to African Americans, they "found that . . . black consumers tended to prefer newer styles." He notes that "African Americans . . . were anything but nostalgic for the old South. As a result, records by black rural artists were marketed not in separate black country series, but in the regular Race catalogs alongside the hottest singers on the contemporary pop scene."[76] The record companies did advertise blues and black religious music's southern roots because much of the black record-buying public were African American immigrants to the North who wanted to get the real thing from the heartland of black culture.

The constant struggle between African Americans and a hostile dominant society and culture creates a need for black music makers to produce music that speaks to their specific needs and historical experience. This empowers the many African retentions and African American creations that keep black music alive and vibrant, expressing its difference from European and European American music. In 1740 an English colonist, Charles Leslie, called the music of African Jamaican banjo and drumming "a very barbarous Melody," and in 1793 Bryan Edwards wrote from Dublin of the "dismal monotony" of the West Indian "Banjo or Merriwong."[77] Such European reactions to black five-string banjo playing read like today's denunciations of hip-hop music by whites and assimilationist blacks. European American and assimilationist African Americans also denounced ragtime, blues, jazz, swing music, bebop, rhythm and blues, and the original rock and roll the same way. Yet European Americans eventually adopted each of these musics and produced Europeanized folk and commercial derivatives of each. Of necessity, such Europeanized products often served different needs and had different musical and social functions from those of the original black musics. They tended to drop distinctive African American aspects of these musics, while developing new, nonblack characteristics.

This cycle of continued white containment of new African American musics fosters the need among black people to produce newer and newer black styles to replace those whose black content and identity have been diminished. Thomas Brothers explains how Charles Keil has developed this idea: "Building on [Amiri] Baraka's views, Charles Keil . . . speaks of an 'appropriation-revitalization process.' In response to white appropriation of their music, African-American musicians revitalize core values. From the revitalization comes a new style, which is eventually appropriated, and the process continues."[78] Black youth, the dancers, singers, and new musicians and creators of new music and dance, accelerate this process of creating new music that the dominant society has not captured with their need to declare their musical independence from previous generations.

African Americans have become so urbanized that the term *urban* has become a synonym for *black*. As African Americans left the rural South for cities and industrial areas in the North and South in the mid-twentieth century, they brought much of their music from the urban and rural South to the cities, especially the blues and religious music. The migrants created new forms of urban blues and greater interaction between country blues and urban blues, ragtime, and jazz. Formerly rural Mississippi musicians like Muddy Waters and Chester Burnett (aka Howling Wolf) became stars in Chicago; Louisiana-born Clifton Chenier became the toast of Houston; and Texas-born T-Bone Walker filled the clubs on Los Angeles's Central Avenue. These new urban mixtures also influenced musicians who stayed in the South and in the country. These musicians were not revivalists of older musics; instead they produced a new synthesis between the rural music and the black urban culture. New musics like gospel, jump blues, Chicago and West Coast blues, rhythm and blues, soul, and funk flowed out of this synthesis.

These new migrants could not take the fiddle-banjo playing with them; it was already dying or dead when they left the South. While the blues became identified with the new immigrants, urbanized African Americans view the five-string banjo — last heard waning in the rural South — as even more old-fashioned and completely "country." No black five-string banjoists remained in the cities to defend the banjo, so they and their banjos passed out of the active African American memory.

Black music producers, especially the youth, do not look back to older black musics but create new musics that they hope remain black. When folklorists located the last representatives of the black five-string banjo tradition, these black banjoists found little hearing from African Americans. Despite the rise of revival black five-string banjo and fiddle playing and the appearance of great African American string bands, those of us who play this music still have primarily European American audiences.

Understanding the last days of the living black banjo tradition requires placing it in the revolution of new black musics since Emancipation. Ragtime, blues, jazz, gospel, and popular musics influenced by them conquered African Americans earlier and more completely than they did whites. Even in the Upper South, where the black banjo tradition persisted longer than anywhere else, it rose and fell with its function: providing rhythm for dancers. When the dances changed, the banjo had no function. Little did they know that a new generation of black banjoists would pick up the banjo.

Notes

I could not have written this chapter without the wonderful examples and continued encouragement of Robert Winans and David Evans and the great discourse that opened when I launched the Yahoo online group Black Banjo Then and Now in April 2004. In particular, I wish to thank David Evans, Robert Winans, Joseph Byrd, and Greg Adams for their close editing and correction of this essay, and Jeff Titon, Jay Scott Odell, Laurent Dubois, and Elijah Wald for their advice.

1. Conway, "Black Banjo Songsters in Appalachia," 149–66.

2. Floyd, "Ring Shout!," 49–70.

3. According to Sterling Stuckey, "The ring shout was the main context in which Africans recognized values common to them—the values of ancestor worship and contact, communication and teaching through storytelling and trickster expressions, and of various other symbolic devices. Those values were remarkable because, while of ancient African provenance, they were fertile seed for the bloom of new forms" (*Slave Culture*, 16).

4. Hazzard-Gordon, "African-American Vernacular Dance," 428.

5. Wilson, "The Significance of the Relationship between Afro-American Music and West African Music," 16.

6. Cohn, liner notes, *Honey Babe Let the Deal Go Down*, 60.

7. Morton and Wolfe, *DeFord Bailey*, 175.

8. Morton and Wolfe, *DeFord Bailey*, 175–76.

9. Morton and Wolfe, *DeFord Bailey*, 109.

10. Gura and Bollman, *America's Instrument*, 75–253; Linn, *That Half-Barbaric Twang*, 5–36.

11. Linn, *That Half-Barbaric Twang*, 86.

12. Abott and Seroff, *Out of Sight*, 48.

13. Abott and Seroff, *Out of Sight*, 56.

14. Abott and Seroff, *Out of Sight*, 56.

15. Abott and Seroff, *Out of Sight*, 453–54.

16. Schreyer, *Banjo Entertainers*, 58.

17. Cantwell, *Bluegrass Breakdown*, 104.

18. Schreyer, *Banjo Entertainers*, 64.

19. Schreyer, *Banjo Entertainers*, 66.

20. Linn, *That Half-Barbaric Twang*, 42.

21. Wald, *Escaping the Delta*, 52.

22. Miller, *Segregating Sound*, 215–40.

23. William E. Lightfoot writes, "The Carter Family's biggest debt to African-American culture was in the area of religious music-spirituals and gospel songs. A rough estimate puts the Carters' repertoire at 19 percent folksongs and novelty tunes, 40 percent parlor music, and 40 percent sacred tunes, with half of that coming from black religious expression" ("The Three Doc[k]s," 181).

24. Miller, *Segregating Sound*, 154.

25. For a good selection of these string bands, see *Alabama: Black Country Dance Bands — Complete Recorded Works, 1924–1949* (Document Records, DOCD-5166); *The Earliest Black String Bands, Vol. 2: 1917–1919* (Document Records, DOCD-5623); *The Earliest Black String Bands, Vol. 3: 1919–1920* (Document Records, DOCD-5624); *The Earliest Black String Bands, Vol. 1: Dan Kildare* (Document Records, DOCD-5622); *A Richer Tradition: Country Blues and String Band Music, 1923–1942*, 4-disc box set (JSP Records, JSP7798); *String Bands, 1926–1929* (Document Records, DOCD-5167); *Texas Black Country Dance Music, 1927–1935* (Document Records, DOCD-5162).

26. *Gus Cannon: Complete Recorded Works in Chronological Order, Vol. 1: 1927–1928* (Document Records, DOCD-5032); *Gus Cannon and Noah Lewis: Complete Recorded Works In Chronological Order, Vol. 2: 1929–1930* (Document Records, DOCD-5032).

27. See take 47002–2-Vi V38515 on *Gus Cannon: Complete Recorded Works in Chronological Order, Vol. 1: 1927–1928*.

28. See Thomas, "Gus Cannon."

29. Linn, *That Half-Barbaric Twang*, 140–41; Morton and Wolf, *DeFord Bailey*, xvi.

30. Bastin, *Red River Blues*, 14.

31. Linn, *That Half-Barbaric Twang*, 49.

32. Linn, *That Half-Barbaric Twang*, 75. Blackface performances by white entertainers outside of institutionalized minstrelsy, amateur fundraising and high school minstrel shows, and minstrel-like depictions of African Americans continued until the rise of the civil rights and Black Power movements put a stop to them.

33. Linn, *That Half-Barbaric Twang*, 75.

34. Ramesh and Rani, *Claude McKay*, 127.

35. McKay, *Banjo*, 49.

36. Linn, *That Half-Barbaric Twang*, 91.

37. Linn, *That Half-Barbaric Twang*, 91.

38. Robinson, "Harlem Renaissance, Plantation Formulas," 132.

39. Robinson, "Harlem Renaissance, Plantation Formulas," 133.

40. Wald, *Escaping the Delta*, 51.

41. Abott and Seroff, *Ragged but Right*, 7.

42. Pastras, *Dead Man Blues*, 6.

43. Pearson, "Appalachian Blues," 39.

44. Pearson, "Appalachian Blues," 39.

45. Charters, *The Country Blues*, 248.

46. Daniels, *One O'clock Jump*, 17; Davis, "Banjo and the Jazz Era," 1.

47. Abott and Seroff, *Out of Sight*, 354.

48. Abott and Seroff, *Out of Sight*, 354.

49. Ramsey, *Been Here and Gone*, 103.

50. Hughes, "Black Misery," 175.

51. Gus Cannon interview by F. Jack Hurley, February 7, 1967, audiotape, Documenting Jazz and Blues in the Memphis Area Project, Oral History Research Office, Department of History, University of Memphis, Memphis, Tenn. I thank Professor David Evans for providing me with a copy of this interview. See Thomas, "Gus Cannon."

52. Algae Mae Hinton interview by Tony Thomas, April 9, 2005 (Black Banjo Gathering CD 9A, digital recording in author's possession).

53. According to his obituary in the June 7, 1890, New York *Clipper*, an entertainment newspaper, the nineteenth century's most famous African American banjoist, Horace Weston, took up the banjo in 1855 when, "having broken his guitar, he borrowed a 'tub banjo'" (Abott and Seroff, *Out of Sight*, 95). Abott and Seroff report that "African American press reports of the early 1890s suggest that during the previous two decades there had been a 'golden era' of guitar playing among African Americans" (254–55). They quote recollections of the 1870s to the early 1880s by George L. Knox, the editor of the *Indianapolis Freeman*, a leading African American entertainment newspaper. On February 11, 1893, Knox wrote, "We recall the time when the 'guitar players' of the race were like the sands of the sea shore in number, but the 'guitarist' is no longer a fad" (255). In each of the examples of banjo playing in New York City cited earlier, banjoists were accompanied by guitarists.

54. See Bruce Bastin's *Red River Blues* (15–19) for a picture of how inexpensive steel-string guitars, the Sears catalogue, and an agricultural depression in the early twentieth century made cheap pawn-shop guitars affordable and available to blacks across the South. While Bastin gives the year 1908 when Sears offered a $1.75 guitar as his example, the change in relative prices of mail-order guitars and banjos came about earlier. In the 1897 Sears catalogue, the range in price in guitars was from $3.95

to $27, while the range in banjo prices was from $2.10 to $21. Only three years later, in fall 1900, Sears offered guitars ranging from $2.70 to $10.80. While they offered a $1.75 banjo, Sears did not "recommend" it. Recommended banjos ranged from $2.95 to $25. Store-bought banjos were now more expensive than store-bought guitars. Just as important for the blues, the 1900 catalogue proclaimed that all Sears guitars featured a "full set of superior steel strings."

55. See take 20144-2-Pm 12571 on *Gus Cannon: Complete Recorded Works in Chronological Order, vol. 1*; Bob Bostick interview by Tony Thomas, Nov. 9, 2010 (video recording in author's possession). One of the few people to actually ask Cannon how he played the banjo, the Memphis guitarist and banjoist Bostick befriended Cannon in the 1960s and 1970s.

56. Broonzy was born on June 26, 1893 (Barlow, *"Looking UP at Down,"* 32).

57. Barlow, *"Looking UP at Down,"* 33.

58. Pearson, "Appalachian Blues," 30.

59. Evans, *The NPR Curious Listener's Guide to Blues*, 87–88; David Evans email to author, June 26, 2007.

60. Charters, "Workin' on the Building," 16.

61. Evans, "Afro-American One-Stringed Instruments," 247.

62. Evans, *Big Road Blues*, 47.

63. Elijah Wald email to author, June 20, 2007.

64. Charters, "Workin' on the Building," 16.

65. Jansen and Jones, *Spreadin' the Rhythm Around*, 224.

66. Winans, "The Black Banjo-Playing Tradition in Virginia and West Virginia," 8–10.

67. Winans, "The Black Banjo-Playing Tradition in Virginia and West Virginia," 8–10.

68. Winans, "The Black Banjo-Playing Tradition in Virginia and West Virginia," 23.

69. Winans, "The Black Banjo-Playing Tradition in Virginia and West Virginia," 10.

70. See Ajaj Kalra's analysis of Uncle Homer's "Rockin Chair Blues," in Kalra, "John 'Uncle' Homer Walker." Two of the blues were bluegrass tunes contributed by Lewis Hairston, who plays the banjo in a two-finger style influenced by bluegrass three-finger playing. His repertoire mixes bluegrass with African American banjo tunes. For example, he plays a version of "Sitting on Top of the World" in the style popular with bluegrass bands since the 1960s, using lyrics and a tune that seem to have issued from Doc Watson's 1960s recordings of the tune for Folkways and Vanguard, not from the African American blues version based on the Mississippi Sheiks covered by Elmore James and Bob Wills.

71. Linn, *That Half-Barbaric Twang*, 141.

72. Wald, *Escaping the Delta*, 31

73. Miller, *Segregating Sound*, 121.

74. Mazor, *Meeting Jimmie Rodgers*.

75. For a deeper discussion of European American nostalgia and romanticism of the rural past, whites from Appalachia, and the banjo, see Linn, *That Half-Barbaric Twang*, 116–63.

76. Wald, *Escaping the Delta*, 52, 32.

77. Abrahams and Szwed, *After Africa*, 282, 292.

78. Brothers, "Ideology and Aurality in the Vernacular Traditions of African-American Music," 43–47, 201.

Old-Time Country Music in North Carolina and Virginia

THE 1970S AND 1980S

Kip Lornell

On September 20, 2007, Joe Thompson, an African American fiddler from Mebane, North Carolina, received a National Heritage Award from the National Endowment for the Arts, the most prestigious recognition for a folk artist in the United States. In addition to the public recognition, this honor came with a hefty $20,000 cash award. The awards ceremony—held just outside of Washington, in suburban Maryland—always includes performances by the award winners. During Joe's fifteen minutes on stage he was accompanied not by his banjo-playing cousin Odell Thompson (fig. 6.1), with whom he had performed for decades until Odell's death in a 1994 car accident. Instead he shared the stage with a mixed-gender, multiracial string band, the Carolina Chocolate Drops.

Following an introduction by the folklorist Nick Spitzer, a professor of American studies and communications at Tulane University and the host of public radio's *American Routes* series, Joe came on stage with his four decidedly younger accompanists. The group, which included banjo and guitars, played four selections, including one gospel number, "I Shall Not Be Moved," that featured Joe's surprisingly powerful singing. When asked by Spitzer to characterize his music, Joe responded quickly, clearly, and succinctly, "I play old-time country music."

Thompson stands as one of the last of the community-based black musicians who came of age when this music represented a vital cultural expression. Into the 1950s this particular brand of country music was largely

FIGURE 6.1. Joe and Odell Thompson, Mebane, North Carolina, 1974.
Photo by Kip Lornell.

performed for square dances and in the homes of black residents in the
Piedmont section of North Carolina and south-central Virginia. Since then,
however, country music performed by black Americans on fiddle and banjo
duets, sometimes with guitar accompaniment, has become far less common
and is nearly extinct today.

In what follows, I recall my own early journey as a folklorist and ethno-
musicologist—an exploration of African American "old-time country
music," as Joe Thompson so aptly described it, that began in 1973—and examine the concept of black country music in North Carolina and Virginia,
with a particular emphasis on African American string-band music in or near
Franklin County, Virginia. Because I view this as a very personal story of
research and discovery, I have woven my own narrative into the essay. So
much of what I found during this period had been overlooked by previous
researchers examining vernacular music (usually called "folk music") in Virginia, most of whom focused on traditional down-home blues musicians
(black) or pre-bluegrass "old-time music" (white).

I'm not, of course, the only twentieth-century scholar to explore the wide
variety of traditional African American music. Foremost among them was
Alan Lomax, whose wide-ranging documentary and scholarly work began
in the early 1930s and continued until he suffered a serious stroke in 1996.

While researching southern black music as early as 1933, Lomax wisely often asked about ballads, work songs, and sacred material—interestingly Lead Belly was among the first musicians he encountered—and also explored the African American fife-and-drum band scene in the hill country of northern Mississippi.[1] Closer to the heart of this essay, Lomax also investigated black traditions in Virginia and North Carolina during his forays for the Library of Congress from the mid-1930s into the early 1940s, recordings of which have been reissued as part of an extensive retrospective of his lengthy career as a field collector of music.[2]

Prior to Lomax's work, "The 'Blues' as Folk-Songs" by Dorothy Scarborough provides a fine example of a pioneering article that cites several songs that are clearly part of the African American ballad tradition. Other scholars have looked at the work song tradition, the development of which is clearly intertwined with the evolution of blues and related forms. Significantly, some of the most interesting and accessible documentation of work songs has occurred on documentary films.[3]

This essay recalls the spirit of wide-ranging inquiry displayed by Alan Lomax beginning in the early 1930s, which I know, from conversations with Lomax, proved a very personal experience for both of us. Such inquiry is built on the desire to go out into the field, find out what's on the back roads and in small communities, and add to the body of knowledge by way of album liner notes, articles, books, and recordings. My recollection and reflections underscore how much more is known about black folk music today, which is found in the ever-expanding body of published aural and written records that are so much more extensive than when I began in the early 1970s.

Upstate New York and Piedmont North Carolina

When I began investigating the contemporary African American fiddle and banjo tradition in the fall of 1973, I had just relocated from upstate New York in order to attend Guilford College in Greensboro, North Carolina. While I was a high school student in Delmar, New York (the suburb immediately southwest of Albany), Paul Oliver's *The Story of the Blues*, *Blues Unlimited* magazine, and listening to reissues of old recordings by Blind Boy Fuller, Charley Patton, Jaybird Coleman, and dozens of other artists who recorded prior to World War II provided my basic education in the blues field. I was particularly intrigued by the sounds of songster-bluesmen like John Jackson and Mississippi John Hurt and profoundly moved by Eddie "Son" House's passionate sound, and I was fortunate to hear him perform twice. Many of these early explorations were shared with the late Mark Tucker, the Duke Ellington scholar who lived about two miles away from us and graduated in the same high school class.

I not only found the music emotionally satisfying; it also opened up a new world well outside of my own personal and musical experiences. I found this world utterly fascinating and very distant and alien from my own suburban existence in upstate New York. Mark and I often wondered why so many of these old blues guys were blind, what their lives were like, and how a crippled guy named Lofton made a piano sound like a train rocking along the tracks.

Sensing an opportunity to add to the body of knowledge about this intriguing musical genre, in the fall of 1970, the start of my senior year in high school, I decided to look for black American down-home blues musicians playing acoustic blues. My search took me to the nearby, predominantly black sections of Albany, principally the streets and alleys abutting Pearl Street. My fieldwork primarily consisted of speaking with people on street corners, inquiring at barber shops, asking after guitar and harmonica players at the local music stores, and eventually knocking on the doors of the people about whom I had heard. In this rather compact section of a small northern city I located enough older local blues musicians — almost all of whom had migrated from Georgia, the Carolinas, and Virginia during the 1940s and 1950s — to annotate and produce two albums as well as write a series of articles for the newly launched *Living Blues* magazine.[4]

Because I was so focused on blues I overlooked other interesting and related forms of music, which I realize now was a serious oversight. Gospel music provides the most obvious example. It never occurred to me to explore the music of local Pentecostal churches, nor did I consider documenting the quartet tradition, eventually the subject of my doctoral dissertation at the University of Memphis.

In retrospect, I only made one truly egregious misstep during my first serious attempt at fieldwork. I recall knocking on the door of an elderly gentlemen living on Clinton Avenue, whom I politely dismissed after a pleasant half-hour conversation. This genial man didn't really interest me because he wasn't a "blues man" who played in juke joints; rather he played fiddle and used to perform with medicine shows. Given the research that lay before me, this example of youthful indiscretion (I was nineteen at the time) now appears eerily prescient.

The year before I moved south, I received a National Endowment for the Humanities grant for a project titled "Field Research into the Afro-American

Music of Georgia and the Carolinas." For two months my mentor, Peter B. Lowry, and I traveled through North Carolina, South Carolina, and central Georgia meeting, interviewing, and recording blues and blues-related musicians. Some of these recordings were issued on Pete's Trix label, while other discoveries, such as Rocky Mount, North Carolina's eccentric and talented Guitar Shorty, found their way onto long-playing recordings released by Flyright Records.[5]

After a lifetime in the Midwest, New England, and upstate New York, my experiences in the southeastern states in the fall of 1972 convinced me to move where the climate was more forgiving and I could purse my musical research, so I carefully investigated colleges in central North Carolina. I thought about Davidson College, which is an excellent school and close to Charlotte but at the time admitted only men. I also considered the University of North Carolina at Chapel Hill but felt that it was too large for undergraduate school. Ultimately I chose Guilford College, on the outskirts of Greensboro, because of its relatively small size, the Quaker values it espoused, its strong interdisciplinary approach to learning, my desire to play varsity tennis and work at a college radio station, and my abiding interest in exploring the local black rural blues music scene.

Inspired by the research of Peter B. Lowry and Bruce Bastin, who were writing articles for magazines like *Blues Unlimited* and recording blues singers in the southeastern United States, I began looking for local blues performers in the style of Blind Boy Fuller. Initially I sought out well-known blues performers such as Richard and Willie Trice, two brothers who lived in and near Durham and who had recorded for Decca and Savoy back in the 1940s. Though hampered by a stroke, Floyd Council, who knew Fuller and had also recorded in the late 1930s as Dipper-Boy Council, lived not far from Greensboro, and I visited him as well. J. B. Long, who had served as an A&R man back in the mid-1930s and who got Fuller and others on record, lived at Elon College, and we became well acquainted after half a dozen visits. But I was interested in original research too, so I set out to find previously unknown blues players.

Eventually my own musical interests expanded as I moved in new directions that continue to serve me well to this day and that eventually inspired me to write books about gospel music and go-go.[6] During my first year in North Carolina I continued to look most closely at the blues tradition. The benefit of this sharp focus resulted in the documentation of several heretofore overlooked blues or blues-related musicians, most especially Guitar Slim from Greensboro.

But my focus on blues also had a downside. Simply put, I (almost) overlooked interesting music that was directly in front of me. For example, I didn't even think about looking at the sacred music traditions, such as gospel quartets or the all-brass "shout" bands that thunder through the halls of the United House of Prayer for All People on Sundays, both of which could be heard in North Carolina in the 1970s. I was young, still relatively new to fieldwork, and, perhaps most significantly, I didn't know what I didn't know. Had I been at least aware of these genres, this knowledge could have enriched and certainly expanded my field research.

Building upon my previous experiences and interests, and finding no one else undertaking similar fieldwork, I basically had the middle of the state to myself. In short order I located James Stephenson, aka "Guitar Slim," a very talented blues pianist and guitar picker living not more than three miles from the college. With a girlfriend in nearby Durham I frequently made the one-hour, fifteen-minute drive from Greensboro, not on Interstate 85 but on Route 40 or the smaller roads running between the two small cities. At small towns and crossroads I would stop at the post office, country store, and people's porches asking about local black musicians playing guitar, harmonica, or piano. I didn't locate any down-home blues players, but I soon ran into Dink Roberts, a black banjo player whom I later recorded and who is the topic of a film by Cece Conway. It was at a stop near Mebane, North Carolina, that one man mentioned Joe Thompson, a black man who lived just down the road about two miles and who played fiddle. Struck by the notion of a black American fiddle player and knowing about both Roberts and John Snipes (a black banjo player living not far away, closer to Chapel Hill), I stopped by to visit Thompson. As he was not home, I decided to visit him on my next trip.

Fortunately Thompson was home when I came by about two weeks later. He was pleasantly surprised that anyone, but perhaps even more so a twenty-year-old white college student, would be interested in his music and his life story. Joe's banjo-playing cousin and longtime partner, Odell Thompson, lived just down the road. Odell happened to be at home, so on that first day I was lucky to hear the two men play together, something they rarely did in the early 1970s.

Beginning in the late fall of 1973, I regularly interviewed and recorded this duo, as well as other guitar-playing old-time musicians, including Jamie Alston, who lived in southern Orange County. In the summer of 1975, I moved to Chapel Hill to work on a master's degree in folklore, which made visits even easier. When it came time to pick a thesis topic, the choice was abundantly clear: a comparison of the local African American string-band tradition with the blues scene found in Durham. Not wishing to tarry, I completed my thesis in August 1976. By the time I moved away from the Piedmont in the late summer of 1976, I'd accomplished enough research to not only write my thesis but to eventually publish a journal article, a documentary record, and a book chapter.[7]

North to Virginia

I moved on to the Blue Ridge Institute at Ferrum College in September 1976 in order to produce a series of twenty-six hour-long radio documentaries for public radio devoted to folk music in Virginia. The Institute's director, Roddy Moore—whom I had first met briefly at a concert by the great delta blues man Son House in 1969 when Moore was a graduate student at the Cooperstown Folklore graduate program and I was a high school student— had obtained a grant from the National Endowment for the Arts to underwrite the series. I had attended the Blue Ridge Folklife Festival several times while an undergraduate at Guilford College and had renewed our acquaintance. Based on our friendship, my fieldwork experience, a newly minted MA in folklore, and my radio background, he asked me to oversee the project. Over the next two years I combed the entire state—from coal country in the far southwest, up and down the Shenandoah Valley, throughout the Piedmont, and over to Tidewater—recording new music, conducting interviews, and searching archives for older material.

In these predigital days, this meant not only lugging a high-quality Nagra tape recorder around; all of the editing was done the old-school way, by cutting and splicing tape. Eventually all twenty-six hour-long shows were completed, the topics ranging from the Carter Family to work songs, blues, and native Virginia ballads. The series was broadcast first over Roanoke's WVWR-FM (now WVTF-FM) and later over most of the other public radio stations located throughout the Old Dominion.

In terms of black country music, I started with the folks about whom I already knew. Well-known northern Virginia songster John Jackson was an obvious choice, and I think it was he who mentioned John Cephas, sometimes known as "Bowling Green" John because of his connections with that small Virginia town. I am, I think, the first person to record John, who went on to have quite an extensive touring career. But in early 1977 he was all but unknown. Both men are now deceased, Jackson in 2002 and Cephas in 2009. Fortunately both recorded many times during their long careers.

Roddy introduced me to Marvin and Turner Foddrell, who lived about one hour due south of Ferrum College in Patrick County, Virginia, just a few miles from the North Carolina state line. Turner ran a small country store, which was a focal point for a family that was riddled with music. Their father, Posey, played music, as did Turner's son, Lynn. The brothers (then in their fifties) played an easy mix of blues, sacred, and "country" music. In this context, Turner referred to what they play as "regular old-time country music," and then broke it down into more typical subgenres, such as blues and bluegrass.

Coming of age as musicians in the late 1940s and 1950s, they fell under the spell of local musicians, older phonograph records, the music heard over the radio, and the newly emerging bluegrass sound. Both men explored the nearby options for music making. Turner, for example, played guitar with a local bluegrass band, really an informal Saturday-night jam session with other musicians living in and around their home in Stuart, Virginia. This informal group occasionally competed in local Patrick County fiddle contests, with Turner as their guitar player. Not surprisingly, he was usually the only black musician involved in these sessions and contests. Nonetheless, according to Turner, his involvement raised no eyebrows, which doesn't surprise me because the family was so well known for their musical talents and their local grocery store and were among the few black families living in that section of the county. Turner told me in an interview in 1977, "We mostly grew up with whites. Danced together, made music together. . . . That's all I been used to."[8]

The Foddrells' father, Posey, born around the turn of the twentieth century, played guitar, organ, piano, banjo, and mandolin. He too played in integrated bands in the 1920s through the 1940s, often in nearby Meadows of Dan, home of the renowned Shelor Family, whose 1927 Victor recordings of "Billy Grimes the Rover," "Big Bend Gal," "Suzanna Gal," and "Sandy River Belle" are considered masterpieces of Virginia string-band music. In other words, Turner was merely carrying on a family tradition of playing with white musicians and learning tunes typically associated with white hillbilly music. In the same interview, Turner mentioned that he learned the standard "Chinese Breakdown" from his father when he was about eight years old, around 1935.[9]

The brothers also enjoyed the down-home blues style of Blind Boy Fuller and performed many of his songs, such as "Rattle Snaking Daddy" and "Flying Airplane Blues." Not surprisingly, they also listened to Lightnin' Hopkins, one of the more accomplished and widely recognized down-home blues musicians to record in the late 1940s and early 1950s. His popular "Black Rat Blues" is one of the songs they performed together.

A decades-long employee of the Hotel Roanoke, Daniel Womack was born in rural Pittsylvania County, Virginia, in the first decade of the twentieth century. When I met him, he had already appeared at the Blue Ridge Folklife Festival, held each October on the Ferrum College campus. Daniel proved to be a trove of expressive culture. Not only a very talented musician, he also told African American "home tales" he learned from his father and members of his community, including a great number of tales of wily animals as well as "Master and John" stories dating from slavery times.

Daniel was in some ways reminiscent of the more famous Reverend Gary Davis, who grew up in the Piedmont of South Carolina. Both men were blind, similar in age, and exceptionally talented guitarists who turned almost exclusively to religious music as adults. As a boy Davis sometimes played banjo, though he was legendary for his prowess on guitar. Aside from Davis's greater fame, Daniel's more well-rounded musical background set the two men apart. In addition to recording Daniel for the public radio documentaries, I spent many hours with him between 1976 and 1983, including a five-day trip to Washington to participate in the Smithsonian Festival of American Folklife. Over the years of interviews and informal conversations, I learned a great deal about black musical life in Pittsylvania County, where Daniel lived before moving to Roanoke after World War II.

In addition to sacred music (mostly from his Baptist upbringing), Daniel was very familiar with the blues tradition. Like Davis, he was not inclined to perform this part of his repertoire nor readily discuss such "worldly" music, but he was happy to share the music of his childhood, which as far as I am concerned comes under the "country music" rubric. Daniel often reminisced at length about playing "marches" on the guitar, usually at the close of the school year. Davis also performed marches on the guitar for similar school closings, as did white artists from Virginia, such as the legendary Grayson County banjo player, Wade Ward.

But Daniel was also full of musical surprises. At the Ferrum College Blue Ridge Folklife Festival (I believe in 1977), Daniel overheard a dulcimer player and casually remarked that he used to play one as a child. This stunned me at first, but the more I thought about it, the less unlikely it seemed. The dulcimer, a plucked instrument predominantly associated with Anglo-American folk music in the Appalachians, eventually found its way into homes outside of Appalachia, so why not into the homes and musical lives of black residents of Piedmont Virginia? Based on Daniel's tip, Roddy Moore, the Blue Ridge

Institute's director, and I eventually tracked down the information about Tom Cobb, a black dulcimer maker and performer who lived not far from Daniel's childhood home. Perhaps he was the source for the instruments that black Americans like Daniel played in the 1920s.

Daniel also surprised me when, overhearing a jew's harp player, he stated that he used to play an instrument like that. In subsequent conversations it became clear that he was not referring to a small jew's harp but to its larger and older cousin, the mouth bow. Single-string mouth bows like the one Daniel played as a child are uncommon in the twentieth-century African American tradition, though they are quite often heard in Africa and diaspora countries such as Brazil, where they are called berimbau and are associated with the Afro-Brazilian martial art capoeira.

While I was quite pleased to visit, interview, and record previously known musicians like Jackson, Cephas, the Foddrells, and Womack, curating this series also provided me the opportunity to conduct fieldwork and gave me the excuse to explore topics of interest to me. Having just completed my master's thesis, "A Study of the Sociological Reasons Why Blacks Sing Blues: Secular Black Music in Two North Carolina Communities During the 1930s," which contrasted the Piedmont blues tradition in Durham with the black string-band tradition in neighboring Orange County, I was curious to check out the local African American string-band tradition in addition to blues. Certainly my experience with the Foddrells, in particular, whetted my appetite for exploring new territory.

Ferrum College is located in south-central Virginia, in the heart of Franklin County, about midway between Roanoke and Martinsville, about forty miles north of the North Carolina border and some one hundred miles northwest of Orange County, North Carolina. The college is only about ten miles from the Blue Ridge Parkway, on the eastern slope of the Blue Ridge Mountains. Franklin County is not only quite lovely, but it's well known as one of the state's premier distillers of untaxed liquor, a trade that proudly continues into the twenty-first century.

South-central Virginia is also well known for string-band music, and one can make a strong case for southwestern-central Virginia (Grayson and Carroll counties in particular) as the birthplace of commercial country music. A significant number of the earliest country music recording artists, including Henry Whittier, Ernest "Pop" Stoneman, and Kelly Harrell, grew up in or near Grayson or Carroll County and helped launch the country music industry. Whittier became one of the first country music recording artists when he traveled to New York City and recorded three harmonica solos for the OKeh record company on December 10, 1923.

The Virginia counties bordering the North Carolina line are particularly noted as a stronghold for (white) string-band music. In a tradition that can be traced back to the nineteenth century, the combination of a fiddle and banjo was quite common, with the guitar or mandolin often added beginning in the early twentieth century. The commercial documentation of Virginia's contribution to this music once again involves Henry Whittier, who brought his Virginia Breakdowners (with James Sutphin and John Rector on fiddle and Whittier on guitar) to OKeh's New York City studio in mid-July 1924. These groundbreaking string-band recordings were soon followed by recordings by other local artists, such as Ernest V. Stoneman and His Dixie Mountaineers, the Hill Billies, and Al Hopkins's Bucklebusters.

Even closer to Ferrum College, string-band music had a slightly different flavor. Franklin and Henry counties became Charlie Poole territory in the 1920s, and he still retains legendary status there. The banjo-playing, hard-drinking Poole (along with his North Carolina Ramblers) recorded most extensively for Columbia Records over a five-year period beginning in July 1925. His versions of "The White House Blues," "Don't Let Your Deal Go Down," and "Can I Sleep in Your Barn Tonight Mister" sold quite well and were highly influential and definitive. Other groups, such as the Floyd County Ramblers, the Roanoke Jug Band, and the Four Virginians, hailed from adjoining counties and also recorded in the late 1920s, but none had the same local impact as Poole and his band.

Blues, Gospel, and African American "Country" Music in Virginia

In Virginia in the mid-1970s, the term *African American folk music* almost always meant blues or, secondarily, gospel music. And blues most often referred to pioneering blues men like Luke Jordan (from Campbell County) and William ("Bill") Moore, who lived most of his life in Westmoreland County on the Northern Neck in Tidewater. Jordan and Moore regularly performed for dances and parties within their own communities and also recorded commercially in the late 1920s. In fact since 2000 the state has erected historical highway markers to them in Lynchburg and Tappahannock, noting their cultural and musical importance.

John Jackson, a northern Virginian and one generation younger than

Jordan and Moore, enjoyed a long and successful career as a touring and recording blues artist from the mid-1960s until his death in 2002. The mantle of "Virginia Piedmont blues man" has now largely passed to John Cephas (born in 1930), who grew up in Caroline County but has lived in or near Washington, D.C., for many years. After 1977 the duo of Phil Wiggins (harmonica) and Cephas toured and recorded extensively until Cephas's death on March 4, 2009.

The gospel music scene across the state is generally more acknowledged than truly researched. Sacred music within black communities throughout Virginia is ubiquitous and comes in many varieties. Even back in 1976 the career of the Golden Gate Quartet, which began in Norfolk in the early 1930s and included scores of recordings, was very well known. There had been hundreds of "vanity" recordings on 78 rpm and 45 rpm single discs as well as albums by various black gospel groups from throughout the state. But even today the breadth of music found in the African American Baptist, Pentecostal, and other sects remains underresearched.

Aside from blues and gospel music, other forms of Virginia's contemporary black folk music were all but unknown to scholars and aficionados. I wondered about a black American ballad tradition. How about instruments not typically associated with black Americans, such as the dulcimer or the accordion? And, given my own recent interests, the question of string-band music and banjo playing came most immediately to mind. John Jackson, for example, mentioned that he occasionally played banjo when he was young, but no one looked to that aspect of his music with great care. In other words, I became interested in exploring the notion of black folk music or black country music in light of what existed in the mid-1970s and how it might expand our understanding of the meaning of African American music.

Historical sources had established that African Americans were playing music on the fiddle as early as the 1690s and on banjos (or banjo-like instruments with various names) as early as the 1770s. The WPA Slave Narratives contain an account of quill playing (similar to the homemade fife, more often encountered in Mississippi in the twentieth century) around Norfolk in the 1850s. Although more commonly associated with polka bands formed by European immigrants, accordions were once favored by black Americans living in Virginia and playing into the early twentieth century. At least one African American dulcimer maker, Tom Cobbs of Pittsylvania County, was known to be living and playing in Virginia into the 1950s.[10]

In addition to the obvious topics, such as the Carter Family, bluegrass, and ballads, the documentary public radio series gave me an excuse to more carefully explore, document, and present the notion of black country music in Virginia in 1976 and 1977. Even though there was some scattered information about the topic as well as a handful of recordings, I knew that it was time to hit the field and look myself. As is so often the case, fieldwork was the only way to proceed.

Time and travel money were not an issue because this project was taking up all of my time for about one year and I had ample money for traveling many miles. But I needed to be both practical and savvy. Knowing that I was situated in a part of the state renowned for string-band music and that contained a substantial black population, instead of chasing around Virginia it made sense to look in my own backyard. So I hit the road with a focus of about fifty miles around Franklin County, which took me directly south into Martinsville (Henry County), to Danville (Pittsylvania County) and Lynchburg (Campbell County) to the west, and north into Roanoke.

In addition to asking local white musicians about what they knew, I also stopped at dozens of country stores and post offices. I drove the country roads, shutting down my trusty 1971 Dodge Dart hundreds of times in order to chat with people (black and white) sitting on their porches or working in their yards. After introducing myself and my affiliation with Ferrum College, I asked about older black musicians who played string music or who picked a banjo, guitar, or fiddle, or even old-fashioned music? My query was deliberately vague because I didn't necessarily want to use terms like *blues music* because it could be misinterpreted or misunderstood. But almost anyone middle-aged or older had a much clearer and expansive version of what *string music* might encompass. Due to my persistence and some good luck (two of the most important fieldwork ingredients), this tactic quickly bore fruit and soon expanded my own vision of what constituted black country music in south-central Virginia.

I stumbled across another unexpected black country music tradition in Woolwine, located along the border of Franklin and Patrick counties. While driving along winding Route 40 on my way to Stuart, I stopped to see an elderly black man named James Garfield Pilson, who someone told me had played music when he was young. In addition to stories about country square dances accompanied by fiddles and banjos, Pilson (born in 1893) mentioned that he used to play a fife, which was often accompanied by drums. Pilson was part of a family band that included his brother, William Green, on bass drum and Benjamin Harrison on kettle drum that performed between about 1910 and into the 1920s. According to Pilson, "We got 'em [fife and drums] from the whites; they was the ones that had them. I took my playing from them. Quite often we'd play on the Fourth of July, sometimes we'd have what they would call a celebration." This interview underscores the musical fluidity in south-central Virginia, where the line that distinguishes conventionally "black" from "white" musical genres was often flimsy at best.[11]

Except among creolized zydeco musicians living in southwestern Louisiana and southeastern Texas, the accordion is another instrument not usually associated with black country music. Nonetheless, during the course of my fieldwork for the NPR radio project and again in the early 1980s, when I returned for summer fieldwork opportunities while pursuing my Ph.D. from the University of Memphis, I located and recorded several African American accordion players across Virginia.

Isaac "Uncle Boo" Curry, who was quite elderly, lived on Virginia's Northern Neck (near the Atlantic Ocean) and was the first of the accordion players I located. Largely out of practice when we met, Curry once more got out his instrument to play. Upon my return several weeks later, he was in good spirits and played a mixture of dance tunes and sacred songs. Curry also recorded a rather fragmented version of one of the best-known American ballads, "Casey Jones," which appears on the Blue Ridge Institute collection *Non-Blues Secular Black Music*.[12]

Like Curry, Frank and John Toliver and their older neighbor Hiawatha Giles played a small-button accordion rather than the larger piano keyboard style favored by most of the modern zydeco musicians. All three lived in Nelson County, in the mountains between Lynchburg and Charlottesville, and I came across them in the summer of 1981 while conducting a summer-long folklife survey.

Cousins Frank and John Tolliver grew up near the small town of Massie's Mill. Both men learned how to play from their uncles Frank and Gilly Tolliver. These men, along with Hiawatha Giles, played for local country dances early in their career and into the 1980s for their churches. Frank played at Zion Hill Baptist Church in nearby Roseland. Sacred music, late nineteenth-century hymns and spirituals such as "Death's Cold Hand Be Leaving Me" and "Go Tell It on the Mountain," constituted their entire repertoire when I recorded them in 1981.

In addition to the musicians and their traditions that I discovered during my Virginia fieldwork, I was convinced that I would locate some still-active African American fiddle, banjo, and guitar players who, to use Turner Foddrell's phrase, continued to play "regular old-time country music." In retrospect, it's not surprising that I should run into Lewis "Big Sweet" Hairston,

FIGURE 6.2. Lewis Hairston, Henry County, Virginia, 1977. Photo by Kip Lornell. Courtesy of the Blue Ridge Institute and Museum of Ferrum College.

or someone like him (fig. 6.2). But it surprised me at the time because I continued to think "old-time," "Charlie Poole," and "Joe Thompson" when I initially heard about a "new" black fiddle or banjo player.

Lewis, a very large man who favored bib denim overalls and often emitted a booming laugh, was the first of the black banjo players I encountered while driving the byways of eastern Henry County, just down the road from Swanson's Mill. The rolling hills near his house contained huge groves of trees, growing taller as they awaited harvesting for one of the local pulp mills. A bit farther south and east the land became flatter and gave way to rows of tobacco. These mills and the tobacco fields provided employment for Lewis and many of his contemporaries.

For decades these industries, along with textile mills, supported the residents of two nearby small cities, Martinsville and Danville. Radio station WMVA signed on the air in 1941, followed six years later by WDVA. Both stations featured local live music well into the 1960s, and bluegrass quickly became one of the staples in their daily line-up. Lewis, along with tens of

FIGURE 6.3. Leonard Bowles and Irvin Cook, Martinsville, Virginia, 1978.
Photo by Peter Hartman. Courtesy of the Blue Ridge Institute and Museum
of Ferrum College.

thousands of eager listeners, caught Jim Eanes and the Shennandoah Valley
Boys or Clyde Moody on live, half-hour, early morning or midday broadcasts
before the group headed out for their evening show date.

Although it was almost entirely white-owned and -oriented well into the
1950s, radio did not hang out either "Whites only" or "No colored" signs on
their broadcasts, and everyone tuned their radio dials to their local station to
find out who had died, the weekly supermarket specials, local sports scores,
and the weather. Hairston told me that he listened to both stations, as did
most of his peers. With the local popularity of bluegrass, it's hardly surprising that Lewis (then in his late forties) enjoyed playing in a fingerpicking
style, favored by bluegrass players. He not only enjoyed bluegrass, but one
of his favorites, Grandpa Jones, helped to fill that gap between old-time and
bluegrass. The first tune that Hairston played for me, in fact, was his interpretation of Jones's King Records version of "Mountain Dew," which was very
popular when Hairston was about twenty.

Within a few miles from Lewis lived another banjo player, Irvin Cook
(born in 1924), and his fiddling partner, Leonard Bowles (born in 1918; fig.
6.3). Their music was more reminiscent of Joe Thompson, mostly down-
stroke or two-finger-style banjo with a highly rhythmic fiddle style, than the

bluegrass favored by Hairston. Although Cook and Hairston were born only six years apart, Cook learned from older relatives who played for local square dances and in a style that predated bluegrass. Their repertoire included many tunes, such as "Shortnin' Bread" and "Mamma Don't Allow," more typically associated with white musicians but that fit comfortably under the "regular old-time country music" rubric suggested by Turner Foddrell.

Leonard Bowles was particularly interesting because of his sense of history and his own musical activity. Known mostly for his fiddle playing in his later years, Bowles also performed in a drop-thumb, clawhammer style. He also displayed a keen sense of the importance of performing this music, which was so ubiquitous among black Americans when he was growing up. He often reminisced about local black square dances and in the early 1980s even helped to recreate one for a Channel 7 (WDBJ-TV) documentary, facilitated by the staff of the Blue Ridge Institute. Moreover he was happy to talk with and play for anyone interested in his music.

I found two other banjo players, John Lawon Tyree and Rufus Kasey, living within a half hour of Ferrum College. Tyree (born in 1915) lived just to the east of Rocky Mount, in his hometown of Sontag, about ten miles from the college. His repertoire included many rural favorites, such as "Fox Chase," "Hop Along Lou," "Sally Anne," and "Coo Coo Bird," that transcend racial boundaries. He learned primarily from his uncle Torrence Wade in the 1930s. Wade favored the frailing (clawhammer) style, which Tyree played his entire life.

Rufus Kasey (born in 1918) lived off a small road in Huddleston, in the southeastern corner of Bedford County, not far from the now thriving Smith Mountain Lake resort region. Like Tyree, he began playing in the 1930s and played in the clawhammer style. Kasey also performed a similar version of the "Coo Coo Bird," along with other standards such as "Georgia Buck Is Dead" and "Hop Light Lou." Both men, as one might suspect, also played for square dances held by local black residents into the 1950s.[13]

Conclusions

This narrative underscores the need for revisiting the concept of country music as it relates to the African American tradition(s) in Virginia and, I would argue, neighboring North Carolina, West Virginia, Maryland, and eastern Tennessee. Most definitions of country music call attention to at least four fundamental themes: country music's rural roots, the importance of its British Isles heritage, its southern geographical origins, and its transition into popular mainstream music following the end of World War II. Except for the seemingly obligatory mention in passing of DeFord Bailey and the Grand Ole Opry, Charley Pride, or the impact of blues, black American musical cultures are rarely, if at all, mentioned in definitions of country music. This is an oversight that is clearly increasingly problematic, simplistic, and incorrect.

It's been all too easy to think of traditional, rural black music in Virginia as blues or (to a far lesser degree) gospel music, but the reality is much more complicated. Blues is undoubtedly an important component of traditional black music, but the research is clear: blues is only one of several secular genres played by rural African American musicians during the twentieth century in Virginia. Gospel music remains, perhaps, an unexpectedly problematic term. Even in the twenty-first century the term encompasses genres as wide-ranging as all-brass shout bands, composed hymns performed by large choirs, a capella spirituals sung on Saturdays by the congregants of the Church of God in Christ and Saints, and the "prayer bands" found on the Eastern Shore. Sacred music is an important part of all forms of country music (one only has to look at the repertoire of the Virginia-based Carter Family for a sterling example), though I have focused on the secular traditions in this essay.

Virginia's black country music certainly includes blues and sacred music, but my research demonstrates that it's a more complex, interesting, and still underresearched topic. The "old-time country music" referred to in the title of this essay also underscores the ongoing interaction between black and white musicians in rural areas. Mid-nineteenth-century minstrelsy marked the first instances of direct, commercialized crossover of black and white musical cultures, but the first dramatic commercial crossover of black music into the cultural mainstream didn't occur until the early to mid-1960s, when Motown battled British Invasion groups for the ears and pocketbooks of popular music consumers. It's clear, however, that the black and white musical interchange in rural areas of Virginia had been an ongoing and dynamic process for many decades before my own research.

Let's return to Turner Foddrell's observation that he performs "regular old-time country music" and Joe Thompson's statement that he plays "old-time country music." Their music has strong ties with the past, comes from rural roots, and contains no mention of race or racial categorizations. More typically the term *old-time* has generally been reserved for pre-bluegrass music, quite often string-accompanied songs or instrumentals with decidedly Anglo-American roots that are performed by white musicians.

Among black American musicians born in North Carolina and Virginia late in the nineteenth century or in the first few decades of the twentieth, the concept of old-time country music is more encompassing. It includes such seemingly disparate categories as blues, string-band music, bluegrass, and sacred music performed on the following instruments or ensembles: fife-and-drum bands, guitar, fiddle, banjo, piano, organ, dulcimer, accordions, harmonica, and mouth bow. The context of these performances is equally wide-ranging: square dances, Fourth of July celebrations, school closings, country dances, and churches. Black Americans also sang ballads, ranging from the widely disseminated "John Henry" to Marvin Foddrell's "Riley and Spencer," that seem to be localized to central counties along the Virginia–North Carolina border. In short, old-time country music in Virginia and North Carolina underscores not only the complexities of black rural music that encompasses genres and instruments not typically associated with this term by scholars, fans, or the commercial record industry, but also the problems and issues related to defining musical terms in the face of racial issues.

Notes

1. See Wolfe and Lornell, *The Life and Legend of Leadbelly* for the relationship between Lead Belly and Lomax. *Traveling through the Jungle: Fife and Drum Band Music from the Deep South* (Testament Records, T-2223) includes tracks recorded by Lomax in the early 1940s as well as selections by David Evans and George Mitchell in the late 1960s.

2. The Rounder Records hundred-part series "Deep River of Song" includes one compact disc, *Virginia and the Piedmont* (Rounder Records 11661-1827-2), that bears the telling subtitle *Minstrelsy, Work Songs, and Blues*. These selections were recorded for the Library of Congress between 1934 and 1942 by, among others, Alan Lomax. The selections include six performances by banjo player Jimmie Strothers and six solo and group work songs. All of the Virginia recordings were done in or near Richmond. Because we don't know where the performers grew up or resided, it's not clear how well they represent traditions from across the entire state.

3. Both *Gandy Dancers* (dir. Barry Dornfeld and Maggie Holtzberg-Call, 1994) and an earlier, less technologically sophisticated (though no less compelling) film, *Afro-American Work Songs in a Texas Prison* (dir. Bruce Jackson et al., 1966) can be seen online at the handy site Folkstreams.net. This free site also streams films about a black medicine show entertainer, *Born for Hard Luck: Peg Leg Sam Jackson* (dir. Tom Davenport, 1976), and the Mississippi fife-and-drum band tradition, *Gravel Springs Fife and Drum* (dir. David Evans et al., 1972).

4. *North Florida Fives*, a piano anthology (Flyright Records 510), and *Goin' Back to Tifton*, a collection of guitar and harmonica players (Flyright Records 509), were

issued in England in 1974. The articles appeared in 1973 and 1974: Lornell, "Albany Blues: Part One"; Lornell, "Albany Blues: Part Two"; Lornell, "Albany Blues: Part Three."

5. *Guitar Shorty: Alone in His Field* (Trix Records CD-3306); *Carolina Country Blues* (Flyright Records 505).

6. Lornell, *Happy in the Service of the Lord*; Lornell and Stephenson, *The Beat*.

7. Lornell, "A Study of The Sociological Reasons Why Blacks Sing Blues"; Lornell, "Pre-Blues Black Music"; *Ain't Gonna Rain No More: Blues and Pre-Blues from Piedmont North Carolina* (Rounder Records 2016); Lornell, "Banjos and Blues."

8. Marvin and Turner Foddrell interview by Kip Lornell, Nov. 18, 1976, digital recording, "bluegrass, and father Posey (talking)," Digital Library of Appalachia, http://www.aca-dla.org/cdm4/item_viewer.php?CISOROOT=/Ferrum43&CISO PTR=1135&CISOBOX=1&REC=8.

9. Marvin and Turner Foddrell interview by Kip Lornell.

10. This research is summarized in Lornell, "Non-Blues Secular Black Music in Virginia."

11. James Pilson interview by Kip Lornell, n.d. (ca. 1970–79), digital recording, "family, fife and drum band, WWI (talking)," Digital Library of Appalachia, http:// www.aca-dla.org/cdm4/item_viewer.php?CISOROOT=/Ferrum43&CISOPTR= 2844&CISOBOX=1&REC=2.

12. *Non-Blues Secular Black Music* (Blue Ridge Institute BRI-001).

13. For more about these and other related black banjo musicians, please refer to *Black Banjo Songsters of North Carolina and Virginia* (Smithsonian Folkways SFW 40079, 1998), which was carefully compiled and annotated by Cece Conway and Scott Odell.

7

"The South's Gonna Do It Again"

CHANGING CONCEPTIONS OF THE USE
OF "COUNTRY" MUSIC IN THE ALBUMS OF AL GREEN
Michael Awkward

In a review that appeared in *Rolling Stone*, the renowned music critic Greil
Marcus boldly asserts — prophetically, it turns out — that Al Green's 1978 *The
Belle Album*, the self-produced, "completely idiosyncratic," religious-themed
album that he released after his split with his mentor and longtime producer,
Willie Mitchell, might "someday" be considered his "best" LP.[1] For some
readers, such a claim must have seemed preposterous, given the fact that
the smooth, subtly delivered albums from his early 1970s heyday such as
Let's Stay Together, I'm Still in Love with You, and *Call Me* are chock-full of
his quintessential hits and definitive tracks such as the title songs "Love and
Happiness," "How Can You Mend a Broken Heart," "You Ought to Be with
Me," and "Here I Am (Come and Take Me)." Interestingly, beyond its primary emphasis on spiritual as opposed to romantic matters, what distinguishes *The Belle Album* in the estimation of both Marcus and Jody Rosen,
who reviewed its 2006 expanded edition for *Blender*, is its rump-shaking beat,
its "earthier, countrified soul sound, spiced with dashes of funk, rhythm, and
Green's own noodling lead guitar." These funky beats and uses of "countrified soul" constitute a "sonic departure" for a singer whose most popular
music is renowned for its light but insistent rhythms and cultivated smooth-
ness.[2]

For R&B enthusiasts and, indeed, for virtually all commentators on Green's
career, well informed or not, "Belle," the centerpiece of this acclaimed
album, constitutes an overtly autobiographical statement of the resolution

of the singer's lengthy struggles to forge a peaceful coexistence between his fleshly secular urgings and grace-conferring divine compulsions. In his surprisingly revelatory autobiography, *Take Me to the River*, the R&B singer and soul-stirring minister proclaims, in words that resonate in fruitful ways with the sentiments of this oft-referenced song, that "God has promised that, one day, He will do for Al Green what Al Green can't do for himself: heal the divided soul and make him whole."[3] Green observers encourage other listeners to recognize such proclamations about the challenges of negotiating the sacred/secular divide on Green's part as central to an understanding of his life and especially of his artistic output. Certainly that perspective helps to explain, for many such observers, his often tortured and highly public movement between R&B and gospel music and hence between the highs and lows of romantic and religious love. According to Green, the internal tension that helped to shape the contours of his own recording career has generally defined—as well as artistically inspired—"black people in America," whom he describes as "always . . . torn between walking with Jesus and wandering in the world, clear back to the times of slavery when we either cried out in captivity by singing the blues or held out for a better hope by singing spirituals." This "struggle," in Green's estimation, "is part of what makes us great as a people . . . and . . . makes our music so powerful."[4] Such a perspective is clearly referenced in the much-cited lines of "Belle," where the persona, seen by commentators as expressing the compulsions of the singer himself, tells a breathtakingly beautiful temptress that in order to be with her, sexually and otherwise, he'd have to leave the Lord, with whom he has been "friends for a mighty long time." Despite his intense attraction to Belle, then, this choice is one that he is unwilling to make because, Green sings, while "it's you that I want . . . , it's Him that I need."

I am not interested in using this occasion to challenge the insistent emphasis of commentators who, in my view, in striving to apply this sentiment to his entire body of work, overemphasize manifestations of the struggle between the flesh and the spirit in Green's music. Instead I want to linger for the length of this essay on another concern expressed in this song, one whose sonic manifestations both Marcus and Rosen recognize and which it shares with "Georgia Boy," another track on *The Belle Album*: its regional specificity. Twice in "Belle" the persona situates himself as a son of the South, a form of self-identification that represents a crucial but underexamined aspect of Green's musical self-fashioning. If we are attentive to this concern with regional identity, we would be better able to understand, among other things, the implications of his fruitful earlier forays into the country music songbook in "I'm So Lonesome I Could Cry" and "Funny How Time Slips Away," widely admired covers of songs by Hank Williams and Willie Nelson, respectively, two of the genre's songwriting stalwarts. Further, we would be in a better position to consider the "earthier, countrified soul sound" that *The Belle Album* offers as a potentially fruitful new musical direction for a talented — and, following his massive commercial success, deeply spiritually and emotionally troubled — R&B performer who had been deemed "the Last of the Great Soul Men." That designation served as a response to the fact that, following the success of a pop-oriented, Detroit-based Motown, the death of soul's gruff-voiced standard-bearer Otis Redding, and the startling demise of Redding's label, the Memphis-based, comparatively roots-oriented Stax, R&B music had begun largely to abandon its southern origins and, as a consequence, its gospel-inspired vocal emphasis on gut-wrenching emotionality.

If it is widely asserted by music critics that soul, in contrast to the pop-oriented R&B represented by Motown, is a more culturally authentic expression of black expressive culture — a formulation with which I have taken issue elsewhere — following his major success on the pop and R&B charts that ended, for all intents and purposes, with the 1974 release, *Al Green Expands Your Mind*, in this final foray into pop music before he abandons it for the world of gospel in the 1980s, Green positions himself most firmly at the sacred/secular divide by calling attention to his own deeply rooted "country" dimensions. At the very least, then, Green's dramatic movement away from Willie Mitchell's "formula" in the self-produced *Belle Album* marks an important stage in his quest for divinely inspired personal "whole[ness]" and an essential product of his achievement of his goal of artistic synthesis. Just as his covers of essential country music songs helped to illuminate the vulnerable persona that enabled his meteoric rise in the early 1970s, his references to the dynamics of "country" and its cultural specificities signaled a "new" approach that allowed him to utilize the entirety of his vocal range, both his mannish brashness and his "feminine" vulnerability, as well as seemingly incommensurable elements of the national cultural landscape — North and South and its still vital musical products, including country, urbane R&B, and a still gritty soul — to reflect the depth and breadth of his place as a spiritually grounded, wildly successful black male singer in the post–civil rights period.

According to Peter Guralnick, like country music, "soul music is Southern by definition if not by actual geography. Like the blues, jazz, and rock 'n' roll, both its birth and inspiration stem from the South," and it reflects "a regional philosophy" combining—and inspired by—the "rapid social upheaval" engendered by the southern-based civil rights movement. This movement, which sought to end the "turmoil" of a "tangled racial history," eventuated in and as a sonic expression of "the Southern dream of freedom."[5] For Guralnick, who comes eventually to embrace Atlantic Records executive and R&B producer Jerry Wexler's view of soul as "just a stage of the music" grouped under the rubric of "rhythm and blues," soul is not "a music of uninhibited emotional release—though at times it comes close"—but a genre "that keeps hinting at a conclusion, keeps straining at the boundaries—of melody and convention—that it has imposed upon itself."[6] In that respect, he asserts, it can "be differentiated . . . from the cultural refinements of Motown which, with equal claim to inspiration from the church, rarely uncorks a full-blooded scream, generally establishes the tension without ever really letting go, and only occasionally will reveal a flash of raw emotion."[7]

If Guralnick is correct that "it is feeling in the end that we are hearing when we listen to soul music, it is feeling that gets the music rocking with that steady beat," one point we might usefully consider in this context is Willie Mitchell's insistence that Green's expressions of "full-blooded" "feeling" must be muted, tamed, and all but eliminated if he is ever to achieve his artistic and commercial potential.[8] Mitchell's comments to Guralnick about this matter are particularly telling:

> Well, you see, after we had done "Tired of Being Alone" and "I Can't Get Next to You," I said, "Al, look, we got to soften you up some." I said, "You got to whisper. You got to cut the lighter music. The melody has to be good. You got to sing it soft. If we can get the dynamic bottom on it and make some sense with pretty changes, then we going to be there." He said, "Man, I can't sing that way. That's too soft. That ain't gonna sound like no man singing." We had the damnedest fights, but I think "Let's Stay Together" really sold him that I had the right direction for him musically, 'cause, see, all the things I told him turned out to be true [Green becoming a major artist in eighteen months]. So we softened and softened and softened.[9]

Softening his protégé's sound, unmanning him, in the singer's own estimation, eventuated in astronomical mainstream success following the release of "Let's Stay Together." But it is precisely that sound, and the predominantly heartbroken romantic sentiments that it is used to present (sounds and sentiments that, according to Green, might best be described as womanish), against which he appears to revolt in The Belle Album. At the very least, it is accurate to say that he rejects the style that Mitchell imposed upon him in favor of a form of expression that Marcus considers a "sonic departure." In truth, however, what Green does in *The Belle Album* is to stage a return to the sort of "man-and-a-half" mode he employed prior to coming under the producer's influence and in the more husky-voiced singing that distinguishes the songs that Mitchell cites (the funky mid-tempo cover of a Temptations rollicking classic and Green's first self-penned hit) from the "soft . . . whispers" that characterize many of his hits including and following "Let's Stay Together." Without going so far as to suggest that this self-produced album (on which none of Hi Record's regular stable of musicians appears) represents Green's wholesale rejection of his former producer's "direction," it is indisputable that, in pursuing a more danceable beat and "earthier, countrified soul sound, spiced with dashes of funk [and] rhythm," Green abandons the stylistic accommodations he'd made in pursuit of a Motown-size (and -style) mass audience. He chooses instead to pursue a roots musical orientation that would appeal to a much smaller, perhaps, and certainly, by its own estimation, a more black musical purist fan base that loudly proclaimed its preference for Stax's grittier, southern-based sound. Interestingly, in his pursuit of a "new," more fully expressive "sound" following his major successes on the pop and R&B charts that ended in 1974, Green calls attention to his own deeply rooted "country" dimensions (fig. 7.1).

In his efforts to convince the enticing Belle — and perhaps his own wavering will in the face of lush temptation — of the depth of his religious convictions, Green's persona characterizes himself as a simple "little country boy" whose worldly endeavors led him "through many drunken country bars" during a boozy, sinful life from which the Lord eventually "brought me safe." Having been saved from the shame of "drunken" degradation, he is born again in Christ and unwilling, as a consequence of his lengthy immersion in His grace, to follow Belle in pursuit of lustful earthly pleasures neither endorsed by nor undertaken in the spirit of the Lord. Instead of giving into the sort of base desires for sexual fulfillment outside of marriage that characterize the relationship between men and women in earlier songs like "Here I Am (Come and Take Me)," where he speaks, with no more than a dash of subtlety, of "a burning deep down inside," the persona of "Belle" luxuriates — sonically, lyrically, and otherwise — in the felt glories of his relationship to the Lord, whom he characterizes as "my bright morning star" and "my everything . . . in the morning / in the evening / in the daytime / [and] in the nighttime." So if this song serves as a graphic instantiation of the battle between the demands of the spirit and the flesh which Green has waged,

FIGURE 7.1. Posed at the edge of a wooded field, in this 1978 promotional photo Al Green highlights his "country" dimensions. Ebet Roberts / Getty Images. Courtesy of Getty Images.

it positions that battle as one between a "little country boy" and a big, bad something that Belle—along with alcohol, sin, and the city—represents.

These references can be illuminated in the context of Green's discussions in his autobiography of his artistic origins and stylistic influences and of his sense of God's intentions as they relate to the sounds that emanate both from nature and, as important, from a confrontation between nature and man-made objects. According to Green, he was most deeply inspired as a child not by singers such as "Elvis or Otis, Jackie Wilson or Wilson Pickett," but by the experience of "just walking alone by myself down a country road, singing a song with no words," and by the experience of "wak[ing] up early to the birds singing in the trees," which led him to "throw open the window just to catch their whistles and chirps." Artistically his "earliest influences," he tells us, were "the rain on the window, the wind in the corn crop, or the water lapping on the banks of the river," all of which he experienced as the voice of "God speak[ing] through His creation and the language he uses is music to those with ears to hear."[10]

Insisting that this musical language is deeply southern, he speaks of being "cut off from the glory of the natural world . . . , [and] feeling . . . forlorn and lonely" when his family moves from rural Arkansas — enlivened by "the warm caressing wind blowing up from the Gulf of Mexico" — to an infinitely more industrial Grand Rapids, Michigan, during his sharecropper father's futile search for better-paying work. For Green, then, the South, his nostalgically referenced birthplace, represents not the site of slavery, Jim Crow, and whipped, chained, charred, lynched, and everlastingly oppressed black male bodies, or, perhaps more accurately, *not simply* the location of those bloody, traumatic racial interactions. Instead, given his extensive discussion of his family's status as impoverished sharecroppers and his passing reference to black American oppression in its fecund lands, Green represents the South primarily as an unparalleled site of musical inspiration.

Hence he emphasizes his sense of pride in his "country" status, characterizing the South as a site and a source of divinely inspired, incomparable sounds unavailable in the North as well as of protection from the addictive lure of comely women and mind-altering substances that pollute "country bars." So when he introduces, in "Georgia Boy," the subject of regional conflict in comments clearly targeted at other fellow southerners who fear that his persona has lost sight of his roots and hence the sense of regional loyalty implied in the prideful claim of being "from the country" ("Just because I'm thinking about New York City / Just 'cause I am, don't mean I ain't thinking about Georgia too"), we might see it as the attempt of a fortunate son of the South to introduce another thematically animating dichotomy into his work — alongside the aforementioned sacred/secular divide and, I would add, stereotypically male (hard) and female (soft) vocal styles — that he feels he has adequately resolved with the apparent resolution of his quest for "whole[ness]." Indeed being able to think about, and to resolve to hold dear, both the Big Apple and the Peach State releases Green's music from a smooth veneer imposed upon it by Mitchell — to my own and countless other listeners' everlasting debt — a smooth style of vocalizing from which he felt initially estranged and by which he ultimately came to feel unmanned and entrapped, sonically and thematically. Mitchell's inventive notions of Green's characteristic sound — "silky on top. Rough on the bottom. Jazz vocal style with those mellow chords and progressions laid lightly over a sandpaper-and-grits R & B rhythm section" — placed the singer's persona in a state of perpetual vulnerability against which an older, wiser, and more fully self-aware (and self-confident) Green appears stylistically to chafe.[11] By the time *The Belle Album* was released, "the Last Great Soul Singer" had ascended and tumbled painfully down the mountain of top-40 success, had mastered and grown disenchanted with Mitchell's formula, which had helped to make him a superstar and which Green himself describes as a "smooth" style of singing that reflected

> something more private and personal, something I was almost afraid to let another person hear. It was a soft, tender, vulnerable side of myself that could only express itself through singing, like a little boy crying out for his mama or a grown man weak for the love of a woman. To sing like that, you've got to let something inside of you loose, give up your pride and power, and let that surrendering feeling well up inside until it overwhelms you and uses your voice to cry out with a need that can't be filled.[12]

If Green's "star story" revolved around his successful projection of "soft," boyish, heartbroken "vulnerability," if, in other words, the mass appeal of songs like "I'm Still In Love with You," "Call Me," and "How Can You Mend a Broken Heart" was tied specifically to his projection of a state of forlornness, irresolution, and weakness that typically is associated with his struggle to accommodate himself successfully to what are often competing earthly and divine compulsions, the "something new" promised in the liner notes of *The Belle Album* applies not merely to its head-bobbing, finger-popping beat or, for that matter, to its refusal to adopt romantic love as its predominant subject. Nor is its "new" direction limited to its emphasis on religious themes or to its attempt to accommodate both New York City and Georgia. What is most "new" about *The Belle Album* is Green's use of all of these seemingly disparate entities to signal his achievement of "whole[ness]": his transcendence of boyish vulnerability, his refusal to fall prey to the seductions of liquor and godless women, and his achievement, in the words of one of the album's most infectious songs, of "good" "feel[ing]" inspired by "King Jesus." Indeed the album's pervasive sense of resolution and accommodation—including and, perhaps especially, to the pleasures that derive from his "country" identity—is crucial to its delivery of the unmistakable, unambiguous sounds of deep-seated joy.

Still, even recognition of how closely the album's synthetic designs are tied to its emphasis on regional identity does not prepare us for the startling line in "Georgia Boy": "South's gonna do it again." (Georgia, of course, is not Green's homeland, but as a consequence of, among other things, its association with Martin Luther King Jr.'s freedom movement and its idyllic status in songs like Ray Charles's cover of "Georgia on My Mind" and Gladys

Knight and the Pips' "Midnight Train to Georgia," it has been positioned as the quintessential black American southern homeland.) Clearly "Georgia Boy" references the battle between country and city, South and North, Georgia and New York, that is manifested elsewhere in R&B of the 1970s in songs with such titles as the Stylistics' "Country Living," the Ebonys' "Life in the Country," the War instrumental, "City, Country, City," and the Stevie Wonder classic "Living for the City." Certainly by the end of the 1970s, when *The Belle Album* appeared, urban blight and the disenchantment caused by widespread perceptions that the lofty promises of the Great Society had gone largely unfulfilled had led black Americans to begin to reassess the nature of their investment—imaginative, financial, and otherwise—in the hustle and bustle of urban landscapes whose economic infrastructures had begun noticeably to erode. But despite his attraction to the bright lights of the City, Green's persona remains as tied to and defined by his status as a "Georgia boy" as his counterpart in "Belle" is by his relationship to the Lord. Given the socioeconomic, political, and cultural changes wrought by the actualization of what Guralnick calls the "Southern dream of freedom," if the South is to "do it again" in the late 1970s, if it is to position itself as a worthy rival to New York and other northern destinations, culturally, economically, or otherwise, for the first time in its storied history it will have to allow its black American citizens full access to and participation in its material, psychic, and spiritual glories.

Struggling to make sense of this utterly nostalgic formulation which, at the very least, ignores the fundamental relationship between black oppression and the "Old South," Greil Marcus speaks of this declaration as "a statement of quiet pride" after "a seven minute slow walk through the piney woods," which, "perhaps in spite of itself, sounds like a warning."[13] However, despite the self-consciousness that distinguishes Marcus's attempt to come to terms with that "doing"—marked, during the recently ended, largely southern-based civil rights movement, by efforts to preserve its long-standing reduction of black people to a second-class citizenship at best—there is nothing I can hear or see that would justify this claim that the song strikes a note of caution. Indeed Green expresses what perhaps can only be experienced as a rather myopic sense of regional pride, albeit one that is consonant with the startling return by black Americans to the Deep South and the impulse to continue to see it as a cultural home in the United States. Green's southernness, the aural signals of deep "country" roots that distinguish his vocal style from those of his Motown and Philadelphia International counterparts in the estimation of many critics, is tied specifically to his heretofore understated expression of pain and suffering. That much-maligned region's forecasted "rise," its reemergence as a site of national power and cultural prestige, has been the subject of extensive academic and journalistic conversations and is confirmed, at the very least, in our electoral presidential politics since the mid-1970s and the continued implementation of Richard Nixon's cynical "southern strategy." It is no accident that, since 1980 and prior to the 2008 election, it has overwhelmingly been sons of the South (Carter and Clinton) or those who have proudly assumed many of its iconic symbols (a spry, smiling, still-rugged Reagan sitting atop a horse wearing what is indistinguishably cowboy attire—hat, shirt, and boots; George W. Bush riding fences on the Crawford, Texas, ranch he purchased just before running for president and sold just after his term ended) who have graced (or disgraced) the Oval Office.

Such perspectives help us to understand not merely the sonic thrust of *The Belle Album* or these otherwise easily dismissed lyrical references to "country" roads, bars, and identity, but the full implication of his earlier engagement of the material of white country artists such as Willie Nelson and Hank Williams. If, as a recent study of black masculinity and the South asserts, it is fruitful to consider "the role of geography in constituting difference and otherness within the category of African American . . . men," white supremacists whose views reflected—and came to determine—that region's racial politics constructed a powerful "myth that cast [black] men as sexually pathological, hyperbolized their phallic power, and construed them as inherently lustful and primitive" because of "the growing panic about racial intermixture . . . that emerged after slavery ended."[14] In the estimation of white traditionalists before, during, and after the successful pursuit of the "Southern dream of freedom," essential to the "ris[ing]" South's resurgence is the containment of a "pathological" black masculinity, a sentiment that seems to motivate the recent rash of overzealous prosecutions of black high school boys for having sex with slightly younger white female peers.

Interestingly, the key to Green's mainstream success, by his own account, was his willingness to recalibrate his performance of masculinity so that, rather than project himself as a brash upstart "full of [his] mannish ways," he exposed "a soft, tender, vulnerable side of [him]self" that sounded "like a little boy crying out for his mama or a grown man weak for the love of a woman" because of being tormented by "a need that can't be filled."[15] If, following the suggestions implicit in Guralnick's formulations—if not actualized in his discussions of the songs produced by movers and shakers of southern soul—we consider Green's stylistic choices and changes in the context, for example, of white supremacist theories of black southern masculinity that characterized it as an uncontrollable ("primitive") force that needed to be altogether neutralized, neutered, and otherwise contained, Green's career-propelling performance of boyish masculinity whose primary subject is unrequited love marks his as an especially palatable form of black masculinity. Utilizing that "formula," as he calls Mitchell's mixture of smooth vocals and gritty instrumental accompaniment, Green affected a style through which, in his use of vehicles he both covered and helped to create, he essayed a seductive, incomparable suite of soul music animated by (black) male vulnerability.

Using that formulation of the pains of desertion and heightened fear of soul-shattering loss in two albums produced in 1972, for example, Green reworked three country music classics into apt templates for his popular personae. The first of these covers, a remake of Kris Kristofferson's "For the Good Times" on *I'm Still in Love with You*, features lyrical, vocally lush efforts to indulge in the sweetness of breakup sex. In it, Green's persona attempts to convince his former partner that despite their pain over the dissolution of their relationship, "this world [will] keep . . . on turning" and that, instead of wallowing in sorrow, they should "be glad that we had this time together." Insistent on communicating the urgency of his persona to get a former mate to "make believe you love me one more time," Green's voice luxuriates in turning what I have identified as a key image he used in his autobiography to signal "God speak[ing] through His creation"—"the rain on the window" or, in Kristofferson's more poetic turn of phrase, "the whisper of the raindrops / falling softly against my windowpane"—to compel her compliance. And even if the song can be read as an attempt at seduction by an insincere cad, the patient, "soft," "vulnerable," and, to reference the title of another of the album's tracks, "simply beautiful" tones of Green's voice suggest that his persona too needs reassurance that he will be able to survive their breakup.

Similarly compelled by the desire to articulate male resolution in the face of romantic heartbreak, Green covers Willie Nelson's "Funny How Time Slips Away" on *Call Me* by utilizing (or, as some might term it, wallowing in) the slow, luxuriant style that marks his covers of songs of romantic breakup like "For the Good Times" and the Bee Gees' "How Can You Mend a Broken Heart." In this case, however, instead of using his vulnerable style to communicate heartbrokenness or hopefulness at the mutual ending of what has been a largely fulfilling love, Green's softened, whispering tenor is stretched to express his persona's desire for cosmic revenge: "remember what I told you in time you're gonna pay." However, his singing style, intended to communicate boyish vulnerability, also expresses both his persona's lingering pain in the face of desertion and a more fresh hurt because he has been told that his former mate has so successfully gotten over him that she has repeated to her "new love" the promise she'd made to him—and on which he had relied—that she would "love him till the end of time." Unlike the aforementioned covers, the album's widely recognized "country" companion to Nelson's much-recorded song, Green's haunting rendition of Hank Williams's "I'm So Lonesome I Could Cry" wallows in unmistakable self-pity from which not even sounds of "God speaking through His creation"—a "blue," "lonesome," "whippoorwill," a "weep[ing]" robin, "the silence of a falling star," a "midnight train grinding low"—can release him.

To reference again formulations Green offers in *Take Me to the River*: the singer uses these early covers of country songs to exemplify the "soft" masculinity he was compelled to perform by Mitchell in order to achieve mainstream success and to suggest the contours of his "star story": "soft, tender, vulnerab[ility] . . . , like a little boy crying out for his mama or a grown man weak for the love of a woman," a boy who has "let that surrendering feeling well up inside until it overwhelms you and uses your voice to cry out with a need that can't be filled."[16] Having abandoned that musical self by the time he goes into the studio to record *The Belle Album* and attempting to pursue a "new direction" that is marked not by unending vulnerability but by psychic, spiritual, and philosophical "whole[ness]," maturity, and synthesis, Green references "country" and its store of meanings for vastly different reasons. His persona does not merely signal romance-inspired forlornness or, for that matter, the baleful historical mistreatment of black Americans that served to define the South and to compel socially, economically, and politically circumscribed black men like Green's father—and Green's persona in "Belle"—to frequent "country bars" in order to dull their attendant pains. Instead the "country," in this critically acclaimed late-1970s album, constitutes a region of hope, a space where disparate aspects of the self—and, by extension, historically divided peoples whose cultures and bloody interactions have come to define the region—can come together productively. For Green, then, if we avoid the pitfalls such as those presented by the lush titular character of the album's centerpiece, the "country" has come to be recognized as a site of "good" long-lasting "joy" and thoroughly satisfying "feel[ing]."

Notes

1. Greil Marcus, "The Belle Album," *Rolling Stone*, Feb. 23, 1978, http://www.rollingstone.com/music/albumreviews/the-belle-album-19780223.

2. Jody Rosen, review of "*The Belle Album (Expanded Edition)*," *Blender*, http://www.blender.com/guide/reissue/53940/belle-album-expanded-edition.html.

3. Green and Seay, *Take Me to the River*, 8.

4. Green and Seay, *Take Me to the River*, 6.

5. Gurnalick, *Sweet Soul Music*, 6–7.

6. Gurnalick, *Sweet Soul Music*, 4, 7.

7. Gurnalick, *Sweet Soul Music*, 7.

8. Gurnalick, *Sweet Soul Music*, 15.

9. Gurnalick, *Sweet Soul Music*, 306.

10. Green and Seay, *Take Me to the River*, 13, 11–12.

11. Green and Seay, *Take Me to the River*, 239.

12. Green and Seay, *Take Me to the River*, 240.

13. Marcus, "The Belle Album."

14. Richardson, *Black Masculinity and the U. S. South*, 4.

15. Green and Seay, *Take Me to the River*, 240.

16. Green and Seay, *Take Me to the River*, 240.

Dancing the Habanera Beats
(in Country Music)

THE CREOLE-COUNTRY TWO-STEP

IN ST. LUCIA AND ITS DIASPORA

Jerry Wever

Shortly after I first arrived in St. Lucia, a former St. Lucian parliamentarian told me this popular joke about how much St. Lucians love country music: "The French police—when they wanted to catch up with the St. Lucians in Martinique who were illegal—you know what they do? Just put up a country dance—a country music dance—and you just catch everybody who is illegal."[1] Despite the fact that St. Lucians are predominantly Afro-Caribbean, the joke was referring to American country music. This essay examines the creolization of American country and western music in St. Lucian society and its diaspora and considers the silences such a phenomenon exposes in black country and country music more generally in the United States. Its inclusion in this volume is a strategic inversion of focus that serves to frame black country music in a more global and African diasporic context. Such deepening and broadening of perspective allows a more comprehensive and powerful exposition of those silences and brings into greater relief the associated stakes as they are arrayed in the nation-building and decolonization processes of a young postcolonial society.

Although the parameters designated by the title of this book would not preclude examining black country music in other parts of the African diaspora, all other chapters focus on primarily U.S. cases and involve a specifically U.S. framing of "race" issues.[2] Even if I were not expanding my discussion to include St. Lucia's diaspora in Brooklyn, New York, the material I present on the St. Lucian country music scene alone is important to more fully contextualize American black country music and the elisions it exposes. The casting of C&W as a white musical form in the United States has made it more difficult for St. Lucians to understand the appeal of C&W for black Caribbean people. Because country is cast as "white" in the United States, its African diasporic roots have been underacknowledged, so that speaking to matters of blackness seems ironic, when in fact a full discussion of country music's simultaneous role in the creation of whiteness in the United States and in compounding identity discussions of blackness and creoleness in St. Lucia is clearly overdue. Moreover, by exporting black C&W singers to Nashville and New York City, St. Lucians are helping to expose the underacknowledged African diasporic roots of American C&W.

With considerable genius, St. Lucians have creolized American country and western dancing much as they creolized European country and court dances in earlier centuries: by Africanizing it. In this instance, however, the music was already more creole than is customarily admitted. And rather than participating in what might otherwise be simplistically read as a case of homogenizing cultural imperialism, St. Lucians make American country and western their own by curating songs with a particular Caribbean resonance, creolizing the dance on habanera beats, and syncretizing it with marginalized St. Lucian folk practices. St. Lucians have claimed C&W as their own, highlighting its underacknowledged but already creole ingredients, merging it with their own Afro-Creole folk forms, and transforming it into a music of black social experience. Nonetheless its popularity has been a thorny challenge for postcolonial identity in such a newly independent, progressive, predominantly black nation.

American C&W has been part of the St. Lucian soundscape since the early 1940s, that is, from an early period in the music's commercial dissemination in North America, when it was still known as hillbilly music. Particularly popular still, to the point of standardization, is a repertoire of classics from the honky-tonk era, curated for its suitability for St. Lucia's unique creolized dance style or for the storytelling in the songs, and oftentimes for both. Newer songs by new traditionalists have been folded into the repertoire. St. Lucians call the music *mizik manmay lakai* (home-children music) or *wèstun* in French Creole (Kwéyòl), and most often just *western* in English.[3]

St. Lucians dance the habanera beats in C&W and other music and curate accordingly for songs foregrounding those beats, be it C&W, 1950s R&B, lover's rock, or dance hall. The beat known as the habanera is a key part of what could be called the Afro-Caribbean creole rhythmic substratum. New

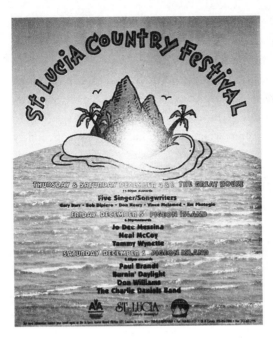

FIGURE 8.1.
St. Lucia's famous Pitons become the ridges of a cowboy hat to advertise the first St. Lucia Country Festival in the late 1990s. Photo by Jerry Wever.

research identifies the habanera with a particular Kongo rhythm whose influences flow from the Kongo through much of the Americas. The Kongo *ngoma* drum rhythm known in Bakongo as "the call to the dance" (*mbila a makinu*) emerged in Cuban *contradanzas* during Haiti's Revolution and was called *habanera* by Spaniards and the "call of the blood" by W. C. Handy.[4] St. Lucians in effect dowse for the habanera beat in American C&W through an intricate network of intercommunity anniversary dances sponsored by typically women-led mutual aid and public service organizations called mothers and fathers groups.

Strangely enough, by curating for the habanera beat, modifying the two-step to reflect that beat and traditional *kwadril* dances, and by establishing the dance as the focal point in predominant Caribbean social traditions, St. Lucians have followed a goal of the work undertaken by the St. Lucia Folk Research Centre (FRC): "To choose from outside without rejecting what is inside."[5] Indeed, although the FRC came under pressure for allowing community process to help define what is creole when that resulted in country and western dances, trust in that process (as opposed to more essentialist top-down preemptive cultural engineering) allowed for the community to assert its very profound creolizations into the identity discussions and creole celebrations.

Popular St. Lucian festivals proudly claim country as a creole form (fig. 8.1), an assertion that carries implications in both St. Lucia and the United States. In both places, recognition of country as a creole form challenges essentialist notions and unveils the complexities of race in a globalized world.

Ethnographic Background
ISLAND BACKGROUND

This study is based on a year and a half of research in St. Lucia over the course of four years, split evenly between rural and urban areas.[6] St. Lucia is part of the Windward Island chain of the Eastern Caribbean and is neighbored by Martinique to the north, St. Vincent to the south, and Barbados to the east. Like most Caribbean islands St. Lucia was colonized by European planters who increasingly relied upon enslaved Africans for labor; these were colonies of exploitation, not settlement.[7] St. Lucia is considered a second-phase sugar island for France and Britain. Long fought over by those two nations, St. Lucia eventually came under long-term British rule beginning in the early 1800s and won independence in 1979. Although St. Lucia is famed for having changed hands between the British and French fourteen times, the reality is that the European influence remained predominantly French in essence for much of the formative colonial era and even far into the remainder of the colonial period, hence the French creole mother tongue and the Africanized French music and dance forms.[8] Sugar was the dominant export crop throughout most of the colonial period, and bananas were the main engine for decolonization. Tourism overtook bananas as the leading source of income at the close of the millennium. The United Workers' Party, in 2006 unseating the St. Lucia Labor Party, which had ruled since 1997, has dominated since the early years of decolonization (1964). There are large St. Lucian diasporic populations in the United Kingdom, United States and Canada, especially in London, Brooklyn, Toronto, Ottawa, Hartford, Boston, Miami, and Washington, D.C.[9]

People of African, Amerindian, English, French, Southeast Asian, and Middle Eastern descent have mixed over the generations to form St. Lucia's creole population.[10] Since Amerindian autonomy ended, there has been a majority of African descent. Early on, enslaved Africans were brought to St. Lucia by French planters from adjacent Martinique. According to a study conducted in the mid-1980s, more than 90 percent of St. Lucia's population of 160,000 are of African descent. Of the remaining population, 5.5 percent are said to be "mixed"; East Indians make up 3.2 percent and Europeans 0.8 percent.[11] All St. Lucians could be said to be creole, but when a St. Lucian is referred to as being "a real creole," it is usually an attempt to mark predominant African descent and the many traditions of the Afro–St. Lucian population.[12] St. Lucia is bilingual at minimum.[13] French Creole (Kwéyòl) is the native language; English was the colonial language and continues to be the main official language.[14]

During colonial times, the Kwéyòl language and lifeways were significantly denigrated, and the stigmas have survived long after independence. Having been stigmatized for so long, creole identity is an emotionally charged issue. The creation of the Jounen Kwéyòl (Creole Day) festival has given rise to the kinds of discourse that raise consciousness about St. Lucia's creole heritage and bilingual reality. This has been an important development for St. Lucians whose first language is Kwéyòl.[15] The festival was established by the Folk Research Centre, founded in 1973 to be the caretaker of St. Lucia's cultural heritage, and other St. Lucian NGOs.[16]

I first studied country and western music in St. Lucia as one of many problems of cultural decolonization, learning about it through debates that came up during the 1997 Jounen Kwéyòl regarding its place in St. Lucian creole culture. Headlines featured questions directed at the Folk Research Centre, imploring, "Is country and western music truly a part of our creole heritage?" and "Since when did country music become part of our culture?"[17]

Wanting my research to be maximally relevant to St. Lucia, at the start of my full year there I asked the current director of the Folk Research Centre which avenues of research would be most beneficial for me to pursue. The FRC requested that I research country and western music: why it has become so dominant, exactly how and when it came into St. Lucian culture, and why it succeeded so well. (There was also a tacit question of what to do about it in terms of decolonizing.) Thus this study is an addition to research the Folk Research Centre had initiated, cooperatively undertaken, or commissioned. Since on the surface it involves modern creole tastes as opposed to the direct renewal or reclamation of deeply historical St. Lucian cultural forms, it has generally fallen outside the parameters of research given first priority by St. Lucian cultural institutions.[18]

COUNTRY AND WESTERN MUSIC IN ST. LUCIA

St. Lucians have a Caribbean-wide and increasingly worldwide reputation for their predilection for American country and western music. Music from the United States has had an impact in St. Lucia since World War II, when a U.S. military base was established there.[19] As early as 1942 the U.S. Armed Forces Radio Service (AFRS) began spreading country and western far and wide, although I was not able to uncover any instances of people tuning in before the 1950s.[20] One informant attributed the spread of C&W in the 1950s not to AFRS but to "early morning radio broadcasts from powerful stations in cities such as Cincinnati, or those in the American South. It was a rural thing right from the start. Rural people would be up early, at 5 a.m., listening as they worked or were getting ready for work."[21] Another suggested that the similarity between the violin in the St. Lucian string bands and the fiddle of country and western helped make the music popular among rural dwellers.[22] Labor migration to the United States and Canada augmented this interest. According to Michael Gaspard, C&W "was further popularized in the '70s by St. Lucian migrant workers who grew to love it in Florida where they had gone to cut cane, and then returned to St. Lucia with a zeal for it."[23]

Soul and country and western were often played by St. Lucian deejays throughout the 1970s.[24] In her book on zouk music, Jocelyne Guilbault noted St. Lucia's affection for country and western in 1993:

> Country and western is extremely popular with the rural population, who consider it equivalent to a slowdance and even categorize it as traditional music. Both country and western and soul are considered to be the best music channels for expressing emotions and represent just about the only genres broadcast in St. Lucia that deal with love and emotional relationships. Because of its strong appeal to a large portion of the St. Lucian population and its association with themes of love and stories about everyday people, country and western is actually used by many local religious groups. In such cases, the lyrics are changed from reflecting on love between men and women to celebrating divine love and calling for peace and harmony.[25]

In the late 1990s the popularity of C&W mushroomed, and it has spread from the country to the city. American country and western music is heard in rum shops, in public minibuses, at dances, blaring from alleys in the nation's capital and from remote rural homes, on the radio and in TV commercials.[26] Huge festivals bring top American performers, and dance competitions stretch out into almost a season. St. Lucians have curated obscure greats from classic American country and western of the late 1950s and 1960s honky-tonk era.[27] For their local repertoires, they curate songs for their suitability to St. Lucia's unique creolized dance style and for their storytelling. The songs are played over and over to the point of standardization. Fiddle- and steel-guitar-filled honky-tonk material that is good for slow dancing is much loved — especially after dark when the gut-wrenching cry breaks pierce the tropical night and people come out to fill the local mothers and fathers groups' dance halls.

In St. Lucia George Jones is king, and duets are favored.[28] The most traditional core comprises songs from the third quarter of the twentieth century. Newer performers who fit that style, such as the new traditionalists, are also popular, with some already crossing over into folksong realm. Favorites are Alan Jackson, Kitty Wells, the Louvin Brothers, the Irishman John Hogan, Jim Reeves, Dolly Parton, the St. Lucians L. M. Stone and Big Brother, Merle Haggard, the Scots Irish Isla Grant, Emmylou Harris, Jim Ed Brown and the Browns, Conway Twitty, Loretta Lynn, Tammy Wynette, Skeeter Davis, Connie Smith, Connie Francis, Red Sovine, Buck Owens, Porter Wagoner, Ray Price, Charley Pride, Hank Williams, Don Williams, Stonewall Jackson, Mo Bandy, the Mavericks, Johnny Cash, George Straight, Vernon Oxford, Faron Young, Bobby Bare, and Patsy Cline, and even very early groups like the Carter Family are popular.[29]

A St. Lucian country and western dance implies about a 60:40 mix of country and western to Caribbean "hot tunes" such as the latest dance hall and soca, or older dub and zouk and *kadans*, or calypso (and occasionally African *soukous* or American 1950s R&B).[30] Sets of four to six country and western songs typically alternate with sets of three to four hot tunes. The proportion of hot tunes to C&W generally increases as the night wears on, to an eventual majority.

Country and western music became firmly institutionalized through an intricate network of intercommunity anniversary dances of mothers and fathers groups, which, despite the name, are typically women-led. These groups emerged to organize communities in the early days of decolonization, in the late 1960s. Rooted in deeply creole traditions of friendly societies, Sunday picnics, and general *koudmen* (lit., "many hands," cooperative work events), the dances mark the anniversary of the group's founding and serve as a magnet to connect far-away communities who come to visit and show support for a day of fellowship. Sunday picnics have brought "the folk" together ever since the days when enslaved St. Lucians had Sundays free to visit one another; on these days, people visited other plantations and would travel great distances for a dance. Like the picnics, the anniversary dances at which C&W is played are part of a celebration that combines worship, shared meals, popular music, and dance.

There are numerous places to dance. On any Sunday night one can count on five or six mothers and fathers groups' anniversary dances, a significant number for an island of only 238 square miles. There are numerous private dance halls regularly featuring a weekly night or nights of country and western music, and always a special dance on holidays. The main market in town, symbolic of the people and exploited as such by politicians, is turned into Nashville Palace on weekends and holidays. Since the mid-1990s radio stations and commercial sponsors have held dances as promotions for upcoming shows and festivals or as a series of dance competitions.

American country and western music provides St. Lucians with a couples dance genre that has risen in popularity alongside the decline in prevalence of the dances played by the string bands of the *kwadril* (quadrille) tradition. It incorporates both a waltz idiom and a two-step repertoire for which St. Lucians have creolized a unique dance along habanera beats.[31] Partly as a result of decolonization efforts, these kwadril traditions, which are based on European court dances, have gone out of style.[32] The string bands that played the dance music have also declined. Interestingly, the country and western "oldies" still preferred by most St. Lucians are songs that remain closer to the string-band roots of American country and western music.[33] The fiddle, banjo, and guitar are common to both St. Lucian and American old-time string bands. It is thus not surprising that the most popular deejay on the island when I first arrived, DJ Hotwatts or Country Watts (his Radio 100 name), is the nephew of the most famous string-band violin player. Not unexpectedly, his sets are full of songs that feature aficionado fiddle playing that is very good to dance to. He now lives primarily in the United States and has bought old American honky-tonk jukeboxes to cull songs to fit St. Lucian tastes.

St. Lucians had already begun borrowing from North American songs before there was such a thing as country and western. First the kwadril tradition was updated with New World source material for dances, particularly for new waltzes. Between tourism, labor and other migrations, intra-Caribbean influences, late-night radio broadcasts from the United States, and the U.S. military bringing records, record players, and the AFRS, there were many possible avenues for the songs to arrive in St. Lucia directly from North America as well as from Europe (during the world wars especially).

Lagging the creolization of the dancing but already afoot is the creolization of the music itself as a form of creole storytelling. St. Lucia's Afro-Caribbean story-song dance traditions (*kont, bélé kont,* etc.) are beginning to reemerge in creolized country and western songs. In general, the storytelling (*listwa*) genre thrives in country and western. One quintessential artist whose compositions about real life and hard times exemplify the intertextuality between country and western and folk song-story traditions is Big

Brother.[34] His storytelling ties in with the Creole listwa and wake stories, utilizing the country and western gospel mode to let the stories build. Words are sung and spoken in Creole, English, and French. His repertoire resembles the song variety of a country and western dance in St. Lucia: zouk or *kadasse* with habanera, reggae, waltzes and two-steps, and duets. Another local artist, Jako, is a renowned creole storyteller and yodeling country and western singer-songwriter.

St. Lucian country and western singers of considerable talent are being exported to the United States and beyond, where they are beginning to find success. One of the most talented exports, whom many compare to George Jones, is L. M. Stone, who uses a gospel testimony and storytelling style in his gospel numbers. Stone won the award for Traditional Country Artist from the Tennessee Country Music Alliance in April 2003. The Living Legend Award—Female that year went to Kitty Wells, one of St. Lucia's beloved favorites. Fully diasporic, Stone is based in St. Lucia and Atlanta.

There is also a large overlap between calypso and country and western, particularly in the storytelling and social commentary of the lyrics. Invader, St. Lucia's most successful and most popular calypsonian for much of the decade straddling the millennium, promoted a series of country and western appearances around the island in the calypso and Carnival off-season.[35] One female calypsonian, Menell, first became famous for a country and western duet and won the Calypso Monarch award—the nation's top prize for calypsonians—at the St. Lucia Carnival in 2007 and 2011. Numerous calypsos critically comment on country and western music. Such connections between calypso, griot, and country and western are not new. Throughout the latter part of the twentieth century, the blind folksinger Coco brought an old-time calypso folk-singing style to his renditions of honky-tonk country and western tunes. He performs weekly in and around the capital during the day at the phone company and at a supermarket.[36]

In 2004 c&w was publicly acknowledged in the cultural section of the national phonebook: "The lack of radio station during the 50s caused locals with radios to tune into American airways broadcasting this music. The locals also developed a unique way of dancing to it." This phonebook explanation, though true, leaves many St. Lucian and Caribbean intellectuals hungering for a more satisfying and comprehensive explanation of the popularity of country and western music in St. Lucia. My interviews yielded relatively consistent reports from people as to why they loved the music and why they thought it was so popular: the meaningful and touching stories and everyday themes; inclusion of instruments like the *vyolon* (fiddle) and banjo, which St. Lucians love, in dance music; and the opportunity it provides for close couple dancing, which continues the style of the kwadril but with little of the colonial formality. But such assertions do not explain the underlying processes at work, nor do they satisfy intellectuals concerned about healthy postcolonial identities.

POSTCOLONIAL IDENTITY CONCERNS

St. Lucia is a predominantly black nation, newly independent, with a legacy of progressive thinkers and a coveted Folk Research Centre that trained St. Lucians in the tasks of ethnography and cultural caretaking to proactively deal with decolonization. The popularity of country and western music thus occasions much healthy critique (especially during Jounen Kwéyòl) on radio talk shows, in newspaper editorials, and in calypsos and other forms of cultural commentary.[37] In his 2001 waltz, "Country and Western Take Over," Calypsonian Smitty, through a metaphor of romantic loss, expresses his frustration at what he suggests is St. Lucians' betrayal of their cultural heritage:

> Deceit is the order
> Western take over
> No more, calypso or soca
> Year I resisted friend
> The fad I said I would end
> Her cheating turned real
> I'm headed for Nashville
> *Chorus*:
> Because Country and Western
> Take Over
> My, in a blaze how I lost her
> Right from the start
> There was her cheating heart.

As the emotional tenor of Smitty's waltz suggests, the list of criticisms leveled at country and western by St. Lucians is substantial. Many feel that its beginnings with the U.S. military base and AFRS make it an artifact of U.S. imperialist hegemony in general, and assert that its pervasiveness constitutes a form of brainwashing that amounts almost to a musical occupation. Many intellectuals have lamented that the presence of the music has grown even after independence, particularly because they see it as an em-

FIGURE 8.2.
Positioning American
country and western
music alongside St.
Lucian folk and popular
music, this album jacket
display in a local record
shop demonstrates the
integration of country into
St. Lucian creole culture.
Photo by Jerry Wever.

bodiment of whiteness and redneck racism inappropriate for a largely black nation. Critics also point to the limited St. Lucian production of country and western music (which has finally started changing) and deplore its role in distracting St. Lucians from creating their own popular music form akin to reggae or zouk. Even the genre's aesthetics attract criticism; some Rastas I interviewed claim simply that C&W is depressing music. For the most part, I heard this criticism from people who are not fans, but even some fans acknowledge the awkwardness of some of the criticism. For some intellectuals, liking the music or dance despite the criticism epitomizes the double bind of colonialism and its stubborn, ever incomplete decolonization.

Nonetheless many St. Lucians view their country and western music as a fundamentally creolized form. One of the things that led me to press on to further investigate the depth of that creolization was a shrine in a Castries record shop displaying country and western album jackets amid those of St. Lucia's own musicians (fig. 8.2). Everything in this shrine is either old honky-tonk C&W or St. Lucian folk and popular music. Most St. Lucian records are on the top and third shelf, except for a kwadril album on the fifth shelf, and the queen of St. Lucian folk, Sessenne, is at the center of the bottom shelf. The display provided a striking visual testament to the integration of country and western music into St. Lucian creole culture.

Several leading intellectuals gave early indications of the depth of this integration. The poet Kendal Hippolyte told me, "People make *kwéyòl* what it is."[38] The historian Gregor Williams similarly explained, "It is creole. The masses have accepted it."[39] Even a leading government spokesperson whose Afrocentric politics went as far as speaking on behalf of Robert Mugabe wrote an editorial that was not entirely critical of country and western music while still being critical of the North-South imbalance, of Folk Research Centre encouragement, and of involvement in Emancipation Day celebrations. All of this was evident even before I was able to transcribe the dance and isolate the habanera rhythm as the curatorial focus of St. Lucian western music in the dance halls, a breakthrough that should, if nothing else, add to the intellectual decolonization of the phenomenon.

St. Lucians Dance the Habanera Beats in C&W Music
HABANERA: THE UNITY IS SUBMARINE

The beat known as the habanera is a key part of what could be called the Afro-Caribbean creole rhythmic substratum, following Edward Kamau Brathwaite's notion of the submarine unity beneath so many different influences and histories on so many different islands.[40] It is found in many musical styles throughout the Caribbean and, by extension, the world. Ned Sublette gives an indication of habanera's ubiquity in the Caribbean and beyond:

> That four-note habanera/tango rhythm is the signature Antillean beat to this day. It's a simple figure that can generate a thousand dances all by itself, depending on what drums, registers, pitches, or tense rests you assign to which of the notes, what tempo you play it, and how much you polyrhythmicize it by laying other, compatible rhythmic figures on top of it. It's the rhythm of the aria Bizet wrote for the cigarette-rolling Carmen to sing (though he lifted the melody from Basque composer Sebastian Yradier), and it's the defining rhythm of reggaeton. You can hear it in the contemporary music of Haiti, the Dominican Republic, Jamaica, and Puerto Rico, to say nothing of the nineteenth century Cuban contradanza. It's Jelly Roll Morton's oft-cited "Spanish tinge," it's the accompaniment figure to W. C. Handy's "St. Louis Blues," and you hear it from brass bands at a second line in New Orleans today. At half speed, with timpani or a drum set, it was a signature rhythm of the Brill Building song writers, and it was the basic template of clean-studio 1980s corporate rock. You could write it as a

TABLE 8.1. Basic St. Lucian C&W Choreography

	1	2	3	4	1	2	3	4	1	2
Beats	1	2	3	4	1	2	3	4	1	2
Steps	3	Shift/turn	1	2	3	Shift/turn	1	2	3	Shift/turn
Woman	R	Shift/turn	L	R	L	Shift/turn	R	L	R	Shift/turn
Man	L	Shift/turn	R	L	R	Shift/turn	L	R	L	Shift/turn

dotted eighth, sixteenth, and two eighths. If you don't know what I'm talking about yet, it's the rhythm of the first four notes of the Dragnet theme. DOMM, DA DOM DOM.[41]

This rhythm that emerged in the Cuban contradanza during the end of the Haitian Revolution (later dubbed the habanera in Spain, as one step en route to global circulation) has been identified by Kongo scholars as the Kongo "call to the dance" (*mbila a makinu*). As Robert Farris Thompson explains in his book, *Tango*:

> In Kongo there is a bass ngoma-drum pattern identical to the bass of the habanera. Bakongo translate its pulses into syllables: *ka*, ka *ka* kan, *ka*, ka *ka* kan. These syllables are close to the ones that tangueros use when verbally notating the beat of the habanera: *da*, ka *ka* kan, *da*, ka *ka* kan. When people are not dancing, and a drummer on the bass or "mother" ngoma drum (the ancestor of the famous conga drum of Cuba) wants to generate action, he repeats this pattern—*ka*, ka *ka* kan, *ka*, ka *ka* kan—on the drum. This is the message: "Now hear this, now hear this, everyone get out there and dance!"[42]

The unique St. Lucian creolized dance step itself could be called the St. Lucian habanera country two-step, but I have called it the St. Lucian creole-country two-step, or more simply the St. Lucian creole two-step. It goes 1-2-3 shift (or turn) over four beats in 4/4 time, with the dance sequence starting at midmeasure of the music (that is, on beat 3). Table 8.1 illustrates the basic footwork. The timeline across the top and bottom marks the four quarter-note subdivisions of a 4/4 measure. Rows 2 and 3 show a full two-measure sequence of the two-step starting midmeasure, with weight on the man's left foot and the woman's right foot. The basic beat of the habanera is usually denoted in 2/4 time due to its historical origin and for ease of notation (fig. 8.3).

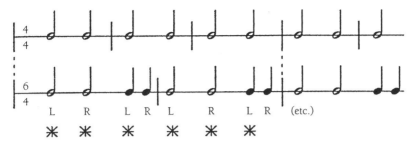

FIGURE 8.4. Metric comparison of basic two-step music and dance patterns. Reprinted from Jocelyn Neal, "The Metric Makings of a Country Hit," in *Reading Country Music*, ed. Cecelia Tichi (Durham: Duke University Press, 1998). Courtesy of Jocelyn Neal.

It is important to understand the differences between American and St. Lucian two-step dance styles not only because this volume is centered in the American country and western world but also in order to grasp the logic of the creolization of the dance in St. Lucia. Figure 8.4, from Jocelyn Neal's work on the American country and western two-step, is useful for comparing with the St. Lucian two-step. For the purposes of comparison, imagine that the two styles of dancing are occurring to the same song, say, a 1960s George Jones two-step. The top line in 4/4 is the music. The bottom dance line in 6/4 denotes the man's footwork pattern, with the asterisks marking the accents in the music. Footwork-wise, the most important differences to note are the American slow-slow-quick-quick and the St. Lucian 1-2-3 shift, or quick-quick-slow shift, which always starts midmeasure.

Table 8.3 provides a simplistic comparison of St. Lucian creole and American standard country and western two-step dance styles. Elsewhere I take up the great diversity of American two-step styles, but stick with the standard here.[47] Again, this example bases the two dance styles on the same song.

What I have described is merely a baseline for comparison. I want to be clear that in the St. Lucian creole-country two-step there is great artistry, unique flair, and other kinds of variation even when it comes to the steps, and also in other aspects, such as Africanized, stylized arm positions. Moreover I am not discussing waltzes, which are more standard in the way they are related to American country and western waltzes and to European, American, and Caribbean waltzes in general.

An important area for future research is to try to understand with greater clarity the technical details of dance creolization, especially in regard to other St. Lucian folk dance mechanics. It is likely that the St. Lucian two-

TABLE 8.3. Comparison of St. Lucian and American C&W Two-Step Dance Styles

Comparison aspect	St. Lucia creole two-step	American standard two-step
Full sequence time (beats or bars in 4/4 time)	8 (2 bars)	6 (1.5 bars)
Full sequence steps	6	4
Smallest unit	Half sequence	Full sequence
Metric unit of significance	Quarter bar	Half bar
Average pace (steps per bar)	$9/3=3$	$8/3=2^{2/3}$
Metachoreography	Independent couples, no set pattern	Progressive (circling the floor counterclockwise), promenading couples
Choreography	1-2-3-shift quick-quick-slow shift	slow-slow-quick-quick
Emphasis	Hips, upbeat fourth beat	Steps, downbeats

Note: In St. Lucia the country and western dancing emphasizes the fourth or final beat of the measure, as do many other Caribbean dance musics. The St. Lucian two-step may be picked up at the start of the measure, but such a start would be out of phase with the rest of the dance, which starts midmeasure, in part due to the habanera beat and the emphasis on the fourth beat. Revisit note 44 to see the way lyrics of loved anthems line up with this second step on the fourth beat standard. The songs curated in St. Lucia tend to have the bass frequently sounding on the fourth beat to match the second footstep. In a technical sense, the American two-step steps on the fourth beat every other bar. In St. Lucia, the fourth beat is stepped every bar. Of the beats most likely to have no bass sounding, it is beat 2, during which St. Lucians are turning or shifting.

step style evolved with little influence from the United States and instead proceeded from a love for the music and, dancing-wise, directly from skill at St. Lucian kwadril forms, including the polka box step, the execution of the other hot tune dances (*gwan won*, *faci*, etc.), the weight shift from the *lakon-met*, the elegance of the kwadril figures, and the spinning from the waltz.[48]

I have interviewed many St. Lucians about why country and western dancing is so loved and popular. Responses include its simplicity and the ease with which it is mastered; the large skill rollover from kwadril and the fact that it is an evolved form of the kwadril, contradance, and square dance types; the applicability of widespread familiarity with dancing to fiddle (vyolon) and banjo; and its status as a couples dance. St. Lucian dancers are thus intensely conscious of the creolized elements in their c&w two-stepping.

THE PEOPLE THAT LOVE C&W ARE THE PEOPLE THAT KNOW THE CULTURE

In my interview with him, House, a Brooklyn deejay, club owner, cultural activist, and kwadril group leader, said this: "The people that love country and western are the people that know the culture. We know that deep within, the culture has country music in it. . . . It's in the culture. It's in the blood. It's like something you have in the blood."[49] He is not saying that people who do not like country and western are not St. Lucian or do not know their own culture. He is talking specifically about the "folk" whose traditions are featured in Jounen Kwéyòl, whose deep creole culture is deemed worthy of reclamation in the cultural decolonization processes of the Folk Research Centre. They are the ones who really love country and western music, and they are the culture bearers; they are the ones who might be stigmatized by some for being too creole, too country, too backward. And yet the neocolonial connotations of country and western music make their commitment to race and decolonization categorically questionable. Thus a full understanding of the implications of this music for St. Lucian postcolonial identity requires us to turn to the stories in the music and the stories of whiteness in the United States.

It's about the Stories:
C&W and the Creation of U.S. Whiteness

When asked why he loved country music, Charlie Parker replied, "The stories, man. Listen to the stories."[50] One of the reasons St. Lucians have taken country and western so deeply to heart is the way the stories are danced, which continues the rich drum-dance traditions that begin with a story and end with a dance. The St. Lucian curation of music is commendable in its own right, and has earned the attention of country and western aficionados in the United States for its music quality, voice quality, instrumentation (crying steel guitars and haunting fiddles), classic sound, and themes. But outside the dance halls the curatorial focus is on the stories.

I knew when I began my research that part of the difficulty in making sense of the country and western phenomenon in St. Lucia lay in the silences regarding the genre in the United States, particularly concerning its African American and African diasporic contributions. African American contributions have helped to define the unique sound of country. For example, Cecelia Conway has shown that the banjo is an African-derived instrument. Moreover the African American blues form provided a basis for country at least from the time of Jimmie Rodgers, and the yodel that he popularized is as Kongolese as it is Swiss. Nor are these contributions limited to North America or to country music. Many of the European dances imposed upon enslaved people in the Caribbean were the same as those imposed upon enslaved people in the United States, and their creolized New World forms became the basis of many popular dance forms in the Americas. The habanera, which developed deep in the Caribbean substratum, greatly influenced Mexican habanera, bolero, New Orleans jazz, and R&B. Ultimately the Kongo New World in Latin America, the Caribbean, and North America found its way into American country and western music and even retained its influence when rock and roll had itself "straightened out" with the British invasion.[51]

St. Lucians have responded not only to European aspects of the music but also, and perhaps especially, to these Africanisms involved in the creation of American country and western. The creolization of country and western in St. Lucia differs significantly from the earlier creolization of the European quadrille tradition in this regard, for, unlike the quadrille tradition, American country and western was already creole in multiple senses. It was born in the New World of Old World sources, and it contained very important formative inputs from African American blues forms, blue yodels, the African-originated banjo, and, most important for the St. Lucian connection, the Afro-Caribbean habanera beat.

In spite of this creole heritage, however, country and western came to be increasingly cast as a "white" form, a process formative to the creation and maintenance of whiteness in the United States. It is now well documented that C&W played a vital role in the creation of whiteness in the United States by denying its African American antecedents, becoming segregated from "race records," and maintaining the marked racism of its minstrel component.[52] (Recent Stevie Wonder concerts, such as the one in Atlanta in 2007, have included a mini teach-in on country and western in his attempt to expose the suppression.) African Americans who showed interest in the music were looked at as strange and even ostracized within their own communities. There are many stories of black people with large collections of country music they kept hidden because it was politically dangerous or uncool.[53] The banjo and the blue yodel became reactionary sounds in the black community. Such are the legacies of racialized slavery and ongoing white supremacy; the wounds and stigmas continue to run deep. Even a recent PBS documentary featured Wynton Marsalis belittling a prominent New Orleans creole banjo player for perpetuating the minstrel stereotype despite the fact that Marsalis knows well the history of the banjo as a timekeeper in New Orleans jazz nearly from its inception.[54]

Attempts to cast country and western as white have prompted African American musical geniuses like Charlie Parker and Ray Charles to stress that it was the stories that drew them to the music.[55] The African American country singer Rissi Palmer has similarly related, "Country music resonated with me the most because of its storytelling aspect. . . . It just tells amazing, real, honest stories. That's why it's been my favorite and that's why I chose to follow this path."[56] More recently, Darius Rucker, front man for Hootie and the Blowfish, has become an established country star, with five hit singles on the country charts from a top-ten album on the country charts, and Jamie Foxx covered a George Strait song at the 44th Annual Academy of Country Music Awards, where he was able to make comedic use of notions of musical segregation. Foxx's portrayal of Ray Charles in *Ray* included a scene in which Charles establishes himself as adept at country music, having grown up hearing and loving it. Like other African Americans performing country, both Rucker and Foxx have had to explain away the surprise, admitting the role the music has had in their lives. By doing so, these two stars have further broadened the range of the contemporary black country experience, as have Palmer and Cowboy Troy.

In spite of these acknowledgments, increased scholarly attention to the deeply African American roots of country, and critiques of raced music in general, racial essentializations of country and western have taken their toll.[57] They elicit nearly hardwired responses of surprise at black appreciation of and attraction to the music, responses that belie the fact that the construction of musical whiteness takes a lot of effort and maintenance. As Geoff Mann argues, "It has taken a great deal of ideological work both to make country the sound of American whiteness, and, at least as importantly, to make it continue to 'call' to white people — to make country music seem not only something that only white people make, but also something that only white people 'hear,' something that recruits white people to their 'whiteness.'"[58]

This musically enacted whiteness is only reinforced by making someone who identifies black feel strange or as though he is somehow betraying his racial commitments by listening to (and worse, liking) country and western music (and worse, dance). But because of the opaqueness of the construction of whiteness—its silence and denials—the admissions are not easily offered, if they can be articulated at all.[59] Mann asks why country music sounds white, but the St. Lucian intervention needed here is perhaps to ask, What is not being heard when country is heard as only "white"? Mann concludes, "Country music sounds white . . . because white people are hailed by, hear, and turn to its sounding. This 'sounding' works in both senses of 'sound': country music is a 'sound of whiteness,' and it 'sounds' whiteness, i.e. sounds its depths."[60] Despite the overdue effort to have a full discussion of whiteness and C&W, his is a circular argument that does not acknowledge people's true agency, the varied roots of country and western music, or people's active role in the creation and maintenance of whiteness. The St. Lucian intervention is important to move forward notions of U.S. whiteness and blackness in relation to country and western, which is, in turn, important to an analysis of the racial and postcolonial dynamics of the genre in St. Lucia.

Conclusion

St. Lucians have transformed American country and western into a music of black social experience.[61] They have creolized American country and western dancing much as they have creolized European country and court dances in earlier centuries: by Africanizing it. In this instance however, the music was already more creole than is customarily admitted, and its greatest popularity came *after* Independence, when Caribbean people should theoretically have been free to choose their own music. The cultural challenge posed by the popularity of country and western has been exacerbated by lack of transparency in the United States about the role of the genre in the creation and maintenance of whiteness and by the corollary denial of the African diasporic contributions to the music. The lessons of St. Lucian creolization thus reach far beyond the island to the United States, where interventions in the racial coding of the music are also sorely needed.

So although creolizations are afoot that are perhaps even deeper than some other efforts at cultural decolonization, it nevertheless goes against common decolonizing sense to stand by and let the pervasive fascination with country and western run its course. What makes it especially difficult for many Caribbean intellectuals to stomach the notion that there may be any redeeming qualities to country and western in St. Lucia is the fact that the creolization of Western culture continues some of the painful colonial music imperatives, such as updating the kwadril tradition while de-emphasizing the

Afro-Creole musical rhythmic sensibility. Furthermore, the seeming whiteness of the music is a constant reminder of the colonial influence. Its growth initially dovetailed with pressures to learn the colonial language (English), even in times of decolonization. Adding salt to the wounds is its mushrooming popularity *after* independence *amid* the tremendous Afro-Caribbean musical blossomings in the region. One elephant in the room asks, So much great music, why this? And especially, why now, of all times, when we are free? The pervasiveness of the music and the seamlessness of its integration takes on an insidious character and becomes a veritable nagging thorn in the side of decolonization and cultural caretaking efforts.

But beneath the blatant contradictions between a seemingly white music and a progressive, new, predominantly Afro-Creole nation and its decolonization ethos, the continuations of Afro-Creole culture within the creolizations of country and western remain a compelling expression for the people who love the music. The continuations are many: the storytelling in the songs; the working-class and real-life themes; the integration of stories with dance events; the social context of the dancing in deep communal cross-island exchanges; the match with instruments and genres from Africa, including fiddle and banjo, yodel and drum; and perhaps most important of all, the Caribbean rhythmic sensibility epitomized by the habanera and upheld in full by the 3-4-1 bass beat matched with a footwork pattern. Given these continuities, the popularity of country and western in St. Lucia seems overdetermined rather than counterintuitive.

So despite the seeming whiteness of the form with which this newly independent nation is enamored, and with which it continues its predominantly African-descended creole folk practices in the postcolonial era, the dowsing is more specific and restorative on a number of fronts. Explaining what he envisioned as the goals of the Folk Research Centre, its founder, Monsignor Anthony, said, "If only we could engender such rootedness [in St. Lucian Afro-Creole culture], we would be enriched by learning from the outside without rejecting what is inside."[62]

The country and western music that St. Lucians have integrated into their lives reflects the importance of the deep roots of their culture in spite of the seeming whiteness of the music they have creolized. St. Lucians in great numbers have chosen from an available form something that honors their inner sensibilities and allows them to continue some of the Afro-Creole forms so dear to them. The selection process is not as open as Monsignor Anthony wishes, and is indeed fraught with undeniable reminders of colonization. For in the Caribbean, colonization eras are the early centuries of globalization, and the postcolonial creolizations often bear the archaeological record of that colonization rather than being a process moving toward true sovereignty. The shortcut of essentialism is often easier. Yet an important part of the decolonization methodology of the Folk Research Centre was a Marxian attention to the will, collective resources, and wisdom of "the people," which resulted in a trust and perceptive openness to formulations of creole identity suggested by the people despite their wandering from the more intellectual Afrocentric paradigms.

Notes

1. Michael Gaspard interview by Jerry Wever, 1998, audiotape in author's possession.

2. This volume makes no attempt to cover the whole African diaspora; thus there are no chapters on the popularity of American country music in Africa, for example. Chapters treating Africa in such a volume would be more reception-oriented.

3. *Country and western* is emic usage. The fact that it is seen as a dated term in the United States, both in academia and in general, and yet remains in high use in St. Lucia further epitomizes the particular St. Lucian love affair with the older eras of the music. Thanks to Jocelyn Neal for encouraging me to emphasize this point explicitly as it underscores my general argument about St. Lucian curatorial prowess.

4. Thompson, *Tango*, 111–18.

5. Monsignor Patrick Anthony, keynote address, delivered at the Islands in Between conference, Sir Arthur Lewis Community College, Morne Fortune, Castries, St. Lucia, 2002. Anthony was the cofounder of the St. Lucia Folk Research Centre.

6. Thanks so much to the people of St. Lucia for sharing your knowledge and wisdom regarding all the traditions I have researched. I hope you find a suitable reflection of your genius in this essay. Above all, I thank Michaeline Crichlow, who mentored me at Iowa. So many people in St. Lucia have helped in the process, from historians to musicians, dancers to music lovers, and most especially Allan and Travis Weekes, Therol and Marcus Hippolyte, and Linus Modeste for the intellectual and practitioner camaraderie that has been my most valuable teacher. Thanks to those who have given sustained assistance: Gregor Williams, Frank Norville, "Charlie" Julian Augustin, Ives Simeon, the FRC, and the people of Boguis, Fon Aso, Monchey, and Brooklyn. I have tried to attribute specific ideas to the people who first or most influentially shared them with me, and yet I alone take responsibility for any errors. Please contact me with any inaccuracies, corrections, suggested improvements, opinions, and any other forms of critique: jwever@spelman.edu.

7. Beckford, *Persistent Poverty*.

8. As for the famed back-and-forth between British and French rule, it is important to note the proximity of St. Lucia to the headquarters (Martinique and Barba-

dos) of these two competing European powers. This unique location accounted for many of the ambivalences and skirmishes to control St. Lucia.

9. Midgett, "West Indian Migration in St. Lucia and London."

10. Brathwaite remarks that the development of creole society presupposes a situation of rule by a foreign ethnic minority, in which a society is caught up in some kind of colonial arrangement with a metropolitan European power on the one hand, and a plantation arrangement on the other, and where the society is multiracial but organized for the benefit of a minority of European origin (*Contradictory Omens*, xv). In general my use of *creole* in this essay refers to society and cultural forms created from old worlds yet forged in a new one. The word is commonly thought to derive "from a combination of two Spanish words criar (to create, to imagine, to establish, to found, to settle) and colon (a colonist, a founder, a settler) into criollo: a committed settler, one identified with the area of settlement, one native to the settlement though not ancestrally indigenous to it" (10). In the Caribbean, *Creole* was originally used to describe colonists of pure European descent born in the New World. The term subsequently came to refer to anyone or anything born or naturalized in the region (Dominguez, "Social Classification in Creole Louisiana"). The first written record of use we currently have is in a letter from Peru in 1567 to describe people born "here" (Fleischmann, "The Sociocultural and Linguistic Profile of a Concept," xv). The Inca Garcilaso's 1602 writings claim that, to quote Maureen Warner-Lewis, "the word was invented by native-born Africans to distinguish themselves from their descendents" ("Posited Kikoongo Origins of Some Portuguese and Spanish Words from the Slave Era," 90). In this case the use of the term apparently implied superiority for those born in Africa, as opposed to being born (into bondage) in the New World. The origin in European languages is traced to Portuguese (*crioulo*) and on back to Latin, possibly deriving from the Latin root *crear* (to create). Scholarly diligence has finally suggested African or Afro-American coinage (Allsopp and Allsopp, *Dictionary of Caribbean English Usage*; Warner-Lewis, "Posited Kikoongo Origins"). Spanish etymologists have suggested African origins (Allsopp and Allsopp, *Dictionary*). Warner-Lewis has posited Kikoongo origins in particular. An important consideration is that, in the case of the suggested African or Afro-American (Brazil) coinage, the origins are neither European nor Caribbean. This may seem ironic given the widespread use and heavy association of the term and its forms with European languages and with Caribbean experience. But this is actually indicative of a central feature of the term. Whatever its origin, it became useful across boundaries, languages, and ethnicities in the process of colonization of the New World and later beyond, and increasingly so where the central economic scheme became a plantation based on slave labor. Members of both African and European societies, and their descendants born in the New World, found it useful, if not necessary, to distinguish between those born in the New World and those born in the Old World (Stewart, *Creolization*). Regardless of its wide historical usefulness and the arguments for its continued relevance, however, its continued use is problematic and should yield in

the context of what Michaeline Crichlow cogently terms the "post creole imagination" (*Globalization and the Post-Creole Imagination*).

11. Kremser, "The African Heritage in the 'Kélé.'" *Mixed* would imply a mixture of African descent and European descent. *East Indian* is the local term for St. Lucians with ancestry from the subcontinent of India.

12. *Afro–St. Lucian* is not an emic term, however, so I will not use it hereafter. I use it here only to distinguish from non–St. Lucians.

13. This is contested. The hegemony of English as being the language of the least resistive route to money-earning power has helped to create a situation in St. Lucian schools where Kwéyòl and English are not taught bilingually; nor is English taught as a second language. Rather English is taught as a first language and the use of Kwéyòl in school is largely discouraged. It is often thought of as an interference in children's abilities to gain "tested" proficiency in English. See Midgett, "Bilingualism and Linguistic Change in St. Lucia"; Samuel, "The Challenge of Bilingual Education in Bilingual St. Lucia"; Samuel, "Towards a National Language Policy in St. Lucia; Devonish, *Language and Liberation*. "Whereas Kwéyòl is the lingua franca of the vast majority of St. Lucians in the rural districts and the repository for their rich cultural heritage as an oral people, English is the official language" (Anthony, "Folk Research and Development," 43). Gains have been made in recognition of bilingualism. In 1998, Kwéyòl was voted recognition as an official language of Parliament.

14. *Creole* and *kwéyòl* are the same word in different languages. For the most part, I use *kwéyòl* when it is clear that I am talking about situations specific to St. Lucia, and the English version, *creole*, when talking about broader processes and identities such as creolization and Afro-Creole. However, the terms are used interchangeably by some writers, and I too fall into this tradition. One of the journalists I quote uses *Jounen Creole*. The term *Patwa* is perhaps most commonly heard when the average St. Lucian refers to the language, but the work of the Folk Research Centre has increased the usage of *Kwéyòl* because of derogatory associations of broken language attached to *Patwa*. Older passages would tend to use *Patwa*. Because of sensitivities involving the stigmatization inherent in this usage, however, I consistently use *Kwéyòl* instead.

Some glosses in *Kwéyòl*, Creole: *Jounen Kwéyòl*, Creole Day Festival; *kwadril*, quadrille; *mizik manmai lakai*, home children music (c&w and quadrille); *wèstun*, country and western; *dansé*, dance.

15. In the rural community where I lived, many of the people had greater competence in Kwéyòl than in English. In an early Jounen Kwéyòl mass, Father Patrick Anthony (founder of the Folk Research Centre) sings (not literally) the praise of Jounen Kwéyòl: "We have removed the veil that told us we were stupid—old foreign coat of negative attitudes against ourselves. Long live Jounen Kwéyòl!"

16. The popular yearly creole festival Jounen Kwéyòl is a twenty-year-old festival created to showcase and celebrate kwéyòl heritage, combat culture loss, and destigmatize and raise national consciousness about kwéyòl and Afro–St. Lucian heri-

tage traditions and identity. The idea for Jounen Kwéyòl was born out of an international kwéyòl conference (of Bannzil) in Louisiana in 1983. Jounen Kwéyòl was spawned collaboratively by MOKWÉYÒL (an intellectual movement for the orthographic standardization and revitalization of Kwéyòl as a national language), the Folk Research Centre, and the National Research and Development Foundation. For a history of the festival, see Charles, "Oral Traditions in St. Lucia."

17. This study grew out of my research in expressive culture, power, and identity in postcolonial St. Lucia. The main focus in my first two months in St. Lucia in 1998 was to document creole revitalization efforts, especially as they related to Jounen Kwéyòl. The Folk Research Centre, a St. Lucian nongovernmental organization, has been at the core of destigmatizing and promoting creole traditions and identity, and beginning before Independence has conducted much and governed nearly all St. Lucian social science research in expressive culture. Afro–St. Lucian traditions were heavily stigmatized in the colonial period, and an important step of the decolonizing process was to reclaim respect for these customs. Significant strides have been made. Jounen Kwéyòl was focused on doing this work, in part through public debates around festival time, on the streets and in the media, about issues important to creole identity. One such issue that came up in the 1997 Jounen Kwéyòl was the appropriateness of including a country and western dance as a part of official celebrations. This opened up space for critical appraisal of current creolization processes such as the integration of American country and western music into St. Lucian society, and it is in this prickly area that my scholarship will contribute to St. Lucian projects.

18. I conducted interviews with dancers, fans, nonfans, musicians (including musicians specializing in kwadril, American country and western, jazz, and calypso), dance and radio deejays, club owners, record shop keepers, dance instructors, other culture workers and kwéyòl activists, sponsors, promoters, and politicians. I surveyed dancing opportunities, including community dances and their social group sponsors, nightclubs having one or more dedicated country and western nights, practices, competitions, festivals, kwadril and associated dances (danced to string-band music), and country and western bands. I also surveyed radio programming and its history in the Eastern Caribbean, program deejays, record store inventories, and St. Lucia's fledgling Country Music Association.

19. Guilbault, "On Redefining the Local through World Music."

20. See Malone, *Country Music USA*, 275.

21. Gregor Williams interview by Jerry Wever, 1998, audiotape in author's possession.

22. Andrea Lionel interview by Jerry Wever, 1999, audiotape in author's possession.

23. Gaspard interview by Wever.

24. Guilbault, "On Redefining the Local through World Music."

25. Guilbault, *Zouk*, 191.

26. St. Lucian tastes concerning country and western are far from monolithic, and varied kinds of programming and CD or cassette mix-making have their own followings. For a sampling of the kinds of country and western music enjoyed in St. Lucia, there are a few St. Lucian C&W radio programs that are accessible on the Internet. The main one until recently was Radio 100. A newer station, Hot FM, rivals R100 on Tuesday nights, 9–12 Eastern Standard Time, and their Sunday morning country and western show is listened to island-wide during Sunday cleaning: http://www .caribbeanhotfm.com. On Radio 100 another show playing country and western music interspersed with talk about kwéyòl healing remedies and stories in Kwéyòl, is by Jako on Sunday mornings, 5–7 Eastern Standard Time, htp://www.htsstlucia .com from 8 p.m.–12 p.m. Eastern Standard Time. Another show, arguably the most popular show in the countryside, alternates country and western music with talk in Kwéyòl by the incendiary social commentator Juke Bois. It airs weekday mornings, 5–5:30, and Monday–Thursday evenings, 6–8, and until recently included a Saturday evening show.

27. I use *honky-tonk* as St. Lucians use it. It has become synecdochic for mid-century popular country and western forms and is used more generally to differentiate that era of music from the more rock- and pop-oriented forms of the 1980s and onward. Within American discourse on country music, *honky-tonk* has a narrower, more specific meaning, and is used to differentiate between country substyles, which include countrypolitan, bluegrass, hillbilly, old-time, western swing, rockabilly, and so on. I thank Tracy Laird for reminding me that the specificity of American usage requires me to clarify the St. Lucian usage. In St. Lucia the distinction is something like what Fox documents in Texas in regard to AM versus FM country (Fox, *Real Country*).

28. Early on I was told by a country and western deejay and taxi driver, "George Jones is the most popular. George Jones is King. Jim Reeves, he is the Prince." I thought it was just one opinion, but I heard it echoed much thereafter. While I was there in the summer of 1999, a leading national newspaper featured a full-page spread on George Jones. Jim Reeves was so popular that in the 1960s there were at least three separate buses named after his songs, for example, "Distant Drums" (Doug Midgett, personal communication, 1998), and the first international St. Lucian country star, Harold Dolor, said that in 1962–63 they would play fifteen Jim Reeves songs in one night at Dennery country and western dances. George Jones has also held that position for the past half century with no sign of letup. On the December 19, 2006, edition of the Hot FM 8–11 p.m. country show, over half the songs played were by George Jones, including a string of over twenty consecutive songs.

29. The anthropologist Ken Bilby confirms that various kinds of American "country" music have long been popular in Jamaica, ranging from very pop-oriented material such as Jim Reeves, Skeeter Davis, Patsy Cline, and Marty Robbins, to relatively noncommercial southern U.S. "white" gospel music (personal communication, 1998).

30. "Dub" refers to Reggae. For example, songs by Jr. Kelley, Eric Donaldson, Kassav, and Mighty Sparrow might make up a hot-tune set, or some local soca (much more soca near carnival season, but the best loved ones are heard year-round).

31. Gregor Williams explained how much in common St. Lucians had with the subjects of American country and western songs in terms of working-class blues: unemployment, migration, losses of land and crops, and more. He compared Appalachia (rural United States) with Babonneau (rural St. Lucia). American country and western music is popular in many former British colonies and territories, including Australia, Ireland, Canada, India, Nigeria, Tanzania, Jamaica, and the British Virgin Islands (Williams interview by Wever).

32. Guilbault, "Musical Events in the Lives of the People of a Caribbean Island"; Guilbault, "St. Lucia Kwadril Evening."

33. Traditional Dance Officer Frank Norville pointed out to me that the American square dance and contradance are not very different at all from St. Lucia's tradition.

34. The length of this chapter does not allow for a full discussion of the intertextual relationships between country and western and folk storytelling traditions. I discuss them in detail in my dissertation, "Dancing the Habanera Beats (in Country Music)." There I go into greater detail on the intertextuality between country and western and St. Lucian drum-dance traditions as well. The important thing to know is that numerous drum-dance traditions such as *kont* and *bélé* begin with a story and then turn into a song that heats up and is danced to drumming. The storytelling (*listwa*) also occurs in great quantity at the beginning and end of the traditional eight-day-long wake (Guilbault, "Musical Events in the Lives of the People of a Caribbean Island"; "On Redefining the Local through World Music"; *Zouk*).

35. This was a spinoff of some of the community-hopping series of country and western dance competitions and concert promotions. Invader has composed several country and western songs which he performs in this venue, and he also showcases a country and western band formed by another calypsonian who writes calypsos for many calypsonians. Even before his more formal entry into the country and western scene, his carnival hit ("Belelesh") had yodeling at the end of it.

36. Some of his original songs get regular airplay on St. Lucian radio stations.

37. Typically, calypsonians are understandably perturbed that their own local Caribbean artistry can go underappreciated while some foreign "white" music with such politically incorrect if not outwardly racist politics has swept the nation by storm. Two examples of calypsos critical of country and western are Paulinus's "Country and Western Take Over We Country," written by a civil servant who writes for many calypsonians, and Lord Believe Me's "Too Many Country and Western Junkies."

38. Kendal Hippolyte interview by Jerry Wever, 1998, audiotape in author's possession.

39. Williams interview by Wever.

40. Brathwaite, *Contradictory Omens*.

41. Sublette, *The World that Made New Orleans*, 124.

42. Thompson, *Tango*, 115.

43. Sublette, *Cuba and Its Music*.

44. A number of songs might serve as examples of musical emphases on the 3–4-1 that is danced. George Jones's "If You Ever Need Me (I'll Be There)" and Isla Grant's "Call on Me" both have the 3–4-1 bass beaten and sung with the three-syllable title (or subtitle, in the case of the Jones song). See note 48 for more detail on the timing of steps to beats. "Humble Man" by John Hogan is the quintessential "call to the dance" at country and western dances in St. Lucia. The steel guitar intro plays a sultry slow habanera high in the mix. Even people standing along the walls all night try to find someone to dance that song with. "There Goes" by Alan Jackson is another anthem that gets everyone on the floor.

45. Brewer, "The Use of Habanera Rhythm in Rockabilly Music." Technically, what Brewer defines as the habanera is really just the tresillo, requiring me to contextualize many of his comments. But for this purpose his argument still holds true.

46. I thank Aaron Fox for equipping me with the parlance of curation to talk about the strategic accumulation of repertoire.

47. Wever, "Dancing the Habanera Beats (in Country Music)."

48. The genius of this postcolonial creolization is illuminating on a number of fronts and provokes the need for further research. In St. Lucia itself, there is an opportunity to better understand the possible Kongo influences in the south of the island, where country and western first took root. It may indeed merely be due to the location of the U.S. military base and its "country" remoteness from "town" (Castries), but the Kongo questions bear further investigation. In the United States it is important to look beyond the Elvis "Hound Dog" moments at midcentury and see the influence of the "basic template of clean-studio 1980s corporate rock" on country and western in order to better understand the spread of implicit habanera tendencies in the music (Sublette, *The World That Made New Orleans*, 124). Although the St. Lucian two-step differs greatly in form and tempo from the zydeco two-step of southwestern Louisiana, they do share the same underlying footwork rhythm and similar regional creolization processes. I thank Jocelyn Neal for pressing me on this last point. While I doubt there was any direct spread of the zydeco two-step to St. Lucia, it is entirely possible. Many soldiers from the U.S. South, some African American, were stationed in St. Lucia during World War II, and it is plausible to imagine that some might have brought the zydeco two-step.

49. House interview by Jerry Wever, 2005, audiotape in author's possession.

50. Hentoff, *Listen to the Stories*, 168.

51. Sublette, "The Kingsmen and the Cha-Cha-Cha," 89–90.

52. Malone, *Country Music USA*; Peterson, *Creating Country Music*; Miller, *Segregating Sound*.

53. McPherson, *Elbow Room*.

54. *American Creole: New Orleans Reunion*, prod. Michelle Benoit and Glen Pitre,

Cote Blanche Productions (PBS, Sept. 7, 2006). This situation further underscores my point on the pressures of racial commitments. *The Dave Chappelle Show* also features ongoing segments on the banjo and minstrelsy. Although banjo reclamation projects are a new renaissance area, as evidenced by the release of Otis Taylor's 2008 CD *Recapturing the Banjo*, it remains on the margins. To Marsalis's credit, though, I should note that his own 2008 album, *Two Men with the Blues*, with Willie Nelson (who also has a reggae C&W album) might signal a shift in perception.

55. Hentoff, *Listen to the Stories*; Ivey, "Border Crossing."

56. Rissi Palmer interview, CMT.com, http://www.cmt.com/videos/interview/rissi-palmer/255134/i-love-the-storytelling-in-country-music-studio-330-sessions.jhtml.

57. Radano, *Lying Up a Nation*.

58. Mann, "Why Does Country Music Sound White?," 83.

59. See Yancy, *What White Looks Like*; Lott, *Love and Theft*.

60. Mann, "Why Does Country Music Sound White?," 83.

61. I thank Aaron Fox for this concept.

62. Anthony, keynote address.

Such fiddling and dancing nobody ever before saw in this world. I thought they were the true "heaven-borns." Black and white, white and black, all hugemsnug together; happy as lords and ladies, sitting sometimes round in a ring, with a jug of liquor between them.
—DAVY CROCKETT (1834)

My belt buckle is my bling-bling. It's just going to keep getting bigger.
—COWBOY TROY (2005)

Playing Chicken with the Train

COWBOY TROY'S HICK-HOP AND
THE TRANSRACIAL COUNTRY WEST

Adam Gussow

Black Hillbillies and Blacknecks

There was no necessary reason why Cowboy Troy's country-rap single, "I Play Chicken with the Train," should have caused such an uproar among country music fans when it was released in the spring of 2005. The song itself is a sonic Rorschach test: not so singular a curiosity as many might think but still a challenge to what passes for common knowledge in the music business. It is animated by a sound and a lyric stance that might strike us, in a receptive mood, as uncanny—at once unfamiliar, a half-and-half blend of two musical idioms that rarely find themselves so jarringly conflated, and strangely familiar, as though the song has distilled the sound of ten-year-old boys filled with limitless bravado, jumping up and down and hollering into the summer afternoon. Compared with other country-rap hybrids, "I Play Chicken with the Train" contains surprisingly few sonic signifiers of hip-hop: no breakbeats, no samples, no drum machines, no scratching. The full burden of audible blackness is carried by Cowboy Troy's decidedly old-school rap, with its square phrasing, tame syncopations, and echoes of Run-DMC. One hears white voices framing, doubling, responding to, supporting that black voice; simultaneously one senses that somebody has torn down the wall that is supposed firmly to demarcate the boundary between twanging redneck euphoria—the lynch mob's fiddle-driven rebel yell—and rap's exaggerated self-projections of urban black masculinity.[1]

The song scans, to receptive ears, as a particularly boisterous example of the male-bonded American pastoral articulated by Leslie Fiedler in *Love and Death in the American Novel*, a transracial masculine idyll stretching its unencumbered limbs across some country and western frontier, "civilized" men throwing off their generic shackles and reinventing themselves as a fraternity of fearless young warriors out to revitalize the world. Or else — to the unreceptive — it is monstrous and must be treated as monsters are treated. In *The Philosophy of Horror*, Noël Carroll defines monsters as entities that are "un-natural relative to a culture's conceptual scheme of nature. They do not fit the scheme; they violate it. Thus, monsters are not only physically threatening; they are cognitively threatening. They are threats to common knowledge." The email blast that alerted potential purchasers to the recording's release fused a kind of King Kong sensationalism with an assertion of scandalous, unprecedented hybridity: Cowboy Troy, we were informed, is "the world's only six-foot, five-inch, 250-pound black cowboy rapper." Was that a threat, a brag, or a promise?[2]

In his follow-up album of 2007, *Black in the Saddle*, Cowboy Troy referenced the antipathy with which some whites and blacks greeted the song and, by extension, his highly conspicuous presence in the country music world. "People I've never met wanna take me body surfing behind a pickup," he sang in "How Can You Hate Me," referencing the infamous dragging death of James Byrd Jr. in Jasper, Texas, at the hands of two white men. As for the black response to his hick-hop persona: the silence from hip-hop precincts, at least publicly, has been deafening, although *Vibe* magazine did take note of *Black in the Saddle* long enough to sneer at Coleman's presumptive audience: "Troy and his twang trust are keen to serve two masters: game ex-urban blacks steeped in country grammar and white fans of post-redneck rock. Together, at last." Coleman's rejoinder to his black critics in "How Can You Hate Me" — "some of y'all sayin' Troy ain't nothing but a Sambo" — suggests that he has indeed taken some heat.[3]

Although it received virtually no airplay on country music radio, *Loco Motive*, the album out of which "I Play Chicken with the Train" was released as the first single, debuted at number 2 on *Billboard*'s Top Country Albums chart on June 4, 2005. Within weeks, Troy Coleman, a former Foot Locker shoe salesman from Dallas, had the number 1 download at iTunes and was a *succes de scandale* in the country music world, along with his producers and backup singers, the alt-Nashville duo of "Big Kenny" Alphin and John Rich. From media reviewers to country music websites such as CMT.com and VelvetRope.com, the nature of Cowboy Troy's scandal seemed evident to his supporters and detractors alike: he had dared to create hybrid art by mixing two musical idioms understood to be racially pure, country and rap, thrusting his hip-hop braggartry into country's pristine white precincts with the help of his renegade white producers. "Stomping middle ground between the Sugarhill Gang and Charlie Daniels," opined *Time*. "A new kind of American music, equal parts metal, country, hip hop, and balls," wrote another reviewer. Admiration was supplanted by disgust in the postings of those who styled themselves country music's defenders. "He has tried to come into country to pollute it with his rap-junk," wrote one. "He is just polluting this awesome genre," wrote another. "This is such an abomination," wrote a third. "A discrace [*sic*] to humanity . . . Troy on stage and the white girls down front dancing for him." The racist tenor of the "pollution" claim becomes unmistakable when juxtaposed with the "abomination" of an imagined race mixing in which black masculine potency looms over compliant white womanhood. (Perhaps it's worth noting that the original film version of *King Kong* was retitled *King Kong and the White Women* for its German release.)[4]

The train that Troy was jousting with in his hit single was, as he readily admitted in interviews, the Nashville country music establishment, a crypto-racist coterie that, with several notable exceptions, had refused to allow black performers to become stars, much less country-rap stars. By the summer of 2006, Coleman, backed by Big and Rich, had performed his train song at the Grand Ole Opry and had a steady gig hosting *Nashville Star*, a country music version of *American Idol*, with Wynonna Judd. But the song, as it happens, references two trains: not just the racist Nashville establishment train but the "big black train comin' around the bend" as a figure for Cowboy Troy himself, an outsized musical revolutionary roaring full tilt into country music's airbrushed myths of whiteness: white origin figures and stars, white aesthetic grounding, white audiences, white rural purity given voice. "I'm big and black, clickety-clack," he bragged, "and I make the train jump the track like that." The self-styled "hick-hopper" and "blackneck" had played chicken with the train, and the train had swerved.[5]

Recent scholarship by Pam Foster, Charles Wolfe, Louis M. Kyriakoudes, Elijah Wald, and others has significantly undercut these myths, above all the myth of Charley Pride, lone black superstar, as the exception that proves the rule about the thoroughgoing whiteness of country. We now know that John Lomax collected canonical versions of "Home on the Range" and "Git Along Little Dogies" from a retired black cow-camp cook; that the founder of the

Grand Ole Opry, George Hay, launched his career by penning newspaper and radio blackface skits; that the harmonicist DeFord Bailey, the first star of the Opry, was the product of an extensive black hillbilly tradition that otherwise remained all but unrecorded; that Hank Williams and Bill Monroe need to be paired with Rufe "Tee Tot" Payne and Arnold Shultz, their early African American partners and mentors; that the Carter Family learned much of their mountain repertoire from their black guitar player, Leslie Riddles; that the Supremes and the Pointer Sisters released country-themed albums in 1965 and 1974, respectively; that a number of talented black country performers have surfaced in subsequent decades, including Cleve Francis, Al Downing, Stoney Edwards, and Trini Triggs; that Merle Haggard, disgusted with contemporary Nashville, insisted in 1994, "I'm just a little blacker than that" and "I'm thinking of doing some tours through the South only for black people"; and that country music has long had a passionate black fan base in Africa and the Caribbean and a significant, if little acknowledged, following among black southerners, including musicians. Questioned by the folklorist Alan Lomax at his home near Clarksdale, Mississippi, in the early 1940s, Muddy Waters proudly listed seven of Gene Autry's hits in his working repertoire, including "Deep in the Heart of Texas" and "Take Me Back to My Boots and Saddle." "You have to play all the Western tunes for the colored these days," insisted another black Delta musician who played on a cowboy music radio show every Saturday afternoon. The prelude to Ray Charles's epochal album, *Modern Sounds in Country and Western Music* (1962) was his late-1940s gig with the Florida Playboys, during which he "yodeled, wore white western suits, and . . . was dubbed 'the only colored singing cowboy.'" "When I played hillbilly songs," Chuck Berry writes in his autobiography, speaking of his days at the Cosmopolitan Club in St. Louis, "I stressed my diction so that it was harder and whiter. . . . Some of the clubgoers began whispering, 'Who is that black hillbilly at the Cosmo?'"[6]

Still, there's a difference between demonstrating mastery of the country idiom, as Berry, Bailey, Charles, and Pride did, and loudly proclaiming your disruptive role in accents that frame your entrance as Blackness Triumphant. According to one Nashville journalist, Troy Coleman was so aware of his polarizing potential that he "briefly toyed with the idea of sending [*Loco Motive*] to radio programmers along with a roll of toilet paper and a bottle of Pepto Bismol. 'I figured [program directors] would need one or the other,' he says, 'depending on how excited they got or how sick they felt' after hearing it." The only major country station that played him, according to the producer John Rich, was KTYS in Dallas, although the album went on to sell more than 340,000 copies. Coleman's contested Nashville ascendance deepens our understanding of his aggressively provocative train song. The audible racial scandal he seems at first to enact—the flagrant mixing of "his" black rap with "white" country music—is, I suggest, merely a screen for an altogether different scandal: his implicit demand that we understand both musical traditions as *already* amalgamated. More specifically, "I Play Chicken with the Train" combines frontier brag-talk of the Davy Crockett variety with urban rap braggadocio in a way that forces us to acknowledge the shared, creolized history of both forms, a history that owes something to African praise-song, something to blackface minstrelsy, and much to life on the western frontier before and after Emancipation (fig. 9.1).[7]

Cowboy Troy's hick-hop is a challenge to our received understandings not just of country and rap but of musical blackness and whiteness more broadly—a transracial "excluded middle" of a sort explored by Christopher Waterman in a recent article on the song "Corrine Corrina." "One effective way to analyze the logics of inclusion and exclusion that have informed the production of racialized music histories," Waterman writes, "is to examine music that springs from, circulates around, and seeps through the interstices between racial categories." Cowboy Troy's hick-hop is merely one example of an emergent country-rap tradition that includes artists such as Trace Adkins ("Honky-Tonk Badonkadonk"), Vance Gilbert ("Country Western Rap"), Bubba Sparxxx ("Comin' Round"), and Insane Shane McKane ("I Put the Ho in Hoedown"). Even considering the liberatory potential of Troy's transracial aesthetics, the long shadow of blackface minstrelsy lingers within his comic self-enlargements and surfaces in the Big and Rich stage show that frames some of his public performances—a show in which Troy shares the stage with a dancing dwarf named Two-Foot Fred. It's worth remembering, in this context, that country music as we know it evolved out of "hillbilly" music, whose early performers came from the ranks of vaudeville and medicine shows, where blacking up was part of the business. Their performances—straight down through the television hit *Hee Haw*—mingle roughshod comic burlesques and the winking self-mockery of the country rube. "Through much of its history," the historian James N. Gregory reminds us, "country music courted ridicule and needed audiences who either enjoyed the joke, missed the joke, or did not care." Although several white artists, including Sparxxx, have configured country-rap as a medium for serious reflection, Cowboy Troy's version of the idiom—it's a scene of playful, wildly self-dramatizing transgression, inflected by Coleman's acknowledged fondness for the World Wrestling Federation and its stagey braggartry—

FIGURE 9.1. Cowboy Troy. Rusty Russell / Getty Images. Photo courtesy of
Getty Images.

is seconded by the recordings of Adkins, Gilbert, and McKane. McKane's double-edged burlesque, in which he mocks black culture *and* redneck culture by mocking his own obscene, rhythmically challenged hip-hop stylings, shows how racist meanings can haunt the "brothers under the skin" aesthetic of the transracial frontier.[8]

Raps, Recitations, and Postmodern Honky-Tonks

The final words of "I Play Chicken with the Train," flung down as an invitation and a challenge on the heels of the completed track, are Troy's: "Get you some of *that*." But what exactly is *that*, apart from the provocative fusion of "white" and "black" music that feels like sacrilege to some and refreshing innovation to others? Coleman's own statements, which offer multiple and conflicting evocations of one hick-hopper's self-fashioning, are a good place to begin this investigation.

In an interview with National Public Radio's Jennifer Ludden during the first rush of postrelease publicity, Coleman insisted that what *sounds* like rap to some people is in fact merely his updating of the "recitation," an established mode within country music itself. "You start listening to old Charlie Daniels records and listening to old Jerry Reed records," he said, "[and] the delivery a lot of times is considered—it was called recitations at that time, but if you listened to it now, you'd probably call it a rap, but it was mostly spoken and everything rhymed." Troy's claim—that he isn't so much hybridizing country with rap as he is highlighting a preexistent strain within the former idiom—positions him, unexpectedly, as the conservator of country music tradition, even as it implicitly rebukes those country fans who view him as a "polluting" interloper. Later in the same interview, however, he offers a different origin narrative in response to the question "Where'd you come up with the idea to put all this together?"

> Well, I think that if you have ever spent any time, for example, in country bars in Texas, as have I and many of my friends, you'll notice that during the first 45 minutes or so of a show, the band or the deejay is playing traditional Top 40 country music. However, during that last quarter of the hour, the deejay begins to play either rap, rock, or, you know some sort of dance music, and the dance floor always gets packed during the rap portion of the hour. And that let me know that I wasn't the only cowboy that like rap music as well as country music. And so I figured, why not make a style of music that appeals to me as

well as to my friends and something that I know that there is a market for?[9]

"If you've been to a country bar recently," he told *Time* in a similar vein, "and seen people dance to a George Strait song followed by a Ludacris song, you know I'm hardly the only person that likes rap and country mixed together." Here Coleman represents himself as an innovator responsive to the needs of an emergent public: the regular crowd in a modern honky-tonk, united in their protean tastes and shaking their denim-clad booties to Dirty South hip-hop grooves. The contemporary country audience's tastes clearly resonate with his own—and do so in a way that highlights the potential for profit that lies within stylistic innovation. In "I Play Chicken with the Train," Coleman brags about his global reach and selling power—"All over the world wide web you'll see / Download CBT on an mp3"—but what he signals in his public statements is a desire to meet an eager audience halfway by synthesizing a hybrid idiom: "I grew up listening to country music, rap music, and rock 'n' roll. . . . I figured, 'Why can't I take my favorite elements of all three and mix them into one style?'" His objective, he told the journalist Farai Chideya in rhyming accents, "is to strive for connection regardless of complexion."[10]

The origin of his aesthetic shifts in Coleman's telling from childhood home to honky-tonk to frat party. As an undergraduate at the University of Texas in Austin, a town celebrated for its musical eclecticism and alt-country temperament, Coleman began performing at frat parties and clubs. "I had my cowboy hat on and would rap over techno," he told the reporter John Gerome. "People started remembering who I was, I guess, because I had the cowboy hat on everywhere I went." The "big blackneck" persona Coleman dramatizes in his country rap hit seems to have had its origins in this collegiate clubbing life. "I'd go to country bars," he told a British journalist, "and I'd be one of two or three blacks in the entire place. Then I'd wear a cowboy hat and boots to a hip hop club. People thought I was brave or crazy."[11]

"Syncretism will always be an unpredictable and surprising process," insists Paul Gilroy. "It underlines the global reach of popular cultures as well as the complexity of their cross-over dynamics." The complexity of Coleman's crossover lies in the tension between the self-evident disruption of his song and cowboy-hatted presence on the one hand and, on the other, the aesthetic and attitudinal continuities he claims in interviews such as these. Even as "I Play Chicken with the Train" organizes its aggressive braggadocio around the tall, dark, unruly figure of Cowboy Troy whooping on (white) Nashville,

Coleman's own statements insist that there *is* no scandal. Country folk and rap folk are actually the same folk, he claims, with their transracial affinities reflected not just in the willingness of white honky-tonk dancers to boogie down to hip-hop grooves but in shared lyrical concerns. In response to Ludden's comment that "one doesn't normally think of a country music audience and a hip-hop audience overlapping," Coleman responds, "Well, that would be a traditional concept . . . but if you really listen to the lyrics of the songs, I mean, many of the themes that are within the music on either side of the fence are quite similar. I mean, a lot of people that listen to rap music like to talk about the cars that they drive or the trucks that they drive. And similarly, in country music, they like to talk about what they drive as well." He continues, "A lot of rap is about drinking and having a good time. Country artists sing about that stuff too." Coleman is not the only black rap artist to have ventured a claim about the thematic continuities between country and rap. In a review of *Loco Motive* titled "Is Nothing Sacred? Country Meets Hip-Hop," the journalist Ernest Jasmine reports a conversation he had with Ice-T in which the topic unexpectedly turned to similarities between rap and country artists. "They are both down to earth and wore jeans and hats to awards shows, [Ice-T] pointed out. He even alluded to hip-hop gangsta, quoting Johnny Cash: 'I shot a man in Reno just to watch him die.' When I joked that he should record a country album, he cut me off, saying something like 'We have different agendas.'"[12]

As Ice-T's bridling response suggests, black rappers have been as quick to discern stylistic affinities with the western half of the country and western dyad—especially hypermasculine frontier mythology involving posses, big guns, and outlaw behavior—as they have been leery of country music per se. In an essay titled "Hip Hopalong Cassidy: Cowboys and Rappers," Blake Allmendinger mentions a series of relevant rap recordings and films, including "Ghetto Cowboy" (Bone Thugs–n-Harmony, 1998), "Westward Ho" (Ice Cube/Westside Connection, 1996), "California Love" (Tupac Shakur, 1995), *Posse* (Mario Van Peebles et al., 1993), and *The Wild Wild West* (1999), the last of which features Will Smith as "the cowboy who outdraws the outlaws, the rapper J. W. G. ('James West Gangsta'), who outrhymes his competitors." Snoop Dogg dedicated his 2008 novelty hit "My Medicine," a southern-fried paean to pimping and pot smoking, to "my main man Johnny Cash, a real American gangster."[13] Yet even as Cowboy Troy dramatizes his emergence onto a Western stage in "I Play Chicken with the Train" with a bravura not unlike Smith's, he rejects the gangsta pose with its emphasis on violence, on being "hard":

Southern boy makin' noise where the buffalo roam
Flesh, denim and bone as you might have known
See me ridin' into town like a desperado
With a big belt buckle, the cowboy bravado

Rollin' like thunder on the scene
It's kinda hard to describe if you know what I mean
I never claimed to be the hardest of the roughest hard rocks
But I'm boomin' out yo' box
Skills got you jumpin' outch'a socks

What distinguishes Coleman's frontier mythology from those of other black rappers is the public for whom he conjures Cowboy Troy: not an inner-city black audience looking to an imagined West for outlaw poses and high-octane gun fetishism, even as it views country music as the soundtrack of rural racism, not a mainstream American audience happy to indulge Will Smith's benign gangsta stagings, but a contemporary country music audience sufficiently heterogeneous that those who take offense at the "pollution" of Coleman's rap are counterbalanced by those happy to dance to Ludacris and George Strait at their local honky-tonk. "Country music today," wrote the sociologist George H. Lewis in 1997, "is not the music of a relatively homogeneous blue collar subculture, as it was, purportedly, in the past." Instead it "has revealed several distinct demographic clusters of country fans." Lewis identifies the expected "hard-core traditionalists" and "transition-30 baby boom listeners," both of whom are attracted to country in part because it aligns with conservative community and family values, but he also identifies a younger "Lollapalooza-age" audience—an alt-country audience, broadly speaking—that embraces everything from Killbilly to the Dixie Chicks. Finally, there are "country converts" who, according to Lewis, "consume the music as part of their extremely varied musical listening pattern. These musical omnivores . . . are the complete postmodern grazers—equally likely to purchase and enjoy the work of Cecilia Bartoli, Phish, and Merle Haggard—and are, by the way, the fastest growing segment of the modern country listening audience, clocking in at nearly 30% of it in 1996." Cowboy Troy's core appeal would seem to lie with the third and fourth demographic clusters, younger alt-country fans and eclectic "grazers." Coleman's own edgy, wide-ranging tastes fit this demographic. The list titled "To My Heroes" at CowboyTroy.com includes Charlie Daniels ("You really struck a nerve with me early on and got me into country music with an edge"), Jerry Reed, Dwight Yoakam, Tim McGraw, Metallica, Bruce

Willis, Will Smith, Denzel Washington, Gretchen Wilson, Run-DMC, and Clint Eastwood.[14]

What sets Coleman apart, again, is the way he counterposes a sincere musical eclecticism with a provocateur's instinct to foreground his bigness and blackness in a way guaranteed to inflame country traditionalists. His producers, "Big" Kenny Alphin and John Rich, never fail to invoke Coleman's height and race in their public statements, even as they emphasize their antiracist bona fides. The hip-hop-tinged name of their production group, Muzik Mafia, stands for "Musically Artistic Friends in Alliance"; their corporate creed, taking direct aim at a Nashville establishment and fan base presumed to be racially retrograde, is "Country music without prejudice"; and their record label, Raybaw Records, is an ethnically inclusive acronym for "red and yellow, black and white." It might be argued that what Big and Rich are offering here, with Cowboy Troy's help, is a corporatized version of racial reconciliation in which all one need do is sing, sing, sing—and buy, buy, buy. But there is also evidence that the singing and buying, along with the temporary community created during live performance, has had a transformative effect on country fan culture. "How many black people show up at your shows?" Chideya pressed Coleman during her 2007 interview. "I have noticed that over the last couple of years," he responded, "there has been a darkening of the audience at our country shows. And I think that that has gotten to the point where . . . people are saying that they are starting to feel more comfortable coming to the shows because, obviously, there has been some, sort of, stereotype about country audiences and it's, you know, semi-unfair."[15]

"I Play Chicken with the Train" limns the paradox that is Cowboy Troy: a spectacularly self-foregrounding black subject who wants to summon us into an expansive country and western clearing where we dance out whatever it is that divides us—the racially restrictive "train" symbolized by Nashville, above all—and rejoin the world transformed:

> People said it's impossible,
> Not probable, too radical
> But I already been on the CMAS
> Hell, Tim McGraw said he like the change
> And he likes the way my hick-hop sounds
> And the way the crowd screams when I stomp the ground
> I'm big and black, clickety-clack
> And I make the train jump the track like that

There is indeed a paradox at work here, but it's not precisely the paradox I've outlined above. If Cowboy Troy makes the train jump the track and ends up hosting *Nashville Star*, it is because his brag-talk, the heart of his game, is neither black nor white but both: Texas-born rapper as a latter-day game-cock of the West, and deeply in the American grain.

Frontier Breakdowns and Transracial Brag-Talk

The most productive way of illuminating the "that" served up by "I Play Chicken with the Train" is to focus on the unabashedly self-inflating voice that dominates the song: not just Troy's rap but also, crucially, the twangy titular refrain sung by Big and Rich that frames and responds to it. To para-phrase the title of a story by Eudora Welty, Where does this voice come from? Out of which cultural wellsprings does it emerge? Some of those wellsprings are indisputably African American. The literature scholar Fahamisha Patricia Brown speaks of "the self-affirming voice" in African American poetry, with its "annunciatory 'I am,'" as having "strong vernacular roots in the boast, a genre of poetry from urban street culture in which young men, in the most hyperbolic manner, affirm their worth in terms of physical strength, sexual prowess, and the ability to inflict harm."[16]

Those hard-core traditionalists who deride Cowboy Troy's brags as "rap-junk" polluting the presumptively white precincts of country music have common cause on this point with Brown: both would demand that we hear Coleman's—and Nelly's, and Ludacris's, and Run-DMC's—self-aggrandizing style as a powerful evocation of blackness. As Waterman notes, "Music [in the United States] has long played a privileged role in the naturalization of racial categories. . . . In musico-historical discourses, the retrospective construction of well-bounded, organically unified race traditions—musico-logical corollary of the infamous one-drop rule—has tended to confine the complexities and contradictions of people's lived experience . . . within the bounds of contemporary ideological categories." "Black music" is one such ideological category, and over the past twenty-five years the most immedi-ately recognizable sign of musical blackness, regardless of how many white kids flock to the music, has been the rapped brag. When the black Brooklyn-ite Radio Raheem thumps his boom box down on the counter of Sal's Piz-zeria in Spike Lee's *Do the Right Thing* (1989), the declamatory tones of Pub-lic Enemy's "Fight the Power" irritate and accuse the white pizzeria owner to precisely the degree that they exhilarate and empower Raheem; the au-dible blackness of black music is being wielded like a club—and by whites and blacks simultaneously, facing each other across an unbridgeable racial divide that the music both incites and reflects. Hard-core white traditionalists who sneer at Cowboy Troy's "pollution" of country music and the far better known cohort of contemporary African American rappers who glory in their own vocalized hustle and flow are recapitulating Sal and Raheem: polarized in every other respect, they're united in the view that rap is black. But is it?[17]

If one wanted to retrospectively construct a "well-bounded, organically unified race tradition" behind Coleman's outsized performance, one could indeed sketch a plausible genealogy. The line of descent responsible for the "urban contemporary vernacular language situation of 'rappin,'" as Brown calls it, leads us back through southern-born boasters and toast-makers like H. Rap Brown, Shine, and Dolemite (Rudy Ray Moore) and into the arms of blues boasters like Bo Diddley ("I walked 47 miles of barbed wire / I used a cobra snake for a necktie") and Willie "Hoochie Coochie Man" Dixon. The blues boaster, according to the folklorist Mimi Clar Melnick, "dreams of personal greatness, . . . brags of his accomplishments, and in no uncertain terms establishes himself as a hero. . . . There is also a strong identification with objects of power and speed—trains, weapons, cars, even large cities— which sometimes perform the boaster's feats for him or which lend him, through his intimacy with them, the attributes of a kind of superman." The black blues boaster in turn takes cultural energy from earlier black badmen such as Railroad Bill, Stagolee, Aaron Harris, and Two-Gun Charlie Pierce, all of whom achieved iconic status in a series of turn-of-the-century ballads in which an admiring black community—rather than the badmen themselves—brag of their exploits, often against symbolic representatives of a larger (white) world understood to be oppressive:

> Railroad Bill he was a mighty mean man
> He shot the midnight lantern out the brakeman's hand
> I'm going to ride old Railroad Bill . . .
> Buy me a pistol just as long as my arm,
> Kill everybody ever done me harm,
> I'm going to ride old Railroad Bill.

The braggart here, to repeat, isn't the badman himself but the singer who has been inspired by his exploits. Still, the line of descent from "Railroad Bill" to "I Play Chicken with the Train" is readily discernible.[18]

As we venture back into the period of antebellum slavery, the trail grows more faint. The cultural historian Lawrence Levine and others tell us that the cocky, boastful, self-affirming black voice was not common on the plantation, and not simply because such self-foregrounding would have incited severe reprisal from the master. Secular slave heroes, according to Levine, "operated by eroding and nullifying the powers of the strong; by reducing the powerful to their own level," and it was only with emancipation that African Americans fashioned "their own equivalents of the Gargantuan figures that strode through nineteenth-century American folklore. Indeed, the presence of such figures in black folklore [i.e., badmen] was, along with the decline of an all-encompassing religiosity and the rise of the blues, another major sign of cultural change among the freedmen."[19]

Leaving aside those Gargantuan figures for a moment, it seems clear that Levine's several claims problematize any argument for the exclusively African American origins of rap braggadocio. Brown herself skirts both the antebellum plantation and minstrelsy, preferring to deep-source rap's tall-talk, with some scholarly justification, in the African praise-song tradition. A tradition of self-foregrounding praise-songs or *ijala* has long flourished among Yoruba hunters. "I am physically sound and in great form," declaims one such hunter at a thanksgiving feast. "I will speak on, my mouth shall tell wondrous things." In the Mandingo epic *Sundiata*, drawing on the warrior side of this tradition, contending princes exchange lines such as "I am the poisonous mushroom that makes the fearless vomit" and "I am the ravenous cock, the poison does not matter to me." According to Brown, such songs of self-praise persisted in African American culture, presumably enduring a forced latency period on the plantation before flowering after Emancipation as stylized braggartry or "self-introductions" in the various forms described earlier. Cowboy Troy's claim that he's "big and black, clickety-clack, and [makes] the train jump the track," in other words, is deep and multiply sourced in the African American cultural past.[20]

The problem with this genealogy isn't that it's wrong but that it's incomplete. It constructs a "well-bounded, organically unified race tradition" by leaving out the other great American tradition of "self-affirming voices" with their "annunciatory 'I am'"s from which Cowboy Troy, and rap as a whole, also draw their inspiration: Davy Crockett, Mike Fink, and the ring-tailed roarers of the old southwestern frontier. In 1831 James Kirk Paulding fictionalized Davy Crockett as the frontiersman Nimrod Wildfire in his play *The Lion of the West* and voiced his larger-than-life persona with memorable concision: "I'm half horse, half alligator, a touch of the airthquake, with a sprinkling of the steamboat." This mode of exaggerated self-presentation was intimately linked, as the historian Elliott Gorn and the literary scholar

Christian K. Messenger have shown, with the evolving practice of rough-and-tumble fighting in the backcountry and the "temporary play communities" such practices established. "By the early nineteenth century," according to Gorn, "simple epithets evolved into verbal duels. . . . Backcountry men took turns bragging about their prowess, possessions, and accomplishments, spurring each other on to new heights of self-magnification. . . . [A frequent] claim [is] that one was sired by wild animals, kin to natural disasters, and tougher than steam engines." The so-called raftsmen's episode in Twain's *Life on the Mississippi* (1883) features two backwoods brawlers who trade threatening self-introductions with as much gusto as any pair of posturing African warriors: "I'm the man they call Sudden Death and General Desolation," announces the first. "I take nineteen alligators and a bar'l of whiskey for breakfast when I'm in robust health," answers the second, "and a bushel of rattlesnakes and a dead body when I'm ailing!"[21]

Although we might be tempted to code such frontier bluster as "white," if only in an attempt to establish it as parallel to and distinct from the African American tradition just outlined, the truth is that both cultural streams have long intermingled. After trading threats and insults, we might remember, Twain's raftsmen and their crew "[get] out an old fiddle, and one played, and another patted juba, and the rest turned themselves loose on a regular old-fashioned keelboat breakdown." African American cultural materials — the juba rhythms but also the plantation-inflected fiddling tradition and the breakdown itself, named after a popular plantation dance — are essential constituents of cross-racial exchange on the frontier. "The backwoodsman and the Negro danced the same jigs and reels," maintains the cultural historian Constance Rourke. "The breakdown was an invention which each might have claimed." Davy Crockett himself was a proficient fiddler and blackface performer. "He should . . . go down in history," argues Leon Wynter, author of *American Skin: Big Business, Pop Culture, and the End of White America*, "as the first American pop star to sport a bit of 'white Negro' persona."[22]

Whatever contributions African Americans may have made to this transracial country West, this brag-talking breakdown-driven culture of the frontier, prior to Emancipation, Levine and others agree that freed slaves and their children and grandchildren embraced that culture and the rhetoric of self-aggrandizement and self-assertion it enabled in various ways, including the so-called badman persona. "I'se Wild Nigger Bill / Frum Redpepper Hill," sings one "Negro youth" sitting near the railroad tracks with a banjo on his knee, in a post-Reconstruction tale related by the folklorist H. C. Brearley. "I never did 'wk, an' I never will. / I's done kill de boss; / I'se knocked down de hoss: / I eats up raw goose widout apple sauce!" Even H. Rap Brown, self-styled as "sweet peeter jeeter the woman beater," drew on the language of the frontier in his signature rap, calling himself "the deerslayer the buckbinder . . . known from the Gold Coast to the rocky shores of Maine."[23]

What is most "black" about H. Rap Brown's pronouncements, in other words, is simultaneously what is most "white" about him: he, like Bo Diddley, Wild Nigger Bill, Davy Crockett, and Twain's blustering raftsmen, is drawing on a multiply sourced, all-American tradition of vernacular self-aggrandizement. Cowboy Troy too draws on this tradition. "I Play Chicken with the Train" is scandalous *not* because it mixes "black" rap with "white" country but because, through the sheer force of unlikely but seamless juxtaposition, it forces us to acknowledge that those two musical styles, at least when they whoop it up, are brothers under the skin.

Black Cowboys Are Real:
Lassoing the Train, Sounding the Train

In seeking the fullest possible sounding of Cowboy Troy's resonant, disruptive hit, we might contextualize Coleman with reference to two African American figures who deserve to be called his precursors: Nat Love, an ex-slave turned cowboy, and DeFord Bailey, the harmonica-playing son of slaves and the first star of the Grand Ole Opry.[24] Both men incarnate the excluded middle, in Waterman's terms. Neither man, like Troy, is "consonant with dominant conceptions of racial difference," and as a result both have often been "elided from academic, journalistic, and popular representations" of their respective fields of achievement. Each man bears a double burden of invisibility: black overachievers in arenas culturally coded as white, unusually mobile in those chosen surrounds, both men find their achievements diminished (as exceptions to the rule) or erased entirely from mainstream histories and African American cultural histories alike. The otherwise definitive *African American Music: An Introduction* (2006), for example, edited by Mellonee V. Burnim and Portia K. Maultsby, makes no mention of Bailey, nor of the multitude of African American claims on country music inventoried, for example, in Pamela E. Foster's *My Country Too: The Other Black Music* (2000).[25] Nat Love and DeFord Bailey help contextualize Cowboy Troy not just because they too work the excluded middle but because the pivotal action of his signature song—playing chicken with a train—finds unexpected purchase in their epic lives.

Both Love and Bailey, as it happens, are born and raised in the vicinity of Nashville. Both men ultimately achieve a fame that spreads their names far beyond that mid-South staging ground. The secondary scene of Love's self-staging is his autobiography, *The Life and Adventures of Nat Love, Better Known in the Cattle County as "Deadwood Dick"* (1907); the primary scene is his career as a cowhand in the company of white western men. Love grows up on the family farm, learns how to break horses in the employ of several white men, and moves out to Dodge City, Kansas, in 1869, where he soon finds work as a brand reader and cowboy living what he repeatedly apostrophizes as "the wild and free life" on the open range. On July 4, 1876, in Deadwood, Dakota, he earns the sobriquet "Deadwood Dick" by beating all comers in a calf-roping and shooting contest. A few years later, shortly before he leaves the cowboy life, a love-struck Love jumps on his horse in a fit of drunken euphoria and decides to lasso the next train that passes through town. "The rope settled gracefully around the smoke stack," he reports, "and as usual my trained horse set himself back for the shock, but the engine set both myself and my horse in the ditch."[26] Love's outsized "play" leaves him none the worse for wear and contributes to his daredevil reputation within the transracial cowboy brotherhood.

Bailey, mildly disabled rather than physically vigorous, was an acknowledged master of the harmonica train song. He opened the inaugural radio broadcast of the WSM Barn Dance in 1925—a Nashville radio show, soon to be renamed the Grand Ole Opry—with his "rousing rendition of 'Pan American Blues,'" a song he'd learned as a boy by playing chicken with the *Dixie Flyer*, a train that blew through town on its daily run from Chicago to Florida.[27] "I'd run and get under the trestle," he told an interviewer. "I'd hold my head down and put something over my eyes to keep cinders out of my eyes. Me and my foster sister would do that. We'd listen to the sound and then I'd play that sound all the way to school":

> I worked on my train for years, getting that train down right. I caught that train down just like I want in a matter of time. I got the engine part. Then I had to make the whistle.
>
> It was about, I expect, seventeen years to get that whistle. . . . It takes years to get it down piece by piece. I got that whistle so it would have a double tone to it, a music tone. . . .
>
> You can tell my train is moving. Every time I blow, you can tell I'm getting further. It's moving out of sight as I blow. The sound of their train is moving, but staying in sight too long. I'm always reaching out. When I get about 115 miles an hour, I can feel it. My normal speed is

95 miles an hour. That don't feel like I'm doing nothing, but my train sure enough moves along.[28]

Cowboy Troy celebrates himself in "I Play Chicken with the Train" as a "Southern boy making noise where the buffalo roam," but Nat Love and De-Ford Bailey too are fearless southern boys, or rather fearless southern-born African American men, who rope the train, play the train, *work* the train, as a way of making space for themselves on a country and western frontier that they refuse to imagine as anything other than hospitable to their gifts. The train ultimately rewards them. Love retired from the open range to ride the rails as a Pullman car porter, a life he depicts in his autobiography as no less satisfying than his earlier career as a cowboy. Bailey enjoyed a celebrated tenure at Opry Land, at least for a while: shoulder to shoulder with his fellow white musicians, he became, ironically, one of the constituent parts of the Nashville-industrial "train" that Cowboy Troy later seeks to derail. In June 2006, as Coleman's hick-hop novelty was ascending the charts, the Big and Rich traveling show featuring Cowboy Troy played in Deadwood, North Dakota, where Nat Love had earned his nickname 130 years earlier. "A crowd estimate is still pending," reported *Black Hills Today*,

> but there is no doubt that this weekend's crowd for Wild Bill Days far exceeded any previous counts for attendance to any Deadwood event. People jammed Main Street Sunday night to hear the Deadwood favorites: Cowboy Troy and Big & Rich. The crowd was not at all intimidated by CMT (Country Music Television) cameras who were filming segments for an upcoming video. . . . Before the duo played the crowd was already on their feet for . . . Cowboy Troy, who prepped [them] with his "hick hop" rap "I Play Chicken with a [*sic*] Train" and "My Last Yeehaw."[29]

This postmodern tableau draws some of its resonance from what it is not: a lynch mob having its way with the isolated black man at its center, a man like Henry Smith (1893) or Jesse Washington (1916), both of whom were tortured and burned before large Texas crowds. Coleman and his producers know these histories and signify wittily — or tastelessly — on them. "My Last Yeehaw," a track from the *Loco Motive* album, begins with John Rich saying "Get freaky! Scare the—somebody scare the s—t out of me right now!," followed by a blood-curdling rebel yell and the sound of a chain saw spluttering to life. "When the black American reads Frederick Jackson Turner's *The Frontier in American History*," Houston A. Baker has argued pointedly, "he feels no regret over the end of the Western frontier. To black America, *frontier* is an alien word; for, in essence, all frontiers established by the white psyche have been closed to the black man."[30] Yet the truth is, lynching in the West was far more often a white-on-white affair during the years when southern lynching was rapidly becoming racialized, and the history of black material and imaginative investments in the West, as an arena of self-actualization and transracial play, is extensive. By 1890 more than 500,000 African Americans lived west of the Mississippi.[31] Some were brought as slaves; others, such as Nat Love, arrived of their own volition, hoping to find a fresh field of action shorn of familiar race-based restrictions and, as Allmendinger notes, became farmers, miners, merchants, members of the military, trappers, scouts, and cowboys—including, in the generations that followed, the rodeo stars Alonzo Pettie and Bill Pickett, the inventor of bull-dogging.[32] "Black Cowboys Are Real," proclaimed the NAACP in a 1940 issue of *The Crisis*—an acknowledgment of the degree to which this important element of African American migrational and employment history had been neglected to that point.[33] Thankfully recent scholarship has begun to tell a fuller story of black investments in the West, a story that, as Baker's dismissal suggests, has been largely ignored by scholars of African American history and culture during decades that saw a remarkable outpouring on virtually every other subject area in those fields.

A few black cowboys, Cowboy Troy among them, are surreal rather than real: self-created, media-savvy manipulators of a powerful symbolic language through which "the cowboy," as a cultural icon, is constituted.[34] Here Troy Coleman's significant precursor is Herb Jeffries. Born in Detroit in 1911 of African, Italian, Irish, French, and American Indian descent, Jeffries traveled west at precisely the moment that Gene Autry was making the so-called singing cowboy—a country singer in cowboy garb—into a pop cultural sensation with *In Old Santa Fe* (1934), *Tumbling Tumbleweeds* (1935), and a series of other films.[35] Jeffries filmed *Harlem on the Prairie* (1937), which he billed as the first "'all-colored' western musical," in Victorville, California, on N. B. Murphy's Dude Ranch, an enterprise founded by a black businessman from Los Angeles. Performing his own stunts, singing songs like "The Cowpoke's Life Is the Only Life for Me" and "Almost Time for Roundup" in a voice that mixed blues, swing, and country, Jeffries followed up his film debut with *The Bronze Buckaroo* (1938), *Two Man Gun from Harlem* (1939), and *Harlem Rides the Range* (1939). The title of that first sequel ended up becoming his nickname.[36]

Deadwood Dick. "Pan-American Blues." The Bronze Buckaroo. Cowboy

Troy. The transracial country West—an alternate field of action traversed by black masculinity in the passage out of slavery into the postmodern moment—begins to reveal its contours when this sort of genealogy is sketched.

I'm Country Like That: Hick-Hop, Hill-Hop, and the King of Country Bling

Although he is arguably the most popular current purveyor of the hybrid genre known variously as country rap, hick-hop, and hill-hop, "Cowboy Troy" Coleman is neither the creator of the genre nor its only significant representative. *Loco Motive* is one attempt among many to build a bridge between America's two most popular and most seemingly irreconcilable musical forms. "In 1998," according to Christopher John Farley, "for the first time ever, rap outsold what previously had been America's top-selling format, country music. Rap sold more than 81 million CDs, tapes, and albums last year, compared with 72 million for country." In one sense, the emergence of country-rap hybrids might have been anticipated: the 1990s were the decade in which the terms *multicultural* and *biracial* achieved currency, a decade capped off by the year 2000 census, in which respondents could, for the first time, self-identify as both white and black. *Rhythm Country and Blues* (1994), a concept album that paired country stars like Willie Nelson, Conway Twitty, and Reba McIntyre in duets with R&B performers like Gladys Knight, Aaron Neville, and Natalie Cole, was a notable attempt to bridge the perceived gap—a precursor and parallel to the country-rap renaissance. By the same token, country and rap have achieved much of their contemporary popularity by configuring themselves in the national imagination as proudly (if not in country's case overtly) racialized genres: the voice of unreconstructed southern pastoral and the rural white working class on the one hand, and the voice of inner-city frustration, gunplay, and rump-shaking Vegas-style fantasy on the other; Buddy Jewel's "Sweet Southern Comfort" facing off with N.W.A.'s "Fuck the Police."[37]

Despite the varied and often occluded black investments in country music, the music's whiteness has asserted itself in a range of ways through the course of its long history, from the blackface routines enacted by George Hay, Jimmie Rodgers, and Gene Autry in the 1920s and 1930s to the late-1960s moment when, according to the historian James N. Gregory, "country music provided the soundtrack for the Silent Majority," South and North, in the face of rock-and-roll integrationism. In 1968 Nashville's Music Row "was practically a battlefield command post for George Wallace," observes the journalist Paul Hemphill; Wallace's third-party presidential candidacy recast the southern segregationist as a populist of national reach at precisely the moment Black Power politics were fueling black urban unrest at multiple points on the compass. Those memories have lingered, for blacks as well as whites. When race is at issue, the trope *country music* has often functioned much like the Confederate battle flag described by the historian John M. Coski as the "expression of an ideological tradition." "[The] only thing country about him is his cowboy hat," insisted one of many irritable contributors to Cowboy Troy's main discussion board at CMT.com, oblivious to the irony attendant on *that* prop of fabricated authenticity. "He has NOT created a new genre, until someone else follows (considering it takes more than 1 person or group to have a genre), which will never happen. Even his own website calls him a rapper. Is part of a bad-intention group called the 'Muzik Mafia,' which is trying very hard to pollute country." As the sociologist Pierre Bourdieu notes, "In matters of taste more than anywhere else, all determination is negation; and tastes are perhaps first and foremost distastes. . . . The most intolerable thing for those who regard themselves as the possessors of legitimate culture is the sacrilegious reuniting of tastes which taste dictates shall be separated."[38]

Self-appointed delegitimizers notwithstanding, country-rap hybrids have proliferated over the past decade. The transracial country West has been reconfigured as a dozen different contact zones, each betraying a different set of aesthetic preoccupations and racial investments. Many of them, surprisingly—or perhaps not—stage white incursions across the color line. Trace Adkins's voyeuristic anthem, "Honky Tonk Badonkadonk" (2005), envisions black-white interchange as the reenchantment of white female flesh with the help of a borrowed (black) gaze, attitude, and vocabulary:

> Now Honey, you can't blame her
> For what her mama gave her
> You ain't gotta hate her
> For workin' that money-maker
> Band shuts down at two
> But we're hangin' out till three
> We hate to see her go
> But love to watch her leave
> With that honky tonk badonkadonk
> Keepin' perfect rhythm
> Make ya wanna swing along

Got it goin' on
Like Donkey Kong.[39]

The rappers Keith Murray, LL Cool J, and Ludacris first introduced the term *badonkadonk* in "Fatty Girl" (2001); Missy Elliott's "Work It" (2002) included the boast, "See if you can handle this badonk-a-donk-donk." Adkins didn't just sample a bit of rap vernacular into his raunchy country hit but invoked a whole hip-hop-inflected attitude of female display and male connoisseurship, with a blues standard, Elmore James's "Shake Your Money Maker," thrown in for good measure. Adkins, a country star, anchors his sexualized gaze in honky-tonk workmanship and the dance it produces— that is, in the ritual of call (his band's performance) and response (the booty in question "keepin' perfect rhythm"). The invocation of Donkey Kong, however—a popular Nintendo character modeled on King Kong—raises questions about the potentially racist undercurrents shadowing such heavy white investments in black cultural materials. The raunchy, late-night revelry evoked by Adkins arguably transforms him, at least in fantasy, into a jungle gorilla animated by a donkeyish phallic "swing."

Insane Shane McKane, who calls himself "the King of Country Bling" and a purveyor of "redneck-rap," fuses country and rap into a very different sort of double-edged burlesque, mocking—in his own boozy brags—both benighted southern whiteness and attitudinizing hip-hop blackness, as though the idiot banjo player in *Deliverance* had decided to ventriloquize the voice of 50 Cent and started spitting out tin-eared rhymes. "The Nobel Peace o' Ass Prize" on *I Put the Ho in Hoedown* (2004) is typical:

You know I deserve it, come on give it up
A cowboy like me knows how to fuck
You put a bone out, a dog's gonna chew it
A woodpecker on a tree, you peck right through it
You put some booty in front of me, I'm gonna screw it
In more positions than I know what to do wit.[40]

McKane's rap is energized by roughly the same proportions of admiration, derision, and ideological confusion that animated blackface minstrels of another era. Blackness here registers as sampled vernacular (booty, kickin', bitch, check that ass, ho), sexual signifying ("You put a bone out, a dog's gonna chew it"), and hip-hop braggartry ("You can't compete with me, you want a piece 'a me"), but all of these materials are transformed into evocations of white trash idiocy. McKane seems to have found a way of balancing both poles of the mythic hillbilly—comic yokel and dangerous degenerate—on the fulcrum of an appropriated, reductive black urban masculinity.

At the opposite extreme from the burlesque lubricity of Insane Shane McKane, voicing white working-class southern pride with a brooding stringency that is its own kind of urban cool pose, stands Bubba Sparxxx, native of rural LaGrange, Georgia. There is no cowboy in Sparxxx, no brag, nothing "racial," just an evident desire to retreat from the big wide world for a spell and recollect himself with the help of hip-hop stylistics, as in this opening stanza from "Comin' Round":

> There's a portion of the south in the spirit of this song
> Keep followin' the fiddle, it'll never steer you wrong
> I've lived a lot of life so my innocence is blown
> I'm headin to LaGrange to replenish it at most
> I've been across the globe and I've seen the world's charm,
> I taught 'em my slang, I didn't mean the world harm
> It makes the soul smile to see what I've accomplished
> I got up out the woods without a map or a compass
> Life does change, and the sun does set
> But my last breath ain't a one gust yet
> As long as daddy know that his son does sweat
> The same as he did for that uncut check
> I'll sleep fine and a child will come
> With the same last name as my poppa's son's
> And you can rest assure that my son will know
> That his Da-da wasn't a one-squeal show.[41]

Sparxxx's album *Deliverance* (2003), on which these lyrics appear, was produced and partially programmed by Timbaland, one of the most influential black producers on the Dirty South hip-hop scene.[42] Like Cowboy Troy's *Loco Motive*, it's a crossover project that juxtaposes "white" and "black" voices—in the case of "Comin' Round," a keening nasal sample from the Yonder Mountain String Band juxtaposed with Sparxxx's taut, inward-turned rap—in a way designed to suggest spiritual convergence, a productive call-and-response ritual. Where Adkins and McKane demand that the blackness they've borrowed license unrepressed (white) sexuality, Sparxxx's crossover move here forsakes the sexual for the sake of establishing a legitimate paternal line. The phrase "one-squeal show," given the album's provocative title, suggests that Sparxxx is working to remake precisely the damaged racial identity—the savage, man-raping white degenerate—that McKane is parading as a kind of backwoods playboy. Self-contained, respectful, and nobody's jailhouse bitch, Bubba neither takes it nor gives it.

When African American artists participate in country-rap hybrids, they, like Cowboy Troy, almost always participate from the "black" side of the divide, which is to say they amalgamate or juxtapose their rap with "white" country inflections provided by others. The one notable exception is Vance Gilbert, an African American singer-songwriter and self-described "ex-multicultural arts teacher and jazz singer" from Philadelphia. It would be fair to say that a listener unfamiliar with Gilbert would, in a blind test, hear a "white" voice and would place him in the programming niche he in fact occupies: a guitar-strumming product of the Cambridge, Massachusetts, New Folk scene and stage-fellow of Shawn Colvin, Martin Sexton, Patti Larkin, and Bill Morrissey. Gilbert's "Country Western Rap" (1994) wittily addresses this dilemma by enacting a seesaw rapprochement between two racialized idioms, alternating his now problematic "white folkie" voice with Jimmie Rodgers–style yodels, followed by burlesque renderings of a "black" rap voice, complete with beat-box stylings. A fiddle-driven western swing groove alternates with low-down crunk to heighten the stylistic collision:

[*sung to western swing*]
Well I was talkin' to my manager about a new plan of attack
He says "You play great folk guitar, but don't forget: you're black!
Now here's a new promotional angle that'll put us on the map.
We'll create a whole new genre, call it country western rap."
Chorus:
Yodelay-ee-hoo [beat box] [repeats]
Yodelya-ee-hoo-hoo-hoo . . . [Can't touch this]
Lay-hee odelay-hee odelay-hee odelay-hee hoo
Now rap they've got New Kids on the Block, and country's got
    Charley Pride
And that's pretty multicultural if you put 'em side by side
But I could be the new breed, yeah . . . the one to fill the gap, mm
    hmmm
The best of the both, that's the ticket: country western rap
[chorus]
[*"black" rap voice over crunk groove*]
Well I was hanging at the crib [just chillin'], popped in a tape and
    my boy was killin'

He was [pumpin' up a jam], I had to have this, ah who was it, it was
    Randy Travis, say [whoa]
Well it's off to the record shop, hell I didn't stop 'till my Visa was
    smokin'
I left Tower Records' charge machine broke . . . yeah, boyeee. . . .
Well I bought [Merle Haggard], Hank Williams too, my homeboy
    said [Whatcha tryin' a do?]
I said Yo, bro, I don't mean to be dissin', but there's beaucoup jams
    that I think we've been missin'
LL Cool J and Dolly Parton, Crystal Gayle and I'm just startin'
Reba McIntyre and MC Hammer, what a double bill it's a bad
    mama jamma
Johnny Cash and Bobby Brown, yippie kai-yo kai-yay get down
With a fresh little jam that's in between . . . it's a little bit a both,
    if you dig what I mean.
[chorus][43]

Gilbert imagines the transracial country West not as a dance-inducing,
community-building frontier breakdown, à la Cowboy Troy, but as a self-
conscious postmodern collage, a comic rejoinder to race-driven expectations. Those expectations pressure him from both sides of the color line. His
(presumptively white) manager sees "country western rap" as a shrewd and
profitable way of heightening his blackness, and in fact his black vernacular voice erupts into the song the moment he begins listening to a Randy
Travis tape. His (presumptively black) homeboy back at the crib, on the
other hand, is understandably dubious about Gilbert's newfound obsession
with twang—an obsession that immediately morphs into Gilbert's roguish
determination to forge the unlikeliest of duets between the country-western
and rap pantheons circa 1994.

Eleven years separate "Country Western Rap" from "I Play Chicken with
the Train." It is tempting to counterpose Gilbert's facetiousness with Coleman's good-natured swagger—a satire of rap braggadocio in the former case,
actual rap braggadocio in the latter—and to read significance into the difference: a failure of the earlier historical moment to sustain country rap, with
the 2000 census and its national certification of bi- and multiracialism as a
watershed moment. The manifest absurdity of "I'm country like that" gives
way to the empowered audacity of "Get you some of *that*." But if the present
investigation of America's musical excluded middle has anything to teach
us, it's that we should begin with the concrete and particular, not with pre-

digested understandings of America's racial landscape. Vance Gilbert comes to the country-rap project as a Cambridge-bred folkie responding to both idioms as a cultural outsider. His parodic distancing is, among other things, a way of asserting solidarity with a particular subculture that values such a stance. Troy Coleman comes to the same hybridizing project as a Dallas-and-Austin-bred rapper with Nashville-centered ambitions and wide-ranging tastes. He has cast his fate with a pair of adventurous white alt-Nashville producer-performers, he's eager to synthesize his aesthetic influences, and he's eager to find profitable common ground with modern honky-tonkers. The audience that remains unrepresented in Gilbert's fantasy, it turns out, is the audience that Coleman conjures up and is embraced by. Gilbert "could be the new breed . . . the one to fill the gap," but Coleman is the one whose "skills got you jumpin' outch'a socks," the one who has "already been on the CMAs," has secured Tim McGraw's approval, and gets the crowd to scream when he "stomp[s] the ground." Race plays a crucial role here, but it does so by spurring both artists, albeit in somewhat different ways, to clear a space in which "blackness," even while summoned up, is playfully merged with its imagined Other in the interest of larger, fuller lives for all parties concerned.

Anyone who presumes to find a utopian moment within "I Play Chicken with the Train" must acknowledge, of course, that Coleman's conservative electoral politics are strongly at odds with his progressive cultural politics. He was an outspoken supporter of the McCain-Palin ticket in its 2008 run against Barack Obama, and he called his appearance at the GOP convention in Minneapolis to sing the national anthem "the biggest thing that has ever happened to me." "I'm conservative," he told the journalist Deborah Corey, "because I think it is important to at least be fiscally sound. . . . As a father and husband, I need to think about college (for my children) and taking care of my family. . . . I support being a Christian and being pro-life because that makes sense to me as a husband and father."[44] Yet even here, in his public embrace of Christian conservatism, Coleman is playing an edgier game than might be apparent: married to a white woman, the father of biracial triplets, he's using "family values" to normalize what the southern heartland has traditionally pathologized and criminalized. Is he, then, an abomination come to pollute country music with his "rap-junk" as the "white girls down front [dance] for him," or a patriotic, God-fearing daddy? Or is he merely a canny performance artist who has figured out a profitable way of getting over? Troy Coleman, as Cowboy Troy, has navigated the shadowed open range of the transracial country West with a combination of brashness and finesse that rewards our attention and deserves our respect.

Notes

Epigraph sources: Wynter, *American Skin*, 13–14; Michael McCall, "Cowboy Troy," *People*, May 30, 2005, 43.

1. Journalist Tom Breihan called Cowboy Troy "the whitest-sounding nonwhite rapper since E-40." "Country-Rap: A Secret History," *Village Voice* blog entry, June 17, 2008.

2. Noël Carroll, *The Philosophy of Horror: Or, Paradoxes of the Heart* (New York: Routledge, 1990), 34.

3. Kandia Crazy Horse, "Revolutions: Music: Cowboy Troy," *Vibe*, July 2007; Cowboy Troy, "How Can You Hate Me," *Black in the Saddle* (Warner Brothers Nashville — WASE 43233, 2007).

4. *Loco Motive* sold 51,273 units in the week of June 4, 2005. See Shelly Fabian, "On the Charts: Billboard's Country Singles and Albums," *About.com: Country Music*, http://countrymusic.about.com/od/charts/a/blcharts060405.htm; Josh Tyrangiel, "The Battle of Troy," *Time*, May 30, 2005; Mike Jahn, "'Hick Hop,' Country, Metal and Cowboy Troy," *The Ancient Rocker* (2005), http://www.geocities.com /theancientrocker/cbt; BeamBeam1, "Accurate Description of CBT!," Cowboy Troy Main Board, posted July 18, 2005, http://www.cmt.com/artists/az/cowboy_troy /message_board.jhtml?c=v&t=574482&m=3750904&o=0&i=0; Tyrangiel, "The Battle of Troy"; Gail Dines, "King Kong and the White Woman: *Hustler* Magazine and the Demonization of Black Masculinity," in *Not For Sale: Feminists Resisting Prostitution and Pornography*, ed. Rebecca Whisnant and Christine Stark (Melbourne: Spinifex Press, 2005), 91.

5. Jennifer Ludden, "Interview: Singer 'Cowboy Troy' Coleman Talks about Hick-Hop," National Public Radio, June 19, 2005; Troy Coleman, John Rich, and Angie Aparo, "I Play Chicken with the Train," Cowboy Troy, *Loco Motive* (Warner Brothers — Raybaw 49316-2, 2005); Fryd, "'The Sad Twang of Mountain Voices,'" 268–69, 272.

6. O'Connor, "Cowboy Blues," 96. See also Wald, *Escaping the Delta*, n. 16; Kyriakoudes, "The *Grand Ole Opry* and the Urban South," 76, 78–79; Morton and Wolfe, *DeFord Bailey*, especially 60; Wald, *Escaping the Delta*, 47; Foster, *My Country, Too*, 9, 12, *passim*; Lewis, "Lap Dancer or Hillbilly Deluxe?"; Imani, "Country Music Gets Some Color"; Foster, *My Country, Too*, 10; Nate Guidry, "Country Music's Blacklist," *Pittsburgh Post-Gazette*, Feb. 18, 2001; Stein, "'I Ain't Never Seen a Nigger,'" 150; Foster, *My Country, Too*, 10, 80; Peter Applebome, "Country Greybeards Get the Boot," *New York Times*, Aug. 21, 1994; Wald, *Escaping the Delta*, 47–53, 97; Foster, *My Country, Too*, 87, 39–40; Berry quoted in Bernard Weinraub, "Sweet Tunes, Fast Beats and a Hard Edge," *New York Times*, Feb. 23, 2003.

7. Phyllis Stark, "Cowboy Troy's Wild Ride," *Billboard* 117, no. 23 (2005): 51; Ken Tucker, "Bigger and Richer," Billboard.com, Apr. 14, 2007.

8. Waterman, "Race Music," 167; Gregory, *The Southern Diaspora*, 175.

9. Ludden, "Interview: Singer 'Cowboy Troy' Coleman Talks about Hick-Hop."

10. Tyrangiel, "The Battle of Troy"; Brian Mansfield, "'Hick-hop' Pioneer Troy Wields a Unique Brand," *USA Today*, Mar. 20, 2005, http://www.usatoday.com/life /music/news/2005-03-20-cowboy-troy_x.htm.

11. John Gerome, "Cowboy Troy Offers 'Hick-Hop,'" *Sun Herald* (South Mississippi), June 23, 2005, http://www.sunherald.com/mld/thesunherald/entertain ment/11962014.htm; Martin Hodgson, "The Hidden Faces of Country," *Observer Music Monthly*, July 16, 2006, Guardian.co.uk.

12. Gilroy, *Against Race*, 181; Ludden, "Interview: Singer 'Cowboy Troy' Coleman Talks about Hick-Hop"; "Artists to Watch," *Rolling Stone*, June 2, 2005, 20; Ernest Jasmin, "Is Nothing Sacred? Country Meets Hip-Hop," *News Tribune* (Tacoma, Wash.), July 15, 2005, http://www.thenewstribune.com/ae/story/5023384p-4583233c.html.

13. Foster cites considerable evidence for this attitudinal claim in *My Country, Too*, even as she rebuts it in a range of ways. See also John Marks, "Breaking a Color Line, Song by Song," *U.S. News and World Report*, Apr. 12, 1999, 4; Allmendinger, *Imagining the African American West*, 81–82; Snoop Dogg, "My Medicine," *Ego Trippin'* (Doggystyle/Geffen, 2008).

14. Lewis, "Lap Dancer or Hillbilly Deluxe?" On the subject of racial stratification and transracialism within contemporary country dancehall culture, see Jocelyn R. Neal, "Dancing around the Subject: Race in Country Fan Culture," *Musical Quarterly* 89, no. 4 (2006), online.

15. See Christie Bohorfoush, "The AngryCountry Interview: Cowboy Troy," AngryCountry.com, Aug. 3, 2005, http://magazine.angrycountry.com/article.php ?story=20050803223557953; Farai Chideya, "The Hick-Hop of Cowboy Troy," *News and Notes*, Jan. 10, 2007.

16. Margo Jefferson, "My Town, Our Town, Motown," *New York Times*, Mar. 5, 1995; Brown, *Performing the Word*, 83.

17. Waterman, "Race Music," 167.

18. For connections between Shine and Dolemite and the rap tradition, see Perry, *Prophets of the Hood*, 30; Melnick, "'I Can Peep through Muddy Water and Spy Dry Land,'" 267–68; Gussow, *Seems Like Murder Here*, 171.

19. Levine, *Black Culture and Black Consciousness*, 400–401.

20. Alabi, "'I Am the Hunter Who Kills Elephants and Baboons,'" 13–23; Smitherman, *Talkin and Testifyin*, 78; Brown, *Performing the Word*, 87.

21. Paulding, *The Lion of the West*, 21; Gorn, "'Gouge and Bite, Pull Hair and Scratch,'" 32; Messenger, *Sport and the Spirit of Play in American Fiction*, 60–61; Twain, *Life on the Mississippi*, 53.

22. On the plantation origins of the breakdown, see Hartman, *Scenes of Subjection*, 78, 226 n. 126; Rourke, *American Humor*, 79–80; Wynter, *American Skin*, 13.

23. Brearley, "'Ba-ad Nigger,'" 569; Brown, *Performing the Word*, 89.

24. Much of what I write in this section is drawn from two sources: Love, *The Life and Adventures of Nat Love*, and Morton and Wolfe, *DeFord Bailey*.

25. Burnim and Maultsby, *African American Music*.

26. Love, *The Life and Adventures of Nat Love*, 123.

27. Kyriakoudes, "The *Grand Ole Opry* and the Urban South," 1.

28. Morton and Wolfe, *DeFord Bailey*, 77–78.

29. "Big and Rich Rock the Black Hills and Cowboy Troy Plays Chicken! Largest Deadwood Crowd Ever Packs Main Street for Wild Bill Days Concert," *Black Hills Today*, June 20, 2005, http://www.blackhillsportal.com/newsarchives /archivedetails.cfm?id=535.

30. Baker, *Long Black Song*, 2.

31. Scott Minerbrook, "The Forgotten Pioneers," *U.S. News and World Report*, Aug. 8, 1994, 53.

32. Allmendinger, *Imagining the African American West*, 33; Douglas Martin, "Alonzo Pettie, 93, Creator of a Black Rodeo," *New York Times*, Aug. 12, 2003, 7.

33. Nicholls, "Westward Migration, Narrative, and Genre in African America," 33.

34. Peterson, *Creating Country Music*, 83.

35. Ibid., 87.

36. Leyda, "Black-Audience Westerns and the Politics of Cultural Identification in the 1930s," 48, 52.

37. Christopher John Farley et al., "Hip-Hop Nation," *Time*, Feb. 8, 1999.

38. Gregory, *The Southern Diaspora*, 313; Coski, *The Confederate Battle Flag*, 301; BeamBeam1, "Accurate Description of CBT"; Bryson, "'Anything but Heavy Metal,'" 886.

39. Trace Adkins, "Honky Tonk Badonkadonk," CowboyLyrics.com, http://www .cowboylyrics.com/lyrics/adkins-trace/honky-tonk-badonkadonk-15326.html.

40. Insane Shane McKane, "The Nobel Peace o' Ass Prize," *I Put the Ho' in Hoedown* (Cockfight Records, 2004), lyrics transcribed by Adam Gussow.

41. B. Kaufman, W. Mathis, and T. Mosley, "Comin' Round," *Deliverance* (Beat Club/Interscope Records B0001147-02, 2003), http://www.actionext.com/names _b/bubba_sparxxx_lyrics/comin_round.html.

42. For more on Sparxxx, see Sarig, *Third Coast*, 234–39.

43. Biographical information from vancegilbert.com; Vance Gilbert, "Country Western Rap" (self-published, 1994), lyrics transcribed by Adam Gussow and reprinted here with permission.

44. Marco R. della Cava, "Grand Old Party Time," *USA Today*, Sept. 4, 2008; Deborah Corey, "Cowboy Troy: Q&A—Outside the Box," *Washington Times*, Oct. 17, 2008.

If Only They Could Read between the Lines

ALICE RANDALL AND THE
INTEGRATION OF COUNTRY MUSIC

Barbara Ching

"She's got her God and she's got good wine, Aretha Franklin and Patsy Cline," sings Trisha Yearwood in her top-selling 1994 single "xxxs and ooos (an American Girl)." Cowritten by Matraca Berg, a Nashville singer-songwriter, and Alice Randall, an African American Harvard graduate, it is one of the first songs written by an African American woman to top the country charts. Randall takes special pride in the "moment of integration" created by naming Franklin and Cline, and such juxtapositions energize nearly all of her writing.[1] Unlike Donna Summer, with her wondrous number 1 hit, Dolly Parton's 1980 "Starting Over Again," Randall has maintained a presence in country music for nearly twenty years, integrating songwriting teams by creating lyrics with many notable writers, including Steve Earle, Matraca Berg, and Marcus Hummons.[2] She has also shaped the visual and intellectual presentation of contemporary country music. She cowrote two of the songs included in Peter Bogdanovich's 1993 film about aspiring Nashville songwriters, *The Thing Called Love*. She worked as a screenwriter on the high-profile video *Is There Life Out There* for Reba McEntire and the made-for-TV movie *xxx's and ooo's*, set in Nashville. Both works were inspired by the complex lives of the American women described in the songs to which the titles refer. The author of *My Country Roots: The Ultimate MP3 Guide to America's Original Outsider Music* (2006, with Carter and Courtney Little), Randall has an

FIGURE 10.1. Alice Randall. Photo courtesy of Getty Images.

encyclopedic knowledge of country songs; *My Country Roots* features one hundred playlists (fig. 10.1).

In a delicious irony, she teaches courses on country music as literature at Vanderbilt University, the place where the Nashville Agrarian and segregationist Donald Davidson, vying with John and Alan Lomax's stunning discoveries of African American songs and singers, taught and wrote about the connections between British ballad literature and country music.[3] Indeed Davidson's work on southern folk music and country music epitomizes the "white sound" of country music as described by Geoff Mann: a nostalgic sense of white grievance conveyed by a southern-inflected "twang." As Mann puts it, "If country sounds white, it is perhaps worth considering the possibility that . . . something like a purportedly American whiteness—however historically baseless—is not *reflected* in country music, but is, rather, partially *produced* by it."[4] In contrast, Randall's writing challenges the "white sound" of country music in both the historical and ideological senses of the term. It not only disrupts the white nostalgia and interpellation described by Mann, but it also draws continual critical attention to class, race, and gender relations in history and daily life. Her writing, in short, talks back to "the Man."

To show how this disruption works, I contrast Randall's work in country music to that of other race-conscious African Americans in the genre.

In addition to offering this historical contextualization, I place the songs Randall has written on a continuum with her literary fiction, especially *Pushkin and the Queen of Spades* (2004), to argue that since the early 1990s, she has used the country music lyric not only to draw attention to the lines that separate high and low culture and black and white culture but also to imagine their erasure. A postmodernist versed in critical race theory, Randall invests history with both personal and communal significance through her writing. Whether they resound in a song, on a screen, or in a book, her words limn lives inflected by the history of slavery in America, by contemporary cultural hierarchies, and by complex networks of love and theft among the races in America.[5] Randall creates characters who tell stories about how these forces shape who they are and how they live and, most important, how they harness these forces to their own ends. Through her use of the country music lyric and the contemporary novel, she imagines an anti-essentialist commonality, a renewed and revalued cultural space, what Josh Kun calls audiotopia: "almost-places of cultural encounter" where we experience American popular "music's utopian potential" to "transform the world we find ourselves in" precisely because of the multiple voices conveyed in the words and sounds.[6]

The fact that much of Randall's writing has been aimed at the mainstream, commercial market increases the likelihood that her songs will seep into our heads; the more "alternative" writing she has done, though, makes clear her commitment to constructing and deconstructing the African American resonance in country music. For the most part, however, Randall seeks to "voice the popular" in her audiotopias, a term I borrow from Richard Middleton to stress popular music's always already subalternity, its status as a "low other" containing "plural, hybrid [and] compromised" voices.[7] She contrasts her fiction to that of Nobelist Toni Morrison by claiming that her work offers intellectual play to readers as opposed to the wrenching memories of slavery and racism that Morrison conjures.[8] Likewise, in place of Morrison's opera libretto *Margaret Garner*, Randall writes lyrics to three-minute songs. Her first novel, *The Wind Done Gone* (2001), an "unauthorized parody" of Margaret Mitchell's *Gone with the Wind*, evoked legal controversy when the Mitchell estate unsuccessfully sued to block publication. But unlike, say, the characters in Morrison's *Beloved*, maimed and haunted by the legacy of slavery, Randall's heroine, half sister to Scarlett O'Hara by virtue of Captain O'Hara's relationship with the slave "Mammy," leaves the plantation and lives elegantly ever after (often with Rhett Butler).

By "voicing the popular," Randall refocuses what skulks about as a mystery, or, as Mann describes it, as mystified innocence, in mainstream country music: the enduring legacy of slavery and segregation. Take, for example, Loretta Lynn's restored plantation home in Hurricane Mills, Tennessee. In *Still Woman Enough*, her second autobiography, Lynn explains that she bought it because the white-pillared mansion "looked like a hillbilly's dream"; she goes on to say that it was haunted by a Confederate soldier (as well as by her late husband's many paramours), so she ultimately chose to build herself a new house.[9] Fans can tour the antebellum dream home, however. Johnny Cash too believed his Jamaican plantation home, Cinnamon Hill (originally owned by Elizabeth Barrett-Browning's family), was haunted. Although he is not as specific as Lynn about the ghost's identity, he implies it is a slave and claims that he was not bothered by it. In *Cash: The Autobiography*, he opens the chapter on his life in Jamaica by obliquely justifying life in the big house: he is descended from Scottish royalty, and the lush Jamaican landscape reminds him of his Arkansas childhood on a cotton farm. He displaces the unanswered questions about justice and complicity on (other) tourists; he doubts that the visitors golfing on "the manicured sod" that surrounds his house know that "thousands of slaves" once lived on the grounds.[10] In contrast, while *The Wind Done Gone* most explicitly demystifies the symbolic nostalgia of (southern) whiteness, several of Randall's high-profile country lyrics also disrupt the subtle nostalgia for the days of unquestioned white supremacy that Mann links to the white sound of country music.

Randall's lyric-writing strategy works particularly well because she does not perform, and her strongest lyrics are evocative ballads rather than first-person expressions of sentiment. Moreover the range of her subjects and the diversity of her song placements demonstrate her skill with country music's standard themes, such as nostalgia for a simpler past (Marie Osmond's "My Hometown Boy"), love (The Woodys' "A Hundred Years of Solitude"), nature (Glen Campbell's "Who's Minding the Garden"), and religion (Moe Bandy's "Many Mansions"), as well as her ability to encompass the regional identities of the genre by setting songs in the West (Radney Foster's "Went for a Ride") and New Orleans (Jo-El Sonnier's "Café du Monde"). Her "Blinded by Stars," cowritten with and sung by the alt-country aspirant Adrienne Young, echoes and contradicts the bellicose flag-waving of Toby Keith's "Courtesy of the Red, White, and Blue (The Angry American)" well enough to be an answer song: "This is my flag, but this ain't my fight," says the chorus. "I'll Cry for Yours If You'll Cry for Mine," a confrontational song about Confederate monuments and memorials, has not found an audience in the United States, although the Danish star Tamra Rosanes recorded it.

Likewise, Randall works in several country music styles, such as the western swing of Walter Hyatt's "Get the Hell Out of Dodge," the old-time string-band sound in her "Ballad of Sally Anne," and the Eagles-esque country rock of her first hit to crack the top ten, Judy Rodman's "Girls Ride Horses, Too." The selections in *My Country Roots* similarly confirm Randall's catholicity; the section of the book titled "What We Sound Like" features playlists devoted to each of fourteen different genres of country music. Throughout, selections include famous country artists from the Carter Family to Toby Keith, little-known ballad singers, and songs performed by Chuck Berry, Leadbelly, Neil Young, the Rolling Stones, and Bruce Springsteen.

In addition to encompassing many forms of country music, Randall articulates the literary value of the country lyric. She studs her lyrics with literary allusions and her novels with allusions to Hank Williams and Tupac Shakur, consciously working to undermine the value-laden distinctions between the literary and the vernacular, the European and the American, and the class, gender, and racial categories that mark country music. In an interview with Robert Birnbaum, she explained that she went to Nashville after graduating from Harvard because she was interested in "the metaphysical poetry that I found in country songs and the connection to the American Metaphysicals that I had read."[11] Such cross-fertilization of "high" and "low" cultural references also feeds her literary writing. For example, in the epigraph to *Pushkin and the Queen of Spades*, Randall quotes the Emily Dickinson poem "Hope Is the Thing with Feathers," which is also the first line of "Many Mansions," the title track from Moe Bandy's 1989 album. More recently her song "A Hundred Years of Solitude" borrows its title from *One Hundred Years of Solitude* (1967) by the Colombian Nobel Prize winner Gabriel García Márquez, an Oprah book club selection. *My Country Roots* frequently notes the literary lineage of the selections, tracing them as easily to the Harvard professor Francis J. Child's nineteenth-century collection of traditional British ballads as to slave songbooks. Similarly the book praises "Pancho and Lefty," performed by Merle Haggard and Willie Nelson and written by Townes Van Zandt as "the *Iliad* and *Odyssey* of country music."[12] Randall's allusions are middlebrow, or at least safely unobscure, but such obviousness is perhaps the best way to make the point that country lyrics can have the complexity and historical resonance that we routinely accord to literary texts even as they retain the resonance of audiotopias.

When Alice Randall came to Nashville in the mid-1980s, country music had portrayed the shared experience of race at extremes of strife or mild tolerance. Charley Pride, the first black country music superstar, was fad-ing from glory, but his career exemplified innocuous tolerance — so much so that his songs resonated little but nostalgia or present-day bliss. Entering the charts in 1967, Pride enjoyed his biggest hits with domesticated love songs such as "Kiss an Angel Good Morning," his first gold record (1971). He won the Country Music Association Entertainer of the Year award that year too. His record company, RCA, chose songs for him, generally written by a stable of white male songwriters. Even so, Pride sang country music like he was born to it; more important, he sang it as if nobody doubted that he should, exemplifying the notion that country music and its largely southern setting had no racial legacy. The closest he ever came to singing about the racial politics of country music may have been the gentle praises of tolerance in a few songs, such as the title track of his 1980 album *There's a Little Bit of Hank in Me*. An introduction to a selection of Hank Williams's covers, the song features a few autobiographical details, such as the memory of singing and listening to Hank's songs during a Mississippi childhood and the addition of an oblique moral: "Music has no boundary it comes from the heart / And where my music comes from Hank you play the leading part."[13] (Nevertheless Pride's cover choices from Williams's repertoire, particularly "Kaw-Liga," the song about a red-faced wooden Indian, and "Honky Tonk Blues," gain an interesting resonance when sung by a black man.) The upbeat 1974 "Mississippi Cotton Picking Delta Town" says nothing about race relations in the home of the blues, and in Pride's 1981 hit, "Roll on Mississippi," the singer expresses his nostalgia by sitting on the riverbank thinking of Tom Sawyer and Huck Finn. He doesn't mention the escaped slave, Jim, whose plight gave the white boys' adventures their knotty moral significance. "All His Children," a 1972 release with Henry Mancini, implicitly advocated colorblindness with a line noting that we are all part of the family of man. The title of 1971's "I'm Just Me" implies that the singer stands apart from ethnic or racial groups, and the lyrics even suggest that any claim to group identity would be an inauthentic expression of grievance. He thus separates himself from people (implicitly African American?) who complain that "life is rough." The chorus, with its gloss on the title, offers a strangely timid pledge to the audience: "Every day I try to be exactly what you see" is juxtaposed with a placating "Every day I'm just me."[14] Again speaking explicitly for himself, Pride told an interviewer, "I don't go for that 'us and y'all and them' stuff. . . . I am and have always been first and foremost an American."[15] When Pride's stream of hits trickled dry in 1985, RCA dropped him. Even so, he charted a few more singles until his last top-40 hit, "Amy's Eyes," in 1990.

While Pride enjoyed his mellow prime, other, less successful black country artists made a point of dramatizing the connections *and* disjunctions between country music and their skin color. Linda Martell, the first black woman to sing on the Opry, released her only country album with the title *Color Me Country* (1969). For the most part, however, this country music dramatized black men speaking to the Man in the tradition of hard country predecessors such as Merle Haggard, "the poet of the working man." Slyly enacting what I have called "burlesque abjection," this tradition makes a spectacle of the failure to exert the privileges of white manhood.[16] It takes country's traditional working-class themes of economic hardship and familial failures and explicitly contrasts them to the suburban sublime. When a black man sings about such woes, however, the blend of ridicule and rage becomes more fraught, particularly in the early 1970s. For example, on a 1972 album title cut, the songwriter and singer O. B. McClinton set his "Obie from Senatobie" (Senatobia, Mississippi) to the melody of Haggard's "Okie from Muskogee," and in place of Haggard's line about rednecks "waving old glory down at the courthouse," McClinton lampooned stereotypes about blacks, claiming, "We still eat watermelon down at the courthouse." While Haggard's song lent itself to both nostalgia for the good old days and satiric, progressive interpretations, McClinton's edge becomes jagged here. Liking the song implies rejecting the racism he burlesques. Similarly juxtaposing black and white working-class identities, he released an album called *Chocolate Cowboy* in 1981 and a single called "Honky Tonk Tan" in 1984.[17]

Likewise, in 1973 Stoney Edwards made a spectacle of abjection by tracing his lineage to the hard country heroes Hank Williams and Lefty Frizzell at the same time that he called attention to his roots in African American music in the single "Hank and Lefty Raised My Country Soul." Written by the (white) songwriting masters A. L. Owens and Dallas Frazier, this song capitalizes on the African American connotations of the term *country soul*. As the gifted popular music chronicler Barney Hoskyns describes it, country soul, while visibly black, arose from overt racial collaboration: the rhythm and blues sound of African American singers (most notably Aretha Franklin, Percy Sledge, Otis Redding, and Solomon Burke) working with white songwriters and integrated studio staffs at Stax and Muscle Shoals, all inflected by a shared experience of southern rural life and religiosity.[18] O. B. McClinton also overtly played with the connection in album cuts like "(Country Music Is) American Soul" and "Country Music, That's My Thing." The claim to shared territory, however, couldn't be made without struggle. Edwards's 1976 single "Blackbird," written by his white producer, Chip Taylor, was a musical manifesto for African American country, the story of a young boy whose fiddling father also taught him to strum the blues with a "string from Robert Johnson's guitar" before he formed a country band. While Pride stood only for himself ("I'm Just Me"), the men in this song hit the road as "a couple of country niggers." In the song, their entry into the country music business meets with resistance from "scarecrows" in the music industry, but the chorus urges "blackbirds" to keep up the fight.[19]

The limited success of these artists could be cited to illustrate the scarecrows' power over blackbirds or the reluctance of the country music audience to confront racial conflict; likewise, it can confirm the suspicion that Pride's high profile served as the exception that proved white rule over country music. The journalist Paul Hemphill went so far as to call Pride "Nashville's house nigger."[20] The spectacle of Hank Williams Jr. performing his white supremacist fantasy "If the South Woulda Won" at the 1988 Country Music Association's Award Show when he was named Entertainer of the Year also speaks uncomfortable volumes. As the writer Jeff Woods noted, "No one assembled at the Opry House . . . revealed the slightest displeasure with Hank," although *Billboard*'s country music journalist Edward Morris resigned from the Association afterward.[21] In the meantime, Music Row record labels, in search of the next Charley Pride, groomed black singers such as the cardiologist Cleve Francis (Liberty) and Trini Triggs (Curb). Francis signed his record deal in 1990, but his upbeat love songs and ballads in the Charley Pride tradition never achieved chart success, and by 1995 he had returned to his cardiology practice.[22] Francis complained that Liberty did little to integrate his act with those of his label mates such as Garth Brooks, one of the era's top concert draws. He told *Nashville Scene*'s music writer Bill Friskics-Warren, "I basically toured by myself. Garth could have put Mickey Mouse on his show and it would have sold, but I never got a chance to open for Garth. In fact, I never did a show with any of my labelmates. What does that mean?"[23] In 1999 a *U.S. News and World Report* article optimistically placed Triggs on "the star track,"[24] but his label released only a CD single, "Straight Tequila" / "Horse to Mexico" (1998), both songs with inconsequential and incongruent Mexican themes. (Darius Rucker, who recently enjoyed two top-selling country hits, may have finally repeated Pride's exceptional success.) At the end of the 1990s black country artists began to express concern about maintaining their presence in the genre. Frustration with limited opportunities prompted the songwriter Frankie Staton to found the Black Country Music Association in 1997. The next year the journalist Pamela E. Foster self-published *My Country: The African Diaspora's Country Music Heritage*, an encyclopedia and manifesto offering "definitive evidence of the close, long-standing and tumultuous relationship between children of the African motherland and the musical core of the American heartland."[25]

Nevertheless, even if new opportunities were declining in the 1990s, Nashville's institutions paid plenty of respectful attention to the *historical* role of African Americans in country music. In 1992 the *Journal of Country Music* devoted an issue (14.2) to black artists in country music. As Charley Pride was disappearing from the country charts, well-publicized 1990s recordings, such as the Country Music Foundation's three-disc box set *From Where I Stand: The Black Experience in Country Music* (1998) and MCA's 1994 biracial duets project, *Rhythm, Country and Blues* documented links between country soul, the blues, and country music for the mainstream. In his introductory essay to the *From Where I Stand* booklet, Bill Ivey, the Country Music Foundation's director, frames the project as a "border crossing" contesting a complex of "conventional wisdom" about the African roots of the blues, the British roots of hillbilly music, and the "suburbanization of country music."[26] Less scholarly, James Hunter closes the liner notes for *Rhythm, Country and Blues* by evoking unobjectionable common ground: "One of the several glories of this collection is that in a day when neither country nor soul is the exclusive province of any one region or spot or race, singers like this can still make their stories, their weather, their luck seem like everyone's."[27] The project gained further industry recognition at the 1995 Grammy Awards: Trisha Yearwood and Aaron Neville's version of "I Fall to Pieces" won for Best Country Vocal Collaboration, and Al Green and Lyle Lovett's "Funny How Time Slips Away" took the prize for Best Pop Collaboration.

But no matter how easy it was to hear shared emotional resonances in country music, blues, and soul from earlier decades, "hot new country" was tied to a tepid, effeminate whiteness, still infused with nostalgia and still conveyed in a hurting, albeit softened, twang. No longer strictly associated with white, working-class southerners, mainstream country music now played in soccer moms' minivans. While it still lay at the bottom of an abstract hierarchy of musical genres, the Opry as opposed to the opera, in the 1990s its popular music "other" was no longer rock, with its artistic ambitions and connections to a college-educated, white, "hippie" counterculture, but rap, emanating from the inner city, and alternative country, located in a rough-hewn haze of country "tradition." Hip urbanites embraced alt-country as a counterculture, looking to older country roots as a way to express their alienation from mainstream popular music of all sorts and reconfiguring burlesque abjection into a familiar, deeply nostalgic form of white guy cool-supremacy in the process.[28] In 1994, when "XXXs and OOOs" reached number 1, the Rick Rubin and Johnny Cash collaboration *American Recordings* debuted, making Cash hip and vindicating his disappearance from country music radio and record charts. In 1995 *No Depression*, the *Rolling Stone* of the alternative country movement, was launched. In its pages, top-selling neocowboys like Garth Brooks were dethroned in favor of other white men, ranging from the Carter-covering country-grunge Midwesterners in the band Uncle Tupelo to dearly departed heroes like Hank Williams.

While alt-country contrasts country's macho past to its white bread feminized present, rap contrasts the urban jungle to the suburban city. As Bruce Feiler wrote in his gushing book on country music in the 1990s, *Dreaming Out Loud: Garth Brooks, Wynonna Judd, Wade Hayes, and the Changing Face of Nashville*, "If, as Public Enemy's Chuck D once famously asserted, rap music is the 'CNN of the ghetto,' country music, in the nineties, became the CNN of the suburbs."[29] He quotes Edward Morris (the *Billboard* country music editor who resigned from the Country Music Association): "Country is fundamentally based on the white experience." Likewise, Tony Brown, then president of MCA Nashville, told Feiler, "Country basically *is* white music." In this climate, Randall skillfully wrote African Americans into the music by assuming that black and white voices had always been joined in song, just as they had also been joined in strife. Her successes mined a more complicated vein of racial self-expression than Pride's bland blackness or the more confrontational hard country of Pride's contemporaries O. B. McClinton and Stoney Edwards. In fact Randall doesn't even mention songs like McClinton's or Edwards's in the vast selection offered in *My Country Roots*, although she does reinforce the sentiment of Pride's "There's a Little Bit of Hank in Me" by including that song on her playlist about country music songs that reflect the black experience.[30] In the book's brief introduction she defines country music by stressing its complexity: "No genre of music deals with a more diverse body of subject matter, provides a more mature perspective, or draws from a wider range of conflicting impulses."[31] Among the conflicts and subjects she lists are race, class, gender, and African American musical heritage, a particularly complex construction at the turn of the twentieth century.

Not all of Randall's songs raise the question of race, but in those that do, the subject gains an intriguing ambiguity in the mouths of white performers, doing what songs do best: getting in your head. At the same time, this ambiguity creates new possibilities for identification by portraying both racism and integration as historical experiences shared by blacks and whites even as blacks have borne the greater burden. In her "Ballad of Sally Anne," sung by the contemporary bluegrass virtuoso John Cowan (1991), racial violence resounds through a community with a simultaneously galvanizing and disarming emotional charge. This song tells of a lynching that takes place right after the wedding of Johnny and Sally Anne, but the listener can't know for certain whether the victim was a black man married to a white woman or a white man married to a black woman. Or are both lovers black? (In *My Country Roots* Randall lists the song in the "Who We Are" section called, simply, "Black," although she still avoids specifying which character is black.) The song's ancestors similarly complicate the story: in the "Ballad of Sally Anne," Randall takes on the whitest strains of country music, the (wordless) Appalachian fiddle showpiece, the product of hillbilly virtuosi, and the ballad, with its British lineage and Harvard-educated collectors. In 1918 the British ballad collector Cecil Sharp described a version he transcribed in North Carolina that introduces a theme that Randall develops: Sally Anne's wedding. But Randall also alludes to more racially complex songs. A model of narrative compression, Randall's "Ballad" opens with Johnny's simple proposal to Sally Anne. In the fourth line, we hear that "the ride from the church bore strange fruit," an easy allusion to Billie Holiday's signature song about lynching. The rousing melody never evokes tragedy, however, and the rest of the lyrics suggest that another union, or at least some sort of reconciliation with the community, could come about. Indeed communal wedding celebrations epitomize such harmony, especially when they feature traditional music. Thus another verse says that Sally Anne "attends every wedding around here," adding that when the fiddle strikes up the tune, her presence can be felt. The song also enacts the joy of a wedding celebration with its infectious fiddle break. The chorus invites someone to dance with Sally Anne, to bring her to the party once again, to create a happy ending, even as the catchy melody could easily lure a crowd onto the dance floor.

Yet strange fruit is not party food, and the other songs stirred into "Ballad of Sally Anne" further embitter the brew. Many song collectors note that "Sally Anne" is related to another folk song, "Sail Away, Ladies," and Randall and O'Connor's song maintains that link; in place of the last chorus ("Who's gonna dance with Sally Anne?"), Cowan sings, "Sail away, ladies, sail away," while O'Connor's fiddle answers. As sung by the Grand Ole Opry star Uncle Dave Macon (1927) or Odetta (1957) or Joan Baez (1959), this song celebrates living happily in Tennessee while expecting an even better home in heaven. Randall and O'Connor's version, however, just sings out the title; it does not pick up these verses. Nevertheless any listener with a submerged memory of this song's history can activate it, and in that respect a version in Thomas Talley's *Negro Folk Rhymes* (1922) offers a more interesting twist, particularly in light of the lynching story: "Sail away, ladies! Sail away! / Nev' min' what dem white folks say."[32] This verse, in particular, prompts memories of Randy Newman's original composition, also called "Sail Away" (1972; covered by Ray Charles in 2002), a song awash in guilt and irony about what white folks said as they lured Africans onto slave ships. Sung by a slave trader, the lyrics promise the captives plenty of food and slyly boast that in America "every man is free to take care of his home and family."[33] Only later would these Africans learn who the free man is and what their relationship to him would be. In Randall's "Ballad of Sally Anne," which reflects all of these songs, listeners too need to figure out their relationship to Sally Anne and the Man.

Similarly listeners must experiment with a range of racial and sexual identities in Radney Foster's 1992 recording of Randall's "Went for a Ride." Race is only one detail in the singer's elliptical account of his lost trail-riding partner, the black cowboy. ("He was black as the sky on a moonless night.") The singer's race is not stated, and the rest of the ballad seems to be about a love triangle such as those that shaped the story of Butch Cassidy and the Sundance Kid or perhaps about a betrayal such as the one obscurely implied in Townes Van Zandt's "Pancho and Lefty" or Randall's earlier "Girls Ride Horses, Too."[34] The singer introduces the complication of a woman (whose race also does not merit mention), noting that there was "blood on the leather and tears in her eyes," but he doesn't say whose blood or what leather. The listener wonders whether the singer killed the dark cowboy because he wanted him for himself, or whether it was the woman he wanted. Or maybe the woman did the killing. "She stole my heart," is as close to an explanation as anything offered, but that only displaces the question, Where did the dark cowboy's heart lie?

Like "The Ballad of Sally Anne," "Went for a Ride" also disrupts nostalgia as it engages American history and race relations through audiotopic intertextuality. With its image of bloody leather, the song references and retunes Tex Ritter's "Blood on the Saddle," first performed in *Green Grow the Lilacs*, Lynn Riggs's play about Oklahoma's transformation from Indian Territory into the forty-eighth state. (Rodgers and Hammerstein would adapt this play for their first musical, *Oklahoma!*) While these musicals blotted the blood from that trail of tears, Randall (and many listeners) can easily (re)-trace it. "Blood on the Saddle," though, displaces the tragedy of the American Indian with a rodeo accident that evokes laughter rather than sympathy. Its diction jarringly blends the emotional instructions offered by traditional ballads with the language of cartoon violence: "Oh, pity the cowboy, all bloody and red / For the bronco fell on him and bashed in his head."[35]

Performed in an ominous midtempo, "Went for a Ride" regains the sense of doom that "Blood on the Saddle" squandered, connecting it to a new understanding of history not only through the songs it evokes and the curiosity it engenders but also through the dramatic flourish that closes the first verse by announcing that history books "got it all wrong." The referent of the pronoun *it*, as usual, is unclear, but what is clear is that the song functions both as an antidote to nostalgia about the Old West, the rip-roaring drama that gives cover to a more painful history, and as a reminder of nearly everyone else's complicity. At the same time, the reminder has the potential to renew the community, much like the invitation to dance with the bereaved Sally Anne. As Kun notes, such structures encourage us to "listen and think audiotopically . . . for music that is already made but not yet heard, music that makes audible racialized communities who have been silenced by the nationalist ear."[36]

No song better illustrates Randall's commonality-building perspective on country music and her gentle disruptions of the "white sound" of commercial country music than "xxxs and ooos," her most successful song to date. It differs remarkably from her first songs about women and family as it places its subject firmly in contemporary middle-class life. When Feiler interviewed Randall to support his argument that "country music is the CNN of the suburbs," she suggested that the African American experience of suburbia was more complex than he imagined; in other words, African Americans live there and deal with both racism and friends and neighbors. He didn't know what to do with that insight, concluding, "This is the reason for the growing segregation [of country music]" in spite of the fact that he was talking to Randall *because* she represents integration.[37] In fact since late twentieth-century suburbs, much like country music, were only *symbolically* the bastion of the white middle class, the argument could just as easily be turned around, finding reasons for the growing integration of country music.

Exploring the complexity of the integrated suburban experience was the theme of Aaron McGruder's *Boondocks*, the enormously successful *and* controversial comic strip (and later a television show) that began national syndication in 1999, and life in a McGruderesque Boondocks is clearly part of the story related in "xxxs and ooos." That the suburbs now shelter the mainstream country audience also becomes clear in the muted treatment of the country/city dichotomy and the upbeat portrayal of middle-class womanhood in the song. In contrast, one of Randall's earliest songs, "My Hometown Boy," recorded by Marie Osmond in 1988, relies on the country/city dichotomy. As Randall puts it in *My Country Roots*, this boy's appeal lies in his ability to see the simple country girl that the successful urban woman once was. The title "Small Towns (Are Smaller for Girls)," recorded by Holly Dunn in 1987, expresses less nostalgia for the simple past but also imagines a way of life in which there is no suburban middle ground. Thanks to the double standard, the girl in this song, growing up in the small-town South, is denied the freedom to explore not only her sexuality but also most other aspects of adult life. She spends her days in restrictive "ribbons and curls," and at night, while the boys enjoy wild times, she plans her getaway, "reading about New York City with her daddy's flashlight."

The woman of "xxxs and ooos," who "*used to* tie her hair up in ribbons and bows," seeks a different kind of recognition and freedom than that longed for in "My Hometown Boy" and "Small Towns (Are Smaller for Girls)." The simple geography of city versus country that structures both songs vanishes as well, even though in other respects this American girl could be Holly Dunn's small-town girl all grown up. In "xxxs and ooos," in addition to "romance and a live-in maid," the woman balances nostalgia for who she once was with proud recognition of who she is now. With verses that list the chores weighing on a career woman's mind, such as finding someone to fix the sink and mow the grass, the setting evokes a home in 1990s suburbia *and* a job downtown, both grounds covered by the aspirational "have it all" feminism of the late twentieth century. At the same time, the multiple imagery of the song sketches the psychological contours of this new geography. In the immediate context, xxxs and ooos seem to signify affection: kisses and hugs, the open intimacy between lovers, friends, and family members. It's worth noting, however, that this symbol is one that the woman in the song *used* to use to close her letters. Now she's working in the man's world ("her daddy's," says the song), where she tries to "keep the balance up between love and money." The xxxs and ooos, then, also signify a sort of conflicted and competitive emotional bookkeeping. The two letters are, after all, the symbols used to play that easily stalemated child's game, tic-tac-toe, and the marks that represent strategies in the more macho, territory-conquering game of football.[38] Whatever the game, the woman is winning. In spite of the precarious emotional balance described, the American girl is not focused on loss or victimhood. She has gained territory and crossed all kinds of lines: "She's got *her* God and she's got good wine, Aretha Franklin and Patsy Cline." This woman's deity doesn't deny her the refined alcohol that old-fashioned southern religiosity would prohibit.[39] Just as heavenly, the songs in this American girl's head feature country-tinged oldies from both sides of the color line. (In Randall's novel *Pushkin and the Queen of Spades*, Aretha is described as "country and colored" [181].)

This song, like O. B. McClinton's "Obie from Senatobie" and Stoney Edwards's "Blackbird," acknowledges the color line by drawing upon it. Unlike those songs, however, this one enters the world of "the (white) man" without dramatic provocation. In its chart-topping incarnation, it was sung by a blonde woman (Trisha Yearwood) who pays the incongruity of Aretha and Patsy no special vocal attention and who draws up an inventory of what an American girl does when she becomes an adult that gives no more emphasis to her playlist than to her hairstyle, which used to feature the girlish trappings of bows and ribbons, but now, evidently, flows free. (Admittedly, untamed hair may have more fraught symbolism for African American women.) As Randall notes in *My Country Roots*, "Yearwood has made a living scoring number one hits which sit softly on the mind and easy on the soul."[40] In this case, when Yearwood's rousing yet bland performance rose to the top of the country charts, most buyers were unaware of the feminist, African American identity of the songwriter. It could be argued that the "unmarked" category, "American" without the "African" modifier, makes it easy to assume that we are hearing about white women. But nothing prevents one from imagining that the "American girl" listening to Aretha Franklin and Patsy Cline could be white, black, or something between the lines.

While "xxxs and oooos" gently insinuates integration between listeners' ears, Randall can underscore grotesque boundaries and their breechings when she chooses. Thus in the long-playing format of her novel *Pushkin and the Queen of Spades*, she recapitulates and deepens the scenarios of "xxxs and oooos," "Sally Anne," and "Went for a Ride." While the plot is difficult to summarize, my discussion here focuses on "the cultural conversation" that takes place when the heroine, Windsor Armstrong, a Detroit-born, black intellectual woman living in Nashville at the end of the twentieth century, integrates country music into her life (213). With a last name that evokes athletic prowess and a first name that she knows to be drawn from the ruling family of England, and, more important, from the suburb that links Detroit to Canada, a place that obscures the border and invites regular crossings (103, 205), Windsor, narrating in the first-person, evokes Randall herself. In this novel, as in her lyrics, Randall consistently juxtaposes high and low culture, the rural and the urban, and Motown and Nashville in order to marry black and white.

Windsor's son, Pushkin X, the hero of what turns out to be a comedy, is a star NFL defensive lineman named after the slave-descended Russian writer *and* after Malcolm X, "the best black brain and the fiercest black heart" (6). Windsor herself plays a sort of defensive linewoman, embarrassed that she, a Harvard-educated, Vanderbilt-tenured specialist in Afro-Russian literary relations, has raised what she sees as a "stereotypical" black male, all brawn and drawn to the status conferred by white women and suburban McMansions. Likewise, pregnant after her rape by a white executive, she once felt that her subsequent pregnancy turned her into a stereotypical unwed black mother. While her years spent in Russia and her Vanderbilt professorship remove her from ghetto stigmas, Pushkin's engagement to Tanya, a Russian lap dancer, threatens her Nashville shelter. Worse, before his wedding, he demands to know who his father is, but Windsor wants to shield him from this information since it would reveal not only his whiteness but also her rape.

The book thus opens with Windsor struggling to find a way to accept what Pushkin has done with his life and a way to answer his question. In the meantime, her hesitation has cost her an invitation to the wedding, but with this conflict structuring the plot, the potential for comedy, a happy reconciliation of the initially grotesque juxtapositions, presents itself from the start. As she drinks in her favorite "hillbilly bar," Windsor writes chapters from her life story, looking for ways to tell Pushkin X what he needs to know. She chooses the bar over her Vanderbilt office and her architect-designed home not only because she needs to drown her sorrows country music–style but also because in Pushkin X's earlier childhood, she had used country music to translate her feelings about their roots in Motown. They listened to the *Smithsonian Collection of Country Classics*, valuable, she explains, because it provided "translations of [her] experience that [she] could share without damaging him" (59). They especially like the song "Detroit City." Moreover the title of the collection announces the bridging between high and low culture that is important to Windsor (and Randall). Many compilations, after all, feature "Detroit City," but a woman like Windsor would choose one that also emphasizes connections with cultural institutions like the Smithsonian and with the cultural capital implied in the word *classic*. Although Windsor doesn't extensively gloss Bobby Bare's lyrics to "Detroit City," the song bemoans a lost southern home, replete with cotton fields and family. She does note, however, that Detroit had been a place of "hard truths" for her, and Pushkin learned to play football in Motown while she was off completing her Harvard degree (64). Perhaps the most relevant wish expressed in this song is the sole line Windsor does cite: the wish that people could "read between the lines." Similarly she hopes her son can learn the painful truth she has to tell him about his patrimony without reliving the humiliation that rape and the stigma of single motherhood caused her.

While Windsor writes in order to give Pushkin a way to read between the lines and discover the essential truth about his patrimony, she too learns to read between the lines of the pain she feels about his impending matrimony. She must, in short, confront her "racism," her reluctance to accept his white bride-to-be (125), a situation similar to the scandalous wedding described in "The Ballad of Sally Anne." Once again country music helps her get between the lines. As she leaves the hillbilly bar to meet her son at the bar in the far more prestigious Hermitage Hotel, named after Andrew Jackson's plantation but evoking as well the art museum and palace of St. Petersburg's doomed White Russians, she affirms her love for Hank Williams as a way to "get in touch with [her own] whiteness" and to acknowledge her son's "complex ethnicity" (212–13). As the novel closes, Windsor realizes that the translations she has created for herself and her son will also connect her to her white daughter-in-law. She thus addresses some of the final paragraphs to Tanya, expressing the hope that she has "blackened [Tanya's] mind" by "pour[ing] blackness into [her] ear" (271, 277). The word choice, as usual, is crucial. The words Windsor has written are on a page, but their impact, like the words to a song, takes place in the ear, particularly through the poem, or rap song, that she has also created by finishing, fixing, and remixing Pushkin's unfinished short story about an impending interracial wedding, "The Negro of Peter the Great." "Words in the air are full of life," she notes, in contrast to the dead if enduring words committed to paper alone (137). So Windsor chooses life when she pours blackness into Tanya's ears by writing a rap song.

At their first meeting, Tanya had enthusiastically talked about rap as poetry, recommending Tupac Shakur to Windsor, who eventually falls in love with some of his songs. When Windsor returns the favor, she hopes that the bride now has what she had long wanted for Pushkin X: the soul of black folks. In fact she had initially planned to give him a first edition of W. E. B. Du Bois's *The Souls of Black Folk* for a wedding gift. In the hillbilly bar, though, she works out that it's more important to give him her own soul along with the knowledge of his white blood (200). Moreover, when the Pushkin remix replaces Du Bois as a wedding gift, Tanya becomes the "Queen of Spades" of the title, and hence the comedy's heroine. Most important, from Windsor's point of view, Tanya will love her son and be the mother of her mixed-race grandchildren. Much like an African American country songwriter, the disc jockey presiding at this wedding celebration orchestrates the racial mix. Windsor notes that he is "invisible in the heat and the history," but the songs go in the new family's ears, and they too speak of a long history of distinct yet blended voices: "I hear you sing America, Walt [Whitman]. I hear you too, Langston. Yep, and now I hear Tupac," she concludes (280). And remember, Windsor wrote her story in a hillbilly bar in Nashville while Hank Williams songs resounded from the jukebox.

While her songs and stories recall the wretched history of American slavery and its aftermath of lynching and sexual exploitation, Randall, on the page and in the airwaves, also empowers our imagination to enter into new stories. These stories take the "white sound" of country music, with its nostalgia and twang, into different relationships with the past and future and, more important, into different relationships with the people who inhabit the real spaces of the world. They are as easy to listen to as a Charley Pride song, even though some evoke the kinds of struggles that O. B. McClinton and Stoney Edwards sang about. Almost all of them also build the better spaces of audiotopia. In Randall's happiest visions, as in the novel that ends as comedies classically do, with a communal wedding feast, racial identities mingle through marriage and procreation rather than through slavery and rape. Happy families proliferate rather than bear strange fruit. Women succeed in the man's world, and the new perspectives they bring with them remake that world. Love and gifts replace love and theft as the epitome of cultural production. Indeed Randall's characters, whether black, white, or in between those lines, convey their struggles and triumphs through resonant gifts of new songs and stories. "Hope is the thing with feathers," says the epigraph to *Pushkin and the Queen of Spades* and the first line of one of Randall's songs. The next line, as Dickinson wrote it, tells us that the thing with feathers "perches in the soul." It also sings.

Notes

1. Ching, Duck, and Menson-Furr, "Finding the Hook That Works."

2. Parton expressed surprise at learning that Summer wrote this song, and by extension, implied that she assumed most songs that her producers proposed to her were written by white songwriters. Roland, *The Billboard Book of Number One Country Hits*, 258. For the sake of simplicity, I generally refer to Randall as the writer of the songs discussed in this essay, though some are cowritten.

3. "A Southern View of Folk Song," typed manuscript, box 27, folder 45, Donald Davidson Collection, Vanderbilt University Library.

4. Mann, "Why Does Country Music Sound White?," 75.

5. I choose the word *resound* here to indicate my debt to Ronald Radano's work

on the discursive construction of "black music," especially in his *Lying Up a Nation: Race and Black Music*. The work of Josh Kun, Richard Middleton, and Geoff Mann grows out of Radano's argument that the racial identities tied to music are best understood as resonances. "In the figure of resonance, of an utterance without beginnings, we locate a key critical concept for imagining a different story of black music. . . . As a resonance is received . . . so is it repeatedly recast, rearticulated, and heard within the social. Conceived as a textural figuration of sound's position within a social 'unconscious' and accordingly existing between and beyond an ever-present discursive sphere, it conjures a flutter of sounds and texts that give shape to resoundingly racialized constructions of difference through the continual engagement of blacks and whites" (11).

6. Kun, *Audiotopia*, 2, 17.

7. Middleton, *Voicing the Popular*, 23.

8. Ching, Duck, and Menson-Furr, "Finding the Hook That Works," 363–64.

9. Lynn and Cox, *Still Woman Enough*, 145–46.

10. Cash, *Cash*, 34. Leigh Edwards skillfully discusses the connections and contradictions among Cash's reggae performances, his portrayal of the cruelty of slave owners in "The Ballad of Annie Palmer," and his evasive discussion of the "home invasion" he suffered in Jamaica in the context of his plantation ownership and colonial nostalgia. See Edwards, *Johnny Cash and the Paradox of American Identity*, 111–12.

11. "Alice Randall, Author of *The Wind Done Gone*, Converses with Robert Birnbaum," *Identity Theory*, July 14, 2004, http://www.identitytheory.com/interviews/birnbaum149.php.

12. Randall, Little, and Little, *My Country Roots*, 180.

13. Written by John Schweers.

14. Written by Glenn Martin.

15. Millard, "Charley Pride," 19.

16. Ching, *Wrong's What I Do Best*, 30–31.

17. Bowman, "O. B. McClinton," 23–29.

18. Hoskyns, *Say It One More Time for the Brokenhearted*, 173–76.

19. Guralnick, *Lost Highway*, 264–75.

20. Hemphill, *The Nashville Sound*, 163.

21. Woods, "Color Me Country," 10.

22. According to the Cleve Francis website (http://www.clevefrancis.com), however, he still performs in the Alexandria, Virginia, area.

23. Bill Friskics-Warren, "That Ain't My Song on the Jukebox," *Weekly Wire*, Sept. 2, 1997, http://www.nashvillescene.com/nashville/that-aint-my-song-on-the-jukebox/Content?oid=1181548.

24. John Marks, "Breaking a Color Line, Song by Song," *U.S. News and World Report*, Apr. 12, 1999.

25. Foster, *My Country*, vii.

26. Ivey, "Border Crossing," 11.

27. Hunter, liner notes, *Rhythm, Country and Blues*.

28. I discuss this phenomenon in greater detail in Ching, "Going Back to the Old Mainstream" and Ching and Fox "The Importance of Being Ironic."

29. Feiler, *Dreaming Out Loud*, 243.

30. Randall, Little, and Little, *My Country Roots*, 43.

31. Randall, Little, and Little, *My Country Roots*, 13.

32. Talley, *Negro Folk Rhymes*, 17.

33. For further discussion of Newman's song, see Erickson, "'Sail Away'" and 'Louisiana 1927,'" 307–11.

34. Randall, Little, and Little, *My Country Roots*, describes Pancho and Lefty as "two drug dealers" (180). Pancho, caught by the "Federales" in Mexico, "loses his life," while Lefty, languishing in Cleveland hotel rooms, "loses his soul" (32).

35. Herndon, "Blood on the Saddle," 300–304. For a history of this song, including a version collected from "a colored boy in the Detention Home, Detroit," see Gardner and Chickering, *Ballads and Songs of Southern Michigan*.

36. Kun, *Audiotopia*, 25.

37. Feiler, *Dreaming Out Loud*, 251.

38. As the narrator of Randall's *Pushkin and the Queen of Spades* puts it, "I know something about college football. . . . When I look at the diagrams of the plays . . . I get tangled up in space amid the x's and o's" (141; subsequent page references to this book are given parenthetically in the text).

39. If the song has any connection to "Big Dreams," Randall's contribution to the soundtrack of *The Thing Called Love* (1993), this god is a woman, since the struggling but happy woman in the soundtrack contribution states that "God must be a woman, too."

40. Randall, Little, and Little, *My Country Roots*, 238.

You're My Soul Song

HOW SOUTHERN SOUL
CHANGED COUNTRY MUSIC

Charles L. Hughes

In the summer of 1977, Buddy Killen, one of Nashville's most powerful music men, wrote and produced "Ain't Gonna Bump No More (with No Big Fat Woman)," the final hit single for the legendary soul star Joe Tex, whom Killen had produced and marketed for the entirety of Tex's fifteen-year run as an R&B hitmaker. Killen wrote "Ain't Gonna Bump" after observing the growing popularity of the titular dance at black nightclubs, venues that had been such fertile ground for previous Tex hits. In disco's pulsating rhythms, the cagey Killen saw a chance to return his semiretired client to the top of the charts. Indeed the raunchy, rowdy song gave Tex ample opportunity to unleash every facet of the chameleonic talent that helped him succeed in the many subgenres that emerged during soul's heyday in the 1960s and 1970s. In this momentous period, soul culture's assertive creativity became intimately linked to simultaneous developments in African American social and political life. "Ain't Gonna Bump No More," recorded in Nashville by the trademark group of "half soul, half country" musicians to which Tex and Killen attributed their success, was a fitting capstone for Tex's storied career: the song reached number 7 on the R&B charts and crossed over to the Pop Top 20.[1]

Killen, though, saw even greater potential in the song's infectious rhythms. His collaborations with Tex and his creation of the R&B label Dial as an outlet for Tex and other soul artists were only a small part of his career in Music City. A veteran musician, Killen wrote and produced a long string of country hits, and his publishing firm, Tree, grew from relatively humble origins in the late 1950s into the largest song house on Music Row. Recognizing an opportunity, Killen took the recorded backing track for "Ain't Gonna Bump No More" (which he owned), assembled another set of lyrics, and recorded the new song, "I Can't Wait Any Longer," with the country star and Grand Ole Opry fixture Bill Anderson. "No one in the country field had done a disco record," Killen remembered. "I felt the climate was right." Released in 1978, Anderson's reworking of Killen's recording of Joe Tex's disco hit topped the country charts.[2]

The success of "I Can't Wait Any Longer" is far from an intriguing anomaly, since many other country stars scored hits with records that possessed clear disco roots. Many of these stars were associated with the genre's popular (and controversial) urban cowboy movement, a phenomenon that paralleled the rise of disco and reflected the continuing importance of cross-racial influences between country music and R&B. Indeed even at the dawn of the racially divisive Reagan era, Nashville country continued to be changed by the music and musicians of southern soul.

This dynamic process was due to a large, interracial group of musicians, songwriters, producers, performers, and executives who had formed the creative bedrock for country, soul, and genre-blending "country-soul" for the previous two decades. All located in a country-soul triangle of Memphis, Nashville, and Muscle Shoals, they defined genres, built careers, and played on literally hundreds of classic records by artists from pop to R&B, rock, country, reggae, and beyond, a musical versatility that paradoxically helped the participants forge artistic identities successful enough to make each city's distinctive sound a sought-after badge of professionalism and integrity.

Despite this rich legacy and subsequent recognition of the interrelationship between country and R&B, almost all the limited literature on connections between the two genres focuses overwhelmingly on the impact of white music and musicians on southern soul. Foundational works like Peter Guralnick's *Sweet Soul Music* and Barney Hoskyns's *Say It One Time for the Broken Hearted* frame their respective analyses in discussions of white "crossover" into black musical spaces, both literal and figurative, centering their discussions on the exceptional individuals who, to quote Hoskyns, "[turned] against their own backgrounds of bigotry and prejudice" thanks to the liberating force of African American music.[3] Guralnick and Hoskyns, whose works remain vital, each use these individual acts of culture crossing to symbolize the larger political moment represented by interracial soul. Guralnick even argues for southern soul as a metaphor for the "Southern dream of freedom," the political energies of which had a temporary moment of prominence during the 1960s, thanks to the combined effects of the civil rights movement and the heyday of southern soul. Each author presents the 1970s as a period of decline, in which both the interracial political "dream" and the interracial musical movement were diminished, even lost, in the wake of Black Power, white backlash, and, importantly, the rise of less "authentic" forms in both genres.

This linkage between genre and politics adds another layer to the strictly expressed teleology adopted by southern soul's chroniclers. Hoskyns explicitly accuses the "black disco style" of "killing off" soul made in the South, and ends his work by wondering if "perhaps [country-soul] was too ingenuous and heartfelt to survive the onslaughts of disco and hip-hop. . . . Can pop music ever regain such innocent intensity?"[4] While less blunt than Hoskyns, Guralnick too parallels the fall of the hopeful politics of the 1960s civil rights movement with the rise of funk and disco in the 1970s, even while basically ignoring the continuing role of southern soul musicians in creating those styles. Like Hoskyns, he firmly asserts a link between the loss of musical "authenticity" and a loss of political opportunity.[5]

Ironically, even though neither Guralnick nor Hoskyns has much to say about country music (particularly "mainstream" varieties emanating from Nashville), this tendency to malign the music of the 1970s in comparison to that of the 1960s has its own parallel in country studies. Indeed though the occasionally tense interplay between traditional and pop country forms is a central element in country's larger historical narratives, the popular 1970s countrypolitan and urban cowboy genres have become stand-in symbols for the overly commercialized abandonment of country's core musical and cultural values, its own disco-esque moment of indulgent opportunism. What makes this particularly noteworthy, especially in light of soul narratives presented by Guralnick and Hoskyns, is that both countrypolitan and urban cowboy benefited greatly from the introduction of soul's sounds and personnel into its musical mixture. This infusion of talent affected all sectors of the Music City's industry and, as Buddy Killen's work with Joe Tex and Bill Anderson demonstrates, continued well out the other side of the chronological barrier erected by Guralnick and Hoskyns. Combined with the fact that southern soul was equally loved by the artists of the insurgent outlaw movement, the embrace of southern soul by Nashville's country establishment makes it the single most important external influence in the development of modern country. It is in fact impossible to imagine the genre in its current state without southern soul's impact and influence.

However, despite soul's foundational importance, it is nonetheless true

that the form's white participants generally enjoyed far greater opportunities within the country sphere than did their African American counterparts,
who—with a few significant exceptions, particularly in the realm of songwriting—ran up against many of the limits that the cross-racial impact of
their music would seemingly contradict. There is no question that, in several
important respects, the interactions between soul and country reflect historical tendencies toward white appropriation and control of black musical
culture. Still, the ubiquity of R&B within country's musical palette, as well
as the degree to which soul players and songwriters made their presence felt
throughout all sectors of the industry, adds an important dimension to these
hegemonic narratives.

Just as country and soul informed each other *musically* throughout this
period, the two musical spheres interacted on every other level as well, and
putting these two aspects of musical creation into conversation greatly clari-
fies the truly exceptional quality of interracial country-soul through the
1960s and 1970s. Many analyses of soul music (from contemporaneous celebrations to the most recent studies) adopt a certain degree of mysticism
in attempting to understand the interracial quality of the genre's southern
variants, but an emphasis on the importance of country (and specifically
Nashville as both city and stylistic marker) as an important participant in the
circuitous exchange of sounds, songs, and personnel helps make these connections clearer and more understandable. Additionally, uncovering these
professional networks reveals that, beyond each genre's working-class roots,
the recordings were the product of working musicians whose success defined them as efficient, versatile professionals. This model was symbolized by
the centrality of Nashville's country industry, which maintained its importance as a creative and commercial model for studios (regardless of genre)
throughout the South. Its booming business made it both a tantalizing destination for music hopefuls and a wealth of resources from which other scenes
could draw. For its part, Nashville's companies actively sought the services of
southern soul musicians, songwriters, and producers (particularly the white
folks), whose record of success grew exponentially from the early 1960s onward. Thus exploring the concrete factors behind these relationships further
enriches a discussion of their racial politics; rather than presenting a temporary, one-way crossover story of 1960s integration, a more fully formed examination provokes deeper questions of artistic authority, cultural "authenticity," and, indeed, interracialism itself.

Tracing the story of soul's impact on country music offers the opportunity
to not only reinterpret but also reimagine this rich and complex moment in

southern popular music. It extends its chronological and stylistic boundaries, greatly complicates its racial and cultural politics, exposes the networks of production and economics that give this often nebulous story a more concrete framework and, most important, makes the country-soul conversation truly a two-way interchange.

"You Better Move On," the 1962 hit by the African American singer-songwriter Arthur Alexander, is generally considered both the creative and the commercial impetus for the birth of the storied Muscle Shoals recording scene, which ultimately inspired significant international attention and praise, much of it centered around the Shoals' reputation as the home of the deepest, strongest, *blackest* soul music of the era. As such, Alexander's cut is an auspicious debut, since—musically—it bears little resemblance to the gritty "deep soul" with which Muscle Shoals became so identified. Alexander's vocal most directly recalls smooth operators like the country crooner Eddy Arnold or R&B statesman Ben E. King (both of whom were among his major influences), and the aching accompaniment by the original Muscle Shoals Rhythm Section also splits the difference between the textured honky-tonk of the 1950s Nashville Sound and the urbanized black pop of the Brill Building. Hoskyns describes the record as "a backwoods version of Ben E. King . . . a hillbilly 'Save the Last Dance for Me,'" which possessed "none of the gospel desperation that typified the Southern soul man."[6] Indeed the funky, unmasked blend of sounds that came to define southern soul is barely traceable in the twangy vocals and cha-cha rhythms of "You Better Move On."

Nonetheless this historic track seems less anomalous in the context of Muscle Shoals' emergence as a recording center, since, as Alexander's biographer Richard Younger chronicles, the scene developed primarily in the hopes of becoming a satellite for Nashville country. In 1956 the locals James Joiner, Kelso Hurston, and Walter Stovall started Tune Records, which served primarily as a venue for the area's aspiring country songwriters to hone their craft and demo their songs for sale on Nashville's Music Row. In 1958 Tune sold a Joiner composition called "A Fallen Star" to Buddy Killen's powerful Tree Publishing.[7] The sentimental "A Fallen Star" was soon recorded in hit versions by the country stars Ferlin Husky and Jimmy C. Newman, among others.[8] Tune's success brought many songwriters, performers, and session players to Muscle Shoals, including Rick Hall, a fiddler with Carmol Taylor and the Country Pals, and Hall's running buddy Billy Sherrill, a saxophone player in a Shoals-area R&B combo called Benny Cagle and the Rhythm Swingers. Joiner liked the pair's material and, through his newfound Nashville contacts, got Hall-Sherrill compositions recorded by the country stars Brenda Lee and Homer and Jethro. While moderately successful, none of their efforts propelled them to immediate fame on the fiercely competitive Music Row. Still, Joiner's assistance provided the growing number of Shoals songwriters with their initial entry to the music business. "I was helping out what I could, going to Nashville and opening the doors," Joiner remembered. "After they went through, they didn't need me."[9]

Hall and Sherrill soon came into partnership with Tom Stafford, a local businessman whom one Nashville musician called "a patron of the arts."[10] With James Joiner, Stafford started a publishing company, Spar, in 1958. Thanks to Joiner's Nashville success, Spar ultimately played host to the core of Muscle Shoals' (and ultimately Nashville's) studio establishment. The Spar roster included future luminaries like David Briggs, Jerry Carrigan, Donnie Fritts, Marlin Greene, Roger Hawkins, Earl Montgomery, Linden "Spooner" Oldham, Dan Penn, Norbert Putnam, and Terry Thompson. All were white, and all made their mark on countless soul, pop, and country sessions over the next twenty years, a disproportionate swath of American popular music that, when Rick Hall and Billy Sherrill are added in, becomes even more impressive.[11]

The cultural contexts that gave rise to this community demonstrate that, from the very beginning, country and R&B coexisted in the minds, and ears, of the musicians who helped create southern soul. Perhaps most important was the existence of three overlapping performing circuits — "frat," "chitlin'," and country — which provided touring musicians with steady work and (perhaps unintentionally) acted as a genre-blending precursor to their later recordings. The chitlin' circuit was, of course, the backbone of African American live performance and a pivotal element in the development of R&B and soul music.[12] In addition, many southern soul musicians honed their crafts touring on the frat circuit, the loosely defined group of southern college campuses (mostly, though not exclusively, white) that served as a grooving greenhouse for regional musicians. Both black and white bands, whether upstarts or established performers, toured the frats, playing a mélange of rock and roll and R&B perfectly suited to the raucous college audiences. The clean musical fit nonetheless came with ambiguous racial politics, since, for black musicians, working frat gigs often required performing desegregated music for all-white, sometimes segregationist crowds. "Even the diehard segregationists loved the black music," remembers Wolf Stephenson, a student at the University of Mississippi during the concurrent heyday of the frat performances and anti-integration protests. "It was like two worlds —

the students danced to the music but the moment the musicians left the stage they would have nothing to do with them."[13] Peter Guralnick, arguing for the centrality of the frat circuit in understanding the roots of southern soul, addressed this dynamic when he suggested that "patronization" by otherwise hostile white audiences at these shows represented "the other side of the romanticization" felt by white soul admirers. Guralnick also recognizes, however, the frat gigs' economic benefits, suggesting that for black performers, they were the best bookings (with facilities and paychecks that usually exceeded the majority of chitlin venues), and for white bands, they were the most consistent source of income.[14]

There was, however, another spatial prologue to country-soul interaction. While almost entirely ignored in most soul histories and given only brief mention in the better works on country, many of those who made up the first southern soul cadre also gained experience in distinctly *country* performing milieus. The eclectic musicians congregating in Muscle Shoals had worked with country artists, including the guitarist Earl Montgomery, who toured with the Wilburn Brothers, or the drummer Roger Hawkins, who toured with Cousin Wilbur, an Opry comedian, before becoming the primary drummer on sessions by Aretha Franklin, the Staple Singers, and many others. All three of Memphis's primary soul studios — Stax, Hi, and American — began as outlets for white country artists; Stax's cofounder Jim Stewart (like Rick Hall) led an unremarkable career as a fiddler before launching the label. The proximity of Nashville's country and R&B scenes provoked inevitable crossover as well. Unsurprisingly, black artists had significantly less access to country venues, but they were not entirely prohibited; for example, Buddy Killen told a story of Joe Tex performing at a Texas honky-tonk, much to the chagrin of the club's owner, who had assumed Tex was white.[15] Most black artists did not share the privilege of alternating between country and R&B performances in the manner of white musicians.

The restrictions of Jim Crow may have circumscribed physical performance spaces, but the radio waves beaming across the rural South remained desegregated. The stylistic overlap that provoked interracial country-soul variants in Memphis, Nashville, and Muscle Shoals reflected the desegregated listening habits of countless southern musicians, of both races, who quite literally dialed between genres as they searched their radios for the powerful signals of R&B stations like Memphis's WDIA or Nashville's WLAC or the country sounds of Nashville's WSM. In the mid-1950s a white disc jockey from the Shoals station WLAY — one of Arthur Alexander's favorites — named Sam Phillips, and his pioneering label Sun Records, provided

southern music hopefuls with both a creative example and a business model.[16] Sun explosively blended blues, country, gospel, and pop, and Phillips's success also gave rise to a slew of independent southern studios and radio stations. By the time of southern soul, Phillips was living in Nashville, applying his golden touch to the making (and marketing) of country records.

Thus Arthur Alexander (fig. 11.1), who emerged as Muscle Shoals' first national recording star, can be considered the product of a musical world informed by deeply heterogeneous — but concrete — roots: the mixture of R&B, rock and roll, and country in the repertoire of working Shoals-area musicians; the country-R&B-pop mixture of the Shoals' early songwriters; the influential coexistence of country and R&B radio stations in southern listening habits; the business example of Sam Phillips's independent (and independently minded) vision of southern musical success; the importance of Nashville as both artistic and commercial inspiration; and, significantly, the idiosyncratic genius of the Shoals' fortuitous ensemble of working musicians.

This singular alchemy illuminates Alexander's genre-blending sound and also helps explain why Alexander, who sang with a doo-wop group and was the first African American presence at Spar, caught the attention of Stafford,

Hall, and Sherrill primarily as a songwriter. While Alexander's uniquely compelling song-craft certainly deserved this attention, the group's decision to market him as a writer and not as a performer was in keeping with their devotion to the economic model of Nashville's Music Row, where songwriters *wrote* songs, singers *sang* songs, and rarely did the two intersect. Alexander reaped the benefits of the Shoals' contacts in Nashville; his "She Wanta Rock," published by Spar, was unsuccessfully cut by Nashville rockabilly Arnie Derksen in 1960. Backing Derksen is an all-star lineup of Nashville studio heavyweights, including Owen Bradley (who owned a popular studio and managed Patsy Cline), Grady Martin (arguably the era's most prolific country guitarist), and Floyd Cramer (whose slippery lines on others' recordings and his own hits like "Last Date" established him as one of Nashville's definitive piano stylists).[17] Their appearance on the first published song of one of Muscle Shoals' "deep soul" pioneers remains historically, if not commercially, noteworthy.

Many of these Nashville pros also recorded in Muscle Shoals during this period, both by themselves and with local artists. The country industry always appreciated the talents of versatile studio musicians and songwriters, so it is not entirely surprising that, from its earliest days, Music City big shots like Gary Walker, Chet Atkins, and (later) Buddy Killen eyed the Spar talent pool with real, if detached, interest. The prolific pianist Hargus "Pig" Robbins even traveled there to record what Richard Younger calls a "melodic rock 'n' roll instrumental" in the style of the Ventures or Santo and Johnny; Tom Stafford and Gary Walker coproduced this Nashville-Shoals hybrid.[18] When Walker and Robbins came to record, Arthur Alexander, along with most of the rest of Stafford's crew, came to watch the storied men in action. Walker and Robbins returned the favor, playing on Alexander's first recordings.[19]

In 1959 Sherrill, Stafford, and Hall expanded Spar to FAME, which stood for "Florence, Alabama Music Enterprises." Despite auspicious beginnings, and almost humorously contradictory to the firm's grand title, the first thing of significance to happen at FAME was a split in 1960, with Hall buying out his former partners.[20] Billy Sherrill sold his share in the company for one dollar, a decision that might be remembered as shortsighted if not for Sherrill's growing disaffection with the rock and roll and R&B now favored in the Shoals. Reversing the trajectory of most of the area's white musicians, who had grown up on country but grew more interested in black music's "deeper" grooves, Sherrill felt pulled toward country. He describes himself as "a rock'n'roller . . . until [he] heard George Jones": "Then I got switched around and came up to Nashville and got caught up in the big country deal and had a lot of fun doing it."[21] He left Spar in 1961.

As Sherrill grew disenchanted with Muscle Shoals, Arthur Alexander became ever more involved, recording "You Better Move On" in 1961. The musicians for the session (produced by Rick Hall at the new FAME Studios) were the definitive grouping of the first Muscle Shoals Rhythm Section: supple piano by David Briggs, Jerry Carrigan's restless drums, thudding bass from Norbert Putnam, and the interlocking guitars of Forrest Riley, Terry Thompson, and Earl Montgomery.[22]

After mixing and mastering "You Better Move On," Rick Hall took the smoldering ballad to Nashville. Failing to arouse any interest from the publishing houses (including giants like Tree and Acuff-Rose), he shopped "You Better Move On" to record labels. At the labels, the song went over, but the singer did not. Richard Younger suggests, "Some of the A&R reps [at Mercury, Decca, and Capitol Records] expressed an interest in having their own singers cut the song, being none too impressed by a vocalist who sounded 'too black . . . [and] wobbly and all over the place.'"[23] Chet Atkins captured this moment of musical separatism: "I'm sure it's a good record, but I don't know anything about black music."[24] Even Sam Phillips's Nashville representative would not buy Alexander's record.

In a surprising show of loyalty between black performer and white executive, Hall refused to separate "You Better Move On" from its creator, finally finding a home for the track at Dot Records. In historical hindsight, this seems surprising, since Dot was previously, dubiously known as the home of Pat Boone's much-maligned covers of Little Richard and Fats Domino, often held up as symbols of inferior (and "inauthentic") white covers of African American material.[25] Still, Dot has a more complicated history. The label's head, Randy Wood, began his tenure by switching Dot from classical to pop, or, more accurately, to a mix of R&B, country, gospel, and white vocal music that he hoped would gain him fans among listeners of the black station WLAC, thus reaching out to the very listeners (and musicians) alienated by the Pat Boone covers.[26] Wood—briefly the head of the prominent black-music label Vee-Jay Records—released "You Better Move On," which became a hit on both R&B and pop charts.

For the next decade, Alexander recorded exclusively in Nashville, often with A Team musicians like Pig Robbins, who expressed such admiration for the musicians in Muscle Shoals. Spooner Oldham, a Shoals keyboardist, even accuses Robbins of directly copying a fluttering piano figure that Oldham played on the demo version of what became Alexander's next hit, the Latin-inflected "Anna (Go to Him)."[27] Robbins, whose presence inspired a standing-room-only crowd in Muscle Shoals two years earlier, now himself participated in bringing the sound of the Shoals to the heart of Music City.[28]

In 1965 the arrival of the Muscle Shoals sound in Nashville became a reality, as the original Muscle Shoals Rhythm Section—Briggs, Putnam, Carrigan, and Montgomery—left FAME Studios. Rick Hall, already smarting from the loss of Arthur Alexander, considered this a final insult from the country establishment. Coalescing around a new studio band, the equally talented Muscle Shoals sound, and the increasingly memorable songwriting of Dan Penn and Spooner Oldham, FAME Studios turned to pop and R&B sessions. Hall was helped in this regard by his recent alliance with the Atlanta-based record producer Bill Lowery, who brought his own cadre of musicians and songwriters—featuring talented young players like Joe South, Jerry Reed, and Ray Stevens—as well as two of his most profitable clients, the white pop star Tommy Roe and the R&B group the Tams.[29]

As FAME ascended, Muscle Shoals expatriates Billy Sherrill, Arthur Alexander, and the Muscle Shoals Rhythm Section arrived in a city and industry in transition. Having cemented its hold on country music's economy in the early 1950s, Nashville's record companies, song publishers, and recording studios embarked on a modernizing mission, actively aiming to make Nashville's country artists—and the genre itself—more palatable to a mainstream audience; as a result, national recording companies took note of the increasingly successful, and explicitly crossover-minded, Nashville sound.[30] Sawing off the "hillbilly" trappings of the early days and replacing the string bands and "old-timey" get-ups of previous years with orchestras and crisply tailored suits, modern Nashville marketed stars like Patsy Cline and Arthur Alexander's idol Eddy Arnold, who flavored country's roots with a presentation that owed as much to Bing Crosby as Uncle Dave Macon. The rock and roll explosion fundamentally challenged this model, and the interracial, sexually ambiguous music (some from studios in longtime rival Memphis) sent Music City temporarily reeling. By the dawn of the 1960s, however, musicians-turned-label-heads like Chet Atkins and Harold Bradley recuperated their commercial reputations with the development of a new generation of stars who blended well-worn Nashville sound formulas with a diluted version of rock and roll's energy and invention. Doing this required the services of a continually refreshing group of musicians, songwriters, and producers, and Sherrill, Alexander, and the Muscle Shoals Rhythm Section entered this booming economy with high creative and commercial aspirations.

Alexander recorded for Dot Records, and later Monument, the eclectic label that recorded everyone from the soul star Joe Simon to a young Dolly Parton. Despite early optimism, Alexander never achieved much success as a recording artist, thanks to a sad string of misfortune and mishap, with blame extending from record company mismanagement to his struggles with drug use and mental illness. Many blame Alexander's lack of commercial success on the very interracial musical identity that distinguished him in the first place; country stations mostly ignored him. His manager Phil Walden boldly suggests, "I don't even think Arthur could get played on many R&B stations. For him, being saddled with Dot was akin to having George Wallace as your manager, if you were an R&B singer."[31] After "Anna," Alexander did not have another sizable hit until 1975's "Every Day I Have to Cry," recorded back in Muscle Shoals. Still others question why Alexander's growing catalogue of superb original songs often wound up as the B sides to his covers of recent pop, R&B, and country hits. For example, he wrote "Every Day I Have to Cry" in 1963, and the song became a minor hit for Steve Alaimo that same year. Following in Alaimo's footsteps, a slew of artists recorded the song, along with other selections in Alexander's increasingly esteemed catalogue. While covers by the Beatles ("Anna") and the Rolling Stones ("You Better Move On") have gained greater attention, Alexander's material also provided a source of material for country artists; Dan Penn's long-held belief that Alexander "could write songs like Hank Williams could write songs" seems especially poignant in this regard.[32]

Some of the country artists who covered Alexander were also his colleagues at Monument Records and at the songwriting collective Combine, which he joined in 1968. At Combine, Alexander joined Dolly Parton, Kris Kristofferson, Ray Stevens (who had visited Muscle Shoals since the days of "You Better Move On"), and others whose idiosyncratic writing helped define country in the 1970s. He was one of the only African Americans on the roster, and his work was a deep source of inspiration for the young Combine writers, with Kristofferson testifying to the group's "great respect for Arthur as a person and as a musician": "When Arthur sang his kind of country, it sounded authentic."[33] Beyond the racially loaded terminology, the role of Arthur Alexander's "authentic" sound as direct inspiration for country musicians from the 1960s to the 1980s points to the vast repertory exchange between country and R&B.[34] Although this exchange has been previously acknowledged, it seems important to stress that, like the musical interplay, this was a truly two-way conversation: songs from each genre traversed the other's pathways with regularity, and songwriters consistently drew inspiration from their fellow artists on the other side of the musical color line. (Perhaps the clearest example of this is the work of Ivory Joe Hunter, the richly talented R&B singer-songwriter whose reputation among country artists and fans resulted in a remarkable 1974 benefit, following Hunter's stroke, at the Grand Ole Opry, in which the soul star Isaac Hayes stood alongside George Jones and Tammy Wynette in honoring him.)[35]

Despite admiration for his work among country's most celebrated songwriters, and despite repeated trips up the country charts for Alexander's songs, the artist himself remained merely at the margins of the city's mainstream music scene, dividing his time between Nashville's R&B clubs and country studios. This was not the case for the Muscle Shoals Rhythm Section, who, upon arriving in 1965, almost immediately became cornerstones of Nashville's studio establishment, opening Quadraphonic Studios and forming Area Code 615, which can be heard on countless country and pop records over three decades. The country music historian David Cantwell deservedly calls the arrival of the Muscle Shoals Rhythm Section "the single most important event in country music after the rise of rock and roll."[36] The fact that Shoals musicians like David Briggs and Jerry Carrigan so easily and successfully slipped into this position seems both a product of racial privilege and a testament to the fact that—despite the degree to which *Muscle Shoals* became shorthand for a certain variant of "authentic" black music—the early years at FAME Studios were defined primarily by *efficiency* and *versatility*. The efficiency came through Rick Hall's ambitious insistence on booking as many sessions as possible, while the versatility grew from the varying styles of early Shoals clients, whether the uptown R&B of the Tams, Sandy Posey's country-pop, or the gritty soul of Jimmy Hughes. The early interest taken by Chet Atkins and others in Shoals professionalism came to fruition with the Music City arrival of the Rhythm Section, who left their mark on dozens of hits.

Of course, the black musicians who accompanied them in Muscle Shoals received far fewer chances to contribute. Even during the Shoals' ascendant period, some black players worried that the African American road bands who backed star performers like Percy Sledge were being replaced by the corps of white musicians at FAME Studios: Andrew Wright, who cowrote Sledge's legendary hit "When a Man Loves a Woman," later remarked that he "[didn't] know what happened. They just got rid of all the black musicians and writers."[37] This situation only worsened in Nashville, even as the Muscle Shoals Rhythm Section played on an increasing number of tracks that demonstrated a debt to the soul music they helped pioneer.

Billy Sherrill produced many of these recordings. Sherrill first worked for Sam Phillips before doing production work at Epic Records. He also continued songwriting, and, in 1965 and 1966, his dual ambitions paid off, with a large hit as a producer (David Houston's "Mountain of Love") and as a songwriter (the oft-covered "Almost Persuaded"). From then on, Sherrill's star rose meteorically, as he produced and wrote hits for Tammy Wynette, George Jones, Charlie Rich, and many others.[38] Sherrill's lush production style is often credited with sparking the countrypolitan movement of the 1970s, an updating of the original Nashville sound that even further amplified the crossover aspirations of the earlier genre. Sherrill recorded some of his most definitive hits with Charlie Rich, a former rockabilly singer and jazz pianist whose career led him from Sun to the early configuration of Memphis's Hi Records to (briefly) Monument, where he joined Arthur Alexander on the roster. Sherrill's work with Rich, with its gauzy arrangements and sophisticated sensibility, paralleled not only the 1970s rise of Philadelphia soul but also the "Quiet Storm" R&B phenomenon of the decade's latter years, with its "bedroom" ballad style and glistening appearance, which were explicitly designed for mature, urban audiences. String-heavy hits like "Behind Closed Doors" and "The Most Beautiful Girl" are not far removed from equally lush Spinners or Smokey Robinson records, while one of Rich and Sherrill's first hit collaborations, 1969's spare, gospel-derived "Life's Little Ups and Downs," is a close musical relative to the churchy "deep soul" made at Stax, FAME, and elsewhere.

Rich was not alone: other Sherrill clients, like Conway Twitty and Barbara Mandrell, demonstrated equal R&B influence in their choice of musical texture and repertoire. (Mandrell's early, Sherrill-produced hits included covers of Joe Tex and Otis Redding.) Sherrill even produced and cowrote a gospel-inflected number 1 Country hit in 1973 for the white former R&B singer Joe Stampley called "Soul Song," in which the title phrase — and the concept of soul, born as a signifier for assertive black politics — becomes a loving central metaphor: "You're my soul song / My everything that I do song / My pick me up when I'm blue song / That's why I sing all the time."

As Sherrill became country's most prominent producer, he remained aware of Nashville's other musical networks. One of his contacts was Freddie North, a deejay at the influential Nashville R&B station WLAC and a participant in Nashville's flourishing R&B scene.[39] In 1971 North recorded a pulsing track called "She's All I Got," cowritten and produced by Jerry Williams Jr. (fig. 11.2), who balanced a career as a songwriter and producer with the recordings of his alter ego, Swamp Dogg, mixtures of rock, soul, gospel, and

FIGURE 11.2.
Like Arthur Alexander, Jerry "Swamp Dogg" Williams Jr. found success as a songwriter in Nashville but remained convinced that African Americans were unlikely to find success in performing roles. Michael Ochs Archives / Getty Images. Photo courtesy of Getty Images.

country that possessed radical politics and a distinctly mind-blowing sensibility. North cut "She's All I Got" (which Williams cowrote with the R&B star Gary "U.S." Bonds) for Williams's independent Fungus label.

North's version of "She's All I Got" became a top-ten R&B hit, and the recording soon came to Sherrill's attention. Sherrill remembered North from WLAC, and also remembered hearing his voice on demo versions of songs recorded by Elvis Presley and others. When the esteemed Nashboro Music publisher Bob Tubert brought Sherrill the recording of "She's All I Got," the combined pedigree was enough to convince Sherrill of the song's potential.[40] Over the next year Sherrill recorded the song on a shockingly extensive list of Nashville's biggest talents, from Loretta Lynn to Marty Robbins, but it was ultimately the faithful arrangement that Sherrill produced for honky-tonker Johnny Paycheck in 1972 that hit pay dirt, hitting number 2 on the country charts. The next year, Gary "U.S." Bonds and Jerry "Swamp Dogg" Williams received the award as Songwriters of the Year from Broadcast Music International (BMI), the powerful songwriters' union based in Nashville. While they attended the awards ceremony, Swamp Dogg long claimed that he was purposely not sent an invitation to the dinner that preceded it, while Frances Preston, head of BMI at the time, swore, it was an honest mistake.[41] Still, despite the winners' absence, it remains notable that, in 1972, at the height of country's mutual embrace of conservative politics, BMI bestowed one of its highest honors on a man whose other songs included "Call Me Nigger" and "God Blessed America (for What?)." Artists from the Commodores to Tracy Byrd recorded Williams's songs in coming decades.

Looking back, Williams clearly, bluntly understands how the country music that was his "first love" made its way into even his funkiest work: "My productions still have country flavor, and that's why I use all of those horns. . . . Everything I write and sing comes out country, and that's why I have to take so much time in arrangements and instrumentation, because— if not—I'd just be cutting a bunch of country records with black people. And we *know* that black people are not makin' it in country."[42] These remarks are notable for multiple reasons. Beyond suggesting that his use of horns was a conscious attempt to associate his recordings with authentically "black" musical textures, Williams also gestures toward the fact that—beyond the significant exceptions of Charley Pride, Ray Charles, and a few others— African American performers were usually unable to become country stars, or at least to enjoy the fruits of Nashville's star-making machinery. Even as country fully embraced soul influences and utilized its talent pool, soul's black performers (from Arthur Alexander forward) could not parlay their affection and gifts for country music into successful recording careers. Millie Jackson, soon to be a huge soul star in Muscle Shoals, summarized this frustration: "I've always been a country-rocker at heart. But it served me no purpose, because no one would let me cross over!"[43]

Although Jackson, Alexander, and other black performers were unable to cross over into country fame, and although the white members of the country-soul triangle's interracial studios found greater opportunities for professional advancement than most of their black contemporaries, the *songwriting* base of country-soul proved the most tenaciously interracial in its impact on Nashville country music: Jerry "Swamp Dogg" Williams was far from alone in proving a genre-crossing success. Joe South, a white Georgian whom Swamp Dogg covered multiple times, compiled a legendary catalogue of country-soul material (including the Grammy-winning "Games People Play") that was covered by everyone from the country-pop singer Billy Joe Royal to the reggae star Johnny Nash. Memphian Charles Chalmers, the white saxophonist from countless soul sessions, toured with Jerry Lee Lewis and Mel Tillis, sang background vocals for Al Green, and wrote hits on both R&B and country charts, including Conway Twitty's number 1 hit "The Clown." Also the steady stream of hit Alexander covers extends even beyond Alexander's 1977 exit from the active music business; Joe Stampley recorded Alexander's "Every Day I Have to Cry" that very year, and, in 1980,

Billy Sherrill came full circle, producing a graceful version of "You Better Move On" for George Jones and Johnny Paycheck.

Even more successful were Alexander's old colleagues Dan Penn and Spooner Oldham, who—separately and together—composed some of R&B's most compelling masterpieces and provided the backbone of studio crews in Muscle Shoals and Memphis. While the duo is deservedly legendary for 1960s soul songs like "I'm Your Puppet," "It Tears Me Up," and "Sweet Inspiration," their respective careers in 1970s country have been relatively ignored. Despite this, both men maintained an active presence in country through the decade, even beyond the fact that their soul hits provided fodder for numerous covers. Spooner Oldham worked with honky-tonker Freddy Weller, who recorded a decade-long series of hits produced by Billy Sherrill, some written by Joe South and many others cowritten by Weller and Oldham. (The pair also wrote "Lonely Women Make Good Lovers," a country number 4 for Bob Luman, and later Steve Wariner.) Dan Penn, who moved to Nashville in the early 1970s, never recaptured the magic of his mid-1960s heyday, but he did work prominently with Ronnie Milsap, producing his 1975 album and writing his top-ten hit "I Hate You."

Before Penn moved to Nashville or began recording country music (which he initially loathed), he cowrote one of soul's defining anthems, "Dark End of the Street." Although the song has been recorded by a wide variety of artists, including Porter Waggoner and Dolly Parton, it is justifiably considered a near-perfect encapsulation of southern soul's musical and thematic characteristics. Penn composed "Dark End of the Street" with Chips Moman, the white producer, songwriter, and guitarist from Memphis who helped launch Stax and later opened American Studios, a prominent recording house visited by everyone from Joe Tex and Bobby Womack to, quite famously, Dusty Springfield and Elvis Presley, who chose American for his country-soul comeback of 1968.[44] Although they remain less famous than other studio bands, the all-white group at American are the only southern studio ensemble to equal the Muscle Shoals players in terms of ultimate prominence in Nashville.

A decade after defining one genre with "Dark End of the Street," Moman (collaborating with American's guitarist Bobby Emmons) defined another, with "Luckenbach, TX," which, when recorded by Waylon Jennings and Willie Nelson, became the unofficial anthem of the outlaw country movement. The outlaws resisted the restrictive rules of Nashville's establishment, priding themselves on conceptions of artistic integrity and genre experimentation that seem very much grounded in the participants' avowed affection for (and involvement with) southern soul. Willie Nelson recorded at Muscle Shoals Sound, the home studio of the Shoals' second great ensemble, and later worked with both Chips Moman and the black Stax luminary Booker T. Jones, who produced Nelson's smash *Stardust*. Kris Kristofferson's connections to southern soul went deeper than just his abiding love for the music of Arthur Alexander, who, Kristofferson later said, "was from Muscle Shoals, the real thing."[45] Kristofferson's road band included the Shoals original Donnie Fritts, and his studio recordings featured a Miami-based soul band, the Dixie Flyers. Fritts also cowrote hits for Jerry Lee Lewis, Hank Williams Jr., and Waylon Jennings, whose mournful version of "We Had It All" appears on his groundbreaking *Honky Tonk Heroes*, generally considered one of outlaw country's foundational albums. Jennings developed a particular attachment to American's guitarist Reggie Young, who remained in his band throughout his career. In 1982, produced by Moman and backed by most of the former American Studios crew, Jennings and Nelson even hit number 13 on the country charts with a cover of Otis Redding's "Sittin' on the Dock of the Bay."

Despite the many abstract and tangible connections between outlaw country and southern soul, however, it would be a mistake to assume that the outlaws were any more attuned to soul than were the major stars of Nashville's 1970s boom period, since many of the era's biggest stars exhibited clear R&B influence in their work and presentation; they include Rich, Twitty, Milsap, Mandrell, Parton, Kenny Rogers (who collaborated with the Alabama-born Motown star Lionel Richie), and Mickey Gilley, who released two chart-topping R&B covers and another that went to number 2. One of these covers, Gilley's version of Ben E. King's "Stand by Me," was featured on the soundtrack to *Urban Cowboy*, whose controversial place in country very much mirrors that of disco in the longer history of R&B. Just as soul chroniclers like Peter Guralnick and Barney Hoskyns use disco as a moment of decadent downfall, most histories of country music treat the urban cowboy phenomenon as a similarly unfortunate point of mediocre, overly commercial indulgence.[46] Beyond the parallel discursive space occupied by disco and urban cowboy, however, other similarities exist. As Tyina Steptoe notes, "urban cowboy" was a large dance movement, hinged very much on complex conceptions of race, class, and sexuality and taking place in large, spectacularly lit venues where groups of well-dressed dancers moved in near-formation to pulsating selections that negotiated the perilous gap between subcultural roots and broad appeal.[47] If nothing else, these similarities speak to the importance of the dance floor to artists in both genres, of which Buddy Killen's work for Joe Tex and Bill Anderson is merely the most obvious example.

Beyond Bill Anderson, artists like the Bellamy Brothers, Lynn Anderson, and Dolly Parton employed disco's trademark "four-on-the-floor" drum pattern and sweeping string sections. The country-soul veterans Jerry "Swamp Dogg" Williams and Dan Penn adopted disco textures into their production techniques, and, much like their predecessors, southern soul stars, including Millie Jackson and Bobby Womack, included both disco tracks and country covers in their mix. Recording at Muscle Shoals Sound, Jackson had a top-five R&B hit with Merle Haggard's "If You're Not Back in Love by Monday" and also recorded a steamy dance track called "Kiss You All Over" a full year before Kentucky group Exile took the same song to the top of the pop charts. Although Exile recorded "Kiss You All Over" before becoming an explicitly country group in the 1980s, the song remains a fixture on the band's greatest-hits collections (as well as several "various artists" country compilations), suggesting that the band's many country fans have little problem with the song's disco-pop stylings.

The rest of Exile's work sounds very little like their first hit, bearing much greater resemblance to the southern rock movement of the 1970s. In fact many of Nashville's biggest 1980s stars who did *not* exhibit a heavy R&B-soul influence were instead reminiscent of the gritty blend of rock, country, and blues made popular by the Allman Brothers Band, Lynyrd Skynyrd, and others. Still, southern rock has its own roots in the desegregated music of the country-soul triangle. Duane Allman gained valuable experience and exposure playing guitar on sessions for Wilson Pickett and Aretha Franklin, and Lynyrd Skynyrd recorded most of its albums in and around Muscle Shoals. Skynyrd's lead singer Ronnie Van Zant even memorialized the Muscle Shoals sound in the song "Sweet Home Alabama," where Van Zant reminds listeners that "in Muscle Shoals, they've got the Swampers," referencing the band's nickname.[48] Hank Williams Jr., one of the most popular of the southern rock–influenced country stars, worked at Music Mill, one of the Shoals' many small recording houses that sprang up in the wake of its emergence as—in the city's words—the "Hit Recording Capital of the World." At Music Mill, Williams cowrote a message song called "Clean Up America" with Arthur Alexander.[49]

Hank Williams Jr. and fellow post–southern rock country superstars Alabama were two of the acts whose careers were guided by Barry Beckett, the keyboard player who left the Muscle Shoals sound in 1985 to become an A&R representative for Warner Brothers in Nashville. Even more than

Billy Sherrill's success or the prominence of the first Rhythm Section, the installment of someone so closely linked to the deep soul of Muscle Shoals into such a high position of power within the country establishment showed how country-soul triangle music and musicians had become fully integrated (or perhaps desegregated) into Music City's most successful circles. (It also further exemplified that, for black talents, many doors remained closed.) Where Rick Hall could not sell "You Better Move On" because it sounded "too black," now Nashville looked to a player whose résumé included funk, reggae, and disco to make some of its most important creative and commercial decisions.

Barry Beckett's tenure as a Warner Brothers executive extended into the 1990s, when he worked with the "hat act" stars Kenny Chesney and Neal McCoy. As Chesney, McCoy, and other country artists of the present day search the songwriting landscape for potential hit material, one of the places they can consistently turn is Rick Hall's FAME Publishing in Muscle Shoals. Nearly forty years after Hall, Sherrill, and Tom Stafford established FAME as a songwriting outpost for Nashville recording companies, FAME has returned to its roots. It counts among its many successful holdings a song called "I Swear," which in 1994 became a Grammy-winning hit on both country and R&B charts for John Michael Montgomery and All-4-One, respectively. In 2006 the finals of the show *Nashville Star*, a country-music version of *American Idol*, came down to two gritty-voiced, soul-loving siblings from Muscle Shoals, Alabama.

The story of interracial musical conversations in the country-soul triangle, and their ultimate impact on country music, should be neither simplified nor romanticized. In fact it can certainly be argued that the story's ultimate lesson is that, once again, white people managed to have black music without at least most of the black people. One by one, the whites who helped produce, play, and even distribute southern black music moved toward a distinctly country base, and African American soul veterans found themselves increasingly marginalized, even as their styles and songs remained popular fixtures on country radio. Still, stamping a defeated or cynical political imprint on the music and musicians of Memphis, Nashville, and Muscle Shoals would be no more useful than previous, wholly triumphant narratives. At its truest and most substantive moments, the saga of the country-soul triangle reasserts the continuing presence of African American music within seemingly white spheres, even during the very moment when country became so closely associated with reactionary racial politics and even racial bigotry. It is, without question, hugely significant that Charley Pride (and Ray Charles) became a country legend, but is it not equally significant that country went disco? Additionally, is it not significant that, from the 1950s through the 1970s, certain black musicians (apart from Pride and Charles) *did* benefit financially from their country connections and participate on levels of the country industry beyond being performers? Beyond this, the fact that southern soul fundamentally changed country music suggests that, contrary to uplifting narratives about the presence of whites in 1960s southern soul music, a full appreciation of the multifaceted ways in which black music and musicians engaged with country music suggests a much richer, and perhaps more troubling, narrative. The journey from the "dark end of the street" to the bright lights of Music City is truly one worth exploring.

Notes

1. Quoted in Ward, *Just My Soul Responding*, 222.

2. Killen and Carter, *By the Seat of My Pants*, 248.

3. Hoskyns, *Say It One Time for the Broken Hearted*, xii.

4. Hoskyns, *Say It One Time for the Broken Hearted*, 208, 217.

5. Guralnick, *Sweet Soul Music*. African American soul historians, like Gerri Hirshey and Nelson George, exhibit similar teleological tendencies. See Hirshey, *Nowhere to Run*; George, *The Death of Rhythm and Blues*.

6. Hoskyns, *Say It One Time for the Broken Hearted*, 97.

7. Younger, *Get a Shot of Rhythm and Blues*, 19–20.

8. The practice of recording multiple versions of the same song, also known as the "cover version" phenomenon, has an odd role in American musical history. While the racial ramifications of this practice ultimately led to exploitation of and resentment among black musicians, it must be said that the process was not always explicitly racial in its application, as exhibited by the case of "A Fallen Star," where multiple versions were recorded among even members of the Nashville country community.

9. Younger, *Get a Shot of Rhythm and Blues*, 21.

10. Younger, *Get a Shot of Rhythm and Blues*, 22.

11. Montgomery's sister Melba, a future country star, also began her career in Muscle Shoals.

12. For a stellar recent history of the chitlin' circuit, see Lauterbach, *The Chitlin' Circuit and the Road to Rock and Roll*.

13. Hoskyns, *Say It One Time for the Broken Hearted*, 162.

14. Guralnick, *Sweet Soul Music*, 163–64.

15. Killen and Carter, *By the Seat of My Pants*, 160.

16. Information on Alexander from Younger, *Get a Shot of Rhythm and Blues*, 10–12. For more on Sun Records, see Escott, *Good Rockin' Tonight*.

17. Younger, *Get a Shot of Rhythm and Blues*, 28.

18. Younger, *Get a Shot of Rhythm and Blues*, 29.

19. Younger, *Get a Shot of Rhythm and Blues*, 30–31.

20. Dobkin, *I Never Loved a Man the Way I Loved You*, 28–29.

21. Younger, *Get a Shot of Rhythm and Blues*, 30–31.

22. Younger, *Get a Shot of Rhythm and Blues*, 30–31. Younger also postulates that the background vocals may have featured Sandy Posey, a country-trained singer who recorded several R&B-tinged singles in Muscle Shoals in 1965 and 1966, before ultimately relocating to Nashville and scoring country hits.

23. Younger, *Get a Shot of Rhythm and Blues*, 43.

24. Younger, *Get a Shot of Rhythm and Blues*, 42.

25. There are many examples of this, but one particularly poignant usage of Boone's covers is in the "Rock and Roll Explodes" episode of the 1995 television series *Rock and Roll*, produced by WGBH (Boston) for PBS.

26. Younger, *Get a Shot of Rhythm and Blues*, 45. Dot even had an R&B hit with a group called the Griffin Brothers.

27. Spooner Oldham interview by Charles Hughes, Jan. 10, 2006, audiorecording in author's possession.

28. Robbins later played a clavinet, associated most strongly with Stevie Wonder's early 1970s recordings, on the Sherrill-produced George Jones single "Her Name Is."

29. Gillett, *Sound of the City*, 361–62.

30. For an extended examination of this period, see Hemphill, *The Nashville Sound*; Kosser, *How Nashville Became Music City, U.S.A.*

31. Younger, *Get a Shot of Rhythm and Blues*, 74.

32. Dan Penn interview by Charles Hughes, Dec. 1, 2005, audiorecording in author's possession.

33. Younger, *Get a Shot of Rhythm and Blues*, 126.

34. Radano, *Lying Up a Nation*.

35. Bob Palmer, "George and Ivory and Tammy and Isaac," *Rolling Stone*, Nov. 7, 1974, 9–10.

36. Cantwell and Friskics-Warren, *Heartaches by the Number*, 85.

37. Younger, *Get a Shot of Rhythm and Blues*, 111.

38. Sherrill also recorded a fascinating album with the future southern soul stars the Staple Singers in 1966, which consists mainly of covers of popular rock, folk, and country songs.

39. Country Music Hall of Fame, *Night Train to Nashville*.

40. Jerry Williams Jr., interview by Charles Hughes, June 14, 2007, audiorecording in author's possession.

41. Bill Friskics-Warren, "Dog Soldier," *Nashville Scene*, Sept. 28, 1998, 17. In a 2007 interview with the author, Swamp Dogg backed off his previous accusation, saying, "It seemed a little ironic that Gary and I would be left off, but shit happens. I'm not pissed at anybody."

42. Williams interview by Hughes.

43. Randall Grass, liner notes, *Totally Unrestricted! The Millie Jackson Anthology* (Rhino 72863).

44. Guralnick, *Careless Lover*, 326–37.

45. Younger, *Get a Shot of Rhythm and Blues*, 134.

46. Daley, *The Nashville Music Machine*, 68; Jennings, *Sing Me Back Home*, 16–17, 105.

47. Steptoe, "Ode to Country Music from a Black Dixie Chick," 26–27.

48. For more on southern rock and its connections to southern soul, see Kemp, *Dixie Lullaby*.

49. Younger, *Get a Shot of Rhythm and Blues*, 147.

12

What's Syd Got to Do with It?

KING RECORDS, HENRY GLOVER,
AND THE COMPLEX ACHIEVEMENT
OF CROSSOVER

David Sanjek

One of the many peculiarities about country music can be illustrated by the fact that however much its practitioners, admirers, and merchandisers venerate its raw and unmediated characteristics, from the start of the professional recording of the genre, there has been a whole lot of mediation going on. The boundaries that have been erected in order to protect the repertoire from the encroachment of heterogeneous musical practices and keep the material true to its roots have proven time and again to be flimsy at best and, perhaps, ultimately misguided. Neither the makers nor the admirers of country music, however, exist in a vacuum. Ultimately, even though the kinds of themes that resonate for the genre's audience more often than not recall and ratify time-honored traditional values, those very powerful metaphors of home, hearth, family, and faith truly achieve their potency only when they are anchored in the stress and strain of the modern world. The appreciators of country music would remain pretty infinitesimal and isolated if the repertoire addressed only this limited, and ultimately limiting, body of ideas. Obviously such has not been the case, because the infusion of subject matter and forms of music-making that might initially seem alien if not intimidating to the genre's core constituency keep breaking in and forcing accommodation with the wide world outside its venerated origins. Country music, in effect, resolutely protects its authenticity by the incorporation of what appears at the time to be anything but immediately acceptable. It stays true to its roots by stretching its branches again and again.

One can observe this willingness to embrace and absorb what superficially came across as alien from the very start of the professional marketing of country music. Profit-seeking entrepreneurs initially presumed the genre to be a more or less solely regional set of practices with limited interest to those outside the material's point of origin. This blunder proved to be an illustration not of the music's limitations but, instead, of those businessmen's blindness. For example, the managers of OKeh Records and the firm's preeminent executive, Ralph Peer, balked at the enthusiasm exhibited by Polk Brockman when in 1923 he advanced the commercial viability of the kind of material he heard at fiddling contests in his native Atlanta. Brockman was the company's wholesale representative in the Southwest and a leading purveyor of what the period pigeonholed as "race records." On a visit to the company's New York City offices, Brockman attended the Palace Theatre in Times Square and watched a newsreel that featured footage of one of those contests. By the light leading out of the aperture to the projection booth, he scribbled a note to himself that their persistent champion, Fiddlin' John Carson, ought to make recordings. He arranged a session for the performer back home and then struggled against the firm's impulse to forgo pressing any copies of Carson's rendition of "Little Old Log Cabin in the Lane." Commentators routinely assume that Peer's hesitation in particular arose out of antipathy to the genre itself, as he is said to have objected to Carson's vocals and condemned the results as "pluperfect awful." Gene Wiggins suggests that the hubbub could just as likely have occurred as a response not so much to the material as the medium on which it was transcribed, for the engineers in charge had never been compelled before to document an individual simultaneously singing and sawing a fiddle.[1] Such a feat must assuredly have tested their technological capabilities.

Brockman eventually wore down the firm's skepticism about the material yet nonetheless initially failed to sway them as to his perspicacity about its audience. OKeh conceded to the manufacture of just five hundred copies of the results on blank disks meant only for Brockman's use on a purely regional basis. Returning to Georgia, Brockman arranged for yet another occasion of instrumental combat to coincide with an Elks convention in order to entice the live audience to become eager consumers of what some categorized as "canned music." Fiddlin' John Carson took to the stage and played the newly minted document of his repertoire. The crowd immediately bought out the available stash of records, and thereby granted credence to Brockman's original business plan. Peer and the company consequently had no choice but to re-press the work as a commercial release and to bring Carson to New York City in order to attempt to repeat the outcome.

The validation of Brockman's intuition about the marketplace's flexibility might be said to constitute the foundation on which the commercial success of country music was established. It illustrates as well the fact that culture never evolves in a straight path or with any kind of cookie-cutter inevitability. Miraculous actions and actors can spring up when and where you least expect, even if a close examination of a particular period of time illustrates how certain factors have a good chance of leading in one particular direction and not another. Take, for example, the period following the breakout of World War II. In the latter part of the previous decade, the record industry, like every other portion of the U.S. economy, deflated in response to the pressures of the Depression. Whether or not the public wished to buy records, few of them had the available resources to do so. As the economy improved, so did the balance sheets of the record labels, if only temporarily. With the outbreak of war, the American music industry predictably faced any number of perils, including but not limited to the tensions on the home front as well as the recurrent fragmentation of the economy due to the need for investment in the war effort. An even greater obstacle, however, proved to come not from enemies abroad but from cohorts at home. Fearful for the job prospects of his members, the president of the American Federation of Musicians, James Petrillo, initiated a strike in 1942 that ultimately shut down production of any new releases of commercial recordings for the foreseeable future. The job action met with heated opposition from the major labels, yet Petrillo held firm, and nearly two years passed before the situation was resolved.

The institutional stagnation that resulted would deter anyone with common sense, you would imagine, from even thinking about breaking into the business, as it seemed for a time that the very musical marketplace might evaporate along with the authority of the world's democracies. And yet this very volatile period coincides with one of the notable peaks of diversification and expansion in the history of the American record industry. Hungry entrepreneurs took the bait, launched a steady stream of independent record labels, and embraced agreements with the union that the majors were unprepared to arbitrate. They also recognized that the public had been galvanized by the uproar brought about by the conflict and were eager to alleviate their anxieties with novel combinations of musical styles. Consequently social upheaval led to artistic experimentation. Rules of behavior and sets of interpersonal expectations that seemed implacable were overturned, and the public stepped over boundaries of taste and temperament that would have seemed insurmountable just a few years earlier.

One of those prescient individuals who benefited from this turn of events was someone whose engagement in the music industry had to be as unexpected if not unprecedented as was the enormous success of Polk Brockman's bet on the commercial prospects of country music. Sydney Nathan was an asthmatic, overweight, nearly blind Jewish businessman whose previous string of unsuccessful professions ranged from running a pawnshop to promoting professional wrestling to operating amusement park concessions. He was born in Cincinnati, hardly a musical hotbed and even less likely a place where someone might carve out an enterprise that could compete with the major record labels located in New York City, Chicago, or Los Angeles. Nearly forty years old in 1943, he thought that he might transform his prospects with a photo-finishing business, coupled with the sale of phonograph records on the side. Soon, however, the receipts from the latter eclipsed the former, and it turned out that most of his customers wanted country releases, despite the urban setting of the establishment.

Buoyed by his success, Nathan convinced his relatives to loan him $25,000 to inaugurate a record company to supply the product directly. Cut off from any professional centers of power, he recognized that he would have to begin his own business from the ground up. He secured an arrangement with the American Printing House for the Blind, located in Louisville, Kentucky, to press his first efforts. So mediocre were the results that he quickly set up his own facility in Cincinnati and in August 1944 acquired a five-year lease on a local factory site. His earliest professional affiliations were with country artists, most of them performers on the local equivalent of the Grand Ole Opry, WLW's *Boone County Jamboree*. By the time the war ended, the label he initially named Queen—Cincinnati having the nickname of the "Queen City"—was renamed King, and he compounded the already confounding details of his enterprise by ascending quickly among the pack of independent companies to secure hits on the professional record charts.

The unexpected outcome of Nathan's gamble paid off even further when he made the unprecedented appointment of a young, African American composer-arranger-performer from the Lucky Millinder orchestra, Henry Glover, to the company as an A&R man who would also contribute material to the label's catalogue. No other black man possessed a position of comparable seniority and responsibility at any other record label at the time, and those who succeeded him would not repeat his array of achievements for some years to come. Concurrent with Glover's employment, Nathan had expanded the company's repertoire beyond country to incorporate a variety of black performance styles, including blues, rhythm and blues, gospel, and jazz. Unsurprisingly Glover was put in charge of much of this material, but, more unusually, Nathan required him to also supervise a portion of the country catalogue. Glover subsequently not only succeeded in this appointment but also tapped possibilities, both aesthetic and economic, in directing those artists to perform material from the other African American genres, and vice versa. He thereby contributed to the careers of such artists as the Delmore Brothers, Wynonie Harris, Hawkshaw Hawkins, Bullmoose Jackson, Wayne Raney, and Moon Mullican, among many others. The result was a sequence of recordings that illustrate some of the most successful and influential examples of the phenomenon known in the music industry as crossover: the recording of a work drawn from a specific musical genre by someone from another and opposing tradition. The delivery of the work is often if not usually influenced by the practices of the adapter, thereby altering the original composition in a potentially innovative manner (fig. 12.1).

Crossover hardly originated with the King label. It could be said to have begun with the very phenomenon of recorded music. Take, for instance, the work of an exceedingly popular white female "coon shouter" from the turn of the twentieth century, May Irwin, whose 1907 release "The Bully" adapted material from the African American folk tradition. Or, closer to the time of Glover's initial association with Nathan and King, "Pistol Packin' Mama." Al Dexter wrote and originally recorded the track in 1944 for Columbia, his laidback vocal interspersed by interludes on accordion and trumpet. It sold over three million copies and became the third most popular song during the war era. Nick Tosches astutely observes that it assembles an array of approaches such that it comes across as "an alembic in which bubbled the forces of old-timey blues, western swing, honky tonk, and outright pop."[2] Bing Crosby and his managers recognized the appeal of the tune to an audience that exceeded the purportedly narrow if fervent constituency for country. He recut the song the same year along with the Andrews Sisters as his first Decca release following the adjudication of the musicians strike and succeeded as well, though in his case pop predominated over any overt allusion to country.

Dexter's tune epitomizes the generic and stylistic flexibility of crossover; later renditions were released by Louis Armstrong, Jimmie Lunceford, Dean Martin, Glenn Miller, Don Redman, Frank Sinatra, Jo Stafford, and Gene

Vincent. And yet the phenomenon cannot be ascribed simply to a matter
of the hijacking of hits, as though the process constituted little more than a
sequence of musical magpies migrating from one stylistic nest to another.
Glover's participation in crossover adds the crucial ingredient of race, as he
supervised the recordings of particular songs by both black and white performers, often had them played by racially mixed ensembles, targeted them
at both black and white audiences, and incorporated in their creation elements of the stylistic agendas associated with both races. One can think,
therefore, of crossover as an act and these recordings as a repertoire that
resembles a musical melting pot, for two (and sometimes more) musical
and cultural traditions consequently collide, fuse, and reformulate. It is the
purpose of this essay to consider the consequences of this process, examine
some of the most successful examples Glover produced, and situate both
the King label and its contributions to crossover in the wider history of the
American record industry and the development of domestic popular music.
In addition, I distinguish crossover from the more frequently analyzed, and
often excoriated, occurrence of cover records. As Michael Coyle comments,

the latter form emerged "only when 'race' records began to have mass appeal on 'white' pop charts," a phenomenon that happened with greater frequency with the advent of independent record labels already discussed and then virtually became a cottage industry in the 1950s with the emergence of rock and roll.[3] White performers (Pat Boone being certainly the most notorious but just as certainly not the most egregious individual) cut versions of successful black records that were marketed to racially identified audiences; furthermore the delivery of the material often duplicated the earlier release in all but essence, as the vocal attack and instrumental accompaniment were more often than not mimicked renditions of the original material while simultaneously doctored — one might be so snarky as to say bleached — in order to efface any overly racial characteristics. Whereas in the case of the cover, a more or less intentional act of appropriation occurs, the crossover by contrast illustrates an evidently complex and multivoiced phenomenon, one in which the process George Lipsitz dubs "discursive transcoding" can be overheard, whereby artists of both races can " 'disguise' their own subjectivities in order to 'articulate desires and subject positions' that they cannot express in their own voices."[4] To put it another way, the individuals engaged in covers resemble interlopers, trespassing upon another race's aesthetic arena, while those attached to the crossover process come across as co-inhabitants of a universe whose boundaries possess exceedingly fluid demarcations.

To begin, let us turn to Syd Nathan's account of the inauguration of King Records and his management philosophy. To a significant degree, these practices and their attendant attitudes led to Nathan's hiring of Glover, his inauguration of and support for the practice of crossover, and an implicit recognition that neither musical genres nor racial categories need be impediments to intersections between cultural practices and social communities that the larger society thought of as radically separate if not potentially incompatible. These points can best be illustrated by a soliloquy he delivered during the course of a sales meeting, an ardent recitation of corporate achievements preserved by the fortunate intervention of someone with a tape recorder:

> The King Record company was started as a mistake. I was a retailer, selling records in a location that nobody could sell a record. It so happens there are several people here who knew of Syd's Record Shop and where it was located, and it was like trying to sell grand pianos out in the desert. But we done business. The King Record Company was started there. Later we developed it into an organization with a plant,

which I hope all of you folks here have been taken on the twenty-eight cent tour. If there is any part of the plant that you haven't seen, we would like for you to see it before you go home. To see what you're part of. You're not part of a small record company, believe me. You're part of a big record company and one that is proud of the way we do business.

Shortly after we started, and we started this business when I was in the record store. I opened the business with sixty-nine accounts. Sixty-nine phonograph operators, jukebox operators. The farthest one being Big Springs, Texas that I shipped. All the records I could manufacture for them in those sixty-nine accounts, I don't know if they used them for soup bowls or records. They could have made beautiful soup bowls, oh, they were beautiful. You could run a little mouse race around them. Beautifully made.

You remember those first independent records. We started the company by accident. Cowboy Copas, Delmore Brothers, Merle Travis, Hank Penny, Grandpa Jones used to come in the store — they were all on local radio stations here — used to come in the store to buy records. They talked me into going into the record business. They were hungry. They wanted to make a five dollar bill or a forty dollar bill. So naturally we started hillbilly for well over two years, maybe three. Then we saw the need to go into other categories of the record business. . . . Mr. Rosen, who was covering how many states? Eleven states, just a small part of the country. He never had time to stop go see customers 'cause he was traveling all the time. But we done business. We saw a need. Why should we go into those towns and sell only the hillbilly accounts? Why can't we sell a few more while we're there? 'Cause you don't make money while your car is rolling. Every time you get in the car and drive fifty miles, it costs me money. If you could only stand still and do business, we'd make more money. But you can't so you have to get to the next town 'cause I said that you're on your own time, not on my time.

So we branched out into the race business, the blues as they like to refer to it today. The sepia. We were afraid that the main business had been accomplished, the King as hillbilly. You automatically said with it hillbilly. So we started the Queen label. . . . Now we later got to a point where we felt we knew what we were doing in the race business. And I said that within three months, I'm going to get new artists and make a push for the race field.[5]

Nathan thereafter recounts in a jocular manner how the company signed up three of the renowned race artists of the day: Bull Moose Jackson, Wynonie Harris, and Ivory Joe Hunter. His tone veers off momentarily into the unappetizing realm of the sarcastic verging on the racially superior, particularly when he underscores Harris's less than sober behavior, makes light of those elements of Jackson's features that earned him his professional nickname, and points out the many labels for which Hunter had recorded. Yet at the same time one clearly discerns beneath that bluster Nathan's sincere appreciation of their audacious personalities and their eagerness to join in the commercial chase for profits.

He continues:

> Now we started to add artists and we immediately dropped the Queen label. We put the name King where Queen was and we substituted on the label the word King. Because we felt that we had accomplished what we wanted by making King as well known as hillbilly. The record speaks for itself. Immediately we became the factor with the race business. We said that we were going to be a factor with the race field. And that was enough. The impossible we can do right now. The absolutely impossible takes a day longer.[6]

Nathan initially delivered these remarks on September 22, 1951. They can be found as one of the final selections included on the fourth CD of an out-of-print collection, *The King R&B Box Set*, released in 1995. I presume the present owners of the label, GML Inc. of Nashville, found the tapes on their premises among the company's recorded repository and intended them as a representation to the general public of the company founder's expansive personality. It is quite possible as well that the material circulated clandestinely among industry and other insiders before its public unveiling. This community often relishes any illustration of what occurs behind closed doors when the lens of public scrutiny has been obscured. Other instances of surreptitiously preserved public behavior have taken on legendary status within the inner circles of the record business, and sometimes elsewhere with particular frequency upon the advent of the digital download. Widely circulated examples include the jazz drummer Buddy Rich's obscene lambasting of his accompanists and the unintended incompetence embodied by Linda McCartney's less than melodic shredding of one of her husband's compositions. Their uncensored and unexpected exclamations reinforce how thin is the veneer that stands between the polished productions that reach the marketplace and the array of unguarded sentiments that produce those wares.

While Syd Nathan possessed a long-standing reputation among his peers as an audacious and often autocratic entrepreneur, what impresses one about this monologue is its unexpected lack of bombast or egotism. If these comments come to us from under the corporate radar, they remain anything but over the top. Nathan speaks with a kind of even modulation and conversational tone that nonetheless exudes an undeniable assumption of authority. He underscores his conviction of the success of the label's methodology by the calculated repetition of the catchphrase "We done business." At the same time, there is something almost avuncular about the presentation, made during a sales meeting. The words come across as though the progenitor of the label were informing his descendents about how the family fortune came to be made. Familiar as the audience might have been with these anecdotes (you imagine they had heard them more than once before their present iteration), you still get the feeling that Nathan's auditors attend to his every word, and not simply out of fear or obligation. His well-rehearsed remarks emanate a kind of experientially acquired wisdom, a comprehension of the musical economy bred through trial and error, triumph, and near catastrophe. He also conveys the sense that this process does not depend on the ideas and ambitions of a solitary individual. Nathan notably draws attention to the contributions of his subordinates and the fact that the company's successes resulted from their collective hard work and savvy decisions, over which he operated as the final arbiter but not the sole intelligence.

Eloquent as this presentation might be, some elements of Nathan's performance collide with the commonly held assumptions about the larger-than-life individuals who inaugurated the array of independent record labels that flourished, like King, in the years following the conclusion of World War II. These ambitious individuals come across in much of the popular literature written about that period as virtual buccaneers who absconded seemingly overnight with the major labels' long-held and fiercely guarded access to the musical sensibilities of the general public. Admittedly, when this purported onslaught occurred, the stranglehold exerted by the principal companies of the time—Columbia, RCA Victor, and Decca—had met with some considerable opposition, including the strike by the American Federation of Musicians that stymied the production of any new material from the majors for nearly two years, while upstart competitors in some cases made agreements independently with the union. Who would be so foolish as to allow a matter of principle to get in the way of the chance for profit-making?

Concurrent with these developments, a seismic shift was taking place among consumers on the home front, many of whom flocked from their rural residences to urban metropolises in pursuit of the attractive wages to be earned as a consequence of the war effort. There they invariably mingled with races and classes from which they were formerly segregated but, more consequentially, encountered an array of musical forms that eradicated any belief they might have transported with them that genres, like people, ought to be kept unique and distinct. Musicians have a tendency to be remarkably indiscriminate when it comes to established categories of expression, and many of them during this period cobbled together combinations of sound that might well have seemed discordant if not downright incomprehensible only a few years earlier.

New hybrids emerged in the course of time, among them rhythm and blues, honky tonk, bebop, hillbilly boogie, and jump blues. The major labels chose by and large either to overlook or underplay the opportunities that ensued, but the independents lapped up both the possibilities and the profits without regard for the status quo. Labels like Atlantic, Chess, Duke-Peacock, Modern, Specialty, Savoy, Mercury, Imperial, and many, many others flourished as a consequence. Some lasted only a few years, some a decade or two; a very few, Atlantic most notably, survived the end of the past century. More than one commentator has referred to the virtually explosive vitality and innovation of this period, roughly 1944–54, as the democratization of American music, yet it would be folly to ascribe altruistic motivations as a prevailing sentiment on the part of the figures who bankrolled the experimentation. If they advanced the ambitions of those who aimed to stretch the envelope of commercial music in this country, they did so with an unwavering obsession with the bottom line. In their minds, profits would trump any kind of pioneer spirit again and again, much as they appreciated, even admired the artists whose efforts augmented their fortunes.

It should come as no surprise, then, that a melodramatic tone adheres to most of the documentation of these executives' efforts. By and large, they emerge as rapacious, regal, self-regarding, often virtually reptilian individuals. By contrast with the more or less faceless occupants of the current corporate boardroom, their avarice or anger wore a very human face. Some of them even seemed in the flesh to be alarmingly life-size caricatures of zealotry, and, sad to say, Nathan was prominent in this company. As the photographs contained in the *King R&B Box Set* attest, his overweight frame and the oversized lenses in his glasses make for a memorably vivid illustration of over-the-top ambition. And Nathan possessed the capacity to be as pig-headed or pugnacious as any of his peers. Working with him in the studio could be something of an ordeal, for his lack of a common language with which to convey his suggestions to performers routinely gave way to bluster and bad temper. Even his savvy commercial instincts ran up against an obstinate aversion to certain kinds of innovation, as when he dismissed the inaugural recording of James Brown's "Please Please Please," as something other than musical. The black hole Brown's innovative practices occupied in Nathan's consciousness did not dissipate for the duration of the artist's presence on the label. He even made him ante up his own cash for the production of the legendary 1962 *Live at the Apollo* recording. Who would pay for the reproduction of an event they could attend in person, Nathan obdurately argued.

These lapses in decorum or discrimination admittedly pale before some of his associates' more egregious gestures. The songwriter Doc Pomus reported that he overheard an assault occur in the offices of Roulette Records' chief Morris Levy and observed a bloodied and unconscious individual removed thereafter from the premises. Little Richard attested that the African American owner of the Duke-Peacock labels, Don Robey, concluded an argument by punching him so hard in the solar plexus that he lost consciousness. One of the most vilified figures in this crew, Savoy's Herman Lubinsky, known to his peers as "Herman the Vermin," exercised his presumed prerogative in a less lethal but equally effective manner. He claimed, for example, that the contractual obligation of the balladeer Little Jimmy Scott to his company overrode any efforts he might make with a competitor and thereby kept the singer unrecorded—and work for both Ray Charles's Tangerine label and Atlantic Records unreleased—until after the unctuous executive's death in 1974. It was only when Sire Records' Seymour Stein (a protégé of Syd Nathan) heard the artist perform at Doc Pomus's funeral in 1991 that Little Jimmy Scott once again could be presented to the public at large.

While Nathan might well have been equally as obdurate and objectionable on more than one occasion, evidence suggests that he avoided the taint of racism that motivated some of his peers to treat their performers as little more than chattel. For a period and a region in which the assumptions of Jim Crow amounted to something of a virtual reflex, Nathan managed to behave in a remarkably open-minded manner, even at times to adopt the attitudes that the crusade for civil rights would eventually make a matter of national policy only a few years later. The company advertised a nondiscriminatory hiring policy, even though popular opinion held that, being a border town, Cincinnati could not support a multiracial workforce. Its proximity to the Deep South colored racial relations indelibly, it was felt. Nonetheless a 1949 *Cincinnati Post* story revealed that more than a token handful of the King Records staff were African American, including an assistant office manager, the foreman of the mill room, a setup man on the production line, an assistant legal secretary, a dozen stenographers, and 20 percent of the factory workers.[7] Applications for employment included the question whether the prospective staff member objected to working with members of other races or religions, though no one was automatically rejected should he or she answer in the negative. It was felt that anyone who did harbor such prejudices would selectively defer from joining the payroll. The staff consequently intermingled at picnics as well as seasonal celebrations. King sponsored a Negro as well as a white team in the segregated Cincinnati industrial baseball league. Nathan himself is also rumored to have contributed to the principal civil rights organizations of the time.

The label made a point of advertising these conditions at a time when racial integration in the workplace was widely considered an aberration, not a positive achievement. Nathan forthrightly addressed the policy in a 1951 *Saga* magazine article, "The Man Who Is King":

> We give everyone an even break. This is because I'm a Jew, and I know what obstacles are. A Jew may have it rough, but a Negro has it a lot rougher. And a good man is a good man; his religion or his race isn't going to make any difference. Listen, I used to pal around with an Irish kid, and I'd go to mass with him. I liked it. It wasn't my religion, but it certainly didn't do me any harm. I guess no religion does a man harm, unless there is one that teaches him to steal and rob and lie. At King we pay for ability, and that's what we get. Our people get along fine together, and we aren't fooling when we say we don't discriminate.[8]

King's personnel manager, Ben Siegel, echoed Nathan's sentiments in the 1949 *Cincinnati Post* piece, in some cases word for word: "We pay for ability, and ability has no color, no race, no religion. Our hiring policy and our promotion system are based only on the question of the individual's capacity to fill a given job."[9]

Nathan's overlooking of racial prejudices carried over to his choice of repertoire. While many independent labels specialized in a single genre, from the start King signed up both white and African American artists and produced definitive catalogues of country as well as blues, rhythm and blues, and jazz releases. For those unfamiliar with the company and its legacy, the roll call of hits remains conspicuously remarkable. In the sphere of rhythm and blues, they recorded James Brown, Wynonie Harris, Bullmoose Jackson, and Ivory Joe Hunter as well as Roy Brown, Johnny Otis, Little Willie John, Esther Phillips, Hank Ballard and the Midnighters, the "5" Royales, Billy Ward and the Dominoes, and Johnny Guitar Watson. In blues, John Lee Hooker, Lonnie Johnson, Champion Jack Dupree, and Freddie King. In jazz, Earl Bostic, a jukebox veteran whom John Coltrane claimed as a major influence, and Bill Doggett. In country, the Delmore Brothers, Merle Travis, Grandpa Jones, Hank Penny, and Cowboy Copas as well as Reno and Smiley, Hawkshaw Hawkins, Homer and Jethro, and Moon Mullican.

The songs these artists added to the permanent repertoire of American music are equally impressive: "Poppa's Got a Brand New Bag" (James Brown, 1965), "Fever" (Little Willie John, 1956), "The Twist" (Hank Ballard, 1959), "Finger Poppin' Time" (Hank Ballard and the Midnighters, 1961), "Good Rockin' Tonight" (Wynonie Harris, 1947), "Train Kept a Rollin'" (Tiny Bradshaw, 1951), "Sixty Minute Man" (Billy Ward and the Dominoes, 1951), "Honky Tonk" (Bill Doggett, 1956), "Work with Me Annie" (Hank Ballard and the Midnighters, 1954), "Drown in My Own Tears / I'll Drown in My Tears" (Lula Reed, 1951), "Hide Away" (Freddie Kin, 1960) and "Blues Stay Away From Me" (Delmore Brothers, 1949).

Before founding the label, Nathan operated two record stores, and his knowledge of diverse audiences must have been accelerated by face-to-face contact with his customers. Like many of his peers, Nathan's understanding of the music business came not, as is so often the case nowadays, from the abstractions of balance sheets and market surveys but from the desires and interests of the public, as well as listening to what they heard over the airwaves. He appears to have intuitively understood and put into commercial practice the injunction Tony Russell makes in *Blacks, Whites and Blues*: "White country music in America would not have its present form if it were not for black musicianship. Indeed, the only way to understand fully the various folk musics of America is to see them as units in a whole; as traditions with, to be sure, a certain degree of independence, but possessing an overall unity."[10]

Nathan's racial inclusiveness and musically open mind might best be illustrated by the most inspired and influential hiring of his career, that of the African American trumpeter, composer, arranger, and producer Henry Glover. The two men first met around 1947, when Glover was an employee of the bandleader Lucky Millinder, whose ensemble was signed to King in 1950. Marketable as the group's material might have been, the company made particularly successful use of their tenor saxophonist and vocalist, Bull Moose Jackson. His smooth, melodious rendition of the ballad "I Love You, Yes I Do," cowritten by Glover and Millinder, reached number 1 on the black charts and number 21 on the pop charts in 1947. Nathan appears to have recognized with notable speed the diverse skills that Glover could offer the company and strenuously urged him to join King as a producer and A&R man. Promising to teach him all he knew about the business, Nathan induced Glover some short time thereafter to work alongside him for six months; then he doubled the young man's salary and managed to keep him a local resident for two years, before Glover returned to New York City as his home base. He remained affiliated with the company through the end of the following decade.

Glover flourished under Nathan's leadership, and the track record he accumulated during the course of his employment at King attests not only to his musical acumen but also to his perspicacious recognition of the ways musical genres could fuse and intermingle. He was instrumental in the label's practice of crossover, simultaneously recording material in two different genres and two different musical styles written by individuals in the company's employ, thereby doubling the company's publishing royalties as well as augmenting its potential domination of more than one niche of the musical marketplace. This practice may not have originated with King, but the label excelled at the opportunities it afforded for musical experimentation and market share augmentation. While Nathan certainly supported the practice and appreciated its fiscal consequences, he does not appear to have been the sole precipitating figure in the exercise. Glover played a determinant role, certainly choosing which artists would participate in the process and the songs they would perform. He intuited that the public was ready for material that bent established conventions and thereby helped to put in place a number of the crucial stylistic parameters that would in time lead to the emergence of rock and roll. Glover undoubtedly could read the artistic temperament of his artists and consistently comprehended which of them would respond to material that stretched their creative potential and which were restricted by intractable instincts. At the same time, one must add that Glover did not pursue these goals with some master plan or coherent aesthetic scheme in mind. When later in life he characterized some of the results in the country field as being novel for the time, such a designation comes across more as a retrospective assessment than as an aim he had while working for Nathan. If anything drove Glover to push the parameters of both specific genres and the performance practices of some of King's artists, it would have been his resistance to convention and willingness to stretch what audiences would appreciate rather than simply catering to their predetermined affiliations.

Henry Glover's remarkable role in the process of crossover and his emergence as the single most responsible and successful African American music executive of his time has been remarked about in a few places, most notably Arnold Shaw's *Honkers and Shouters*, Barney Hoskyns's *Say It One Time for the Broken Hearted: Country Soul in the Deep South*, my essay "One Size Does Not Fit All: The Precarious Position of the African-American Entrepreneur in Post-WWII American Popular Music," and *King of Queen City*, the full-length history of the King label by John Hartney Fox, who brings to his credentials a period of time in the employ of GML Inc. Hoskyns writes of the label and Glover's efforts, "The wily Syd Nathan didn't drop his black artists once he'd hit paydirt with whites but instead traded songs back and forth between them and enjoyed hits in both markets."[11] Nonetheless Glover's achievements remain something close to a well-kept secret or a matter shared only by a close circle of cognoscenti, even though only one individual prior to him, J. Mayo Williams, possessed anything resembling his posture in the music industry. (Williams worked for the Paramount label, one of the premiere blues rosters of the 1920s and 1930s, and later played a similar role in the 1940s at Decca. On the side, he sold masters he produced to King during the early days of the company.) Part of that erasure from public memory may also be due to the fact that there exists, to my knowledge, only one extended oral history that details his career. John Rumble of the Country Music Hall of Fame conducted it in 1984 and 1990 and thereafter wrote the sole extended commentary on Glover's career in the 1991 special issue of the *Journal of Country Music* devoted to the role of African Americans in the genre.[12]

So considerable are his achievements and so commanding are his skills that one can easily forget how young Glover was when Nathan elevated him to a managerial status few if any among his race held at this point in time, or since for that matter. Barely in his midtwenties when he cowrote Bull Moose Jackson's hit, Glover had been a professional musician since his teens as well as completed an undergraduate and nearly a graduate degree. More than that, he appears to have acquired a degree of confidence unblemished by arrogance that permitted him to work comfortably alongside others far older and with more established credentials than his own as well as with members of other races. One of his associates at King dubbed Glover "the Hillbilly in Technicolor," a memorable designation that simultaneously draws attention to how he seemed to manage effortlessly to cross barriers of race, class, region, and genre at one and the same time.

One can credit such a track record to Glover's apparent possession of an even-tempered disposition that refused to give in to the vitriol so easily bred by the infection of racism. He even apparently managed to weather the frequent eruptions of Nathan's personality and separate the man from his malcontent behavior. Perhaps Glover's equanimity can be traced back, in part, to the tenor of his upbringing as well as the temper of his teachers. He was born in Hot Springs, Arkansas, where his father served as an attendant in the medicinal springs made famous by Franklin Delano Roosevelt as he sought solace from polio in their waters. Despite the town's and the state's position in the nation, Glover felt it avoided the prevalent factionalism of either region or race: it was "liberal in the sense that they didn't have a set population of what one would call today rednecks." He adds, "I didn't hear much about black and white and rednecks and niggers until I got out of Hot Springs, and I began to hear all of these things, and really races were at odds." While one does not wish to second-guess Glover's view of his own experience, it remains incontestable that Arkansas experienced its fair share of the national taint of racism, and even a cursory examination online of the incidence of lynching over the course of the period from 1860 to 1930, as documented by Richard A. Buckelew, illustrates a lamentable recurrence of violent and unwarranted death. Buckelew documents 318 lynchings, of which 224 were of black males and six of black females. Many of the deeds are said to have been committed in retaliation against violent or criminal acts (ranging from murder to rape to theft), while others are connected to activities that bear no evident association with any abrogation of the law.[13]

Four key episodes stand out in this context. In September 1891, ten black men were hanged in retaliation for a cotton picker's strike, and but a few days later, two more lost their lives in subsequent rioting. In 1904, over a four-day crescendo of atrocities, at least eleven black men were killed in the city of St. Charles in Arkansas County for no clear precipitating cause. The so-called Elaine Massacre that erupted in September 1919 was driven by community fear and distrust of a black-led organizing drive in Phillips County. When about a hundred African American sharecroppers attended a meeting of the Progressive Farmers and Household Union, whites retaliated by killing an untold number of black citizens; five of the whites involved in the episode themselves lost their lives. Finally, a notorious event of individual calamity occurred in Little Rock itself in 1927, when Glover was but a child, though certainly old enough to have known perhaps directly about the outcome if he did not hear about it from his family, other adults, or his peers. Following the murder of a twelve-year-old white girl, the alleged culprit was spirited away to Texarkana in order to avoid lethal retaliation. A few days later, a thirty-seven-year-old African American named John Carter was accused of yet another alleged assault on a white woman and her daughter. A mob estimated at over five thousand members sought out Carter, hanged him from a telephone pole, shot the body, set it on fire, and eventually dragged the remains through the streets into the midst of the city's black district. Three hours passed before the governor deployed National Guard troops to restore order; upon arrival, they discovered a member of the mob directing traffic with the aid of the charred arm of the deceased Carter.[14]

Glover was potentially acquainted with some of the worst behavior that Jim Crow culture could perpetuate. Any number of these episodes, and others, may well have come to his attention through tales told in the black community; one can only assume that he had some direct experience with the aftermath of Carter's ignominious death. The degree to which he succeeded in surmounting the rage and rancor that could easily follow such experiences remains a matter for conjecture. Certainly his parents encouraged Glover and his siblings to excel, and even though they initially frowned upon his attachment to music, Glover amply fulfilled their wishes by graduating high school in 1939 and attending Alabama Agricultural and Mechanical College. He then went on to begin, and nearly complete, a master's degree in social studies with a minor in education at Wayne (now Wayne State) University in Michigan, though by the time of his entrance there in 1943, he was already making his mark as a professional musician.

Glover comes across in his conversations with John Rumble as a naturally talented musician and a self-schooled composer. He never took a class in composition or officially mastered the use of keyboards, for, in his own words, he "developed a skill at mastering chord structures" and intuited the tenets required to write music such that he came in second in a national songwriting contest while still in high school. He also recognized that the acquisition of certain kinds of expertise permitted him access to opportunities that sheer talent alone would not allow. Consequently he lapped up whatever his teachers could pass on and appears to have been particularly sensitive to the matters of temperament with which they imbued the curriculum. He states, "The school experience was a reminder that if I were to [go] further in music or whatever, I had to master what the masters had set forth for us to master." When speaking to Rumble just a year before his death, Glover recalls in detail the names of his instructors, both black and white, and their recognition of some nascent skill at leadership on his part, which they appreciated and encouraged. He recounts that they joked about the consequences of a black man taking charge or occupying a place of power as the solitary person of color in an all-white enterprise, yet these jibes were clearly a means of strengthening his resolve and not suffocating his ambition. He clearly never forgot or failed to put into practice the admonition made to him by the black bandleader under whom he studied at Alabama Agricultural and Mechanical College, James Wilson: "Well, you can't be afraid of the foe. You can't fear the foe. You gotta go with the foe."

Glover crossed over from private life onto the bandstand at a young age, both as a participant with white adolescents and as part of all-black ensembles that performed at white-owned and white-attended establishments in Hot Springs. He learned quickly the complexities and contradictions of that world, if for no other reason than by virtue of the gigs he played at the Southern Club. Its proprietor, Owney Madden, had been the owner of Harlem's celebrated Cotton Club before his retirement to the Midwest. (Madden had bought the establishment from the famous, but lamentably bankrupt, black boxer Jack Johnson.) Jerome Charyn asserts that Madden was the "nearest thing that Manhattan ever had to a crime czar"; an English immigrant to America, he led one of New York City's most celebrated and lethal aggregations of lawbreaking adolescents, the Gopher Gang, served nine years in Sing Sing for murder, and became the metropolis's most successful bootlegger during Prohibition.[15] Madden successfully left that location and that specific occupation, if not a streak of criminality, behind when he moved to Hot Springs, where he ran several illegal gambling operations, including the Southern Club, and held the contract for the local wire services in order to facilitate his control of racetrack betting. He simultaneously maintained a local façade of avuncular prosperity, as he was married for over thirty years to the daughter of the local postmaster, lived next door to the Catholic church, avidly supported the Boys Club, and was respected as a soft touch for appeals to alleviate instances of individual indigence or other forms of the loss of security.

Glover certainly succeeded in following Wilson's advice and going with the foe when he solidified his relationship with Nathan. From the start, they must have intuited in one another a certain simpatico that would allow them to overlook or simply obliterate the potential obstacles of race and religion. Glover said of him to Rumble, "He spoke to me very freely about blacks and everything. I didn't feel the man had a lot of prejudice." Nathan appeared to treat Glover as more than simply a business associate. He went so far as to help Glover and his wife find a place to live when they settled in Cincinnati: right next door to the boss in what was clearly a building dominated by white residents. That did not dissuade Nathan from standing up for his colleague and his spouse, and even coming to their defense when another white man verbally abused the black couple. Glover reports to Rumble that Nathan tackled the man to the floor: a singular gesture under the circumstances of the times and even more of one when you consider that Nathan was overweight, asthmatic, damn near blind, and burdened with a weak heart.

You get the sense that Glover and Nathan took the fair measure of one another; each apprehended how his colleague operated and strove to create the least possible resistance that might intrude upon the satisfaction of those skills. Glover memorialized their collaboration to Rumble with great affection tinged by amusement at Nathan's gruff exterior:

> Based on the fact that he put me, as a black man, in pretty high regard, because it wasn't one of those things where I was just hired there, like a flunky, or something, anything else. I had stock, and I was part of the thing, you know. I had a contract, agreements, and things, and he had a little respect for me because of my intelligence, because in many cases he would ask me in a manner that required—how did he put it?—"Come help me mastermind this, with your big time education," as he would put it.

Nathan went so far as to equalize the relationship by offering to make Glover a partner, but he declined. He did not, however, turn down the chance to co-own one of the label's publishing firms and retain the copyrights in his material. Their collaboration collapsed, in the end, during the course of the hubbub over payola that nearly crippled the music industry as the 1950s waned. Nathan dismissed the practice as an inevitable byproduct of the status quo, how "we done business." Darren Blase reports in a 1997 tribute that Nathan flippantly remarked that he "never paid more than $10 a month to any one disc jockey, although some firms might have paid as much as $300–400 to get their records plugged."[16] Glover followed the dictates of the front office, but covered his professional posterior by keeping receipts for any cash laid out or the stubs of whatever checks he signed.

Nonetheless, in the investigations that ensued, Glover was made to appear little more than a co-conspirator and inevitably severed his relationship with the label. One imagines he wished that Nathan had come once more to his aid as vigorously as he did when that racist resident denounced him and his wife in that apartment hallway. Lingering bonds of friendship and camaraderie did not, however, altogether evaporate, for Glover returned to the company in the aftermath of Nathan's demise and did so once again in the 1970s in the interim before GML purchased the catalogue. Maybe he felt a debt of gratitude to his deceased employer; maybe he just wanted to ensure that his stake in the company's assets was not undervalued. Whatever the case, Glover never failed to calibrate carefully either his talents or his contributions to the formidable enterprise that Nathan inaugurated. His pride was more than justified, and he drew attention to the source of that sentiment in his conversation with Rumble: "I knew what I was doing, and the people had me there because I could be a benefit to the artists or whatever."

Indeed so obvious were those skills that Nathan immediately put Glover in charge of performers from both the country and the rhythm and blues portions of his roster. He also apparently instructed Glover to oversee the company's small presence in the gospel market, although the present-day inaccessibility of most of that material makes it hard to assess these achievements. An early example of the synergies Glover sensed between the seemingly divergent musical spheres of country and rhythm and blues occurred when he produced work by the now too little known country bandleader Hank Penny, whose catalogue reflects a sophisticated sense of song structure and a pointed wit that does not often appear in the country arena. Like his label mate Merle Travis, Penny routinely bypassed the genre's recourse to sentiment and upgraded its occasional sympathy for sass. Glover recorded him in Los Angeles, where Penny kept up an active live schedule as well as a presence on radio, combining his musical repertoire with abundant skills at comedy. One of the first major crossover successes Glover achieved at King was when the boisterous blues shouter Wynonie Harris covered Penny's "Bloodshot Eyes" in 1949. Whereas the white performer played up the surprising metaphor in the song's central image, Harris lent it his customary brash approach and infused the material with ardent audacity. In his study of Harris's career, Tony Collins comments, "Whereas Hank Penny had played up the novelty aspect of the song, Wynonie keeps the humor but at the same time sounds like a man who is not to be mess[ed] with as he lays down the law."[17]

Glover comprehended how the bizarre metaphors and twists of logic that Penny composed could appeal to Harris's sense of humor and larger-than-life stage persona. That ability not only to read performers but also to maintain a supportive atmosphere in the studio was apparent to his co-workers. The saxophonist Hal Singer, who is featured on Harris's signature song "Good Rockin' Tonight" (1949), remarked, "Glover was a guy that had a knack of gathering good material and seeing something in artists. Glover could see where talent was and what this talent needed to be pushed and he was very good at that. [In the studio] he knew what he wanted and you had to give it to him or else you wouldn't be on the date any more. Glover was a nice musician and creative and not hard to get along with."[18]

Glover continued to glean the possibilities for intermingling genres when he apprehended the intriguing novelty of "Why Don't You Haul Off and Love Me," written and performed in 1949 by the harmonica-playing country artist Wayne Raney. The lyrics partake of some of the romantic obsession and outright oddity of Phil Spector's 1962 track for the Crystals "He Hit Me (and It Felt Like a Kiss)," though it lacks this work's unappetizing allusion to sadomasochism. Glover induced Raney to stagger his delivery of the first three words in the title when they appeared in the chorus, giving one the sense that the protagonist was temporarily dumbstruck by the sheer physicality of his partner. That same year, Glover passed the material along to Bull Moose Jackson, who showed skill at formats other than the romantic ballad. He was particularly adept at delivering lyrics laced with witty wordplay, most notably the double entendre form that King made a specialty and which certain critics condemned at the time for their "leer-ics." Jackson took that route with the memorable "Big Ten Inch" (1952) and tackles Raney's material with a similar forthright declamatory style. He does not adopt Raney's hesitation, however, and, in so doing, transforms the earlier recording's tentativeness into something verging on a taunt. Where Raney remains shy, Jackson emerges as altogether shameless.

Significant and successful as was the shift from country to the rhythm and blues repertoire under Glover's administration, even more impressive were the achievements of the country artists whom he induced to unleash their inner equivalent of a barrelhouse blues shouter. In Glover's view, one of the most pliable country artists on the roster was Hawkshaw Hawkins. Of him, Glover remarked to Rumble, "I've never seen a guy try any harder than Hawkshaw Hawkins used to try, you know, to grasp what I was trying to get across of the changes coming, the little changes comin' on. Hawkshaw had that flexibility. What I could have worked with had he continued, you know, like at King that Moon [Mullican] had. Hawkshaw could have been a rock singer." You can overhear that willingness to cast aside categories in Hawkins's rendition of Little Willie John's "Let Them Talk" (1962) or Ruth Brown's "Teardrops from My Eyes" (1950). Hawkins must have appreciated, or his producers themselves encouraged, the liberation of those sensibilities, as he repeated the practice on his next label, RCA Victor. One of his 1955 releases was a two-sided engagement with black popular music: the Charms' "Ling Ting Tong" (1954) and Gene and Eunice's "Ko Ko Mo (I Love You So)" (1955). (Additional versions of these songs by the King R&B ensemble Otis Williams and the Charms were released in 1954 and 1955, respectively.) Glover also cut Hawkins performing a solo rendition of "I'm Just Waiting on You," originally a duet for John Carroll and Annisteen Allen (both released 1951). One does not know enough about Hawkins's sense of his own identity other than to conjecture what kind of investment he made in this repertoire. It would be revelatory to be able to ask of him some of the same questions that Michael Awkward addresses to the career of Janis Joplin: Did Hawkins seek "empowerment through the 'emotional fervor' of [his] own version of the blues aesthetic" or did he simply employ "black stylistic elements without attempting to project [himself], either as a performer or a person, as someone who embodies the attitudinal elan associated with some of its celebrated practitioners"?[19] Whatever the case, from Glover's perspective, Hawkins remained "a country singer with a rhythm and blues blend." Unfortunately circumstances did not allow him to elaborate upon the potential permutations of this scenario, as he accompanied Patsy Cline and Cowboy Copas (another King artist) on the fatal flight that crashed in the forests of Tennessee in 1963.

Of all the artists Glover assisted in achieving crossover, perhaps none succeeded as completely in unifying the two spheres of performance as the keyboard-playing vocalist Aubrey "Moon" Mullican. A native of East Texas, he learned to play piano from Joe Jones, a local black sharecropper. He adapted those skills to his household's organ, though Mullican's parents probably flinched when they heard boogie woogie patterns emanating from its pipes. Those sounds proved to be infectious to the young man, and he subsequently left home at sixteen to become a professional musician. It therefore seems undeniable that, to some degree, his engagement with black music allowed Mullican a means of establishing a unique identity and, possibly, "enabled [him] to address [his] own ambivalence about the white American-middle-class community from which [he] emerged."[20] The manner in which he successfully completed that transfer of allegiance allows listeners to consider, in Awkward's words, "race as something more than a strictly biological category. In fact, [Mullican] encourages them to see it — or, perhaps, to *hear* it — as, amongst other things, a group of vocal behaviors from which talented singers of contemporary popular music choose in constituting their own styles."[21] His amalgamation of keyboard techniques from the African American repertoire only amplifies this possibility.

Mullican first recorded as a sideman as early as 1936, when he became a member of Leon "Pappy" Selph's Blue Ride Playboys. He soon thereafter teamed up with Cliff Bruner, a participant in the late Milton Brown's Musical Brownies, one of the first and best ensembles to codify the emerging genre of western swing. Signed to Decca along with Bruner, Mullican was the group's pianist and lead vocalist from 1937 to 1944. As engaging as these performances can be (frequently spurred by the sonic depth charges set off by Bob Dunn's steel guitar, as he had similarly jump-started the Brown repertoire), to these ears they remain more than pleasant but still stalled in second gear. Is it perhaps the absence of drums as well as our accelerated contemporary eardrums that make them so? The pumping instigation of Mullican's left hand compensates, to some degree, but you can sense just whispers of the opportunities that the pianist encountered when Glover encouraged him, as he had others, "to get away from some of the old, hard-core country arrangements."

Mullican joined the King roster in 1946 and quickly climbed the charts that same year when he cut a version of the Cajun classic "Jolie Blon" under the title "New Pretty Blonde." It went to number 2 in the country market. Glover was first paired with Mullican in 1949, when he produced and co-wrote the popular "I'll Sail My Ship Alone," one of the most endearing tunes in Mullican's repertoire. The following year Glover gave Mullican the opportunity to launch into overdrive when he covered the black bandleader Tiny Bradshaw's blazing up-tempo "Well Oh Well." He stomps out the engaging rouser as though the only alternative would be to revert to silence. Glover told Rumble that Mullican was the first white artist for whom he assembled a biracial backup band. The drummer was one Eagle Eye Shields, and the bass player, Clarence Mack, had performed the same function with Bradshaw's group. Picking up on the foundation they laid down was a matter of instinct for Mullican. Glover reports, "I didn't have to tell Moon where to come in or where not to come in or how many bars. He was perfect with time." Mullican apparently sought out similar professional circumstances outside the recording studio, for he welcomed playing in black clubs whenever possible. Glover's considerable admiration and affection for the musician comes across in a heart-felt statement he made to Rumble:

Moon had such a great soul. He was just like a black man to me, you know, like he thought, felt and expressed himself and everything else.

Like we say, he had a whole lot of soul, Moon did. . . . It was kind of hard for me to characterize Moon as a western musician, but he was not. He really was not. He liked the sound of them, maybe, but he wanted to go in a different direction. He wanted to be country, which he was. But very advanced country, even at his age, when I first met him; he was advanced country. And like you saw some of the records I made with him at the piano and everything, he could play.

You can hear that "advanced country" in one of the last tracks Mullican made during his King affiliation, "Seven Nights to Rock," released in 1956. (On this recording, and several others cut at the same session, Mullican is accompanied by the white rock ensemble Boyd Bennett and His Rockets, who had scored a major rock hit for King the year before with "Seventeen.") It echoes the energetic sounds being made at the same time by musicians less than half his age, yet Mullican evidences unfettered intensity that evaporates the curse of chronology. Hearing such material as well as the similar sides that preceded it reminds us that Elvis Presley did not emerge from a wood pile or Jerry Lee Lewis conceive of his style on a whim. Individuals before them had felt a similar urgency to rip it up or climb aboard the mystery train. Like many others, I first became acquainted with musicians like Mullican through the profiles written by Nick Tosches that originally appeared in *Creem* magazine and were collected in *Unsung Heroes of Rock 'n' Roll: The Birth of Rock in the Wild Years before Elvis.* Tosches's effervescent style can stir the interest of anyone other than the oxygen-deprived to want to road test his enthusiasms by seeking out examples of the original material. When doing so, some individuals rise to the challenge; others falter. (I should know, as I bought my way through virtually all of the book's discography; in so doing, I discovered that Amos Milburn, for example, merits copious amounts of time, but not so Merrill Moore. Milburn's output amounts to something more than simply a sequence of encomiums to the superiority of bottled spirits—"One Bourbon, One Scotch and One Beer" [1953] or "Bad, Bad Whiskey" [1950], to name but two—while Moore only occasionally added some dollops of personality to rather pedestrian boogie woogie.)

Mullican remains one of the certifiable keepers, a remarkable performer whom time has unfairly shoved aside. He was similarly ostracized from the commercial spotlight when tracks like "Seven Nights to Rock" appeared, as the emerging adolescent audience preferred lean and lanky contemporaries to overweight and balding middle-aged men who probably reminded them of their uncles. While Bill Haley could temporarily obscure his less than svelte appearance and the degree to which he was tonsorially challenged (much more than a little dab of Brylcream kept that ostentatious spit curl in place), Mullican was dropped from King and demoted back to the country stable. Ghettoized thereafter until his death in 1967 by the restrictive prescriptions of genre, he wandered from label to label: Coral, Starday, Kapp, Musicor, Spar, and Sterling. One can only imagine what he might have achieved had the association with Glover not been severed by contractual obligations.

These are but some of the crossover recordings overseen by Henry Glover that stand out in the King catalogue. Others that might prove equally exciting and informative are not easily accessible at the present time. GML has tended to erect surprisingly restrictive domestic obstacles that prohibit access to the company's considerable achievements, and that of other catalogues they own, for reasons known only to its owner, Moe Lytle. For many years the company squirreled away the King master tapes and only recently allowed the English import label Ace and a few other companies to reissue selective chunks of the complete archives. The domestic disposition of the material remains a rather different matter, for only the most well-known tracks are easily purchased. Consequently one can at present only be tantalized by what might have been achieved when the rhythm and blues ensemble the Swallows perform Don Gibson's country classic "Oh, Lonesome Me" (1958), or wish to experience how the York Brothers gave a bluegrass twist to the salacious lyrics of Billy Ward and the Dominoes' "Sixty Minute Man" (1951). The latter can be found only on a reissue put out by an accessible but relatively obscure European-based specialty label, Collector Records. Finally, there is the easily located and almost altogether surprising instance of the Stanley Brothers taking on Hank Ballard and the Midnighters' "Finger Poppin' Time" (1960). At the conclusion of a session that included such venerable items as the Carter Family's "Wildwood Flower," the duo acceded, apparently without any regret or dissension, to Syd Nathan's request that they endeavor to broaden their audience. The tune was initially laid down with the group's standard instrumentation. Later, finger snaps and drums were overdubbed. The seeming incongruity of this performance only escalates if you consider that, in an *Esquire* article just the year before, Alan Lomax incrementally boosted bluegrass's public image by dubbing it "folk music in overdrive with a silvery, rippling, pinging sound."[22] Progenitors of the genre, such as Bill Monroe and Lester Flatt and Earl Scruggs, were subsequently concerned to maintain allegiance to the repertoire's formal purity even as they endeavored to maximize the genre's potential mass appeal. By contrast, what the Stanley Brothers accomplished — albeit on a single track in a career committed fervently to traditional parameters — might be compared in automotive terms to placing all possible pressure on the accelerator. For contemporary audiences who know Ralph Stanley solely through the *O Brother Where Art Thou?* soundtrack and his dourly stirring rendition of "Oh, Death," the Ballard material would be something of a revelation.

Having attended to the abundant appeal in Glover's intermixture of genre, the potentially troubling question of what distinguishes these recordings from the contemporary practice of covers remains. How can one artist's replication of material by a member of another race and practitioner of a divergent body of expression come across as ambitious and adulatory while another seems little more than illicit and unscrupulous? The body of covers that appeared on the charts during the middle and later 1950s is commonly identified with a small but often commercially quite successful group of white performers who recorded nearly identical versions of material by black artists. Identical, perhaps, in arrangement and sometimes even in interpretation, yet a yawning chasm exists between the specious swagger of a Pat Boone or a Gale Storm and the certifiable savoir faire of Fats Domino or any number of his contemporaries.

The aesthetic failure of these recordings, such as Boone's evisceration of "Ain't That a Shame" or Storm's of "I Hear You Knockin'," comes about not simply through the predictably painful attempts at racial impersonation that veer off into embarrassing caricature. Where Glover seemed interested in helping to manufacture parallel spheres of excellence that meant to co-exist with one another and never supplant their predecessors, the creators of the covers seemed convinced that if they did no more than ape those they copied, they could effectively annex the position they occupied in the public imagination. If one might think of the two bodies of recordings in the language of public accommodation, the covers initiated a kind of aesthetic urban renewal, an attempt to strip away the presence of a foreign population from the record charts, whereas the crossover material aimed at the kind of mixed housing that was the dream of those who aspired to racial integration.

To speak in such terms intimates that Glover, or Nathan for that matter, possessed motives other than the monetary, that they were prepared to jettison commercial objectives and jack up a social agenda. If the latter occurred, it would be a desirable but certainly not a predetermined consequence. We are wise to keep firmly in mind when thinking about the catalogue of crossover recordings released by King the repeated mantra of Nathan's monologue: "We done business." And yet ulterior social motives, even motives that might reside just barely below the surface of the conscious mind, can coexist quite comfortably with fiscal objectives. The manner in which commercial recordings sink into the public imagination and unleash emotions and aspirations only barely hinted at in the notes played or the words sung proves time and again to be as mysterious a process as why a person intuits that a certain individual was meant to be his mate. Something as seemingly innocuous or unmotivated as a look in the eyes or the disposition of a body's stance or, correspondingly, the manner with which a singer inflects a word or a musician bends a note can change a life or even electrify a nation. Sometimes a social soapbox can be erected on a piece of vinyl or in the coded language found on a compact disc or a digital download.

One person who never professed to lobby for the unloosening of the national psyche nonetheless helped quite considerably to detach the impediments that stood in the way of the public embrace of black performers. It would be uncharitable not to admit that the owner of Dot Records, on which Boone and Storm appeared, was much more than a fair-weather friend of rhythm and blues. Randy Wood of Gallatin, Tennessee, the proprietor of Randy's Record Shop and an extensive mail-order business, advertised his wares on the popular station WLAC, broadcast out of Nashville. Their signal encompassed a wide swath of the nation and relayed the material recorded by the most successful black artists of the time. It remains an abiding irony of popular music history that one of the most successful purveyors of rhythm and blues recordings was simultaneously one of the most engaged eviscerators of that very same repertoire. His nose for material carried over to personnel, as he endeavored, unsuccessfully, to sign Glover to a two-year contract for $50,000. Wood tends to be vilified if he is mentioned at all in the historical literature; James Miller's *Flowers in the Dustbin: The Rise of Rock and Roll, 1947–1977* remains one of the very few volumes to speak of his career in detail, and in a balanced manner at that. He astutely compares Wood to Sun Records' Sam Phillips as "an entrepreneur with a vision," even though some might dissent and dismiss Dot's owner as possessed by an attenuated imagination.[23] If Phillips remained committed to the unique characteristics of his roster, Wood put a damper on anything that might confer any idiosyncrasy on his performers. Nonetheless Wood's influence on American popular music of the time and the audience that consumed it was considerable. More than likely, a significant percentage of the white adolescents who bought the work of black artists before that practice reached widespread social sanction did so surreptitiously through mail order from

Wood, who therefore acted as one of the undercover agents, intentionally or not, in the integration of the record charts, and American society altogether.

It is with this complex and sometimes contradictory assembly of motives and intentions in mind that I turn to the final and perhaps most confounding instance of crossover overseen by Henry Glover: the Delmore Brothers' 1949 release "Blues Stay Away From Me." It is one of the most successful songs in their substantial repertoire and certainly one of the principal factors in the duo's installation in the Country Music Hall of Fame in 2001 and the Bluegrass Hall of Fame, as well as helping to instigate Syd Nathan's induction in the Bluegrass Hall of Fame in 2006. The Delmores, Rabon and Alton, were members of the Grand Ole Opry and on the roster of both Columbia and RCA Victor-Bluebird long before they became among the very first artists to sign with King. In the near half-dozen years before the creation of this track, they added amply to their achievements, particularly as they had played a key role in the initiation of the subgenre known as hillbilly boogie, whose ebullient syncopation prefigured the even more raucous rhythms that would energize rock and roll. Clearly Alton and Rabon Delmore were predisposed to pressing the artistic envelope while still remaining in touch with the prescriptions of the country repertoire. Their repertoire also consistently drew upon elements of the African American tradition, and comments in Alton's posthumously published autobiography, *Truth Is Stranger Than Publicity*, underscore the duo's interactions with black performers, particularly the harmonica player DeFord Bailey, who was featured on but never fully assimilated by the Grand Ole Opry. They admired his musicianship and treated him without overt attention to his race; as Alton comments, "There weren't any United States soldiers standing with bayonets drawn to make us like and respect him. We all just did it because it was the right thing to do, and we all thought just as much of DeFord as we did our white friends.[24] (One overhears a less than subtle but ideologically sympathetic reference to the military intervention in efforts at racial integration in Alton's language.) Just the kind of temperament that Glover appreciated and believed he could encourage to take the extra step in order to leap over the inhibitions prescribed by the sometimes rigid construction of musical genres.

The artistic odyssey that led to the recording of "Blues Stay Away From Me" meanders through a sequence of earlier compositions by Glover and even takes a detour into the courts in order to settle the issue of authorship. Apparently the initial impetus came from Nathan. He asked Alton if he was acquainted with a national hit at the time, the saxophone instrumental "The Hucklebuck," written and performed by the black musician Paul Williams. "I want you to write me a hillbilly Hucklebuck. I want a beat, but I want it to be hillbilly," he explained.[25] The Delmores came to Glover with a rudimentary track that they were collaborating on with Wayne Raney, but felt they needed help with the final product. Glover in turn recognized that the piece needed something novel to ground it and make the track potentially deserve the nomenclature of "new country." He did so by providing their material with an insinuating bass line that propelled the languid lyrics and lazy syncopation in an absolutely memorable fashion. The origin of that bass pattern goes back a few years and illustrates, with more than an ounce of irony, the complex trajectory that music can travel before achieving its impact on the public consciousness. In the mid-1940s Glover had written a piece for the well-loved African American comedienne Moms Mabley called "Boarding House Blues" that appeared in a film of the same name meant exclusively for the black audience. Another arranger in the Millinder aggregation copied the material and passed it on to the saxophonist Williams. It soon thereafter was transformed into "The Hucklebuck," soared up the charts, and became the track most associated with Williams for the remainder of his career. Meanwhile the composition simultaneously had metamorphosed in Glover's hands into another work for the Millinder band, "D Natural Blues." These complications led Glover to take Williams before a board of the American Federation of Musicians in order to settle the claims of authorship. Before they reached a decision, Glover and Williams settled the matter between themselves; each would keep their works and allow the audience to determine the superior composition. Williams undeniably achieved that goal. Left out in the cold, Glover recalls, "I went to Cincinnati and got the Delmores together and came up with 'Blues Stay Away From Me,' based on the same melodic structure and the bass doing the same moving at the bottom, with the *bom-ba-pa, dum-ba-pa-dum*, and we came up with 'Blues Stay Away From Me.'"

The ingredients that fed the composition of this tune remind us that, even when we pigeonhole a piece into a single genre, we fail to acknowledge how it partakes, in an indelible fashion, of some elements of other and seemingly incompatible modes of performance. And that counts equally, if not more emphatically, for the racial designation of forms of cultural expression in America. At the same time, for a large part of the public, country music has traditionally been associated with whiteness; as Geoff Mann states, "Country music is widely perceived to be 'white' music—produced by white people, consumed by white people, apparently appealing almost exclusively to white people, at least in North America."[26] He goes on to reinforce how virtually every scholar of note on the genre—Paul Hemphill, Richard Peterson, Bill Malone, Paul DiMaggio, Jack Esco Jr., Barbara Ching, Robert Cantwell, David Fillingim, Aaron Fox, and James Gregory—confirms this piece of purportedly received wisdom. And yet, as Mann reminds us, nothing about this proposition is self-evident, as its incontestable confusion arises from the fact that, first, "there is no such thing as a 'pure' white American ethnicity or culture" and, second, even the most cursory examination of the genre reinforces how "a complicated mix of musics, including those of Mexico, Africa and African-Americans, contribute to what is now called country music."[27] The phenomenon of crossover and the constellation of individuals with whom Henry Glover interacted amplify the veracity of Mann's correction to this dubious but doggedly persistent proposition. The voices of various cultures emanate from the bandstand whenever the country repertoire is retrieved. While Glover might well have originally pursued the creative strategy of crossover for pragmatic reasons as a fundamental means of accessing as wide as possible an audience for the King catalogue, over the course of time his practices would become foundational to the very essence of American popular music. Syd Nathan may well have convinced himself, and others, that in the management of King Records he simply "done business," but an ancillary element of his economic agenda ratified the pluralistic essence of our national character.

Sometimes, as in the case of "Blues Stay Away From Me" and other numbers included on the national jukebox, a song ambles along such a circuitous path that it seems it might never reach a final destination. And sometimes a career takes off on trajectories that nothing can predetermine. The experiences that the "Hillbilly in Technicolor" possessed over a creative and commercially successful career may have come about in part because Henry Glover had been inured against the ravages of racism by any number of factors, including but not limited to his teachers' admonition that he "go with the foe." However, even those individuals might never have been able to imagine at the time how far his resilient attitude would take him. That urge to merge that Glover embodies with individuals and bodies of music that might well have been kept isolated illustrates how the inhibitions that cripple America socially can prove to be surprisingly porous in the cultural realm. One may not immediately intuit the role that Moms Mabley, Lucky Millinder, or Paul Williams in combination with Henry Glover, Syd Nathan, Alton and Rabon Delmore, and Wayne Raney played in the creation of "Blues Stay Away From Me," yet they are each indelibly etched into its effortlessly appealing, languidly loping beat. And if that is not an illustration of *e pluribus unum*, then I don't know what is.

Notes

This essay benefits immeasurably from the research completed by John Rumble into the career of Henry Glover. He conducted four interviews with Glover on February 15 and March 1, 1983, and April 25 and 26, 1990, which are now part of the oral history collection of the Country Music Hall of Fame and Museum, where Rumble is the senior historian. He published his revelatory essay on Glover's career in a 1991 issue of the *Journal of Country Music*. He kindly made copies of all four interviews available to me, and the quotations from Glover contained in this essay are found in those documents. I am also grateful for the help given to me in the past on the subject of King Records by Darren Blase, who completed a senior honors thesis on the label at the University of Cincinnati in 1995.

1. Wiggins, *Fiddlin' Georgia Crazy*, 75.

2. Tosches, "Al Dexter," 4.

3. Coyle, "Hijacked Hits and Antic Authenticity," 134.

4. Lipsitz, *Dangerous Crossroads*, 158.

5. "Syd Nathan and Eli Oberstein Address a Sales Meeting, September 22, 1951," *The King R&B Box Set* (King CD-7002).

6. "Syd Nathan and Eli Oberstein Address a Sales Meeting, September 22, 1951," *The King R&B Box Set* (King CD-7002).

7. Jerry Ransohoff, "Record Firm Here Smashes Jim Crow," *Cincinnati Post*, Mar. 21, 1949.

8. Richard Gordon, "The Man Who Is King," *Saga*, Jan. 1951, 63–65.

9. Tracey, *Going to Cincinnati*, 121.

10. Russell, *Blacks, Whites, and Blues*, 10.

11. Hoskyns, *Say It One Time for the Broken Hearted*, 33.

12. Rumble, "Roots of Rock 'n' Roll."

13. Buckelew, "Racial Violence in Arkansas."

14. Brian D. Greer, "John Carter (lynching of)," in *The Encyclopedia of Arkansas History and Culture*, http://www.encyclopediaofarkansas.net/encyclopedia/entry-detail.aspx?search=1&entryID=2289; Brent E. Riffel, "Lynching," in *The Encyclopedia of Arkansas History and Culture*, http://www.encyclopediaofarkansas.net/encyclopedia/entry-detail.aspx?search=1&entryID=346.

15. Charyn, *Gangsters and Gold Diggers*, 97.

16. Blase, "The Man Who Was King," 13.

17. Collins, *Rock Mr. Blues*, 97.

18. Collins, *Rock Mr. Blues*, 79.

19. Awkward, *Soul Covers*, 143–44.

20. Awkward, *Soul Covers*, 143.

21. Awkward, *Soul Covers*, 152–53.

22. Lomax, *Selected Writings*, 200.

23. Miller, *Flowers in the Dustbin*, 100.

24. Delmore, *Truth Is Stranger Than Publicity*, 178.

25. Delmore, *Truth Is Stranger Than Publicity*, 289.

26. Mann, "Why Does Country Music Sound White?," 74.

27. Mann, "Why Does Country Music Sound White?," 74–75.

Bibliography

Abott, Lynn, and Doug Seroff. *Out of Sight: The Rise of African American Popular Music, 1889–1895.* Jackson: University Press of Mississippi, 2002.

———. *Ragged but Right: Black Traveling Shows, "Coon Songs," and the Dark Pathway to Blues and Jazz.* Jackson: University Press of Mississippi, 2007.

———. "'They Cert'ly Sound Good to Me': Sheet Music, Southern Vaudeville, and the Commercial Ascendancy of the Blues." In *Ramblin' on My Mind: New Perspectives on the Blues*, ed. David Evans, 49–104. Urbana: University of Illinois Press, 2008.

Abrahams, Roger D., and John F. Szwed. *After Africa: Extracts from British Travel Accounts and Journals of the Seventeenth, Eighteenth, and Nineteenth Centuries Concerning the Slaves, Their Manners, and Customs in the British West Indies.* New Haven: Yale University Press, 1983.

Acosta, Yvonne, and Jean Casimir. "Social Origins of the Counter-Plantation System in St. Lucia." In *Rural Development in the Caribbean*, ed. P. I. Gomes, 34–59. New York: St. Martin's Press, 1985.

Adrian, Peter. *Metayage, Capitalism and Peasant Development in St Lucia 1840–1957.* Mona, Jamaica: Consortium Graduate School of Social Sciences, 1996.

Alabi, Adetayo. "'I Am the Hunter Who Kills Elephants and Baboons': The Autobiographical Component of the Hunters' Chant." *Research in African Literatures* 38.3 (2007): 13–23.

Allmendinger, Blake. *Imagining the African American West.* Lincoln: University of Nebraska Press, 2005.

Allsopp, Richard, with Jeanette Allsopp. *Dictionary of Caribbean English Usage.* Oxford: Oxford University Press, 1996.

Anderson, Bobby. *That Muhlenberg Sound.* Beechmont, Ky.: MuhlBut Press, 1993.

Andrews, Natalie, and Eric Larson. "Bill Livers Recalls." *Adena: A Journal of the History and Culture of the Ohio Valley* 2 (Fall 1997): 42–52.

———. "Child of the Lord." *Southern Exposure: A Journal of Politics and Culture* (1977): 14–18.

Anthony, Patrick A. B. "Folk Research and Development: The Institutional Background to the Folk Research Centre, St. Lucia." In *Research in Ethnography*, ed.

M. Kremser and K. R. Wernhart, 37–55. Vienna: Verlag Ferdinand Berger and Söhne, 1986.

Auguste, Joyce, ed. *Oral and Folk Traditions of Saint Lucia*. Castries, St. Lucia: Lithographic Press, 1986.

Austerlitz, Paul. *Merengue: Dominican Music and Dominican Identity*. Philadelphia: Temple University Press, 1997.

Averill, Gage. *A Day for the Hunter, a Day for the Prey*. Chicago: University of Chicago Press, 1997.

——— . "Popular Music in the English-, French-, and Creole-Speaking Caribbean." In *Garland Encyclopedia of World Music*. Vol. 2: *South America, Mexico, Central America, and the Caribbean*, 95–99. New York: Garland, 1998.

Awkward, Michael. *Soul Covers: Rhythm and Blues Remakes and the Struggle for Artistic Identity*. Durham: Duke University Press, 2007.

Baker, Houston A. *Long Black Song: Essays in Black American Literature and Culture*. Charlottesville: University of Virginia Press, 1990.

Baraka, Amiri. *Blues People: Negro Music in White America*. 1963. New York: Harper Perennial, 1999.

Barker, Hugh, and Yuval Taylor. *Faking It: The Quest for Authenticity in Popular Music*. New York: Norton, 2007.

Barlow, William. *"Looking Up at Down": The Emergence of Blues Culture*. Philadelphia: Temple University Press, 1989.

Bastin, Bruce. *Never Sell a Copyright: Joe Davis and His Role in the New York Music Scene, 1916–1978*. Chigwell, Essex, U.K.: Storyville Publications, 1990.

——— . *Red River Blues: The Blues Tradition in the Southeast*. Urbana: University of Illinois Press, 1986.

Beckford, George. *Persistent Poverty: Underdevelopment in Plantation Economies*. New York: Oxford University Press, 1972.

Benitez-Rojo, Antonio. *The Repeating Island*. Trans. James E. Maraniss. London: Duke University Press, 1996.

——— . "Three Words toward Creolization." In *Caribbean Creolization: Reflections on the Cultural Dynamics of Language, Literature, and Identity*, ed. Kathleen M. Balutansky and Marie-Agnes Sourieau, 53–61. Gainesville: University Press of Florida, 1998.

Ben-zvi, Yael. "Setting Instincts: Origin Fictions of Native-Born Settlers." Ph.D. diss., Stanford University, 2003.

Bernabé, Jean, et al. "In Praise of Creoleness." *Callaloo* 13 (Autumn 1990): 886–909.

Bertrand, Michael. "I Don't Think Hank Done It That Way: Elvis, Country Music, and the Reconstruction of Southern Masculinity." In *A Boy Named Sue: Gender and Country Music*, ed. Kristine M. McCusker and Diane Pecknold, 59–85. Jackson: University Press of Mississippi, 2004.

Blase, Darren. "The Man Who Was King." *Cincinnati Citybeat*, March 27–April 2, 1997, 13.

Bogert, Pen. "Ramblin' around Kentucky: The Booker Family, Part 1." *Blues News: The Newsletter of the KYANA Blues Society* (July 1994): 1.

———. "Ramblin' around Kentucky: The Booker Family, Part 2." *Blues News: The Newsletter of the KYANA Blues Society* (August 1994): 1.

Bolland, Nigel. "Creolization and Creole Societies: A Cultural Nationalist View of Caribbean Social History." In *Intellectuals of the Twentieth-Century Caribbean*. Vol. 1: *Spectre of the New Class: The Commonwealth Caribbean*, ed. Alistair Hennesey, 50–79. London: Macmillan, 1992.

Bowman, Rob. "O. B. McClinton: Country Music, That's My Thing," *Journal of Country Music* 14.2 (1992): 23–29.

Brackett, David. *Interpreting Popular Music*. Berkeley: University of California Press, 2000.

Brasseaux, Ryan André. *Cajun Breakdown: The Emergence of an American-Made Music*. New York: Oxford University Press, 2009.

Brathwaite, Edward Kamau. "Caribbean Man in Space and Time." *Savacou* 11/12 (1975): 1–11, 106–8.

———. *Contradictory Omens: Cultural Diversity and Integration in the Caribbean*. Mona, Jamaica: Savacou Publications, 1974.

———. "Jamaican Slave Society: A Review." *Race and Class* 9 (July 1968): 331–42.

Brauner, Cheryl A., and Barry Lee Pearson. "John Jackson's East Virginia Blues." *Living Blues* 63 (January–February 1985): 10–13.

Brearley, H. C. "Ba-ad Nigger." In *Mother Wit from the Laughing Barrel: Readings in the Interpretation of Afro-American Folklore*, ed. Alan Dundes, 578–85. Englewood Cliffs, N.J.: Prentice-Hall, 1973.

Brewer, Roy. "The Appearance of the Electric Bass Guitar: A Rockabilly Perspective." *Popular Music and Society* 26 (Fall 2003): 351–66.

———. "The Use of Habanera Rhythm in Rockabilly Music." *American Music* 17 (Fall 1999): 300–317.

Brooks, Tim. *Lost Sounds: Blacks and the Birth of the Recording Industry, 1890–1919*. Urbana: University of Illinois Press, 2004.

Brothers, Thomas. "Ideology and Aurality in the Vernacular Traditions of African-American Music." *Black Music Research Journal* 17.2 (1997): 169–209.

Brown, Fahamisha Patricia. *Performing the Word: African American Poetry as Vernacular Culture*. New Brunswick, N.J.: Rutgers University Press, 1999.

Bryson, Bethany. "'Anything but Heavy Metal': Symbolic Exclusion and Musical Dislikes." *American Sociological Review* 61.5 (1996): 884–99.

Buckelew, Richard A. "Racial Violence in Arkansas: Lynchings and Mob Rule, 1860–1930." Ph.D. diss., University of Arkansas, 1999.

Burnim, Mellonee V., and Portia K. Maultsby, eds. *African American Music: An Introduction*. New York: Routledge, 2006.

Burroughs, Wilbur G. *The Geography of the Western Kentucky Coal Field*. Frankfort: Kentucky Geological Survey, 1924.

Calt, Steve. Liner notes. *Mississippi John Hurt: 1928 Sessions*. Yazoo 1065.

Calt, Stephen, Don Kent, and Michael Stewart. Liner notes. *Mississippi Sheiks: Stop and Listen*. Yazoo 2006.

Campbell, Bebe Moore. *Your Blues Ain't Like Mine*. 1992. New York: Ballantine, 1995.

Campbell, Gavin James. *Music and the Making of a New South*. Chapel Hill: University of North Carolina Press, 2003.

Cantwell, David, and Bill Friskics-Warren. *Heartaches by the Number: Country Music's 500 Greatest Singles*. Nashville: Vanderbilt University Press / Country Music Foundation Press, 2003.

Cantwell, Robert. *Bluegrass Breakdown: The Making of the Old Southern Sound*. Urbana: University of Illinois Press, 1984.

Carlin, Bob. *String Bands in the North Carolina Piedmont*. Jefferson, N.C.: MacFarland, 2004.

Carter, Dan T. *The Politics of Rage: George Wallace, the Origins of the New Conservatism, and the Transformation of American Politics*. Baton Rouge: Louisiana State University Press, 2000.

Cash, Johnny. *Cash: The Autobiography*. New York: Harper, 2003.

Chaplan, Joyce E. "Creoles in British America: From Denial to Acceptance." In *Creolization: History, Ethnography, Theory*, ed. Charles Stewart, 46–65. Walnut Creek, Calif.: Left Coast Press, 2007.

Charles, Embert. "Oral Traditions in St. Lucia: Mobilisation of Public Support—*Jounen Kwéyòl*." In *Research in Ethnography and Ethnohistory of St. Lucia*, ed. Manfred Kremser and Karl R. Wernhart, 57–69. Vienna: Verlag Ferdinand Berger and Söhne, 1986.

Charles, Ray, and David Ritz. *Brother Ray: Ray Charles' Own Story*. New York: Da Capo Press, 2004.

Charters, Samuel B. *The Country Blues*. New York: Da Capo, 1975.

———. "Workin' on the Building: Roots and Influences." In *Nothing but the Blues: The Music and the Musicians*, ed. Lawrence Cohn, 13–31. New York: Abbeville Press, 1993.

Charyn, Jerome. *Gangsters and Gold Diggers: Old New York, the Jazz Age, and the Birth of Broadway*. New York: Thunder's Mouth Press, 2003.

Cherry, Hugh. Liner notes. *The Atkins-Travis Travelin' Show*. BMG, BVCP 7396.

Cherry, Richard. Liner notes. *Vintage Mandolin Music, 1927–1946: Rags, Breakdowns, Stomps and Blues*. Document DOCD-32-20-3.

Ching, Barbara. "Going Back to the Old Mainstream: *No Depression*, Robbie Fulks, and Alt.Country's Muddied Waters." In *A Boy Named Sue: Gender and Country Music*, ed. Kristine M. McCusker and Diane Pecknold, 178–95. Jackson: University Press of Mississippi, 2004.

———. "The Possum, the Hag, and the Rhinestone Cowboy: Hard Country Music and the Burlesque Abjection of the White Man." In *Whiteness: A Critical Reader*, ed. Mike Hill, 117–33. New York: New York University Press, 1997.

———. *Wrong's What I Do Best: Hard Country Music and Contemporary Culture*. New York: Oxford University Press, 2001.

Ching, Barbara, Leigh Anne Duck, and Ladrica Menson-Furr. "Finding the Hook That Works: A Conversation with Alice Randall on Race, Literature, and Music in the American South." *Safundi: The Journal of South African and American Studies* 13.3–4 (2012): 357–71.

Ching, Barbara, and Pamela Fox. "The Importance of Being Ironic: Towards a Theory and Critique of Alt.Country Music." In *Old Roots, New Routes: The Cultural Politics of Alt.Country Music*, ed. Barbara Ching and Pamela Fox, 1–27. Ann Arbor: University of Michigan Press, 2008.

Clarke, Donald. *The Rise and Fall of Popular Music*. New York: St. Martin's Press, 1995.

Cohen, John. "The Folk Music Interchange: Negro and White." *Sing Out!* 14 (January 1965): 42–49.

Cohen, Norm. "Computerized Hillbilly Discography: The Gennett Project." *Western Folklore* 30.3 (1971): 182–93.

———. " 'I'm a Record Man': Uncle Art Satherly Reminisces." In *Exploring Roots Music: Twenty Years of the JEMF Quarterly*, ed. Nolan Porterfield, 45–51. Lanham, Md.: Scarecrow Press, 2004.

———. *Long Steel Rail: The Railroad in American Folksong*. Urbana: University of Illinois Press, 1981.

———. "Tapescript: An Interview with Doc Roberts (T7–279)." *John Edwards Memorial Foundation Quarterly* 7 (Summer 1971): 99–103.

———. "Tapescript: Interview with Welby Toomey (T7–197)." *John Edwards Memorial Foundation Quarterly* 5 (Summer 1969): 63–65.

Cohn, Lawrence. Liner notes. *Honey Babe Let the Deal Go Down: The Best of the Mississippi Sheiks*. Columbia/Legacy Records, CK 65709.

———, ed. *Nothing but the Blues: The Music and the Musicians*. New York: Abbeville Press, 1993.

Collins, Tony. *Rock Mr. Blues: The Life and Music of Wynonie Harris*. Milford, N.H.: Big Nickel Publications, 1995.

"Commercial Music Documents: Number Five." *John Edwards Memorial Foundation Quarterly* 5 (Winter 1969): 146.

Conway, Cecelia. *African Banjo Echoes in Appalachia: A Study of Folk Traditions*. Knoxville: University of Tennessee Press, 1995.

———. "Black Banjo Songsters in Appalachia." *Black Music Research Journal* 23.1/2 (2003): 149–66.

Cooper, Daniel. "Take Me Down to That Southern Land." In liner notes, *Ray Charles: The Complete Country and Western Recordings, 1959–1986*. Rhino, R2-25328.

Coski, John M. *The Confederate Battle Flag: America's Most Embattled Emblem*. Cambridge: Harvard University Press, 2005.

Country Music Hall of Fame. *Night Train to Nashville: Music City Rhythm and Blues, 1945–1970*. Nashville: Country Music Foundation Press, 2004.

Coyle, Michael. "Hijacked Hits and Antic Authenticity: Cover Songs, Race, and Postwar Marketing." In *Rock over the Edge: Transformations in Popular Music Culture*, ed. Roger Beebe, Denise Fulbrook, and Ben Saunders, 133–57. Durham: Duke University Press, 2002.

Crichlow, Michaeline A. "Globalization and the Post-Creole Condition: Notes on Fleeing Globalization and the Plantation." Unpublished manuscript. University of Iowa, 2004.

———. *Globalization and the Post-Creole Imagination: Notes on Fleeing the Plantation*. Durham: Duke University Press, 2009.

Daley, Dan. *The Nashville Music Machine: The Unwritten Rules of the Country Music Business*. New York: Overlook, 1997.

Daniels, Douglas Henry. *One O'clock Jump: The Unforgettable History of the Oklahoma Blue Devils*. Boston: Beacon, 2006.

Davis, Eddy. "Banjo and the Jazz Era." *Resonator* 32.3 (2004): 1, 6.

Delmore, Alton. *Truth Is Stranger Than Publicity*. Ed. Charles K. Wolfe. Nashville: Country Music Foundation Press, 1995.

Devonish, Hubert. *Language and Liberation: Creole Language Politics in the Caribbean*. London: Karia Press, 1986.

Dixon, Robert M. W., and John Godrich. *Recording the Blues*. New York: Stein and Day, 1970.

Dixon, Robert M. W., John Godrich, and Howard Rye. *Blues and Gospel Records, 1890–1943*. 4th ed. 1964. Oxford: Clarendon Press, 1997.

Dobkin, Matt. *I Never Loved a Man the Way I Loved You: Aretha Franklin, Respect, and the Making of a Soul Music Masterpiece*. New York: HarperCollins, 2005.

Dominguez, Virginia R. "Social Classification in Creole Louisiana." *American Ethnologist* 4.4 (1977): 589–602.

Doucet, Michael. "Amédé Ardoin's Blues: An Introduction." Liner notes. *"I'm Never Comin' Back": Amédé Ardoin, Pioneer of Louisiana French Blues, 1930–1934*. Arhoolie 7007.

Durman, Chris. "African American Old-Time String Band Music: A Selective Discography." *Notes* 64 (June 2008): 797–810.

Eatherly, Pat Travis. *A Scrapbook of My Daddy*. Self-published, 2000.

Edwards, Leigh H. *Johnny Cash and the Paradox of American Identity*. Bloomington: Indiana University Press, 2009.

Ellis, Chris. Liner notes. *Blue Yodelers, 1928–1936: Jimmie Rodgers, Emmet [sic] Miller, Roy Evans*. Retrieval RTR 79020.

Epstein, Dena J. *Sinful Tunes and Spirituals: Black Folk Music to the Civil War*. 1977. Urbana: University of Illinois Press, 2003.

Erickson, Steve. "'Sail Away'" and 'Louisiana 1927.'" In *The Rose and the Briar: Death, Love and Liberty in the American Ballad*, ed. Sean Wilentz and Greil Marcus, 307–11. New York: Norton, 2004.

Escott, Colin. *Good Rockin' Tonight: Sun Records and the Birth of Rock and Roll*. New York: St. Martin's Press, 1991.

Escott, Colin, George Merritt, and William MacEwen. *Hank Williams: The Biography*. Boston: Little, Brown, 1995.

Evans, David. "Africa and the Blues." In *Write Me a Few of Your Lines: A Blues Reader*, ed. Steven C. Tracy, 63–68. Amherst: University of Massachusetts Press, 1999.

———. "Afro-American One-Stringed Instruments." *Western Folklore* 29.4 (1970): 229–45.

———. *Big Road Blues: Tradition and Creativity in the Folk Blues*. 1982. New York: Da Capo Press, 1987.

———. "Black Musicians Remember Jimmie Rodgers." *Old Time Music* 7 (Winter 1972–73): 12–14.

———. *The NPR Curious Listener's Guide to Blues*. New York: Pedigree-Penguin, 2005.

Faragher, Scott. *Music City Babylon: Inside the World of Country Music*. New York: Birch Lane Press, 1982.

Feder, J. Lester. "'Song of the South': Country Music, Race, Region, and the Politics of Culture, 1920–1974." Ph.D. diss., University of California, Los Angeles, 2006.

Feiler, Bruce. *Dreaming Out Loud: Garth Brooks, Wynonna Judd, Wade Hayes, and the Changing Face of Nashville*. New York: Avon, 1998.

Filene, Benjamin. *Romancing the Folk: Public Memory and American Roots Music*. Chapel Hill: University of North Carolina Press, 2000.

Fleischmann, Ulrich. "The Sociocultural and Linguistic Profile of a Concept." In *A Pepper-Pot of Cultures: Aspects of Creolization in the Caribbean*, ed. Gordon Collier and Ulrich Fleischmann, xv–xxxvi. New York: Matatu, 2003.

Floyd, Samuel. *The Power of Black Music*. New York: Oxford University Press, 1995.

Floyd, Samuel A., Jr. "Ring Shout! Literary Studies, Historical Studies, and Black Music Inquiry." *Black Music Research Journal* 22, Supplement: Best of BMRJ (2002): 49–70.

Foreman, Ronald Clifford, Jr. "Jazz and Race Records, 1920–1932: Their Origins and Their Significance for the Recording Industry and Society." Ph.D. diss., University of Illinois, 1968.

Foster, Pamela. *My Country: The African Diaspora's Country Music Heritage*. Nashville: My Country, 1998.

———. *My Country, Too: The Other Black Music*. Nashville: Publishers Graphics, 2000.

Fox, Aaron. "Alternative to What? *O Brother*, September 11, and the Politics of Country Music." In *Country Music Goes to War*, ed. Charles K. Wolfe and James Edward Akenson, 164–91. Lexington: University Press of Kentucky, 2005.

———. *Real Country: Music and Language in Working-Class Culture*. Durham: Duke University Press, 2004.

———. "White Trash Alchemies of the Abject Sublime: Country as 'Bad' Music." In *Bad Music: The Music We Love to Hate*, ed. Christopher J. Washburne and Maiken Derko, 39–61. New York: Routledge, 2004.

Fox, Aaron, and Christine Yano, eds. *Songs Out of Place: Country Musics of the World*. Durham: Duke University Press, forthcoming.

Fox, John Hartley. *King of Queen City: The Story of King Records*. Urbana: University of Illinois Press, 2009.

Fryd, Vivien Green. "'The Sad Twang of Mountain Voices': Thomas Hart Benton's *Sources of Country Music*." In *Reading Country Music: Steel Guitars, Opry Stars, and Honky-Tonk Bars*, ed. Cecelia Tichi, 256–85. Durham: Duke University Press, 1998.

Gardner, Emelyn Elizabeth, and Geraldine Jencks Chickering, eds. *Ballads and Songs of Southern Michigan*. Dalton, Ohio: Gardner Press, 2007.

Gaspar, David Barry. "A Fiction of Freedom." Unpublished manuscript. Folk Research Centre, Castries, St. Lucia, 1975.

———. "La Guerre des Bois: Revolution, War and Slavery in Saint Lucia, 1793–1838." In *A Turbulent Time: The French Revolution and the Greater Caribbean*, ed. David Barry Gaspar and David Patrick Geggus, 102–30. Bloomington: Indiana University Press, 1997.

Gaspar, David Barry, and David Patrick Geggus, eds. *A Turbulent Time: The French Revolution and the Greater Caribbean*. Bloomington: Indiana University Press, 1997.

Geggus, David P., ed. *The Impact of the Haitian Revolution in the Atlantic World*. Columbia: University of South Carolina Press, 2001.

George, Nelson. *The Death of Rhythm and Blues*. New York: Penguin, 2003.

Gerstin, Julian Harris. "Traditional Music in a New Social Movement: The Renewal of *Bèlè* in Martinique (French West Indies)." Ph.D. diss., University of California at Berkeley, 1996.

Gibson, George R. "Gourd Banjos: From Africa to the Appalachians." BanjoHistory.com, http://www.banjohistory.com/article/detail/1_gourd_banjos_from_africa_to_the_appalachians, Oct. 1, 2001.

Gillett, Charlie. *Sound of the City: The Rise of Rock and Roll.* New York: Dutton, 1970.

Gilroy, Paul. *Against Race: Imagining Political Culture beyond the Color Line.* Cambridge: Harvard University Press, 2000.

———. "Sounds Authentic: Black Music, Ethnicity, and the Challenge of a 'Changing' Same." *Black Music Research Journal* 11.2 (1991): 111–36.

Goldsmith, Thomas, ed. *The Bluegrass Reader.* Urbana: University of Illinois Press, 2004.

Gorn, Elliott J. "'Gouge and Bite, Pull Hair and Scratch': The Social Significance of Fighting in the Southern Backcountry." *American Historical Review* 90.1 (1985): 18–43.

Goudie, Sean X. *Creole America: The West Indies and the Formation of Literature and Culture in the New Republic.* Philadelphia: University of Pennsylvania Press, 2006.

Green, Al, with Davin Seay. *Take Me to the River.* New York: Harper Entertainment, 2000.

Green, Archie. "Commercial Music Graphics: Sixteen." *John Edwards Memorial Foundation Quarterly* 7 (Spring 1971): 25–26.

———. "A Discography/Biography Journey: The Martin-Roberts-Martin 'Aggregation.'" *Western Folklore* 30.3 (1971): 194–201.

———. "Hillbilly Music: Source and Symbol." *Journal of American Folklore* 78 (July–September 1965): 204–28.

Gregory, James N. *The Southern Diaspora: How the Great Migrations of Black and White Southerners Transformed America.* Chapel Hill: University of North Carolina Press, 2005.

Gronow, Pekka. "Ethnic Recordings: An Introduction." In *Ethnic Recordings in America: A Neglected Heritage,* ed. Judith McCullogh, 1–49. Washington, D.C.: American Folklife Center, Library of Congress, 1982.

Guilbault, Jocelyne. "Fitness and Flexibility: Funeral Wakes in St. Lucia, West Indies." *Ethnomusicology* 31 (Spring–Summer 1987): 273–99.

———. *Governing Sound: The Cultural Politics of Trinidad's Carnival Musics.* Chicago: University of Chicago Press, 2007.

———. Liner notes. *Musical Traditions of St. Lucia, West Indies: Dances and Songs from a Caribbean Island.* Smithsonian Folkways CD SF 40416.

———. "Musical Events in the Lives of the People of a Caribbean Island: St. Lucia." Ph.D. diss., University of Michigan, 1984.

———. "On Interpreting Popular Music: Zouk in the West Indies." In *Caribbean Popular Culture,* ed. John Lent, 79–97. Bowling Green, Ohio: Bowling Green State University Popular Press, 1990.

———. "On Redefining the Local through World Music." *World Music* 35.2 (1993): 33–47.

———. "Oral and Literate Strategies in Performance: The La Rose and La Marguerite Organizations of St. Lucia." *Yearbook of Traditional Music* 19 (1987): 97–115.

———. "St. Lucia Kwadril Evening." *Latin American Music Review* 6 (Spring/Summer 1985): 31–57.

———. "St. Lucian Musical Traditions." In *Garland Encyclopedia of World Music.* Vol. 9: *Music of Latin America and the Caribbean,* 938–46. New York: Garland, 1998.

———. *Zouk: World Music in the West Indies.* Chicago: University of Chicago Press, 1993.

Guilbault, Jocelyne, et al. *World Music in the West Indies.* Chicago: University of Chicago Press, 1993.

Gura, Philip F., and James F. Bollman. *America's Instrument: The Banjo in the Nineteenth Century.* Chapel Hill: University of North Carolina Press, 1999.

Guralnick, Peter. *Careless Lover: The Unmaking of Elvis Presley.* New York: Back Bay, 2000.

———. *Last Train to Memphis: The Rise of Elvis Presley.* Boston: Little, Brown, 1994.

———. *Lost Highway: Journeys and Arrivals of American Musicians.* New York: Harper and Row, 1979.

———. *Sweet Soul Music: Rhythm and Blues and the Southern Dream of Freedom.* Boston: Little, Brown, 1986.

Gussow, Adam. *Seems Like Murder Here: Southern Violence and the Blues Tradition.* Chicago: University of Chicago Press, 2002.

Hall, Stuart. "Race, Articulation, and Societies Structured in Dominance." In *Black British Cultural Studies: A Reader,* ed. Houston A. Baker Jr., Manthia Diawara, and Ruth H. Lindeborg, 16–60. Chicago: University of Chicago Press, 1996.

Handy, W. C. *Father of the Blues: An Autobiography.* 1941. New York: Da Capo Press, 1991.

Harmsen, Jolien. "The East Indian Legacy in St. Lucia." *Visions* 10.1 (2002): 50–53.

———. *Sugar, Slavery, and Settlement: A Social History of Vieux Fort St. Lucia, from the Amerindians to the Present.* St. Lucia: St. Lucia National Trust, 1999.

Hartman, Saidiya V. *Scenes of Subjection: Terror, Slavery, and Self-Making in Nineteenth-Century America.* New York: Oxford University Press, 1997.

Hazzard-Gordon, Katrina. "African-American Vernacular Dance: Core Culture and Meaning Operatives." *Journal of Black Studies* 15.4 (1985): 427–45.

Hemphill, Paul. *The Nashville Sound: Bright Lights and Country Music.* New York: Simon and Schuster, 1970.

Hentoff, Nat. *Listen to the Stories: Nat Hentoff on Jazz and Country Music.* New York: HarperCollins, 1995.

Herndon, Jerry A. "'Blood on the Saddle': An Anonymous Folk Ballad?" *Journal of American Folklore* 88.349 (1975): 300–304.

Higman, B. W. *Slave Populations of the British Caribbean 1980–1834*. London: Johns Hopkins University Press, 1984.

Hirshey, Gerri. *Nowhere to Run: The Story of Soul Music*. New York: Da Capo Press, 1994.

Hobsbawm, Eric. "Introduction: Inventing Tradition." In *The Invention of Tradition*, ed. Eric Hobsbawm and Terence Ranger, 1–14. Cambridge: Cambridge University Press, 1983.

Hoskyns, Barney. *Say It One Time for the Broken Hearted: Country Soul in the American South*. London: Bloomsbury, 1998.

Hughes, Langston. "Black Misery." In *The Collected Works of Langston Hughes*. Vol. 11: *Works for Children and Young Adults: Poetry, Fiction, and Other Writing*, ed. Dianne Johnson, 170–76. Columbia: University of Missouri Press, 2003.

Humphrey, Mark. "Merle Travis." In *Country on Compact Disc*, ed. Paul Kingsbury. New York: Grove Press, 1993.

Hunter, James. Liner notes. *Rhythm, Country and Blues*. MCA Nashville, B0000020R2.

Imani, Dunkor. "Country Music Gets Some Color." *Black Issues Book Review* 2.5 (2000): 28–29.

Ivey, Bill. "Border Crossing: A Different Way of Listening to American Music." In liner notes, *From Where I Stand: The Black Experience in Country Music*. Warner Brothers CD 9 46428-2.

———. "The Bottom Line: Business Practices That Shaped Country Music." In *Country: The Music and the Musicians*, ed. Paul Kingsbury, Alan Axelrod, and Susan Costello, 280–311. 1988. Revised edition. New York: Country Music Foundation and Abbeville Press, 1994.

Jansen, David A., and Gene Jones. *Spreadin' the Rhythm Around: Black Popular Songwriters, 1880–1930*. New York: Schirmer Books, 1998.

Jennings, Dana. *Sing Me Back Home: Love, Death and Country Music*. New York: Faber and Faber, 2008.

Jensen, Joli. *The Nashville Sound: Authenticity, Commercialization, and Country Music*. Nashville: Country Music Foundation and Vanderbilt University Press, 1998.

Jesse, Charles. *The Amerindians in St. Lucia*. Castries, St. Lucia: St. Lucia Archaeological and Historical Society, 1968.

———. "An Houre Glass of Indian Newes." *Caribbean Quarterly* 12.1 (1966): 46–67.

———. *Outlines of St. Lucia's History*. 1956. Castries, St. Lucia: Voice Publishing, 1964.

———. "A Peep into St. Lucian History." Radio St. Lucia broadcast, audiotape, Sir Arthur Lewis Community College Archive, 1979.

Jones, Max, and John Chilton. *Louis: The Louis Armstrong Story, 1900–1971*. Boston: Little, Brown, 1971.

Joseph, Tennyson S. D. *Decolonisation in the Era of Globalisation: The Independence Experience in St. Lucia.* Cambridge: University of Cambridge Press, 2000.

Kalra, Ajay. "John 'Uncle' Homer Walker." Hutchings Library Special Collections and Archives, Berea College, http://community.berea.edu/hutchinslibrary /specialcollections/amfp/UncleHomerWalker.pdf.

Kelley, Robin D. G. "Notes on Deconstructing 'The Folk.'" *American Historical Review* 97.5 (1992): 1400–1408.

Kemp, Mark. *Dixie Lullaby: A Story of Race, Music and New Beginnings in a New South.* New York: Free Press, 2004.

Kennedy, Rick. *Jelly Roll, Bix, and Hoagy: Gennett Studios and the Birth of Recorded Jazz.* Bloomington: Indiana University Press, 1994.

Killen, Buddy, with Tom Carter. *By the Seat of My Pants: My Life in Country Music.* New York: Simon and Schuster, 1993.

King, B. B., with David Ritz, *Blues All around Me: The Autobiography of B. B. King.* New York: Avon Books, 1996.

King, Christopher C. "Bayless? Bailey? A Rose by Another Name." *78 Quarterly* 12 ([2004]): 59–68.

Kosser, Michael. *How Nashville Became Music City, U.S.A.* Milwaukee: Hal Leonard Press, 2006.

Kremser, Manfred. "The African Heritage in the 'Kélé': Tradition of the 'Djiné.'" In *Research in Ethnography*, ed. Manfred Kremser and Karl R. Wernhart, 103–20. Vienna: Verlag Ferdinand Berger and Söhne, 1986.

Kun, Josh. *Audiotopia: Music, Race, and America.* Berkeley: University of California Press, 2005.

Kyriakoudes, Louis M. "The *Grand Ole Opry* and the Urban South." *Southern Cultures* 10.1 (2004): 67–84.

La Chapelle, Peter. *Proud to Be an Okie: Cultural Politics, Country Music, and Migration to Southern California.* Berkeley: University of California Press, 2007.

Laird, Ross. *Brunswick Records: A Discography of Recordings, 1916–1931.* 4 vols. Westport, Conn.: Greenwood Press, 2001.

Laird, Tracey E. W. *Louisiana Hayride: Radio and Roots Music along the Red River.* New York: Oxford University Press, 2005.

Lauterbach, Preston. *The Chitlin' Circuit and the Road to Rock and Roll.* New York: Norton, 2011.

Lawrence, Keith. "Arnold Shultz: Godfather of Bluegrass?" *Bluegrass Unlimited* 24 (1989): 39–43.

———. "The Greatest (?) Guitar Picker's Life Ended before Promise Realized." *John Edwards Memorial Foundation Quarterly* 17 (Spring 1981 [1980]): 3–8.

Levine, Lawrence. *Black Culture and Black Consciousness: Afro-American Folk Thought from Slavery to Freedom.* Oxford: Oxford University Press, 1977.

Lewis, George H. "Lap Dancer or Hillbilly Deluxe? The Cultural Constructions of Modern Country Music." *Journal of Popular Culture* 31.3 (1997): 163–73.

Leyda, Julia. "Black-Audience Westerns and the Politics of Cultural Identification in the 1930s." *Cinema Journal* 42.1 (2002): 46–70.

Licht, Michael S. "Harmonica Magic: Virtuoso Display in American Folk Music." *Ethnomusicology* 24.2 (1980): 211–21.

Lightfoot, William E. "It All Goes Back to Arnold Shultz." *Merle Travis Newsletter* 2 (1988): 6–7.

———. "Mose Rager from Muhlenberg County: 'Hey, C'mon, Bud, Play Me a Good Rag.'" *Adena: A Journal of the History and Culture of the Ohio Valley* 4:2 (1979): 3–41.

———. "A Regional Musical Style: The Legacy of Arnold Shultz." In *Sense of Place: American Regional Cultures*, ed. Barbara Allen and Thomas J. Schlereth, 120–37. Lexington: University Press of Kentucky, 1990.

———. "The Three Doc(k)s: White Blues in Appalachia." *Black Music Research Journal* 23.1/2 (2003): 167–93.

Linn, Karen. *That Half-Barbaric Twang: The Banjo in American Popular Culture.* Urbana: University of Illinois Press, 1994.

Lipsitz, George. *Dangerous Crossroads: Popular Music, Postmodernism, and the Poetics of Place.* London: Verso, 1994.

———. *Rainbow at Midnight: Labor and Culture in the 1940s.* Urbana: University of Illinois Press, 1994.

Lomax, Alan. *Selected Writings. 1934–1997.* Ed. Ronald D. Cohen. New York: Routledge, 2003.

Lornell, Christopher. "Spatial Perspectives on the Field Recording of Traditional American Music: A Case Study from Tennessee in 1928." In *The Sounds of People and Places: A Geography of American Folk and Popular Music*, ed. George O. Carney, 77–84. 1981. Lanham, Md.: Rowman and Littlefield, 1994.

Lornell, Kip. "Albany Blues: Part One." *Living Blues* 14 (Autumn 1973): 25–29.

———. "Albany Blues: Part Two." *Living Blues* 15 (Winter 1973): 22–25.

———. "Albany Blues: Part Three." *Living Blues* 16 (Spring 1974): 27–29.

———. "Banjos and Blues." In *Arts in Earnest: Field Studies in North Carolina Folklife*, ed. Daniel W. Patterson and Charles G. Zugg, 216–31. Durham: Duke University Press, 1989.

———. *Happy in the Service of the Lord: African-American Sacred Vocal Harmony.* Knoxville: University of Tennessee Press, 1995.

———. "Non-Blues Secular Black Music in Virginia." In *American Musical Traditions.* Vol. 2: *African American Music*, ed. Jeff Todd Titon and Bob Carlin, 42–49. New York: Schirmer Reference Books, 2002.

———. "North Carolina Pre-Blues Banjo and Fiddle." *Living Blues* 18 (Autumn 1974): 25–27.

———. "Pre-Blues Black Music in Piedmont North Carolina." *North Carolina Folklore Quarterly* 23.1 (1975): 27–32.

———. "A Study of the Sociological Reasons Why Blacks Sing Blues: Secular Black Music in Two North Carolina Communities during the 1930s." M.A. thesis, University of North Carolina, Chapel Hill, 1976.

Lornell, Kip, and Ted Mealor. "A & R Men and the Geography of Piedmont Blues Recordings from 1924–1941." *ARSC Journal* 26 (Spring 1995): 1–22.

Lornell, Kip, and Charles Stephenson. *The Beat: Go-Go's Fusion of Funk and Hip-Hop*. New York: Billboard, 2001.

Lott, Eric. *Love and Theft: Blackface Minstrelsy and the American Working Class*. Oxford: Oxford University Press, 1995.

Love, Nat. *The Life and Adventures of Nat Love, Better Known in the Cattle Country as "Deadwood Dick."* 1907. Lincoln: University of Nebraska Press, 1995.

Lucas, Marion B. *A History of Blacks in Kentucky*. Vol. 1. Lexington: Kentucky Historical Society, 1992.

Lydon, Michael. *Ray Charles: Man and Music*. New York: Routledge, 2004.

Lynn, Loretta, with Patsi Bale Cox. *Still Woman Enough: A Memoir*. New York: Hyperion, 2002.

Malone, Bill C. *Country Music USA*. Austin: University of Texas Press, 1985.

———. *Don't Get above Your Raisin': Country Music and the Southern Working Class*. Urbana: University of Illinois Press, 2002.

———. *Southern Music, American Music*. Lexington: University of Kentucky Press, 1979.

Mann, Geoff. "Why Does Country Music Sound White? Race and the Voice of Nostalgia." *Ethnic and Racial Studies* 31.1 (2008): 73–100.

Manuel, Peter Lamarche, Kenneth M. Bilby, and Michael D. Largey. *Caribbean Currents: Caribbean Music from Rhumba to Reggae*. Philadelphia: Temple University Press, 1995.

Mattern, Mark. "Let the Good Times Unroll: Music and Race Relations in Southwest Louisiana." In *Fiddles, Accordions, Two Step and Swing: A Cajun Music Reader*, ed. Ryan A. Brasseaux and Kevin S. Fontenot, 97–106. Lafayette: Center for Louisiana Studies, 2006.

Maultsby, Portia. "West African Influences and Retentions in U.S. Black Music: A Sociocultural Study." In *More Than Dancing: Essays on Afro-American Music and Musicians*, ed. Irene V. Jackson, 25–55. Westport, Conn.: Greenwood Press, 1985.

Mazor, Barry. *Meeting Jimmie Rodgers: How America's Original Roots Music Hero Changed the Pop Sounds of a Century*. New York: Oxford University Press, 2009.

McKay, Claude. *Banjo*. 1929. New York: Mariner, 1970.

McPherson, James. *Elbow Room*. New York: Fawcett Press, 1972.

Meckna, Michael. *Satchmo: The Louis Armstrong Encyclopedia*. Westport, Conn.: Greenwood Press, 2004.

Melnick, Mimi Clar. "'I Can Peep through Muddy Water and Spy Dry Land': Boasts in the Blues." In *Mother Wit from the Laughing Barrel: Readings in the*

Interpretation of Afro-American Folklore, ed. Alan Dundes, 267–76. Englewood Cliffs, N.J.: Prentice-Hall, 1973.

Messenger, Christian K. *Sport and the Spirit of Play in American Fiction*. New York: Columbia University Press, 1981.

Middleton, Richard. *Voicing the Popular: On the Subject of Popular Music*. New York: Routledge, 2006.

Midgett, Douglas Kent. "Bilingualism and Linguistic Change in St. Lucia." *Anthropological Linguistics* 12 (May 1970): 158–70.

———. "Performance Roles and Musical Change in a Caribbean Society." *Ethnomusicology* 21 (1977): 55–73.

———. "West Indian Migration in St. Lucia and London." Ph.D. diss., University of Illinois, Urbana-Champaign, 1977.

Millard, Bob. "Charley Pride: Alone in the Spotlight." *Journal of Country Music* 14.2 (1992): 18–22.

Miller, James. *Flowers in the Dustbin: The Rise of Rock and Roll, 1947–1977*. New York: Simon and Schuster, 1996.

Miller, Karl Hagstrom. *Segregating Sound: Inventing Folk and Pop Music in the Age of Jim Crow*. Durham: Duke University Press, 2010.

Morgenstern, Dan. Liner notes. *Louis Armstrong: Portrait of the Artist as a Young Man, 1923–1934*. Columbia/Legacy C4K 57176.

Morton, David C. "Black and White Notes: From WSM Grand Ole Opry Pioneer DeFord Bailey." Paper presented at Afro-American Culture and History 12th Annual Local Conference, Tennessee State University, Nashville, February 10, 1993, DeFord Bailey website, http://defordbailey.info/news/2007/01/black_white_notes_from_wsm_grand_ole_opry_pioneer_bailey.

Morton, David C., with Charles K. Wolfe. *DeFord Bailey: A Black Star in Early Country Music*. Knoxville: University of Tennessee Press, 1991.

Neal, Jocelyn. "The Metric Makings of a Country Hit." In *Reading Country Music*, ed. Cecelia Tichi, 322–37. Durham: Duke University Press, 1998.

Nevins, Richard. Liner notes. *Before the Blues: The Early Black Music Scene*. Vol. 1. Yazoo 2015.

———. Liner notes. *Kentucky Mountain Music: Classic Recordings of the 1920s and 1930s*. Yazoo 2200.

Nicholls, David G. "Westward Migration, Narrative, and Genre in African America." In *A Casebook Study of Ishmael Reed's* Yellow Back Radio Broke-Down, ed. Pierre-Damien Mvuyekure, 32–50. Champaign, Ill.: Dalkey Archive Press, 2003.

Nzengou-Tayo, Marie-José. "Haitian Callaloo: What You Ask For Is Certainly Not What You Get!" *Callaloo* 30.1 (2007): 175–78.

O'Connor, Patrick Joseph. "Cowboy Blues: Early Black Music in the West." *Studies in Popular Culture* 16.2 (1994): 95–103.

Oliver, Paul. "Jerry's Saloon: Oscar Buddy Woods." In *Blues Off the Record: Thirty Years of Blues Commentary*, 89–94. 1984. New York: Da Capo Press, 1988.

———. *Songsters and Saints: Vocal Traditions on Race Records*. Cambridge: Cambridge University Press, 1984.

———. *The Story of the Blues*. 1969. Boston: Northeastern University Press, 1998.

Oliver, Paul, et al. *Yonder Comes the Blues: The Evolution of a Genre*. Cambridge: Cambridge University Press, 2001.

Otto, John S., and Augustus M. Burns. "Black and White Cultural Interaction in the Early Twentieth Century South: Race and Hillbilly Music." *Phylon* 35.4 (1974): 407–17.

Pastras, Phil. *Dead Man Blues: Jelly Roll Morton Way Out West*. Berkeley: University of California Press, 2002.

Paulding, James Kirke. *The Lion of the West*. 1831. Retitled *The Kentuckian, or A Trip to New York*. Ed. James N. Tidewell. Stanford: Stanford University Press, 1954.

Pearson, Barry Lee. "Appalachian Blues." *Black Music Research Journal* 23.1–2 (2003): 23–51.

———. "Archie Edwards: Barbershop Blues." *Living Blues* 63 (January–February 1985): 22–26.

Pearson, Barry Lee, and Bill McCulloh. *Robert Johnson: Lost and Found*. Urbana: University of Illinois Press, 2003.

Pecknold, Diane. *The Selling Sound: The Rise of the Country Music Industry*. Durham: Duke University Press, 2007.

Perry, Imani. *Prophets of the Hood: Politics and Poetics in Hip Hop*. Durham: Duke University Press, 2004.

Peterson, Richard A. *Creating Country Music: Fabricating Authenticity*. Chicago: University of Chicago Press, 1997.

Pickard, Claude Eugene. "The Western Kentucky Coal Field: The Influence of Coal Mining on the Settlement Patterns, Forms and Functions." Ph.D. diss., University of Nebraska, 1969.

Pollak, Bill. "John Jackson's Good-Time Blues." *Living Blues* 37 (March–April 1978): 26–27.

Porterfield, Nolan. *Jimmie Rodgers: The Life and Times of America's Blue Yodeler*. 1979. Urbana: University of Illinois Press, 1992.

———. Liner notes. *Jimmie Rodgers: The Singing Brakeman*. Bear Family BCD 15540 FI.

Radano, Ronald. *Lying Up a Nation: Race and Black Music*. Chicago: University of Chicago Press, 2003.

Ramesh, Kotti Sree, and Kandula Nirupa Rani. *Claude McKay: The Literary Identity from Jamaica to Harlem and Beyond*. Jefferson, N.C.: McFarland, 2006.

Ramsey, Frederic, Jr. *Been Here and Gone*. New Brunswick, N.J.: Rutgers University Press, 1960.

Ramsey, Guthrie P., Jr. "Editor's Introduction: Becoming: Blackness and the Musical Imagination." *Black Music Research Journal* 28.1 (2008): v–xiv.

Randall, Alice. *Pushkin and the Queen of Spades*. New York: Houghton Mifflin, 2004.

Randall, Alice, with Carter Little and Courtney Little. *My Country Roots: The Ultimate MP3 Guide to America's Original Outsider Music*. Nashville: Naked Ink, 2006.

Richardson, Riché. *Black Masculinity and the U.S. South: From Uncle Tom to Gangsta*. Athens: University of Georgia Press, 2007.

Rinzler, Ralph. 1975. "Bill Monroe." In *Stars of Country Music: Uncle Dave Macon to Johnny Rodriguez*, ed. Bill C. Malone and Judith McCulloh, 202–21. Urbana: University of Illinois Press, 1975.

Robinson, Joyce Henri. "Harlem Renaissance, Plantation Formulas." In *Picturing the Banjo*, ed. Leo G. Mazow, 115–43. University Park: Palmer Museum of Art, Pennsylvania State University Press, 2005.

Roland, Tom. *The Billboard Book of Number One Country Hits*. New York: Billboard, 1991.

Rosenberg, Neil. *Bluegrass: A History*. Urbana: University of Illinois Press, 1985.

———. "Ethnicity and Class: Black Country Musicians in the Maritimes." In *Canadian Music: Issues of Hegemony and Identity*, ed. Beverley Diamond and Robert Witmer, 138–56. Toronto: Canadian Scholars Press, 1994.

Rounder Collective. "The Life of Blind Alfred Reed." *John Edwards Memorial Foundation Quarterly* 7 (Autumn 1971): 113–15.

Rourke, Constance. *American Humor: A Study of the National Character*. 1931. New York: Anchor Books, 1953.

Roy, William G. "'Race Records' and 'Hillbilly Music': Institutional Origins of Racial Categories in the American Commercial Recording Industry." *Poetics* 32 (June–August 2004): 271–75, 277–78.

Rumble, John. "Roots of Rock 'n' Roll: Henry Glover at King Records." *Journal of Country Music* 14.2 (1991): 30–42.

Rumble, John W. "The Artists and the Songs." Liner notes. *From Where I Stand: The Black Experience in Country Music*. Warner Brothers CD 9 46428-2.

Russell, Tony. *Blacks, Whites, and Blues*. New York: Stein and Day, 1970.

———. "Country Music on Location: 'Field Recording' before Bristol." *Popular Music* 26.1 (2007): 23–31.

———. "The First Recording of Black French Music?" *Old Time Music* no. 29 (Summer 1978): 20.

———. "Key to the Bushes: Johnson Boys." *Blues Unlimited* 67 (November 1969): 19.

———. Liner notes. *Black Fiddlers: The Remaining Titles of Andrew and Jim Baxter, Nathan Frazier and Frank Patterson, the Complete Recorded Works of Cuje Bertram (1929–c. 1970)*. Document DOCD-5631.

———. Liner notes. *Fiddlin' Doc Roberts: Complete Recorded Works in Chronological Order.* Vol. 1: *1925–1928.* Document DOCD-8042.

———. Liner notes. *Governor Jimmie Davis: Nobody's Darling but Mine.* Bear Family BCD 15943 EI.

Russell, Tony, with Bob Pinson, assisted by the staff of the Country Music Hall of Fame and Museum. *Country Music Records: A Discography, 1921–1942.* New York: Oxford University Press, 2004.

Rust, Brian. *Jazz Records 1897–1942.* 1961. 5th revised and enlarged edition. 2 vols. Chigwell, Essex, U.K.: Storyville Publications, 1982.

Samuel, Kennedy. "The Challenge of Bilingual Education in Bilingual St. Lucia." M.A. thesis, University of Southampton, 1990.

———. "Towards a National Language Policy in St. Lucia." *Media Development 1: Journal of the World Association for Christian Communication* 35 (1992): 11–13.

Sanjek, David. "One Size Does Not Fit All: The Precarious Position of the African American Entrepreneur in Post–World War II American Popular Music." *American Music* 15.4 (1997): 535–62.

Sarig, Roni. *Third Coast: OutKast, Timbaland, and How Hip-Hop Became a Southern Thing.* New York: Da Capo Press, 2007.

Savoy, Ann Allen, ed. *Cajun Music: A Reflection of a People.* Vol. 1. Eunice, La.: Bluebird Press, 1984.

———. "Dennis McGee." Liner notes. *The Complete Early Recordings of Dennis McGee, 1929–1930: Early American Cajun Classics.* Yazoo 2012.

Scarborough, Dorothy. "The 'Blues' as Folk-Songs." *Journal of the Folklore Society of Texas* (1916): 52–66.

Schreyer, Lowell H. *The Banjo Entertainers: Roots to Ragtime, a Banjo History.* Mankato: Minnesota Heritage Publishing, 2007.

Seroff, Doug. "Polk Miller and the Old South Quartette." *78 Quarterly* 1 (1988): 27–41.

Shaw, Arnold. *Honkers and Shouters: The Golden Age of Rhythm and Blues.* New York: Macmillan, 1978.

Smith, Chris. Liner notes. *Mississippi Sheiks: The Complete Recorded Works in Chronological Order.* Vols. 1–4. Document DOCD-5083 — DOCD-5086.

Smith, Leslie Shively. *Around Muhlenberg County, Kentucky: A Black History.* Evansville, Ind.: Unigraphic, 1979.

Smith, Richard D. *Can't You Hear Me Callin': The Life of Bill Monroe, Father of Bluegrass.* New York: Da Capo Press, 2001.

Smitherman, Geneva. *Talkin and Testifyin: The Language of Black America.* 1977. Detroit: Wayne State University Press, 1985.

Snyder, Jared. "Amédé's Recordings." Liner notes. *"I'm Never Comin' Back": Amédé Ardoin, Pioneer of Louisiana French Blues, 1930–1934.* Arhoolie 7007.

Spottswood, Richard. *Ethnic Music on Records: A Discography of Ethnic Recordings*

Produced in the United States, 1893 to 1942. 7 vols. Urbana: University of Illinois Press, 1990.

———. Liner notes. *The Tommie Bradley–James Cole Groups, 1928–1932: Complete Recorded Works in Chronological Order*. Document DOCD-5189.

Stein, Daniel T. "'I Ain't Never Seen a Nigger': The Discourse of Denial in Lee Smith's *The Devil's Dream*." *European Journal of American Culture* 22.2 (2003): 150.

Steptoe, Tyina. "An Ode to Country Music from a Black Dixie Chick." *Oxford American* 54 (2006): 26–27.

Stewart, Charles, ed. *Creolization: History, Ethnography, Theory*. Walnut Creek, Calif.: Left Coast Press, 2007.

Stoneman, Roni, as told to Ellen Wright. *Pressing On: The Roni Stoneman Story*. Urbana: University of Illinois Press, 2007.

Stuckey, Sterling. *Slave Culture: Nationalist Theory and the Foundations of Black America*. New York: Oxford University Press, 1987.

Sublette, Ned. *Cuba and Its Music: From the First Drums to the Mambo*. Chicago: Chicago Review Press, 2005.

———. "The Kingsmen and the Cha-Cha-Cha." In *Listen Again: A Momentary History of Pop Music*, ed. Eric Weisbard, 69–84. Durham: Duke University Press, 2007.

———. *The World That Made New Orleans: From Spanish Silver to Congo Square*. Chicago: Lawrence Hill Books, 2007.

Sudhalter, Richard M. *Lost Chords: White Musicians and Their Contribution to Jazz, 1915–1945*. New York: Oxford University Press, 1999.

Talley, Thomas. *Negro Folk Rhymes*. Ed. Charles Wolfe. Knoxville: University of Tennessee Press, 1991.

Thomas, Rebecca. "The Color of Music: Race and the Making of America's Country Music." Ph.D. diss., University of Missouri, Columbia, 2000.

———. "There's a Whole Lot o' Color in the 'White Man's' Blues: Country Music's Selective Memory and the Challenge of Identity." *Midwest Quarterly* 38.1 (1996): 73–89.

Thomas, Tony. "Gus Cannon—The Colored Champion Banjo Pugilist of the World." In *The Banjo: Roots and Branches*, ed. Robert Winans. Urbana: University of Illinois Press, forthcoming.

Thompson, Robert Farris. "The Song That Named the Land: The Visionary Presence of African American Art." In *Black Art: Ancestral Legacy. The African Impulse in African-American Art*, ed. Alvia Wardlaw and Maureen McKenna, 97–141. Dallas: Dallas Museum of Art, 1989.

———. *Tango: The Art History of Love*. New York: Vintage, 2005.

Tisserand, Michael. *The Kingdom of Zydeco*. New York: Arcade, 1998.

Titon, Jeff Todd. *Early Downhome Blues: A Musical and Cultural Analysis*. 1977. 2nd ed. Chapel Hill: University of North Carolina Press, 1994.

———. *Old-Time Kentucky Fiddle Tunes*. Lexington: University Press of Kentucky, 2001.

Tosches, Nick. "Al Dexter." *Old-Time Music* 22 (Autumn 1976): 4–8.

———. *Country: The Twisted Roots of Rock 'n' Roll*. New York: DaCapo Press, 1996.

———. *Unsung Heroes of Rock and Roll: The Birth of Rock in the Wild Years before Elvis*. New York: DaCapo Press, 1999.

———. *Where Dead Voices Gather*. Boston: Little, Brown, 2001.

Tracy, Steven C. *Going to Cincinnati: A History of Blues in the Queen City*. Urbana: University of Illinois Press, 1993.

———. *Write Me a Few of Your Lines: A Blues Reader*. Amherst: University of Massachusetts Press, 1999.

Twain, Mark. *Life on the Mississippi*. 1883. New York: Viking Penguin, 1984.

"The Unseen Hand: How Producers Shape the Country Sound." *Journal of Country Music* 12.2 (1987): 2–3.

Visser, Joop. Liner notes. *Lonnie Johnson: The Original Guitar Wizard*. Proper Properbox 81.

Wald, Elijah. *Escaping the Delta: Robert Johnson and the Invention of the Blues*. New York: Amistad, 2004.

Ward, Brian. *Just My Soul Responding: Rhythm and Blues, Black Consciousness and Race Relations*. Berkeley: University of California Press, 1998.

Ware, Burnham. "Kentucky Blues." *Living Blues: A Journal of Black American Blues Tradition* 51 (Summer 1981): 31.

Warner-Lewis, Maureen. *Central Africa in the Caribbean: Transcending Time, Transforming Cultures*. Kingston: University of West Indies Press, 2003.

———. "Posited Kikoongo Origins of Some Portuguese and Spanish Words from the Slave Era." *America Negra* 13 (1997): 83–95.

Waterman, Christopher. "Race Music: Bo Chatmon, 'Corrine Corrina,' and the Excluded Middle." In *Music and the Racial Imagination*, ed. Ronald M. Radano and Philip V. Bohlman, 167–205. Chicago: University of Chicago Press, 2001.

Wells, Paul F. "Fiddling as an Avenue of Black-White Musical Interchange." *Black Music Research Journal* 23.1/2 (2003): 135–47.

Wever, Jerry Lowell. "Dancing the Habanera Beats (in Country Music): Empire Rollover and Postcolonial Creolizations in St. Lucia." Ph.D. diss., University of Iowa, 2011.

Whitburn, Joel. *Top Country Singles, 1994–1997*. Menomonee Falls, Wisc.: Record Research, 1997.

Wiggins, Gene. *Fiddlin' Georgia Crazy: Fiddlin' John Carson, His Real World, and the World of His Songs*. Urbana: University of Illinois Press, 1987.

Wiggins, Gene, with Tony Russell. "Hell Broke Loose in Gordon County, Georgia." *Old Time Music* 25 (Summer 1977): 9–21.

Wilson, Joe. Liner notes. *Altamont, Black Stringband Music from the Library of Congress*. Rounder 0239.

———. Liner notes. *Eddie Pennington Walks the Strings . . . and Even Sings*. Smithsonian Folkways 40146.

Wilson, Olly. "The Significance of the Relationship between Afro-American Music and West African Music." *Black Perspective in Music* 2.1 (1974): 3–22.

Winans, Robert B. "The Black Banjo-Playing Tradition in Virginia and West Virginia." *Journal of the Virginia Folklore Society* 1 (1979): 7–30.

Wolfe, Charles K. "Black String Bands: A Few Notes on a Lost Cause." *Old-Time Herald* 1 (Fall 1987): 15–18.

———. "The Bristol Sessions: The Cast of Characters." In *The Bristol Sessions: Writings about the Big Bang of Country Music*, ed. Charles K. Wolfe and Ted Olson, 40–53. Jefferson, N.C.: McFarland, 2005.

———. "The Bristol Syndrome: Field Recordings of Early Country Music." In *Country Music Annual 2002*, ed. Charles K. Wolfe and James E. Akenson, 202–21. Lexington: University Press of Kentucky, 2002.

———. "Columbia Records and Old-Time Music." *John Edwards Memorial Foundation Quarterly* 14 (Autumn 1978): 118–25, 144.

———. *The Devil's Box: Masters of Southern Fiddling*. Nashville: Country Music Foundation Press and Vanderbilt University Press, 1997.

———. "Early Country Music in Knoxville: The Brunswick Sessions and the End of an Era." *Old Time Music* 12 (Spring 1974): 19–31.

———. *A Good-Natured Riot: The Birth of the Grand Ole Opry*. Nashville: Country Music Foundation Press and Vanderbilt University Press, 1999.

———. *Kentucky Country: Folk and Country Music of Kentucky*. 1982. Lexington: University Press of Kentucky, 1996.

———. "The Legend That Peer Built: Reappraising the Bristol Sessions." In *The Bristol Sessions: Writings about the Big Bang of Country Music*, ed. Charles K. Wolfe and Ted Olson, 17–39. Jefferson, N.C.: McFarland, 2005.

———. "A Lighter Shade of Blue: White Country Blues." In *Nothing but the Blues: The Music and the Musicians*, ed. Lawrence Cohn, 233–63. New York: Abbeville Press, 1993.

———. Liner notes. *The Bristol Sessions: Historic Recordings from Bristol, Tennessee.* 2-CD set. Country Music Foundation CMF-011-D.

———. "Ralph Peer at Work: The Victor 1927 Bristol Sessions." *Old Time Music* 5 (Summer 1972): 10–15.

———. "The Rest of the Story: Other Early Recordings Sessions in the Tri-Cities Area." In *The Bristol Sessions: Writings about the Big Bang of Country Music*, ed. Charles K. Wolfe and Ted Olson, 235–56. Jefferson, N.C.: McFarland, 2005.

———. "Rural Black String Band Music." *Black Music Research Newsletter* 4 (Fall 1980): 3–4.

————. "Rural Black Stringband Music." *Black Music Research Journal* 10.1 (1990): 32–35.

Wolfe, Charles K., and Kip Lornell. *The Life and Legend of Leadbelly*. New York: HarperCollins, 1992.

Wolfe, Charles K., and Tony Russell. "The Asheville Session." *Old Time Music* 31 (Winter 1978–79): 5–12.

Woods, Jeff. "Color Me Country: Tales from the Frontlines." *Journal of Country Music* 14.2 (1992): 9–12.

Wyatt, Marshall. Liner notes. *"Folks, He Sure Do Pull Some Bow!" Vintage Fiddle Music, 1927–1935*. Old Hat CD-1003.

————. Liner notes. *Violin, Sing the Blues for Me: African-American Fiddlers, 1926–1949*. Old Hat CD-1002.

Wynn, Ron. "This Is My Country." In liner notes, *From Where I Stand: The Black Experience in Country Music*. Warner Brothers CD 9 46428-2.

Wynter, Leon E. *American Skin: Pop Culture, Big Business, and the End of White America*. New York: Crown, 2002.

Yancy, George, ed. *What White Looks Like: African American Philosophers on Whiteness*. New York: Routledge, 2004.

Younger, Richard. *Get a Shot of Rhythm and Blues: The Life of Arthur Alexander*. Tuscaloosa: University of Alabama Press, 2000.

Zwigoff, Terry. "Black Country String Bands." *American Visions* 6.1 (1991): 50–52.

————. Liner notes. *Early Mandolin Classics, Vol. 1*. Rounder CD 1050.

————. Liner notes. *String Bands, 1926–1929: Complete Recorded Works in Chronological Order*. Document DOCD-5167.

Zwonitzer, Mark, and Charles Hirshberg. *Will You Miss Me When I'm Gone? The Carter Family and Their Legacy in American Music*. New York: Simon and Schuster, 2002.

Contributors

MICHAEL AWKWARD is Gayl A. Jones Collegiate Professor of Afro-American Literature and Culture in the Department of English at the University of Michigan. His publications include *Soul Covers: Rhythm and Blues Remakes and the Struggle for Artistic Identity (Aretha Franklin, Al Green, Phoebe Snow)* and *Burying Don Imus: Anatomy of a Scapegoat.*

ERIKA BRADY is a professor in the Department of Folk Studies and Anthropology at Western Kentucky University. Her publications include *A Spiral Way: How the Phonograph Changed Ethnography* and *Healing Logics: Culture and Medicine in Modern Health Belief Systems.* She is the host of *Barren River Breakdown*, a weekly radio show on WKYU-FM featuring American roots music, for which she won a 2011 Governor's Award in the Arts.

BARBARA CHING is a professor in and the chair of the Department of English at Iowa State University. She is the author of *Wrong's What I Do Best: Hard Country Music and Contemporary Culture* and the coeditor of *Old Roots, New Routes: The Cultural Politics of Alt.Country Music* and *Knowing Your Place: Rural Identity and Cultural Hierarchy.*

ADAM GUSSOW is an associate professor of English and southern studies at the University of Mississippi. He is the author of *Seems Like Murder Here: Southern Violence and the Blues Tradition* and *Journeyman's Road: Modern Blues Lives from Faulkner's Mississippi to Post-9/11 New York*, among other works. His essays have appeared in *Southern Cultures, African American Review, Harper's*, and many other publications. He is a professional harmonica player and instructor and a member of the blues duo Satan and Adam.

PATRICK HUBER is a professor of history at Missouri University of Science and Technology in Rolla. He is the author of *Linthead Stomp: The Creation of Country Music in the Piedmont South*, which won the 2010 Wayland D. Hand Prize of the American Folklore Society, and the coauthor of *The 1920s: American Popular Culture through History*. He is currently producing a two-CD boxed set for Dust-to-Digital of Atlanta.

CHARLES L. HUGHES is the Mellon Post-Doctoral Fellow at the Memphis Center at Rhodes College. He received his Ph.D. in U.S. history from the University of Wisconsin, Madison in 2012, after completing a dissertation on race and the recording industry in the American South in the 1960s and 1970s. His essays and reviews have appeared in a variety of publications. He is a musician and songwriter, and he was a 2010–11 predoctoral research fellow at the Smithsonian Institution.

JEFFREY A. KEITH is a professor of global studies at Warren Wilson College in Asheville, North Carolina. He is a cultural historian interested in both U.S. foreign relations and the American South, and his essays and reviews have appeared in journals as varied as *Diplomatic History* and the *Journal of the Society for American Music*. He regularly performs string-band music as a member of the Red State Ramblers, and he teaches in Warren Wilson College's traditional music program. He is currently at work on a book about Western perceptions of Saigon during the Second Indochina War.

KIP LORNELL teaches music and ethnomusicology at George Washington University. His most recent books include *Shreveport Sounds: Ark-La-Tex Music in Black and White* (with Tracey E. W. Laird), *The Melody Man: Joe Davis and the New York Music Scene, 1916–1978* (with Bruce Bastin), and *Exploring American Folk Music: Ethnic, Grassroots, and Regional Traditions in the United States*. He received the 1993 ASCAP-Deems Taylor award for *The Life and Legend of Leadbelly* (with Charles Wolfe) and a 1997 Grammy for coauthoring the program notes for the *Anthology of American Folk Music* (Smithsonian/Folkways).

DIANE PECKNOLD is an associate professor of women's and gender studies at the University of Louisville. She is the author of *The Selling Sound: The Rise of the Country Music Industry* and the coeditor of *A Boy Named Sue: Gender and Country Music* (with Kristine M. McCusker). She has contributed essays on country music to a number of collections, including *Pop When the World Falls Apart, Waiting for a Train: Jimmie Rodgers' America*, and *Old Roots and New Routes: The Cultural Politics of Alt.Country Music*.

DAVID SANJEK was the head of the Popular Music Research Centre and a professor in the School of Media, Music and Performance at Salford University in England. Prior to that appointment, he served as the director of the BMI Archives in New York for sixteen years. His essays on popular music appeared in *South Atlantic Quarterly, American Music, Popular Music and Society,* and the *Journal of Popular Music Studies,* among many other publications, and he served as an advisor to the Rock and Roll Hall of Fame, the Rhythm and Blues Foundation, the Blues Foundation, and the Experience Music Project Museum. He also served on several committees for the National Academy of Recording Arts and Sciences and was a member of the National Recording Preservation Board at the Library of Congress. He passed away on November 29, 2011.

TONY THOMAS is a leading scholar of the African American banjo tradition. He is the founder of Black Banjo Then and Now, an Internet listserv devoted to black banjo history and performance. In 2005 his work with the list produced the first Black Banjo Gathering in Boone, North Carolina, an event that served as a catalyst for the recent recognition and revival of African American old-time music. He has contributed essays and reviews to *Banjo Newsletter* and the *Old-Time Herald,* among others, and served as contributing historian to the documentary film *The Banjo Project.* He has taught a number of courses on black banjo, including programs at the Banjo Collectors Gathering, Banjo Camp North, the Blue Ridge Old Time Music Week, and Suwannee Banjo Camp. He plays banjo and guitar with the Ebony Hillbillies.

JERRY WEVER is an assistant professor of anthropology at Spelman College, where he teaches courses on ethnomusicology, the Caribbean, and the anthropology of globalization. He received his Ph.D. from the University of Iowa for his dissertation "Dancing the Habanera Beats (in Country Music): Empire Rollover and Postcolonial Creolizations in St. Lucia." His essay "Mizik Manmay Lakai (Home-Children Music)" is forthcoming in *Songs Out of Place: Global Country,* edited by Aaron Fox and Christine Yano.

Index

music, 20, 33–34, 52, 66, 101, 146, 163; on
King Records, 310, 318; old-time music
as opposition to, 26–27; in race record
series, 22, 60; and rockabilly, 113–14; as
southern music, 193. *See also* African
American banjo playing; African Ameri-
can banjoists; banjo; minstrelsy: African
American; *Modern Sounds in Country and
Western Music*
"The Jazz Fiddler," 46, 68n54
Jeffries, Herb, 2, 252
Jennings, Waylon, 82, 299–300
Jewel, Buddy, 253
Jim Crow. *See* segregation
"The Jockey Blues," 29, 63n25
Joe Tex (Joseph Arrington, Jr.), 283–85, 289,
296, 299, 301
"Joe Turner Blues," 156
John, Little Willie, 327
"John Hardy," 156
"John Henry," 38–41, 189
Johnson, Alonzo "Lonnie," 34, 44, 65n32,
68n51, 319
Johnson, Amos, 114
Johnson, James P., 35, 65n33
Johnson, Jay Cee "J. C.," 34, 65n32, 65n34
Johnson, Lonnie, 161
Johnson, Robert, 101–2, 116n6
The Johnson Boys, 44
The Johnson Brothers, 32–33, 64n29
Johnston, Jess, 55
Joiner, James, 287–88
Jones, Bob, 159
Jones, Booker T., 300
Jones, George, 94, 210, 212, 218–19, 230n28,
232n44, 292, 295–96, 299, 304n28
Jones, Kennedy, 104–5, 107–8, 115, 117n17
Jones, Louis "Grandpa," 114, 162, 186, 313, 319
Jones, Samuel (Stove Pipe No. 1), 38–39,
52, 123
Joplin, Scott, 43–44
Jordan, Louis, 2
Jordan, Luke, 181–82
Jounen Kwéyól (Creole Day), 208, 213, 221,
228n14, 228n15, 228–29n16, 229n17

Journal of Country Music, 96, 271, 321, 337
"Just Out of Reach," 86

"Kansas City Blues (I'm Going to Kansas
City)," 147
Kasey, Rufus, 159–60, 187
"Kaw-Liga," 268
Keith, Toby, 266–67
Killen, Buddy, 283–85, 287, 289, 291, 301
King, B. B., 157
King, Ben E., 287, 300
King, Martin Luther, Jr., 128, 198
King Kong, 235, 236, 255
The King R&B Box Set, 314–16
King Records, 85, 186, 306, 309–11. *See also*
blues: on King Records; Glover, Henry;
jazz: on King Records; Nathan, Sydney;
rhythm and blues: on King Records
Kingston Trio, 162
Kirtley, Pat, 101
"Kiss an Angel Good Morning," 268
"Kiss You All Over," 301
Knight, Gladys, 253; Gladys Knight and the
Pips, 198–99
"Knox County Stomp," 43
"Ko Ko Mo (I Love You So)," 328
Kristofferson, Kris, 5, 94, 201, 294, 300
Ku Klux Klan, 37, 121
Kun, Josh, 265, 275, 281n5

Landress, George "Bud," 32
Lang, Eddie, 65n32, 68n51
"Last Date," 291
"Laughin' and Cryin' Blues," 48
"Laura," 83
"La Valse a Austin Ardoin," 31
Lawrence, Keith, 106, 116n2
Lead Belly, 173, 189n1, 267
Lee, Albert, 104
Lee, Brenda, 288
Lee, Spike, 245
"Let Me Be Your Side Track," 32
"Let Me Call You Sweetheart," 44
"Let's Stay Together," 194, 195
Let's Stay Together, 191

radio, 112, 289–90, 294, 313; African American singers and musicians on, 34, 41, 83, 237, 250; country format radio, 10, 87, 89–91, 235, 238, 273, 294, 302; folk and bluegrass music on, 162, 171, 177, 179, 182–83, 185–86; as influence on musicians, 124, 178, 185–86, 289–90; rhythm and blues on, 89, 289, 294; rock and roll on, 87; in St. Lucia, 208–9, 211–13, 229n18, 230n26; WSM (Nashville), 39–40, 147, 289. *See also* Grand Ole Opry

Rager, Mose, 107–8, 113–15

ragtime, 43–44, 100–101, 144, 146, 153, 158, 166

"Railroad Bill," 246

Rainey, Gertrude "Ma," 154

Randall, Alice, 10, 263–80. See also *My Country Roots*; *Pushkin and the Queen of Spades*

Raney, Wayne, 310, 327, 334, 336

rap and hip-hop, 6, 10–11, 240–43, 245–47, 249, 255, 261n18, 271, 279, 285. *See also* country-rap; hick-hop

Rascal Flatts, 97

"Rattle Snaking Daddy," 178

Ray, 97, 223

Ray, Aulton, 28, 50–51

Raybaw Records, 244

RCA Records, 87, 268. *See also* RCA-Victor Records

RCA-Victor Records, 19, 30–34, 36, 37, 40, 48, 54–55, 61n18, 315, 327, 334. *See also* RCA Records; Victor Records

Recapturing the Banjo, 143, 233n54

record companies: advertising of, 22–24, 26–27, 35, 41, 50; disguising black artists in hillbilly series, 3, 22, 43, 46–52; and early marketing of records, 22–24, 47–49, 53–55, 61n18, 150, 164; field recording sessions of, 32–33, 36, 40–43, 46, 53, 60n16; and foreign language recordings, 23, 50, 60n15; hillbilly and race series of, 22–25, 47–56, 58n9, 60n13, 60n14; and racial categorization of vernacular music, 3, 22–23, 61n17, 69–70n65, 149–50; racially cross-listed

records of, 29, 34–35, 38–52, 53, 57–58n8, 60n13, 69n58; use of pseudonyms, 48–49, 55. *See also specific record labels*

Rector, Steve, 113, 115

"Red Nightgown Blues," 36

Redding, Otis, 193, 196, 269, 296, 300

Reed, "Blind" Alfred, 37

Reed, Jerry, 104, 105, 115, 240, 243, 293

Reese, Nat, 153

Reeve, Phil, 64n28

Reeves, Jim, 88, 90, 93, 210, 230n28, 230n29

Reinhardt, Django, 115

"Release Me," 90

revivalism: and African Americans, 2, 143, 164–66; and bluegrass, 144; and European Americans, 161–64; and folk music, 120, 129, 132, 135, 161–62; and old-time music, 144, 163

rhythm and blues, 5, 93–94, 205, 290–92, 296, 299, 316; as black music, 144, 165; and country and bluegrass music, 103, 284, 286, 294–96, 300–301, 326–27; as cultural threat, 117n11; and habanera rhythm, 222; influence of, on rock and roll, 90, 109; on King Records, 12, 310, 319, 326–27; marginalization of, in music economy, 83–84, 93; in the music of Al Green, 191–94, 197. *See also* country soul; cover records; Nashville: rhythm and blues in; radio: rhythm and blues on; soul

Rhythm, Country, and Blues, 253, 271

Rice, Hoke, 48

Rich, Charlie, 296

Rich, John, 235, 237, 244, 251. *See also* Big and Rich

Rich, Spider, 113

Richardson, Doc, 115

Riddle, Lesley, 1, 237

"Riley and Spencer," 189

Rinzler, Ralph, 102–3, 116n9

Ritter, Tex, 274

Roanoke Jug Band, 181

Robbins, Hargus "Pig," 291–92, 304n28

Robbins, Marty, 230n29, 297

Roberts, Dink, 159, 176

Roberts, Dock "Fiddlin' Doc," 29, 62n10, 63n23, 109

Robison, Carson, 48

rockabilly, 12, 104, 113–14, 117n11, 230n27, 232n45, 296

rock and roll, 312; country music as an influence on, 57n4, 104, 329–30, 334; as cultural threat, 87, 116–17n11, 164, 271, 293; influence of, on country music, 293, 295; influence of, on musicians, 241, 291–92, 296, 298; and interracial musical exchange, 109, 146, 222, 253, 284, 288, 290, 320, 329–30; revivalism, 164; as southern music, 193–94. *See also* radio: rock and roll on; rockabilly; southern rock

Rodgers, Jimmie, 1, 3, 19–20, 32–34, 36, 37, 52, 56–57n3, 64–65n30, 94, 114, 118n58, 146, 149, 150, 163, 222, 253, 257

The Rolling Stones, 267, 294

"Roll on Mississippi," 268

Rose, Bayless, 58n9

Rosen, Jody, 191–92

Rosine, Kentucky, 102, 103, 109–11, 112

Rucker, Darius, 5, 6, 11, 223, 270, 14n14

Rumble, John, 64n28, 321, 323–24, 327, 329, 337

Run-DMC, 234, 244, 245

Rushing, Jimmy, 153

Russell, Tony, 21, 36, 38, 42, 57–58n8, 59n12, 319

sacred music, 23, 27, 29–30, 39, 109, 144, 147, 149–50, 160, 164–65, 167n23, 173, 176, 178–79, 182, 184, 188–89, 192

"Sail Away," 274

"Sail Away, Ladies," 273

"Sally Anne," 187, 273

Salnave, Théophile, 41–42

"Salty Dog," 29, 38, 42

"Sandy River Belle," 178

"Saturday Night Stroll," 36–37

Savoy Records, 316–17

Scarborough, Dorothy, 173

Schaffer, Ed "Dizzy Head," 36–37, 66n36

Scott, Little Jimmy, 317

Scruggs, Earl, 161, 331

Seaney, Uncle Jim (Ernest V. "Pop" Stoneman), 49, 61n18, 180–81

"See See Rider," 156

segregation, 84, 96, 136, 145, 265–66, 288–89; African American memory of, 135, 144, 163–64, 197, 254; impact of, on African American musicians, 84, 119, 132–33; impact of, on musical practice, 3–4, 8, 28, 48, 289; interracial musical practice and, 22, 30, 55, 82, 111–12, 126, 317–18; support for, among white country artists, 37, 253–54

self-affirming voice, 245–47

"Separation Blues," 55

"Seven Nights to Rock," 330

"Sewing Machine Blues," 36

"Shake Your Money Maker," 255

"Shakin' That Thing," 123

Shakur, Tupac, 242, 267, 279, 280

"She Goes All the Way," 97

"The Sheik of Araby," 46

"The Sheik Waltz," 46, 68n54

The Shelor Family, 78

The Shennandoah Valley Boys, 186

Sherrill, Billy, 287–88, 290–94, 296–97, 299, 302, 304n28, 304n38

"She's a Hum Dum Dinger from Dingersville," 36, 65n35

"She's All I Got," 296–97

Sholes, Steve, 87

"Shortnin' Bread," 187

The Shreveport Home Wreckers, 36

Shultz, Arnold: early life of, 107; guitar style of, 102–3, 105–7; influence of, on bluegrass, 1, 101–3, 115–16, 237; influence of, on Western Kentucky thumbpickers, 1, 4, 101–8, 115–16; mythologies regarding, 100–102; and race relations in rural Kentucky, 109–12

Silas Green Show, 153–54

Sims, Raymond, 128

Sinatra, Frank, 310

singing cowboys, 47, 252, 274; African American, 2, 5

Virginia, 2, 8, 128, 156, 159, 172–73, 177–79; Campbell County, 181, 183; Caroline County, 182; Carroll County, 180–81; Franklin County, 172, 180, 181, 183; Henry County, 181, 183, 185; Nelson County, 184; Orange County, 176, 180; Patrick County, 178, 183; Pittsylvania County, 179, 182, 183; Westmoreland County, 181. *See also* Piedmont region

The Virginia Breakdowners, 181

Vocalion Records, 23–25, 40, 42–43, 54, 64n27, 65n34

Wagoner, Porter, 210, 299

Wald, Elijah, 149, 152–53, 158, 162, 164, 236

Walker, Aaron "T-Bone," 165

Walker, Gary, 291

Walker, Malcolm, 102, 114

Walker, Owen, 63n23

Walker, "Uncle" Homer, 159–60, 169n70

Wallace, George, 9, 82, 253–54, 294

Waller, Thomas "Fats," 34, 115

Walter Jacobs and the Carter Brothers, 46

Wanted: The Outlaws, 82

War, 199

Ware, James "Jimmy," 124, 127–28, 133, 135

Washington, Denzel, 244

Washington, Dinah, 83, 87

Waterman, Christopher A., 11, 24, 61n17, 238, 245, 249

Waters, Muddy, 153, 161, 165, 237

Watson, Doc, 104, 115, 169n70

Watson, El, 32–33, 64n29

"Weary Yodelin' Blues, Parts 1 and 2," 34–35

"Well Oh Well," 329

Wells, Kitty, 210, 212

"Went for a Ride," 266, 274–75, 277

western swing, 46, 47, 267, 310, 329

"Westward Ho," 242

Wexler, Jerry, 86, 90, 194

"What'd I Say," 84

The Wheat Street Female Quartet, 39, 52, 67n42

"Wheel in a Wheel," 39, 67n42

"When the Saints Go Marching In," 39

"White House Blues," 181

whiteness: aural signifiers of, 8, 222, 224; and black country artists and fans, 4–6, 120, 135, 222–23; of country music, 2–3, 8–9, 12–13, 22, 27, 38, 57n5, 85, 120, 214, 222–25, 236, 253–54, 271–72, 275, 335–36; as identity claim, 4, 8–9, 48, 255; and nostalgia, 8, 56, 264, 266, 271, 280, 281n10; in popular music, 238; production of, through country music, 3–4, 5, 94, 97, 205, 221–24, 245, 264–65

white supremacy, 5, 120, 121–22, 127, 133, 200–201, 222, 266

Whittier, Henry, 180–81

"Who Is Job? Parts 1 and 2," 39, 67n42

"Who's Minding the Garden," 266

"Why Don't You Haul Off and Love Me," 327

Wiggins, Phil, 182

The Wild, Wild West, 242

Williams, Hank, 1, 11, 87–88, 93–94, 193, 200, 202, 210, 237, 267–69, 272, 279–80, 294

Williams, Hank, Jr., 270, 300–301

Williams, J. Mayo, 321

Williams, Jerry, Jr. (Swamp Dogg), 296–99, 301, 304n41

Williams, Paul, 334–36

Wilson, Gerald, 93

Wilson, Gretchen, 244

Wilson, Jackie, 196

Wilson, Olly, 146

Wilson, Sule Greg, 143

Wilson, Teddy, 109

Winans, Robert, 148, 159, 160

The Wind Done Gone, 265, 266

Wolfe, Charles K., 2, 39, 50, 59n12, 69n63, 70n65, 106, 109, 147, 236

Womack, Bobby, 299, 301

Womack, Daniel, 179–80

Wonder, Stevie, 199, 222, 304n28

Wood, Randy, 292, 333–34

Woods, Oscar "Buddy," 36–37, 66n36

Work, John, III, 155

"Work It," 255

work songs, 64n30, 173, 177, 189n2